LIGHTNING STRIKES

STRIKES

≡ THE LOCKHEED P-38 ≡

STEVE BLAKE

FONTHILL

Fonthill Media Language Policy

Fonthill Media publishes in the international English language market. One language edition is published worldwide. As there are minor differences in spelling and presentation, especially with regard to American English and British English, a policy is necessary to define which form of English to use. The Fonthill Policy is to use the form of English native to the author. Steve Blake was born and educated in California; therefore American English has been adopted in this publication.

Fonthill Media Limited
Fonthill Media LLC
www.fonthillmedia.com
office@fonthillmedia.com

First published in the United Kingdom and the United States of America 2020

British Library Cataloguing in Publication Data:
A catalogue record for this book is available from the British Library

Copyright © Steve Blake 2020

ISBN 978-1-78155-788-4

Typeset in 10pt on 13pt Sabon
Printed and bound in England

Acknowledgments

I would like to offer my sincere thanks for the encouragement and help I received for this project from my colleagues Mike Bates and John Stanaway—particularly for sharing their extensive P-38 photo collections with me, to the considerable benefit of my book. Also to Hayman Tam, the talented warbird photographer, who permitted me to use some of his great photos of the surviving P-38s. My very special thanks to my wife, helpmate, and collaborator Marjorie Blake, for her patience and encouragement during this nearly year-long and often exhausting project, and most especially for her amazing photo editing skills. To be successful, a project like this really does 'take a village'—a network of colleagues, experts, and technical wizards. No such work is a solo effort.

Steve Blake

Contents

Glossary

1Lt.	First Lieutenant
2Lt.	Second Lieutenant
A/D	Airdrome
AA	Anti-Aircraft
AAB	Army Air Base
AAF	Army Air Field
AF	Air Force
ASC	Air Support Command
ATG	Air Transport Group
BAD	Base air depot
BC	Bomber Command
BG	Bomb Group
Brig. Gen.	Brigadier General
BS	Bomb Squadron
BU	Base Unit
CCTS	Combat Crew Training Station
CG	Composite Group
CMS	Combat Mapping Squadron
CO	Commanding Officer
Col.	Colonel
Cpl.	Corporal
D-Day	June 6, 1944 invasion of Normandy
DFC	Distinguished Flying Cross
DSC	Distinguished Service Cross
DUC	Distinguished Unit Citation
e/a	Enemy aircraft
ELINT	Electronic Intelligence
ETO	European Theater of Operations
FC	Fighter Command

FEAF	Far East Air Force
FG	Fighter Group
FRS	Ferrying Squadron
FS	Fighter Squadron
FTC	Fighter Training Center
FTG	Fighter Training Group
FTS	Fighter Training Squadron
FW	Fighter Wing
Gen.	General
hp	Horsepower
IJN	Imperial Japanese Navy
JAAF	Japanese Army Air Force
JNAF	Japanese Naval Air Force
KIA	Killed in Action
LAC	Lockheed Aircraft Corporation
Lt.	Lieutenant
Lt. Col.	Lieutenant Colonel
Lt. Gen.	Lieutenant General
MACR	Missing Aircrew Report
Maj.	Major
Maj. Gen.	Major General
MIA	Missing in Action
mph	Miles per hour
MTO	Mediterranean Theater of Operations
NFS	Night Fighter Squadron
OES	Operational Engineering Section
OTU	Operational Training Unit
PG	Pursuit Group (to May 1942)
PG	Photographic Group
PMS	Photographic Mapping Squadron
POW	Prisoner of War
PR	Photographic Reconnaissance
PRG	Photographic Reconnaissance Group
PRMG	Photographic Reconnaissance and Mapping Group
PRS	Photographic Reconnaissance Squadron
PS	Pursuit Squadron (to May 1942)
PS	Photographic Squadron
PTO	Pacific Theater of Operations
RAAF	Royal Australian Air Force
RAF	Royal Air Force
RCAF	Royal Canadian Air Force
RCM	Radio Countermeasures
RFC	Reconstruction Finance Corporation
RG	Reconnaissance Group

RNZAF	Royal New Zealand Air Force
rpm	Revolutions per minute
RTU	Reconnaissance Training Unit
RTW	Reconnaissance Training Wing
RW	Reconnaissance Wing
S/Sgt.	Staff Sergeant
Sgt.	Sergeant
SWP	South West Pacific
T/Sgt.	Technical Sergeant
TAC	Tactical Air Command
TEAFTG	Twin-Engined Advanced Flying Training Group
TEAFTS	Twin-Engined Advanced Flying Training Squadron
TRG	Tactical Reconnaissance Group
TRS	Tactical Reconnaissance Squadron
USAAC	United States Army Air Corps
USAAF	United States Army Air Forces
USAF	United States Air Force
USMC	United States Marine Corps
USN	United States Navy
WASP	Women Air Service Pilots
Wg. Cdr.	Wing Commander

Introduction

Most World War II aviation historians agree that Lockheed's P-38 Lightning was the most versatile aircraft of that conflict. Designed primarily as an interceptor, it also served, very successfully, as a long-range escort fighter, a fighter-bomber, and, as F-4s and F-5s, that war's premier photo reconnaissance aircraft.

Lightnings were active in every World War II American combat theater and USAAF overseas combat air force, and they were still serving in each of them in considerable numbers as of the cessation of hostilities. Their destruction, in aerial combat, of 3,789 enemy aircraft—1,865 Japanese in the Pacific theaters and 1,924 of the European Axis—was just one of its many contributions to the Allied victory.

This book is dedicated to the men and women who designed, built, test flew, ferried, and maintained Lockheed's Lightnings—and especially to the men who flew them in combat against American's enemies.

1

The Lockheed Corporation and the Design and Production of the Early P-38s

In February 1937, the U.S. Army Air Corps (USAAC) issued its Specification X-608, which outlined its requirements for a new fighter/interceptor. It would have been difficult to believe back then that one of the companies pursuing that contract—the Lockheed Aircraft Corporation (LAC)—would end up producing one of the most famous, versatile, and successful military aircraft of all time, especially given the fact that it had never before built one that it had designed as such.

The origin of LAC was the Alco Hydro-Aeroplane Company, which was established in San Francisco, California, in 1912 by the brothers Allan and Malcolm Loughhead. As indicated by its name, their focus was on designing and building seaplanes. In 1916, the company was renamed the Loughhead Aircraft Manufacturing Company and moved to Santa Barbara, California. The first aircraft it produced was the model F-1 ("Flying-boat One"), which in 1918 set the distance record for seaplanes, flying non-stop from Santa Barbara to San Diego. The company's next effort, a revolutionary monocoque aeroplane called the S-1 ("Sport-1"), was a failure, as then was the company, which in 1921 ceased to exist temporarily.

In 1926, it was reborn as the Lockheed Aircraft Company, named after one of its partners, Allan Loughhead—Lockheed being the actual pronunciation of Loughhead. In fact, Allan then legally changed the spelling of his name to Lockheed. The other partners were Jack Northrop (who would later establish a very successful aircraft company of his own) and Kenneth Jay. The company was now located in Hollywood, California, where it designed and built its first commercially successful aircraft, the Vega, a single-engined, high-wing monoplane airliner that utilized much of the technology it had developed for the S-1. In 1928, the company moved to nearby Burbank, which became its famous permanent home. In July 1929, the company's majority shareholder sold 87 percent of it to the Detroit Aircraft Corporation, and the following month, Allan Lockheed resigned from it.

Despite the popularity of the Vega, the Great Depression that began soon after Lockheed's resignation temporarily undermined the civilian aircraft market and the company went bankrupt. It was bought out of receivership in 1932 by a group of investors headed by the brothers Robert and Courtland Gross and Walter Varney, for just $40,000. Allan Lockheed had planned to bid on it himself but did not do so because he had "only" $50,000, which he felt would not be sufficient. Nevertheless, the company continued to use his name, and it then became the Lockheed Aircraft Corporation, with Robert Gross as its chairman of the board.

The company resumed production of the Vega, with which famous aviators such as Amelia Earhart and Wiley Post made record-setting flights. It then developed what was to be an even more popular civil aircraft, the Model 10 Electra, a small twin-engined transport. Earhart was flying an Electra when she and her navigator disappeared over the Pacific Ocean in 1937. The Model 10 was followed by the Model 12 Electra Junior and the Model 14 Super Electra, which flew for the first time in 1937 and of which 119 were license-built in Japan by the Tachikawa Aircraft Company for the Imperial Japanese Army Air Force—and during the war received the Allied code name "Thelma."

Specification X-608 had been preceded in 1936 by a USAAC Request for Proposal (RFP) for a new fighter aircraft, which it described as an interceptor. It had called for a top speed of at least 360 mph at 20,000 feet, and the proposed aircraft was to reach that altitude in six minutes. It also had to have the endurance to fly at full throttle for an hour. Meeting these performance specifications would require that its engine—or engines—be turbo-supercharged. A Lockheed design team had been working on the fighter proposal for the past year, in anticipation of the full, official USAAC specification. Chosen to lead that team by Lockheed's new chief engineer Hall Hibbard was Clarence L. "Kelly" Johnson, who had then been employed by Lockheed for the past two years, working initially on the Electra.

Until then, the company had not, in all those years, designed any purely military aircraft, let alone a state-of-the-art fighter. As of 1936, only five Lockheed aircraft were serving with the U.S. military—Model 10s that were being used as personal transports for high-ranking officers of the Navy, Coast Guard, and Army Air Corps. But that changed as the winds of war began blowing through Europe and Asia in the mid-1930s and then ignited World War II in 1939. Britain, in particular, was desperate for military aircraft and ordered hundreds of Lockheed's new twin-engined Hudson patrol bomber that was based on the Super Electra,

This is one of the two Lockheed Vegas purchased by the U.S. Army Air Corps in 1931. (*Lockheed photo*)

as did the USAAC, which was soon to become the U.S. Army Air Forces (USAAF). The Air Corps designated it, depending on its utilization, as either the B-34, the A-28, the A-29, or the AT-18. This had all begun in 1938, when, in response to an upcoming visit to the U.S. by a British commission purchasing military equipment, including aircraft, the company built a mockup of a Model 14 converted to a reconnaissance bomber in just ten days.

The Hudson turned out to be an extremely versatile and popular design. A larger, heavier derivative with more powerful engines, called the Ventura, was manufactured by the Vega Aircraft Company, a subsidiary of Lockheed. A few examples of the U.S. Navy's (USN) version of the Ventura, the PV-1 (the "P" standing for Patrol and the "V" for Vega), were even transformed into night fighters.

What Kelly Johnson's interceptor design team—which was soon named Advanced Development Projects but was popularly known, by 1943, as Lockheed's "Skunk Works"— came up with in response to the RFP and Specification X-608 was a very radical aircraft for 1937, with numerous innovations. It would feature butt-jointed and flush-riveted aluminum skin plus metal control surfaces at a time when they were typically fabric covered. It would also feature a rare (for a fighter) tricycle landing gear, which would make taxiing much easier, and, most importantly, to meet the aircraft's speed and altitude requirements, two engines. The powerplant chosen for it was the Allison inline V-1710 engine, the first inline engine to develop 1,000 hp, and the only American liquid-cooled V12 to see military usage in World War II (the Allison Engine Company was a subsidiary of General Motors). Each would be combined with a General Electric Type B-5 two-stage, exhaust-driven turbo-supercharger. They were to be mounted at the forward ends of two long booms, which also housed the turbo-superchargers and which merged at the rear of the aircraft into its twin tails.

What was to become the P-38's center fuselage pod, or gondola, was also unique, containing as it did both the cockpit and, directly in front of it, the guns, which would produce an easily aimed, concentrated barrage. By the end of the war, in nearly one-quarter of the P-38s built, the guns had been replaced by cameras for its F-4 and F-5 photo reconnaissance (PR) models.

On June 23, 1937, the Air Corps placed its contract order number AC-9974 with Lockheed for an experimental prototype, the XP-38, Lockheed Model 022-64-01, for which it agreed to pay $163,000. Work began on it immediately, and it was finally completed in January 1939, whereupon it was partly disassembled and trucked to March Field, in nearby Riverside, California, to be prepared for its first test flights there.

The other, less successful USAAF fighter resulting from Specification X-608 was Bell's P-39 Airacobra. Like the P-38, the P-39 was a radical design for its time. It also featured tricycle landing gear, plus automobile-type doors for the pilot, an engine located in the fuselage behind the cockpit and connected to the propeller by means of a driveshaft running under it—and a very sleek design. Its prototype turned out to be almost as fast as the XP-38, likewise utilizing a two-stage turbo-supercharger, but after Bell added armor and armament and was forced to revert to a single-stage turbo-supercharger, its top speed and climb rate quickly deteriorated. Although the P-39 was used in fairly large numbers in the Pacific and North Africa early in the war, its greatest success was with the Soviet Air Force, which received a large percentage of them—though it hardly matched the P-38's.

Above: One of several Model 10 Electras operated by the USAAC. (*Lockheed photo*)

Below: Lockheed's Hudson assembly line. (*Lockheed photo*)

Although the Lockheed Model 22's original specs did not call for counter-rotating propellers, it was decided during the XP-38's construction to utilize that innovation to counter the engines' torque, which turned out to be an inspired decision. One of the unique features of the Allison V-1710 was its ability to turn the output shaft either clockwise or counter-clockwise by assembling it with the crankshaft turned end-for-end and installing an idler gear in the drive train to the supercharger and camshaft plus a starter that turned in the proper direction—as well as rearranging the ignition wiring on the correct side to accommodate a change in the firing order.

The XP-38's canopy was a semi-bubble type with very little framing, but the need for the heavily framed canopy that was so noticeable later would become obvious after they started coming off during pullouts from high-speed dives, which resulted in the insertion of a metal strap across the top of the canopy and the soon-to-be familiar cross braces on its side panels.

Chosen to fly the XP-38 initially was the USAAC's 1Lt. Benjamin S. Kelsey, who had an aeronautical engineering degree from MIT and was a skilled test pilot. At that time, he was head of the Air Corps' Pursuit Projects Office at Wright Field, Ohio, so his impressions of the P-38 would definitely hold a lot of weight.

Kelsey first made some preliminary high-speed taxi tests, which revealed the aircraft's inadequate braking system. The XP-38 experienced minor damage when it skidded off the March Field runway at one point, but it was quickly repaired. Its first flight took place on January 27, 1939, and it, too, was problematic. During it, three of the four aluminum mounts for the flaps broke, causing some severe vibration, but Kelsey was able to land it OK. The mounts were replaced by superior steel versions, and he test flew it six more times, during which flights it proved itself to be what was then the fastest fighter in the world, with an official top speed of 413 mph at 20,000 feet. The XP-38's climb rate was six and a half minutes to that same altitude and its service ceiling was 38,000 feet.

Ben Kelsey would have already been aware of the P-38's very high wing loading (weight divided by wing area) and very low power loading (weight divided by hp), and he was happy to confirm that the latter definitely improved the aircraft's maneuverability. Mainly due to its large wing area, rolling was not to be one of the P-38's strong points, at least until the addition of hydraulically boosted aileron controls in 1944, but the extreme tapering of its wings tended to help somewhat in that regard. On the other hand, that tapering also restricted the size of the ailerons, which had the opposite effect, requiring aggressive input on the controls by the pilot to maintain a decent roll rate.

Despite some other potentially worrisome problems that had been revealed during the flight tests at March Field—most notably inadequate engine cooling and buffeting, or flutter, in the plane's tail section—it was decided to make a cross-country flight to bring the XP-38 and the Air Corps some added publicity. So it was that on February 11, 1939, 1Lt. Kelsey took off from March *en route* to a refueling stop in Amarillo, Texas, and then on to his home base, Wright Field, where he was met by Gen. Henry H. "Hap" Arnold, Chief of the Army Air Corps.

Kelsey had averaged 360 mph on his flight from California, and Gen. Arnold ordered him to continue on to Mitchel Field, on Long Island, New York. However, on his approach to Mitchel, he experienced carburetor icing, which caused the engines to fail and Kelsey to crash-land on a golf course a half mile short of the runway. Although he was unhurt, the XP-38, having accumulated just eleven hours and fifty minutes of flying time in a little over two weeks, was destroyed—a serious setback to the aircraft's development.

Over the full 2,400 miles, Kelsey had averaged 340 mph, including the unofficial achievement of 420 mph at one point between Ohio and New York. The cross-country flight had certainly demonstrated the aircraft's potential, and two days after the crash, Kelsey and Arnold traveled together to Washington, D.C., to ask the government for more funding for it. The result, on April 27, was a contract for thirteen YP-38s for evaluation by the Air Corps—the "Y" being its designation for prototype aircraft. They were delivered in September, and at least four of them were provided to the 1st Pursuit Group (PG) at Selfridge Field, Michigan, for the planned service evaluation.

One of the YP-38s was flown to Langley Field, Virginia, for wind tunnel tests to hopefully locate the source of the disturbing tail buffeting problem. It was thought initially that the propwash created by the tips of the counter-rotating props turning inward may have contributed to it, so on subsequent models, they switched the engines so the propellers turned outward. This did not solve the problem, however, and the actual solution turned out to be the installation of aerodynamic fillets where the wing roots joined the fuselage, thereby smoothing the air flow from the gondola over the tail. The first of them were installed on the P-322 Lightning I model that was ordered by the British.

As to the engine cooling problem, although it would not be completely solved until the appearance of the redesigned P-38J in late 1943, some measures were taken to at least alleviate it. The radiators on the outside of each boom were enlarged, and two oil cooler air intakes were inserted underneath each engine.

Once the evaluation of the YP-38s had proven the aircraft to be considerably more than satisfactory, Lockheed began manufacturing continually improved production models. First there was the P-38, with no suffix letter designation, of which twenty-nine were built (the other thirty-six aircraft in the order for which being completed as P-38Ds), and then the P-38E, one of which would be the first Lightning to shoot down an enemy aircraft (e/a).

In 1940, the company purchased the Union Air Terminal adjacent to its Burbank factory and renamed it the Lockheed Air Terminal. It would be utilized to test fly the new P-38s coming off its assembly lines prior to their acceptance by the Air Corps—and to commence their ferry flights to military air bases around the country and later to ports on both coasts for shipment overseas.

In the late summer and fall of 1941, the 1st PG's Republic P-43s and new P-38s participated in the army war games comprised of the Louisiana and the Carolina Maneuvers. The opposing forces were the Red and the White, and their supporting aircraft displayed temporary red or white crosses on their noses and wings to indicate which side they were on.

When the Japanese bombed Pearl Harbor, Hawaii, on December 7, 1941 and the U.S. suddenly found itself at war with their empire and with Germany, P-38 production had really just gotten underway, nearly three years after the type's initial flight. As of December 5, there were sixty-nine Lightnings in the USAAF's inventory. The first P-38E had been delivered to it just a few days earlier, and it would be three months before it received the first Lightning PR aircraft. None of them were ready to engage the enemy at that point,

YP-38s on the Lockheed production line. (*Michael Bates collection*)

Above: This YP-38 was displayed by the 1st PG at Selfridge Field, Michigan, on Army Day, April 6, 1941. (*Michael Bates collection*)

Below: These early model 1st PG Lightnings were photographed at Little Rock, Arkansas, in mid-1941. (*Michael Bates collection*)

May 6, 1941: Lockheed workers finishing the last of the YP-38s, 39-701. (*Michael Bates collection*)

Some of the thirty-six P-38Ds that were built during the summer of 1941. In the background are several RAF Hudsons. Lockheed was just beginning a huge expansion and space was limited—hence their final assembly outdoors in the California sunshine. (*Lockheed photo*)

July 1941: P-38s are being completed outside under arc lights by Lockheed's night shift. (*Michael Bates collection*)

Above and below: P-38Ds of the 1st PG that participated in the 1941 Army war games, sporting the white crosses of the White Force. The top photo was taken during the Carolina Maneuvers. (*Michael Bates collection*)

Above: A red-crossed 1st PG P-38D of the Red Force during the 1941 Army maneuvers in the American south. (*Michael Bates collection*)

Below: A nice shot of a 1st PG P-38D in flight over southern California. (*USAF photo*)

but it would not be too long before they did. The first F-4 photo recon mission over enemy territory (New Guinea) was flown in May 1942 and the P-38's initial combat action would take place over Alaska's Aleutian Islands the following August.

By the end of 1942, there would be a huge demand for the latest models of the P-38 and of its new PR version, the F-5, and Lockheed continued to make the improvements and upgrades to the Lightning that would culminate a year and a half later in the ultimate P-38, the L model, which would prove to be one of World War II's best fighters. This process would require the co-operation of Lockheed engineers and test pilots with P-38 maintenance personnel and company technical representatives in the field.

2

Stateside Lightnings

During World War II, Lightnings were a common sight in the skies of the U.S.'s Southwestern and Pacific Coast states, although much less so east of the Mississippi River. One area where they could be spotted in particularly large numbers was southern California.

The U.S. Army Air Forces (USAAF) had been created in June 1941, with the old U.S. Army Air Corps (USAAC) as one of its components. The USAAC designation was finally discontinued in March 1942, although it remained in popular use for some time afterward.

Over a period of two and a half years, eight USAAF fighter groups trained on P-38s in California prior to deploying to Britain. Besides being conveniently close to the Lockheed plant, the source of their aircraft, the weather there was among the world's best for flight training, and the terrain was usefully varied: the Pacific Ocean, a large urban area (Los Angeles), mountains, and a huge desert. Twelve airfields throughout the southern California area were utilized for P-38 training, some of them dedicated military bases and others private or municipal airports that were taken over by the USAAF for the war's duration.

Two of these groups that were training in California in early 1942 were pre-war units that were in the process of converting to the P-38. At the time of the Japanese attack on Pearl Harbor, the 14th PG was based at March Field, near Riverside, where a P-38 had flown for the first time nearly three years earlier. Its 49th Pursuit Squadron (PS) had received the group's first Lightnings the previous October, but its re-equipment with them would not be completed until the following spring, as its 48th and 50th Squadrons did not receive their first P-38s until early in the new year.

The first several months of the U.S.'s involvement in the war were rather chaotic for the 14th PG as it trained to become proficient with its new aircraft while providing part of the air defense of southern California (a carrier attack on the area was considered a distinct possibility, at least until the Imperial Japanese Navy's (IJN) defeat in the Battle of Midway in June). Its squadrons moved around a lot initially; although officially based at March Field, they spent time at the Muroc Lake Bombing and Gunnery Range in the Mojave Desert, at the North Island Naval Air Station on Coronado Island in San Diego, and at Long Beach Army Air Field (AAF), adjacent to Daugherty Field, that city's airport. In February, Group H.Q. moved back to Hamilton Field, near San Francisco, where it had been activated the year before. The 49th Squadron transferred to nearby Mills Field, San Francisco's municipal airport, and the 50th Squadron moved to the Oakland Airport. The 48th Squadron remained in southern California, alternating between March and North Island.

In May, the 14th, now redesignated a 'fighter' group, was split in two, with half of its experienced personnel transferring to the new 78th FG, from which it got in exchange some inexperienced replacements. The following month, it received orders for its deployment to England, which commenced on July 1.

The 1st PG had served with distinction in World War I, and since 1922, it had been based at Selfridge Field in Michigan. Two of its World War I squadrons, the 27th and 94th, were still assigned to it and had been joined in early 1941 by the 71st PS. In the late spring of that year, the 27th PS had been the first operational Air Corps unit to receive P-38s, for service testing, shortly after which it utilized them in that year's army maneuvers in the Southeastern U.S. The first operational P-38 accident—and fatality—occurred when 2Lt. Guy L. Putnam was killed in the crash of YP-38 serial number 39-699 at Selfridge Field on June 23. The 71st and 94th Squadrons were assigned their first Lightnings later that year, and by early 1942, the group was operating a mixture of YP-38s, P-38s (no model designation), P-38Ds, and P-38Es.

On December 7, 1941, the 94th PS's pilots were flying across Texas to California for detached duty at March Field. When they arrived there the following day, they were redirected to North Island. Within a few days, the 94th had been joined by the rest of the group, which was now also part of southern California's air defense.

In late December, the 27th PS moved to Mines Field, near Los Angeles. In early January, the 94th was reassigned to Long Beach, and in mid-February, the 71st transferred to the Grand Central Air Terminal in Glendale. The group flew numerous defensive patrols that were uneventful other than the loss of three pilots in accidents.

Second Lieutenant Jack M. Ilfrey, who had graduated with USAAF pilot training Class 41-I on December 12, 1941, was assigned to the 94th PS at North Island later that same month, where and when he was introduced to the P-38 and quickly learned to fly it, as he later recalled:

> In those days we first read the flight manual over, several times. We walked around and around the P-38 with the flight leader. We were taught the proper procedures and fired up the engines. Practiced taxiing until we got the gallop out of it. Then we were ready for our first takeoff. No piggy-backs [two-seaters] in those days. It was the biggest thrill of my then young life. If you got it back on the ground, you were then a qualified P-38 pilot. Some didn't.

In April, the 1st PG traded twenty-three of its officers and 338 enlisted men to the 82nd PG, newly arrived in California, for an approximately equal number of its less experienced personnel. Also that month, the group was informed of its imminent deployment to England and its pilots picked up their new P-38Fs—featuring the new underwing pylons that would allow them to carry auxiliary fuel tanks and bombs—at the Lockheed factory.

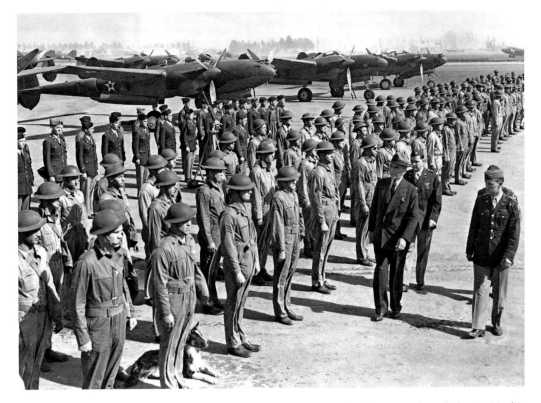

March 1942: America's World War I "Aces of Aces," Eddie Rickenbacker (in civilian clothes), visits his old squadron, the 94th Pursuit, at the Long Beach, California, Airport. The P-38s in the background include several "D" models, easily identifiable by their unique gun enclosure tubes. (*Michael Bates collection*)

The 82nd PG, comprised of the 95th, 96th, and 97th PSs, had been activated at Harding Field, near Baton Rouge, Louisiana, in February. It was an unusual unit, due to the fact that most of the pilots that were assigned to it initially were not officers, but rather enlisted men—staff sergeants.

Due to the potential threat to the U.S. posed by Germany's military successes in Europe, and especially that posed by the Imperial Japanese Empire in the Pacific, by 1941, it had become obvious that the country's military needed to be greatly expanded, and soon. That included the USAAC, which desperately needed more units, more planes, and more pilots. So, the two years of college requirement for prospective Air Corps pilots was scrapped, until the end of the upcoming war; henceforth, they would only be required to possess a high school diploma and be able to pass rigid mental, physical, and aptitude tests.

The Air Corps started that ball rolling in June 1941 by offering its already serving and qualified young enlisted men the opportunity to become aviation cadets. The first class that included these men was 42-C, which graduated in March 1942, and most of its ninety-three new staff sergeant pilots were assigned in April to the 82nd PG. From Harding Field, they, along with a small cadre of officers and non-flying enlisted men, were transported at the end of that month to Muroc, California, where they were to be taught to fly the P-38 on its huge dry lake bed.

The group also then received that aforementioned infusion of experienced pilots and ground crewmen from the 1st PG, the former then taking on its leadership roles—headquarters officers and squadron and flight leaders. The new group CO, Lt. Col. William F. Covington, Jr., who had been a squadron commander in the 1st PG, later commented on the unique aviators under his command:

> We began to receive pilots of a type I had never expected. They were all staff sergeant pilots! And enough of them to assign about twenty-five to each squadron. I can't say enough good things about these men; they fell right into line and were all eager to fly a P-38. No disciplinary problems at all. We set up a ground school which gave them what our organization expected of them and also a thorough briefing on the P-38. The P-38 was a very forgiving airplane and, while we had a few accidents, we were able to check out all the pilots with no washouts.[1]

One of those staff sergeant pilots, the 96th Squadron's Fred J. Wolfe, later recalled his first flight in a Lightning at Muroc:

> When my turn came to check out in the P-38 I taxied out to the takeoff position and waited for tower clearance. While waiting I was nervous as a cat. My knees were shaking like a leaf as I tried to hold the brakes. As I sat there, a big black cloud billowed up on the other side of the lake bed. I found out later that a new pilot had tried to do a loop during his checkout flight and was killed. He was from one of the other squadrons. The tower gave me takeoff clearance and a new P-38 pilot was born.[2]

After two weeks at Muroc, its sergeant pilots having learned the basics of flying the Lightning and having gotten itself somewhat organized, the 82nd FG moved to the Los Angeles area to take the place of the departing 1st FG—the 95th FS to Mines Field, the 96th to Glendale, and the 97th to Long Beach. Group H.Q. initially relocated to downtown Los Angeles, but it joined the 96th Squadron at Glendale in August. Also at that time, the group received a few junior officer pilots from the 55th FG in Washington State.

Seven of the 82nd's sergeant pilots would die in flying accidents in the U.S. The first was Rudolph O. Dear of the 95th PS, who bailed out of P-38E 41-2004 over Muroc on May 6. His parachute did not fully open, and it was believed that he had hit the tail of the aircraft after exiting the cockpit. This was the accident Fred Wolfe had witnessed just before taking off on his first flight in a P-38.

In early September, the 82nd received its orders to proceed to the British Isles. While most of the group's personnel departed Los Angeles by train, some of the pilots delivered P-38s to Newark, New Jersey, for shipment overseas. On September 19, the 95th Squadron's S/Sgt. Samuel P. Bradshaw, Jr., took off from Harrisburg, Pennsylvania, in P-38F-5 42-12584 for the last leg of his ferry flight to Newark. Shortly thereafter, he flew into a cloud-covered hill and was killed. His fellow sergeant pilots all received their commissions before departing for Scotland on the ocean liner *Queen Mary*.

Immediately replacing the 82nd PG at Muroc at the end of April 1942 was the 78th PG, which had been activated at Baer Field, near Fort Wayne, Indiana, on February 9, and which it left on April 25. In mid-May, Group H.Q. and its 83rd and 84th Squadrons moved

Right: Armorers working on No. 45, a 95th FS P-38 named *Frances*, at Mines Field. (*Author's collection*)

Below: Pilots of the 95th FS, 82nd FG on a training flight along the southern California coast. Leading them, in his No. 40, P-38E 41-2223, is the squadron commander, Capt. Robert E. Kirtley. (*Author's collection*)

More P-38s of the 95th FS over southern California. After the 82nd FG left for England in September 1942, P-38F 41-7506 (No. 59) was transferred to the 331st FS, a new P-38 operational training unit, with which it was destroyed in a take-off accident on December 7. P-38E 41-2092 (No. 43) was flown by S/Sgt. William J. Schildt, a future ace. This aircraft was subsequently transferred to the 54th FS in the Aleutians, where it was destroyed in a crash on December 29, 1944. (*Author's collection*)

north to the San Francisco area—Hamilton Field, Mills Field, and the Oakland Airport, respectively, although the 83rd also moved to Hamilton the following month. The 82nd Squadron stayed in southern California, at San Diego.

Robert E. Eby was then, as a second lieutenant, the 78th's Assistant Group Operations Officer. He remembered later:

> All squadrons were constantly on alert with one flight of four pilots in readiness with the planes warmed up and ready to scramble on orders from [IV] Fighter Command. Many times a civilian would advise Fighter Command of a Japanese balloon off the Golden Gate and we would scramble a flight out. Invariably it turned out to be a cumulous cloud on a moonlit night.[3]

The USAAF had divided the continental U.S. among four of its subordinate numbered air forces, mostly for training purposes. They were the First, in the Northeast; the Second (Northwest); the Third (Southeast); and the Fourth (Southwest).

When the 78th PG began its move to England in early November, it was at Hamilton Field, except for the 82nd Squadron, which had just moved from San Diego to March Field.

P-38 OTUs

It had become obvious that requiring the P-38 groups training in the U.S. to teach newly assigned pilots, most of them fresh out of advanced flying schools, how to actually fly the Lightning was inefficient, as it took time and personnel away from their primary task of preparing the units for combat. It would be much more practical to have those novice military pilots become proficient in the P-38 *before* being assigned to them—specifically by completing a course with a P-38 operational training unit (OTU). So it was that the first of such units, the 329th FG, was activated on the West Coast in July 1942.

The 329th FG and its three squadrons, the 330th, 331st, and 332nd, were activated at Hamilton Field on July 10 but moved to Paine Field in Washington four days later. In September, they moved to southern California, but to different bases. Group H.Q. and the 330th FS went to Glendale, the 331st to nearby Inglewood (Mines Field), and the 332nd to the Orange County Airport in Santa Ana. The 330th and 331st moved again in November, to San Diego and the Van Nuys Metropolitan Airport, respectively. They all then stayed put until August 1943, when the 331st was transferred to Olympia Army Air Base (AAB) in Washington State (a satellite of McChord Field, near Tacoma) and the 332nd to Ontario AAF, also in southern California—although it moved back to Santa Ana two months later. The 331st moved to Ellensburg AAF, in Washington, in early November and then joined Group H.Q. at Ontario at the end of December.

In November 1942, the 337th FS, which had been activated two months earlier in Iceland with the 342nd Composite Group (CG), also joined the 329th FG at Glendale, and likewise moved to Ontario in December 1943.

Due to the demand for P-38 pilots, another OTU, the 360th FG, was activated at Glendale in January 1943 to help produce them. Its squadrons were the 371st, 372nd, and

Lt. Harvey Honeycutt, Jr., who was undergoing P-38 operational training with the 332nd FS at the Orange County Airport in California, experienced a "landing accident due to mechanical failure" on February 21, 1944, in P-38G-10 42-13261. Honeycutt later served with the 14th FG in Italy. (*Michael Bates collection*)

Pilots of the 330th FS, a P-38 operational training unit, relax in their ready room at the North Island Naval Air Station in San Diego. (*Author's collection*)

Above left: Unidentified pilots in training with the 330th FS at San Diego in 1943. The aircraft is P-38H-5 42-66814, named *LADY LUCK*, on which has also been bestowed the less formal moniker *Boogie Woogie Pete*. (*Author's collection*)

Above right: An unidentified 330th FS instructor pilot shares some words of wisdom with his students, who have recently won their wings and are now being taught to fly the P-38. Most of the unit's instructors were combat veterans of either North Africa or the Pacific Theater. (*Author's collection*)

Below: On March 3, 1944, during a training flight out of the North Island Naval Air Station, P-38G-10 42-13469 of the 330th FS ended up on a nearby beach when its pilot ran out of fuel and had to crash-land it. (*Author's collection*)

P-38 pilots of the 337th FS, flying from Glendale and Ontario, California, did some of their operational training over the Mojave Desert, as in this photo. P-38H-5 42-66765, in the foreground, was badly damaged in a landing accident at Glendale's Grand Central Air Terminal on December 18, 1943. (*Michael Bates collection*)

373rd. The group moved to Muroc AAB in April, where it was joined by the 446th FS, which was activated there in May. In September, the group moved to Salinas AAB in central California—without the 373rd Squadron, which had transferred to the Lomita Flight Strip, near Long Beach, in July. In January 1944, Group H.Q. and the 371st and 372nd Squadrons moved to Santa Maria AAF, also in central California, and the 373rd and the 446th to Van Nuys.

One of the 360th FG's instructor pilots at Muroc was John A. Stege, a veteran of the 14th FG in North Africa, who recalled that experience years later:

> Our students came from Williams Field [Arizona], where they had just completed the twin-engine course in the AT-10. They had no prior experience in the P-38. So to acclimate them to the plane we had what were called "piggy-backs." The student would sit in the rear section of the P-38 where the radios had been. The trainee sat on a shelf-like structure and would be leaning over the pilot, known as the piggy-back driver, who occupied the pilot's seat. The student got about an hour and a half ride in this position, which included some single-engine operation. This part of the training was done at Palmdale Army Air Field. Additional training was given in formation flying, gunnery and cross-country, where we never got over 200 feet. Most of the planes were "war-weary" P-38Fs.

When these pilots completed their operational training, they were either assigned to P-38 units training in the States in preparation for overseas combat duty or sent overseas as P-38 replacement pilots and assigned to combat units there.

Both groups were disbanded effective March 31, 1944, and a reorganized operational pilot training program went into effect. The new OTUs were initially designated as Base

Lockheed test pilot Milo Burcham (seen addressing the crowd from the wing of P-38L-1 44-24070) visited the 433rd BU at Chico, California, in early August 1944. Besides delivering a pep talk, he also gave a flight demonstration. (*Lockheed photo*)

Units (BU), and then, starting in the fall of 1944, as Combat Crew Training Stations (CCTS). Although Lightnings would be utilized by many of them, those that specialized in P-38 operational fighter training were the 430th at Ephrata AAB in Washington; the 433rd at Chico AAF in northern California; the 434th at Santa Maria (taking over from the now defunct 371st and 372nd FSs); the 441st at Van Nuys, replacing the 446th FS; and the 443rd at Ontario, which replaced the 331st FS. Ephrata was originally a Bell P-39 and P-63 training facility, but it switched to P-38s in November 1944. As had been true of the units they replaced, most of the instructor pilots in these OTUs were P-38 combat veterans.

An Ontario AAF newsletter describes how the 443rd BU's participation in the USAAF's Replacement Pilot Training Program worked. It states, in part:

At OAAF, the trainee pilot receives a rapid but thorough pre-checkout training in P-38 aircraft immediately upon arrival at this station. After satisfying his particular Section Commander that he understands all factors of the P-38 he is checked out. After several hours of Engineering or Transition flying the trainee proceeds on into combat training. This training consists of Elementary Formation, Altitude Formation, Simulated Camera and Aerial Gunnery (both at low and high altitude), Individual Combat, Acrobatics,

P-38s of the 434th BU on a formation flight over northern California. The second photo is a close-up of P-38L-5 44-25301, No. 701. (*Author's collection*)

June 21, 1944: A P.E. class being conducted in front of 434th Base Unit P-38s at Santa Rosa AAF in California. (*Author's collection*)

Night Flying, Ground Gunnery, Dive and Skip Bombing, Fighter Instrument and Navigation.

Due to the rigidness of the course as set up by FAF [Fourth Air Force], it is possible to ascertain shortly after a trainee starts flying fighter aircraft whether he is suited for this type of combat duty. If a man is not adaptable to fighters, he is removed from this training unit.

There was also a unique training program for future P-38 pilots at Williams Field outside Glendale, Arizona, a suburb of Phoenix. Its advanced flight-training syllabus produced more Lightning pilots than any other. The aviation cadets at Williams trained initially in the single-engined North American AT-6; those chosen for twin-engined training (the potential P-38 pilots) moved on to the Curtiss-Wright AT-9 and then Lockheed RP-322s, the "castrated" Lightnings that had originally been ordered for the Royal Air Force (RAF). The official USAF history *The Army Air Forces in World War II* notes that "during 1943 and a part of 1944, Williams Field was unique in that it was the only P-38 transition school in the country."

Of the 143 RP-322s built, at least eighty-five are known to have been utilized to train those future P-38 pilots at Williams Field. They were assigned there initially to the 318th Twin-Engined Advanced Flying Training Group (TEAFTG) and its two squadrons, the 981st and 982nd Twin-Engined Advanced Flying Training Squadrons (TEAFTS), but in mid-1943, those units were consolidated into the new 535th TEAFTS. Relatively few of its RP-322s survived until the end of the war, having been flown constantly for several years mostly by very inexperienced pilots. They were involved in numerous flying accidents at Williams, in which many were destroyed and twelve of their pilots killed.

Dick Bong flew this Lightning he named *Marge*, after his fiancée—P-38J-20 44-23481—for publicity purposes while on leave in the U.S. during the spring and summer of 1944, during which time he visited a number of stateside training bases. This aircraft later saw service with the Fifteenth AF in Italy. (*John Stanaway collection*)

Two stateside P-38s creating smokescreens with airborne smoke generators. P-38L-1 44-24356, in the foreground, is known to have served with the 430th Base Unit at Ephrata AAB in Washington in 1944. (*Michael Bates collection*)

Right: In early 1945, these two combat veterans were instructor pilots with the 441st Combat Crew Training Station at the Van Nuys Metropolitan Airport in southern California. In the Lightning's cockpit is 1Lt. Kenneth R. Frost, who had recently completed a tour with the 82nd FG in Italy. Observing him is Capt. Thomas D. Harmon, the former All-American football player, who had served with the 449th FS in China. (*USAF photo*)

Below: July 27, 1945: The aforementioned 1Lt. Ken Frost (on the far left), now a rocket-firing gunnery instructor, and some of his students with the 444th Combat Crew Training Station at the Daggett Municipal Airport in California's Mojave Desert. Frost was killed less than two months later, on September 17, when his P-38 stalled at low level and crashed during a training mission. (*USAF photo*)

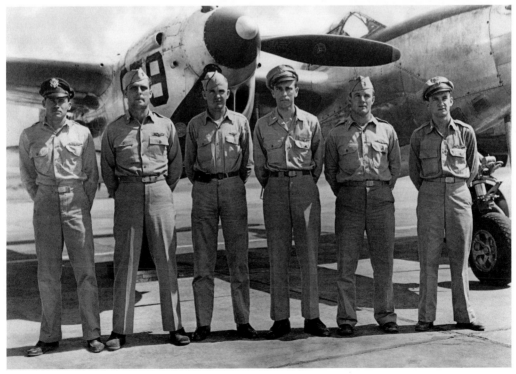

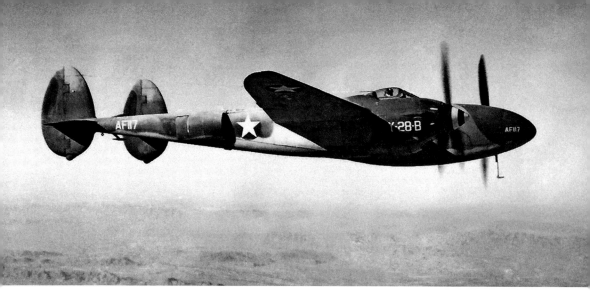

Above: March 25, 1943: Lightning II AF117 over the nearby desert during a training flight from Williams Field, Arizona. (*Michael Bates collection*)

Left: September 1943: Sgt. Robert D. Morris was the crew chief of another of Williams Field's "castrated" Lightnings, AF 126. Note the absence of guns. (*Michael Bates collection*)

Two more West Coast P-38 units departed the U.S. for England and the Eighth AF during the summer of 1943. They were the 20th FG, then based at McChord Field in Washington State, and the 55th FG, at March Field in California.

The 20th FG, comprised of the 55th, 77th, and 79th FSs, had been active all through the 1930s. Shortly after its arrival at Paine Field, Washington, 25 miles north of Seattle, in September 1942, its P-39s and P-40s were replaced with P-38s. In early January 1943, the group moved to March Field, from which it left for England in mid-August.

The 55th PG, which had been activated in January 1941, was based at the Portland-Columbia Airport in Oregon when the U.S. entered the war; its assigned squadrons were then the 37th, 38th, and 54th. In early 1942, the group traded in its Republic P-43s for P-38s, by which time it had been transferred to Washington—H.Q. and the 54th PS going to Paine Field, the 38th PS to McChord Field, and the 37th PS to the Olympia Airport. In May, the 54th, now a "fighter" squadron, was transferred to the Eleventh Air Force (AF) in the Aleutians and was replaced several months later by the 338th FS at McChord. The group also lost the 37th Squadron in February 1943 when it was sent to North Africa to join the reorganized 14th FG. It was replaced by the 343rd FS, also at McChord. During that time, many of the 55th's more experienced pilots had been transferred to other P-38 units prior to their moving overseas. The group left for England at the end of August.

The Eighth AF's next future P-38 unit, the 364th FG, with the new official designation TE (Twin Engine) was activated at Glendale, California, on June 1, 1943 (the Twin Engine designation for P-38 units had gone into effect the previous November). It moved to nearby Van Nuys in August, but in October, the group's three squadrons split up. H.Q. and the 384th FS went to Ontario; the 383rd to the Oxnard Flight Strip, on the Pacific Coast north of Los Angeles; and the 385th to Santa Maria, with H.Q. and the other two squadrons joining it there in December. The 364th's personnel left by train from Santa Maria for New York on January 14, 1944, *en route* to England.

Southern California continued to be the birthplace of new P-38 units. On August 1, 1943, yet another was activated there, at Glendale. This was the 474th FG (TE), comprised of the 428th, 429th, and 430th FSs.

On August 8, the fledgling 474th received six well-used P-38Hs on loan from the 337th FS, the OTU that was also based at Glendale. As soon as they were operational, the group commander, Lt. Col. Clinton C. Wasem, began giving his pilots who had not yet flown a P-38 piggy-back rides in one of them, a two-seater that had been modified for that purpose. A 474th FG historian noted that "It saved him [Wasem] and other busy officers a lot of valuable time. The trainee pilot could see how the P-38 was flown and feel the plane's power."

The 474th moved to Van Nuys in mid-October, having finally begun to receive some of its own P-38s. Most of them were high-time Fs and Gs, but two new J-10s were received on November 2. Its pilots' real training then began, this including gunnery at the Muroc range. In mid-November, the group received an infusion of more than forty new pilots from the 360th FG, with which they had just completed their P-38 operational training.

The first of the five fatal accidents the 474th FG would suffer in the States took place on November 11, when 2Lt. James G. Ware of the 429th FS, flying P-38G-3 42-12797, was killed during an instrument flight when he crashed into a mountain. Another pilot on that

June 4, 1943: The leaders of the 55th FG—squadron commanders and Group H.Q. pilots—pose for a formal photographic portrait at McChord Field, Washington. The aircraft in the background, P-38G-13 43-2312, was assigned to the 343rd FS but was flown by the group commander, Lt. Col. Frank B. James (center). (*Michael Bates collection*)

In this P-38 training accident 2Lt. Norman F. Bettin of the 364th FG's 383rd FS stalled out and crashed RP-38E 41-1995 while landing at the Oxnard Flight strip in southern California on November 15, 1943. (*Author's collection*)

flight crash-landed in a riverbed, destroying his plane but emerging from it unhurt. Two 428th Squadron pilots died in separate accidents on November 29. Pilot fatality number four took place the very next day, when another 428th pilot crashed into the desert north of Lancaster.

As was typically the case, the group's three squadrons split up to train individually until it was time to ship out to England. Group H.Q. and the 430th Squadron went to Oxnard, the 428th to Palmdale, and the 429th to Lomita. Its last pilot death in the U.S. was experienced by the latter squadron on January 17, 1944, when 2Lt. Merle V. Ogden, flying P-38J-10 42-67693, was killed in a crash-landing at Lomita. The whole group reunited at Santa Maria AAF in early February and began its "Overseas Movement" from there on the 15th.

The last USAAF fighter group to train on P-38s in the U.S. prior to deploying to an overseas combat theater was the 479th, which was made up of the 434th, 435th, and 436th FSs. It was activated at Glendale, California, on October 28, 1943. Its first CO, Lt. Col. Leo F. Dusard, Jr., was soon transferred to the Pacific Theater, where he took command of the Thirteenth AF's 347th FG. His replacement was to have been Lt. Col. William E. Dyess, a hero of the disastrous Philippines campaign of 1941–42; however, he was killed at Glendale on December 22 while checking out in a P-38 with the 337th FS when he lost an engine on take-off and crashed. He was replaced by Lt. Col. Kyle L. Riddle, after whom the group was later nicknamed "Riddle's Raiders."

The 479th's squadrons split up temporarily in early February 1944, with Group H.Q. and the 434th Squadron moving to the Lomita Flight Strip; the 435th to the Oxnard Flight Strip; and the 436th to Palmdale AAF, in the Mojave Desert near Muroc. Although there were, inevitably, a few flying accidents as the pilots familiarized themselves with the P-38, the only death took place on March 12, when Deputy Group Commander Maj. Robert C. Twyman suffered fatal injuries when he parachuted from his P-38 while practicing some aerobatic maneuvers.

The 436th Squadron's Capt. Jules D. Biscayart had a rather harrowing experience on March 25 while flying P-38F-13 43-2043, as he later recalled:

I was called on to take a last minute late afternoon aerial gunnery training mission over San Nicholas Island, about fifty miles off the coast, with a flight of four trainees. Out there, my right engine gave a couple of puffs of smoke, followed by a loud bang, and caught fire. I immediately turned toward shore, hoping to be able to belly in on the beach, as I knew there were sharks out there and it being late in the day the rescue people might not be able to find me.

I continued on, with my mates telling me the engine was smoking badly and to bail out. I made it to within gliding distance of the beach then realized that Van Nuys Airport was only a few miles farther, so I attempted to make it there. I was cleared in, but about a mile out on final approach the engine exploded and I bailed out, landing in an orange tree![4]

The 479th reunited at Santa Maria in early April and on the 15th departed for England.

P-38J-10 42-67695 was initially assigned to its 436th FS while the 479th FG was training in southern California but was later reassigned to the 332nd FS, the Santa Ana-based P-38 operational training unit. It was destroyed in a crash-landing on March 17, 1944. (*Author's collection*)

Capt. Jules Biscayart of the 436th FS while training in southern California. Note how the P-38's canopy hinges backward. (*Author's collection*)

Stateside Photo Reconnaissance Training

The first utilization of aircraft in warfare, during World War I, was for reconnaissance, initially just visual and then with cameras—photo reconnaissance. By 1941, the USAAC realized that it was going to be even more important in the war in which it would almost certainly soon be involved. The British RAF was already proving that to be true, and it would assist the new USAAF in that area when the time came.

It did not take long after America's entry into the war in December 1941 for the Air Forces to initiate a photo reconnaissance training program that was run by the Photo Reconnaissance OTU, which was activated at Colorado Springs, Colorado, in April 1942. The location chosen for it was adjacent to the Colorado Springs Municipal Airport, 7 miles east of the city. Construction of the new army air base began in May, and the runways were completed in early August, shortly after which its first aircraft, Lockheed F-4-1s, arrived. It would be the center for USAAF PR training during the first two years of the war. Colorado Springs had been chosen for a number of reasons, the two main ones being the clear air and generally good weather and its proximity to the Air Forces' Photographic School at Lowry Field in nearby Denver.

The PR training at Colorado Springs AAB actually commenced in June, under the supervision of the 2nd Photographic Group (PG), which had been activated in early May and included the 6th, 7th, and 10th Photographic Reconnaissance Squadrons (PRS). They continued to be the USAAF's primary photo recon training units until they were disbanded, effective May 1, 1944. Since there were no PR aircraft available to them initially, ground school classes were the order of the day, although the pilots were able to get in some flight time in utility or training aircraft from the runway at the adjacent civilian airport.

Two USAAF PR units, the 8th and 9th Photographic Squadrons (PS), were already serving overseas when PR training commenced at Colorado Springs. Both had been activated on February 1, 1942—the 8th at March Field in California and the 9th at Mitchel Field in New York. Part of the 8th PS shipped out to Australia in March, and the rest of the squadron joined it there in June. The 9th PS moved to Bradley Field in Connecticut in March and then across the country to Felts Field, near Spokane, Washington, the following month before shipping out to India in May.

Another PR group, the 3rd, was activated at Colorado Springs on June 20, 1942. It was comprised of the 5th, 12th, 13th, and 14th PRSs and the 15th Photographic Mapping Squadron (PMS), all of which would eventually see action in England or North Africa, although not necessarily as part of the 3rd PG. (The 12th PRS, which had been assigned to the 2nd PG since its activation in May, was transferred to the 3rd when it was activated.)

Once the first F-4s arrived on August 4, there soon followed the inevitable first accidents, both of them fatal. On August 7, Lt. William H. Borgersing of the 6th PRS was killed in a collision on the ground in F-4-1 41-2198. The following day, 1Lt. Edward J. Peterson, a Coloradan, was killed when an engine of 41-2202 failed on take-off and he crashed in it. The airfield was renamed Peterson Field in his honor on December 13.

The 3rd PG was not at Colorado Springs very long, as it moved to England in mid-August. Its only original squadron that would be assigned to it there was the 15th. The 12th and 13th Squadrons were sent overseas independently in October; the former ended up in Morocco, while the latter also went to England. The 14th left for England in April 1943.

While in training with the 7th Photographic Squadron of the 2nd Photographic Reconnaissance Group at Peterson Field, Colorado, 2Lt. John R. Richards bailed out of this F-4-1, serial number 41-2200, on May 23, 1943 after one of its engines caught fire. In the second photo, he is posing with another F-4 at Peterson. Richards later flew F-5s and Spitfire PRs with the 7th Photo Group in England. (*Author's collection*)

Meanwhile, the 2nd, which would be redesignated Photographic Reconnaissance and Mapping Group (PRMG) in May 1943, increased its training activities as the air forces' need for photo recon pilots grew. Peterson Field was a very busy place that year, as more photo recon units were activated and trained there before moving on to overseas combat theaters. One of them was the 4th PRG, which was activated on July 23, 1942. It had four squadrons assigned to it initially, only two of which accompanied it to the island of New Caledonia in the South Pacific in October 1942. They were the 17th PRS, which became the Thirteenth AF's first Lightning photo recon squadron, and the 18th PMS, which trained on Lightnings initially but switched to North American B-25 Mitchells before moving to the Pacific.

The 5th PG was activated at Colorado Springs on the same day as the 4th and moved to North Africa in July 1943. It had two Lightning squadrons at Peterson Field, the 21st and 22nd PR, but neither of them went with it to North Africa, where some new squadrons were assigned to it. The 21st was transferred to China and the Fourteenth AF in April 1943 and the 22nd was sent to England (the Eighth AF) in May.

The 6th PG was activated at Peterson on February 9, 1943 and left for Australia (the Fifth AF) in September. It was assigned a B-25 squadron and three F-5 squadrons, the 25th, 26th and 27th. The 25th and 26th accompanied it to Australia, but the 27th stayed in Colorado another month before transferring to England and the Eighth AF.

Another PR group that was based at Peterson very briefly was the 10th Photographic Group (Reconnaissance), formerly the 73rd Reconnaissance Group (RG), whose headquarters moved there in December 1943 but left for England and the Ninth AF the following month. It had no squadrons assigned to it in Colorado but would receive several in England.

The USAAF moved its PR training from Peterson Field to Will Rogers Field in Oklahoma City in October 1943, Peterson then becoming a heavy bomber training base. What was now the 2nd Photographic Reconnaissance Group (PRG) moved to Will Rogers early that month, at which time the 29th PRS was also assigned to it. After the 2nd was disbanded in May 1944, it was replaced at Will Rogers by the Reconnaissance Training Unit (RTU),

P-38J-20 44-23314 served as a modified two-seat trainer (TP) with the 379th Base Unit, a photo reconnaissance OTU, at Coffeyville AAF in Kansas. When this photo was taken, it was carrying neither cameras nor guns. It was rescued from postwar salvage when the USAAF donated it to USC's Hancock College of Aeronautics. No. 44-23314 subsequently went through several other civilian owners and is currently Planes of Fame's *23 SKIDOO*. (*Michael Bates collection*)

which in July became the 348th BU and in April 1945 the 348th Combat Crew Training Station. Two more PR training bases were established at Coffeyville AAF, Kansas, (the 379th BU) and at Muskogee AAF, Oklahoma, (the 349th BU).

From the fall of 1943 through the spring of 1944, eight new photo recon squadrons passed through Will Rogers Field for final training before moving to overseas combat theaters:

The 28th PRS: This unit had been activated at Peterson Field on May 1, 1943 along with the 7th PRMG, to which it was assigned until the following month, when it was attached to the 2nd PRMG. At the end of September, it was reassigned to the 89th Reconnaissance Training Wing (RTW), with which it moved to Will Rogers in October, and then, in November, was attached to the 9th PRG there. It transferred to Hawaii (Seventh AF) in January 1944. As to the 9th PRG, it was activated at Will Rogers on October 1, 1943 and was strictly a training unit, utilizing a variety of aircraft that included F-4s and F-5s. It was disbanded on May 6, 1944.

The 30th PRS: This unit had been activated on the same day as the 28th and was also assigned to the 7th PRMG initially. It, too, moved to Will Rogers Field in October 1943, where it became part of III Reconnaissance Command (RC). It moved to England (the Ninth AF) in January 1944.

The 31st PRS: This unit was formerly the 70th Reconnaissance Squadron (Fighter), but it was redesignated in August 1943, at Morris Field, North Carolina. It moved to Will Rogers in October and was also assigned to III RC. It likewise transferred to the Ninth AF in England in February 1944.

The 32nd PRS: This unit was previously the 45th Reconnaissance Squadron (Fighter), but was redesignated at Gainesville AAF, Florida, in August 1943; it too became part of III RC. It was transferred to Will Rogers in January 1944 and then to Italy and the Twelfth AF in March.

The 33rd PRS: Formerly the 24th Reconnaissance Squadron (Bombardment), this unit was also redesignated in August 1943 and assigned to III RC at Morris Field; it moved to Gainesville at the end of November and to Will Rogers in January 1944. It transferred to England (the Ninth AF) in April 1944.

The 34th PRS: This unit was renumbered and redesignated from the 126th Reconnaissance Squadron (Fighter) in August 1943 and also assigned to III RC, at Thomasville AAF, Georgia, but moved to Peterson Field at the end of that month. It transferred to Will Rogers in mid-October and was assigned there very briefly to the new 8th PRG, which had been activated earlier that month. (The 8th PRG moved to Gainesville later that month, without any squadrons having been assigned to it, and then to India in February 1944.) The 34th Squadron transferred back to III RC in January 1944 and moved to England and the Ninth AF in March.

The 35th PRS: This unit was renumbered and redesignated from the 123rd Reconnaissance Squadron (Bombardment) on August 11, 1943 at Redmond AAF, California. It then became part of the 77th Tactical Reconnaissance Group (TRG) but was soon attached to the 70th TRG until the end of October, shortly after which it moved to Gainesville and was transferred to III RC. It then trained with F-5s at Will Rogers Field from February 1944 until it left for India in April. The squadron joined the 14th AF in China in September of that year.

The 40th PRS: Formerly the 103rd Tactical Reconnaissance Squadron (TRS), this unit was renumbered and redesignated as such in October 1943 at Reading AAF, Pennsylvania, and was assigned to III RC. It moved to Birmingham AAF, Alabama, in November, to Will Rogers in February 1944, and to India and the Tenth AF three months later.

Four more new F-5 PRSs passed through Muskogee for their final stateside training during 1944:

The 36th PRS: This unit was previously the 28th TRS; it was renumbered and redesignated in October 1943 at Camp Campbell AAF, Kentucky, and assigned to the 74th TRG. Now part of I Tactical Air Division, it moved to Muskogee in April 1944 and then left for New Guinea and the Fifth AF in November 1944.

The 37th PRS: Formerly the 152nd TRS, this unit was renumbered and redesignated in October 1943—a very active month for USAAF PR units, at least organizationally. It was assigned to the 69th TRG at Camp Campbell, moved to Esler Field, Louisiana, in November and then to Muskogee in April 1944, having been reassigned to II Tactical Air Division the previous month. It then moved to Italy (Fifteenth AF) in November 1944.

The 39th PRS: Previously the 101st PMS, this unit was renumbered and redesignated effective March 29, 1944 at Thermal AAF, California, and assigned to III Tactical Air Division. It moved to Muskogee two weeks later and to the Ninth AF in France in December 1944.

The 41st PRS: This unit was renumbered and redesignated from the 1st Reconnaissance Squadron (Special) at Pounds Field, Texas, as of November 25, 1944 and transferred to Muskogee on December 7. It was sent to Hawaii in early April 1945 and assigned there to the Seventh AF.

As is amply clear from the above, the situation, organizationally, with the Army Air Forces' photo reconnaissance units could be quite bewildering, especially in the U.S., what with their constantly changing designations, parent units, and bases. Part of the reason was the huge demand for them, in every overseas combat theater and air force, and the pressure to provide them as expeditiously as possible.

Ferrying Lightnings

During the war, aircraft had to be ferried from the U.S.'s many aircraft factories to military air bases around the country and to ports of embarkation on either coast for shipment overseas. For the USAAF, this was the responsibility of the Ferrying Division of its Air Transport Command (ATC).

P-38s coming off Lockheed's assembly lines had to be flight tested from the company's adjacent Air Terminal before being accepted by the USAAF and then ferried to their initial stateside destinations. P-38H-5 42-67079, which certainly went through that process, later served with the 55th FG in England and then with the Fifteenth AF in Italy. (*Lockheed photo*)

While the majority of ATC's ferry pilots were male Army Air Forces officers, many of them were civilian contract employees, including hundreds of women—the famous WASPs (Women Air Service Pilots). The majority of the WASPs did not fly fighters, which required a special P-Class rating that could only be obtained by attending the Pursuit Flight Transition School at Palm Springs AAF, California. Even fewer flew P-38s, which required them to check out in one at Long Beach, California, after obtaining their P-Class rating. In fact, only twenty-six WASPs are known to have flown Lightnings by the time they were disbanded in December 1944.

Those female Lightning ferry pilots served with one or more of four USAAF ferrying groups: the 2nd at Wilmington, Delaware; the 5th at Dallas, Texas; the 6th at Long Beach; and the 21st at Palm Springs. P-38s and (early on) F-5 photo reconnaissance Lightnings were flown from the Lockheed Air Terminal to nearby Long Beach, from where they would commence their ferry trips. Starting in early 1944, there was a major change on the P-38 production lines. Instead of continuing to build F-5s at Burbank, it was decided to fly newly built P-38Js (and later P-38Ls) to Lockheed's Modification Center at Love Field, Dallas, to be converted to camera ships. From there, the new F-5s would be flown by both male and female pilots of the 5th Ferrying Group to their initial destinations.

The only WASP to be killed while flying a P-38 was twenty-four-year-old Evelyn G. Sharp of the 6th Ferrying Group, while in the process of transporting a new P-38J-15, 43-28750, from California to New Jersey, during which she had a problem with its left engine. She made a scheduled stop at Harrisburg, Pennsylvania's New Cumberland Airport, and when she took off from there on the morning of April 3, 1944, black smoke began pouring from the problematic Allison. With just one functioning engine and at low speed, Sharp was unable to clear a hill just beyond the runway, crashed, and was killed.

As the war progressed, many other stateside USAAF units operated Lightnings at one time or another. Among the training units that also utilized P-38s were the 445th FS of the 50th FG at Orlando, Florida, in late 1943 and early 1944; the 904th BU at Kissimmee, Florida; the 2539th BU at Foster Field, Texas; and the 3028th BU at Luke Field, Arizona.

Above left: WASP ferry pilot Iris Cummings, who served with the 6th Ferrying Group at Long Beach, California. Cummings was one of the twenty-six women who were qualified to fly P-38s. (*Larry Bledsoe collection*)

Above right: Ruth Dailey, another WASP ferry pilot, was assigned to the 5th Ferrying Group at Love Field near Dallas, Texas. (*Larry Bledsoe collection*)

Below: Barbara Erikson, the leader of the 6th Ferrying Group's WASP pilots. (*Larry Bledsoe collection*)

3

Lightnings in Action:
The Pacific Theater of Operations
(Fifth, Sixth, Seventh, Eleventh, and Thirteenth Air Forces)

Fifth Air Force, New Guinea

In early April 1942, the first Lightnings to serve outside the continental U.S. arrived at Melbourne, in southeastern Australia, by ship. These were the F-4-1 photo reconnaissance aircraft of the 8th Photo Squadron's "A" Flight, which had been activated two months earlier at March Field, California. In Australia, it became part of the USAAF's Far East Air Force (FEAF).

That month, the Japanese Empire was nearing the zenith of its rampage through the South West Pacific (SWP). It already controlled most of the Philippine Islands; the last Allied servicemen would surrender there the following month. Its forces had captured vital ports and airfields in the Dutch East Indies and had recently begun air attacks from there on the port of Darwin in northern Australia. They had also just occupied much of the northern and eastern coasts of New Guinea and from airfields there had begun attacks on that huge island's most important base, Port Moresby, on its southern coast. The capture of Moresby and its port and airfields was next on the Japanese agenda, and from there they planned to start bombing other parts of Australia. Fortunately, an invasion fleet was turned back by the USN at the Battle of the Coral Sea in early May.

The need for the 8th PS's long-range photo reconnaissance capabilities was obvious: the Allies needed to know what the Japanese were up to—specifically, the numbers, the location, and the movements of their troops, ships, and aircraft. The squadron's F-4s were reassembled and flight tested and its pilots received additional training and briefings in Australia prior to becoming operational. It moved from Melbourne to Brisbane, on Australia's east central coast, at the end of April and then to Townsville, far to the north, from which flights could be made to New Guinea, in early May. It was from Townsville that "A" Flight's first mission was flown by the squadron commander, Capt. Karl L. Polifka, who, based on his exploits in the SWP and later in the Mediterranean Theater, was to become the USAAF's premier photo reconnaissance pilot.

The rest of the 8th Photographic Reconnaissance Squadron (as it had been redesignated on June 9), arrived from the States in late July. The whole unit moved from Townsville to

F-4-1 41-2130, which had been given the colorful name *Malaria Mabel*, was assigned to the 8th PRS in New Guinea in September 1942. When it was photographed at 14 Mile Drome at Port Moresby in October 1943 its paint had been stripped away to expose its bare aluminum skin. (*John Stanaway collection*)

Port Moresby's 14 Mile (Durand) Drome in early September. Moresby's airfields, which were referred to as airdromes—or simply dromes—were initially designated according to their distance from the city, but they then began to be also named after Allied pilots who had been killed while flying from them (the eponymous Durand was a P-39 pilot). As if two names were not sufficient, 14 Mile was also known as Laloki, after the nearby river. The 8th PRS was now attached to V Bomber Command (BC), and specifically to its 19th Bomb Group (BG), for whose use its photos were primarily taken. The squadron would be awarded a Distinguished Unit Citation (DUC) for its vital photo reconnaissance work over New Guinea from July 1942 to January 1943.

Since the Royal Australian Air Force (RAAF) had no PR aircraft comparable to the F-4, in the late summer of 1942, the FEAF decided to loan it two of the 8th PRS's aircraft. These were serial number 41-2158, which received the RAAF serial A55-1, and 41-2159, which became A55-2. They were both repainted in RAAF colors and markings, including roundels in place of the USAAF stars. They began their operational service with 1 Photographic Reconnaissance Unit (PRU), which was then based near Darwin, in October and flew their first mission, to the East Indies, on November 3. A55-2 was destroyed and its pilot killed in a landing accident on November 20. It was replaced with 41-2122 (which became A55-3) the following March.

The P-38s Arrive

The first P-38s—thirty of them—arrived in Australia in August, and then sixty-five more followed in September. These were mostly P-38F-5s in the 42-12600 serial number range. The FEAF had decided that they would be assigned to the 35th FG's 39th "Flying Cobras"

FS, which was then fighting in New Guinea with Bell P-39 Airacobras. The 39th returned to Australia at the end of July, and the following month began training at Townsville with its new P-38s. It returned to New Guinea with them in mid-October, sharing Port Moresby's 14 Mile Drome with the 8th PRS, which later moved to 17 Mile.

Having failed at a seaborne invasion in May, the Japanese began a land offensive against Port Moresby at the end of July, over the treacherous Owen Stanley Mountains. They also commenced one against the strategic Allied base at Milne Bay, on New Guinea's eastern tip—both of them from their newly captured base at Buna. These were extremely hard-fought campaigns, but the Imperial Japanese Army (IJA) was eventually turned back; its forces advancing on Milne Bay were in retreat by September 10 and those heading for Port Moresby were finally halted at the end of that month, only 30 miles from their objective.

The result of these successes was that the Allies were then able to begin a counteroffensive against Japanese forces and bases in New Guinea, gradually either capturing or isolating the latter—usually after devastating aerial bombardments—until all the important parts of the island would finally be under their control by the summer of 1944. The new Fifth Air Force's P-38s and F-5 photo recons would play a vital role in that long campaign. The Allies took Buna on December 14 and soon thereafter began the construction of a new airfield nearby at Dobodura—the first of what was to be a major complex of them that its occupants would refer to as "Dobo."

Although the FEAF had been redesignated the Fifth AF in February 1942, the latter was not officially activated in Australia until September 3. Its V Fighter Command (FC) became active there in November, when its headquarters arrived from the U.S.; the following month, it moved to Port Moresby.

While flying P-38s, the 39th FS would operate under the direct control of V FC rather than the 35th FG. It encountered little aerial opposition initially. Finally, while dive bombing

The 39th FS P-38s lined up on 14 Mile Drome at Port Moresby in November 1942. (*USAF photo*)

the enemy airfield at Lae, New Guinea, on November 25, the 39th claimed its (and the Fifth AF's) first aerial victory by a P-38, although it was scored in a very unusual manner. As their bombs went off on the field, a Zero that was taking off was knocked down by the explosion of Capt. Robert L. Faurot's 500-pounder, and he was credited with its destruction. One of Faurot's squadron mates, 1Lt. Curran L. "Jack" Jones, was a witness to this unusual event:

> We echeloned to the left and approached Lae from the northwest. We dove in a fairly shallow dive and released on Faurot's estimation, as flight leader, two 500-pound bombs each. As we made a gentle climbing turn to the right I could see Zeros taking off and did witness Bob Faurot's bombs go off at the end of the runway and a Zero make a 180-degree turn and pancake in the water. I think we had some chatter on the radio about that, and of course we kidded Bob after we got back.

It was not until the end of December that the 39th's P-38 pilots really began to score—heavily. The 49th FG's 9th "Flying Knights" Squadron was slated to become the Fifth AF's next P-38 squadron, and it would relinquish its old P-40s in early January to begin that transition. A few of its pilots had already been attached to the 39th FS temporarily to gain combat experience in the Lightning. One of them was a slight, mild-mannered second lieutenant named Richard I. Bong. Bong had been training in P-38s with the 14th FG in California earlier that year when, mainly because of some unauthorized "buzzing," he was transferred to Australia. If it had not been for that youthful indiscretion, it is doubtful that many people would still remember Dick Bong.

In just five missions, from December 27, 1942 to January 8, 1943, Fifth AF P-38 pilots would score fifty-five confirmed victories, probably destroy fifteen e/a, and damage fifteen more (55-15-15) for the loss of just one of their own. On the 27th, they intercepted a combined Japanese Army Air Force (JAAF) and Japanese Naval Air Force (JNAF) raid on Dobodura by Aichi D3A "Val" dive bombers escorted by Nakajima Ki-43 "Oscars" and Mitsubishi A6M "Zekes" (Zeros). This air battle resulted in thirteen confirmed kills, including a Val and a Zeke by Lt. Bong, two Zekes (plus another probably destroyed) by 1Lt. Hoyt A. Eason, and two Oscars by Capt. Thomas J. Lynch. Lynch had already scored three victories with the 39th's P-39s, so this made him an ace.

During a bomber escort to Lae on the 31st, the P-38 pilots downed ten Zeros, of which Lt. Eason was credited with three (making him the Pacific Theater's first P-38 ace), Capt. Lynch with two, and Lt. Bong one.

They scored on three successive days in January. On the 6th, the 39th FS participated in an attack on an enemy relief convoy heading for Lae. Its pilots dive-bombed the ships, unsuccessfully, and then protected the real bombers from attacks by some Oscars, of which they were credited with destroying nine, plus five more as probably destroyed or damaged. USAAF planes attacked the convoy again the following day, with two 39th FS flights providing top cover. They and 49th FG P-40s fought off a large number of Oscars, resulting in the Lightning pilots' credits for 5-2-5, of which Dick Bong was credited with 2-1-1 and Tommy Lynch with one confirmed and one damaged.

The climax of this series of eventful missions occurred on January 8, when three separate bomber escorts were flown to Lae, resulting in P-38 aerial credits totaling 16-6-6 Oscars,

Lt. Norman D. Hyland was one of the 9th FS pilots like Dick Bong who were TDY with the 39th FS from November 1942 to January 1943. Hyland scored a confirmed kill and a probable while flying with the 39th and two confirmed and a damaged later with the 9th. He is seen here posing with a shark-mouthed 39th Squadron Lightning shortly after scoring his first victory on December 31. (*USAF photo*)

Ken Sparks (top) and Tommy Lynch of the 39th FS pose with one of the unit's P-38s in early 1943, these photos showing the detail of the artwork on the shark mouth design its personnel had chosen for them. Typically, the discoloration caused by the anti-corrosion sealing tape utilized for its long ocean voyage to Australia are visible on this early model green-and-gray painted ship, especially along the seams of the panels. (*USAF photos*)

2-1-1 of them to Dick Bong, giving him a total of five confirmed and making him an ace. Hoyt Eason was credited with 1-1-1. The 39th Squadron's 1Lt. John H. Mangas was missing in action; he was the Fifth AF's first P-38 combat casualty.

It was shortly after those Lae missions that the 9th FS began to receive its first P-38s, at Port Moresby. Its pilots flew the squadron's first Lightning mission from 17 Mile (Schwimmer) Drome on January 19. The 9th moved to 14 Mile later that month, by which time it had received two dozen P-38s. Its pilots began operating from the new Horanda airstrip at Dobodura during the day before the whole squadron moved there with the rest of the group in early March. It scored its first Lightning victory from Dobo on February 6, when 1Lt. David F. Harbour shot down an Oscar during a fighter sweep to Lae. The squadron's initial P-38 loss was on February 28, when 1Lt. William A. Levitan went missing over the Coral Sea while ferrying a Lightning from Townsville to Port Moresby.

That was also the day on which the IJN dispatched from its base at Rabaul, New Britain, eight transports carrying 7,000 troops to reinforce Lae, plus supplies—escorted by eight destroyers and covered by JNAF and JAAF fighters. They were spotted the following day and on March 2–4 were under constant attack by Allied aircraft, these actions becoming known as the Battle of the Bismarck Sea, which body of water is bordered by the islands of New Guinea, New Britain, and New Ireland. The two P-38 squadrons were heavily involved, most particularly on March 3, when the 9th FS scored nine confirmed kills and the 39th ten. An entire three-plane 39th FS flight was shot down, however, and all its pilots, including Bob Faurot and Hoyt Eason, were killed. Just four of the destroyers, none of the transports, very little of the supplies, and less than 3,000 of the men survived these

April 5, 1943: *Elsie*, a 9th FS P-38, came to grief while being landed at Dobodura by 2Lt. John G. O'Neil, due to a broken nose strut that resulted from its hitting a hole in the runway. The white vertical stripe on No. 88's tail indicates that its assigned pilot was a flight leader, in this case Capt. Clay Tice, Jr. (*USAF photo*)

attacks—and only about 900 of the latter actually made it to Lae. The 9th and 39th FSs were credited with a total of 27-8-4 Zekes and Oscars.

The 80th "Headhunters" Squadron of the 8th FG had been selected to be the Fifth AF's third P-38 squadron. Like the 39th, it had been fighting in New Guinea with P-39s but was recalled to Australia—specifically, Mareeba, near Cairns in Queensland—in late January to begin its transition to the Lightning. It returned to Port Moresby in March and flew its first P-38 mission, a bomber escort to Finschhafen, New Guinea, on the 30th, from 3 Mile (Kila) Drome. It scored its first Lightning air victories on April 11, when the squadron intercepted some JNAF aircraft attacking Allied shipping in Oro Bay, near Dobodura, and shot down three Vals and a Zeke.

From March through July 1942, RAAF Kittyhawks (Lend-Lease P-40s) and USAAF P-39s had intercepted numerous air raids on Port Moresby, but Japanese aircraft were seldom seen there after that as they were then needed more urgently elsewhere. The JNAF did fly one last major raid to Moresby on April 12—by forty-five Mitsubishi G4M "Betty" bombers escorted by sixty fighters. They were intercepted by P-39s, P-40s, and P-38s, which claimed more than two dozen kills. The 9th FS was credited with two Bettys and an Oscar destroyed, the 39th FS with three Bettys and a Zeke, and the 80th FS with a single Betty. The 9th's 2Lt. Grover E. Fanning, a future ace (who was on his first combat mission), was credited with two Bettys destroyed and another damaged, plus two Oscars—one destroyed and the other probably destroyed.

On April 29, the 80th FS suffered its first P-38 pilot fatality when 2Lt. John F. McIntyre crashed G-15 43-2383 while attempting a loop at too low an altitude over 3 Mile Drome.

As more P-38s were becoming available in the spring of 1943, the Fifth AF was granted "special authority" to organize a new Lightning group in the theater. This was the 475th FG, comprised of the 431st, 432nd, and 433rd FSs, which was activated at Amberly Field near Brisbane on May 14. One of the reasons the 475th would become so immediately successful was that many combat experienced pilots were transferred to it from the 8th and 49th FGs. Its first CO was Lt. Col. George W. Prentice, who had previously commanded the 39th FS.

After three months of training in Australia, the 475th FG moved to Port Moresby temporarily in early August while it waited for a new airstrip at Dobodura to be readied for it. It flew its first combat mission from Moresby on the 12th and scored its first victories four days later. While escorting some transport aircraft to the new Allied airfield at Tsili Tsili, near Marilinan in the highlands of New Guinea west of the Huon Gulf, the 431st FS, flying from 12 Mile, encountered enemy fighters, of which its pilots were credited with shooting down twelve. (The 432nd Squadron was based at 5 Mile (Ward's) Drome and the 433rd at 7 Mile.)

The 475th, which would soon become famous as the "Satan's Angels" group, commenced operations just in time to participate in the massive aerial campaign against the four enemy airfields at and near Wewak, on New Guinea's north central coast. On the eighteenth, the whole group flew a bomber escort to Wewak, and its pilots were subsequently credited with 15-3-2 enemy fighters, for the loss of the 431st Squadron's 2Lt. Ralph E. Schmidt, who disappeared while covering some B-25s at low level over the target, in P-38H-1 42-66572. Schmidt was the group's first combat loss, although two of its other pilots had been killed in flying accidents. Scoring his first victories in this action (two Oscars and a Tony) was the 431st's 1Lt. Thomas B. McGuire, Jr., whose name was soon to become very well known.

Although most of the fighters claimed on August 18 were identified as Zekes, they were, in fact, all Oscars. By the late spring of 1943, the JAAF had largely taken over the air

First Lieutenant Richard I. Bong in the cockpit of his P-38 on March 6, 1943, shortly after the 9th FS arrived at its new base at Dobodura, New Guinea. Bong had scored his sixth victory three days earlier when he shot down an Oscar (and probably destroyed another) during the Battle of the Bismarck Sea. (*USAF photo*)

This 9th FS P-38 was destroyed during a JNAF raid on its airfield, Dobodura No. 4—also known as Horando—on March 11, 1943. (*USAF photo*)

Above: 39th FS ace Lt. Charles S. Gallup and his assigned P-38F-5 42-12627, which displays some rather threatening artwork and the name *Loi*. (*John Stanaway collection*)

Below: The 39th FS's Lt. Dick Suehr and his P-38F-5 *Regina*. (*John Stanaway collection*)

operations in New Guinea, while the JNAF was primarily occupied in the nearby Solomon Islands. The Zeke and the Oscar did look very similar, and early on, they were both usually identified as Zeros.

During the next two months, on twenty-two missions from August 20 to October 17, the 475th FG would be credited with 123 confirmed kills, the 80th FS with fifty-eight, the 9th FS with thirty-four, and the 39th FS with nineteen. Most of these victories were scored either on bomber escort missions to Wewak or while defending Allied ships, ports, and airfields in the Huon Gulf area between Buna and Finschhafen from aerial assaults.

Over and near Wewak on August 21, the P-38 pilots were credited with thirty-five kills: twenty-three by the 475th FG, eleven by the 80th FS, and a single victory by the 39th FS. Lt. McGuire downed two Zeros to become an ace. The 475th was awarded a Distinguished Unit Citation (DUC) for its August 18 and 21 Wewak missions. It finally began moving to its new airfield at Dobodura, Horanda West No. 4, later that month.

On September 2, Capt. George S. Welch from 8th FG H.Q., who was flying P-38G-15 43-2203 with the 80th FS, shot down three Oscars over Wewak around 10 a.m., and forty-five minutes later, he destroyed a twin-engined Mitsubishi Ki-46 "Dinah" reconnaissance aircraft. Welch had famously shot down four JNAF carrier aircraft over Hawaii on December 7, 1941 with a P-40, and during his tour with the 8th FG had added three more in P-39s and five in P-38s, the latter while assigned to the 80th FS. His four victories on September 2 brought his final score to sixteen. The 9th, 39th, 80th, and 433rd FSs scored a total of fourteen that day.

Two days later, Welch's squadron mate 1Lt. Jay T. Robbins matched his one-day score by downing four Zekes over the Huon Gulf (and probably destroying two more) out of the eighteen victories scored by the 39th, 80th, and 433rd Squadrons. This brought his total to seven. The mission was in support of the Allied landings at Lae, which was captured on the 16th. Four months later, then-Capt. Robbins would assume command of the 80th FS,

September 14, 1943: 80th FS Lightnings in their revetments at Port Moresby's Kila (3 Mile) Drome. The one in the center is P-38G-13 43-2212, which was assigned to Capt. Norbert C. Ruff. Its squadron letter was "X," and he had named it *Ruff Stuff*. Ruff would shoot down a Hap fighter over Wewak the following day for his fourth and final victory—all of them scored with *Ruff Stuff*. (*USAF photo*)

Above left: Maj. Sidney S. Woods, CO of the 9th FS, and his assigned P-38, F-5 42-12655. Woods scored two confirmed victories and a probable with the 49th FG and later flew another combat tour in England with the famous 4th FG—during which his only scoring in the air consisted of shooting down five Fw 190s in one fight. (*John Stanaway collection*)

Above right: The 80th FS's Lt. Jess R. Gidley poses with his assigned aircraft, P-38F-5 42-12661, which sported the name *Ravishing Lil* and the squadron letter "R." During the summer of 1943, Gidley shot down three enemy planes and probably destroyed two more. (*John Stanaway collection*)

Below: Six of the 39th FS's aces pose with Maj. Tom Lynch's assigned aircraft, P-38G-5 42-12859. It is easy to determine when this photo was taken, as there are ten victory symbols on its fuselage and Lynch scored his tenth on August 20, 1943 and his eleventh the following day. *Standing, from left to right*: Lt. Richard C. Suehr, Lt. John H. Lane, and Lt. Stanley O. Andrews. *Kneeling, left to right*: Capt. John P. Sullivan, Maj. Lynch, and Lt. Kenneth C. Sparks. (*John Stanaway collection*)

Ground crewmen of the 25th PRS work on one of the unit's F-5As at Nadzab, New Guinea, in March 1944. (*USAF photo*)

by which time his victory total had reached thirteen. The 80th was awarded a DUC for its successes over New Guinea from August 20 through September 15, 1943 while under Maj. Edward Cragg's command.

Tommy Lynch had assumed command of the 39th FS at the end of March and was promoted to major three months later. Shortly after scoring his sixteenth victory, on September 16, he completed his combat tour and returned to the U.S. Capt. Dick Bong had scored his sixteenth on July 28, making him the top scoring P-38 pilot. Before he went home two months later, Bong would score five more.

Also in September, the 8th PRS received six of the new P-38Hs that were now arriving in theater, to provide its own fighter cover. Two of its pilots were then exchanged for two experienced 80th FS pilots. The 8th, like the rest of the USAAF's Lightning PR squadrons, had been redesignated Photographic Squadron (Light) effective February 6—and likewise reverted to its PRS designation on November 13, the day it was assigned to the 6th Photo Group, newly arrived in Australia, which already included the 25th and 26th PRSs. Their main tasks would be to obtain pre- and post-mission target photos that were utilized by Fifth AF intelligence officers to help plan bombing missions and to assess their results.

Rabaul

Rabaul, at the northeastern tip of the island of New Britain, was the IJN's main base in the SWP. Its large, protected Simpson Harbor provided a haven for ships—transports that provided supplies and reinforcements to Japanese forces in the Solomon Islands and New Guinea and warships that protected the transports and engaged Allied ships. From Rabaul's four airfields (Lakunai, Vunakanau, Rapopo, and Tobera), JNAF and JAAF units in those areas would receive replacement aircraft and pilots, and air raids were flown against Allied ships and bases.

Rabaul had been targeted by small groups of unescorted USAAF and RAAF bombers and reconnaissance aircraft ever since it was captured by the Japanese in January 1942, some of which were shot down by the Zeros that were based there. It was not until the fall of 1943 that the Fifth AF had enough long-range escort fighters (P-38s) to protect the North American B-25 Mitchells and four-engined Consolidated B-24 Liberators that would now be attacking Rabaul in force, with the help of the 8th PRS's target photos.

The first in this series of Rabaul missions was flown on October 12 by sixty-three B-24s and 107 B-25s escorted by 106 P-38s, the fighters staging through Kiriwina Island in the Solomon Sea south of New Britain, which had been seized from the Japanese in late June. Twenty-six e/a were claimed shot down (though only three of them by the P-38s—one each by pilots of the 80th, 432nd, and 433rd FSs), 100 more as destroyed on the ground by the bombing, and two ships as sunk. Four B-24s and one B-25 were lost, but no P-38s.

Three days later, the JNAF decided to retaliate by attacking Allied shipping in Oro Bay on the assumption that the bombing of Rabaul was a preliminary to its invasion. In a series of air battles that morning, USAAF fighters were credited with 54-8-2 e/a, including thirty-six confirmed kills by 475th FG pilots, a dozen by those of the 9th FS—in both cases without loss—and the rest by 49th FG P-40s. First Lieutenant Tom McGuire was credited with a Val destroyed (his tenth confirmed victory) and two Zekes probably destroyed.

The Japanese planes returned on the 17th, and thirty-six more were claimed destroyed, plus six probables. This time the 9th FS's share was 6-2-0 and the 475th FG's 19-1-0, in the latter case for the loss of two P-38s. The 475th received another DUC for these two missions.

Fifty B-25s attacked Rabaul's airfields on the 18th, *sans* escort. The B-24s that targeted it on the 23rd were escorted by P-38s, which were credited with 13-4-1 enemy fighters— eleven of the confirmed kills being scored by 475th FG pilots, one of whom was the only loss that day.

The Rabaul missions continued the next two days. The Lightning pilots were hugely successful on the 24th, with their six squadrons being credited with a total of 40-9-6 e/a. The 80th Squadron's Lt. Jay Robbins was credited with four "Hamps" (clipped-wing A6M3s) destroyed and another probably destroyed. The only losses that day were two B-25s.

Most of the aircraft attacking Rabaul on the 25th turned back because of the miserable weather; only one B-24 group, escorted by two flights of 475th FG P-38s, made it to their target. Maj. Charles H. McDonald, the 475th's deputy group commander, scored the only victory, shooting down a Zeke—his fourth. There were no American losses that day.

The P-38 squadrons returned to Rabaul with the B-24s on the 29th. Their pilots claimed 15-5-2 Zekes (2-0-1 of them by Capt. Dick Bong), and the Liberators claimed ten more destroyed in the air and nine on the ground. The only loss was a single 475th FG P-38 and its pilot. So far the losses on these missions had been relatively light, but that would not be the case with the next one.

Bloody Tuesday

The Fifth AF delivered what was intended to be its *coup de grâce* against Rabaul on Tuesday, November 2, in support of the landings on Bougainville in the Solomon Islands. The 475th FG's pilots were escorting some B-25s over their targets at low level when they were attacked by numerous enemy fighters, of which sixteen were subsequently credited as destroyed to the P-38 pilots and one to the bombers, which also claimed sixteen destroyed on the ground with their bombs at Lakunai. Three of these Mitchells and five 475th Lightnings also went down.

As the other three P-38 squadrons swept over Simpson Harbor, they were also heavily engaged by the Zekes. The 80th was credited with eight confirmed kills and no less than ten probables—indicating the frantic nature of its actions—and lost two of its pilots. The 9th scored eight kills, also for the loss of two P-38s, and the 39th just one. Their credits totaled 33-19-3 for the loss of six B-25s and nine P-38s. Typically, the actual results were considerably less than those that were claimed, and this mission was far from a knockout blow against Rabaul. In fact, a USN carrier raid three days later did a lot more damage.

The last of these missions was flown on November 7, when the P-38 pilots covered the Liberators as they bombed Rabaul's Rapopo Airfield. Sixty enemy fighters—including some JAAF Kawasaki Ki-61 "Tonys"—were engaged, of which the Lightning pilots were credited with destroying six and probably destroying four, for the loss of one P-38 each by the 9th, 39th, and 80th Squadrons.

The 9th and 80th were awarded DUCs for these missions. While these raids and the USN's had resulted in considerable destruction of and damage to Rabaul's aircraft, ships and facilities, it was a long way from being neutralized, and it would be Allied air units based in the Solomon Islands that finally completed what they had begun, three months later.

A top Fifth AF P-38 ace and leader was KIA on November 9. Capt. Daniel T. Roberts, Jr., had scored four victories with the 80th FS (two with a P-39 and two with a P-38) before transferring to the 475th FG's 432nd Squadron earlier that year. He had then assumed command of its 433rd Squadron on October 3. Roberts had racked up ten confirmed kills plus one probably destroyed with the 475th, four of them and the probable over Rabaul. His last, an Oscar, he shot down over Alexshafen, New Guinea, just before his P-38, H-5 42-66834, collided with H-1 42-66546, flown by his wingman, 2Lt. Dale O. Meyer, resulting in the deaths of both pilots.

The 6th PRG H.Q. joined the 8th PRS at Port Moresby in early December and moved to a new Allied airfield at Nadzab, in the Markham River Valley west of Lae, in February 1944, along with the 25th PRS from Brisbane; they were joined there by the 8th the following month. The 26th PRS transferred from Brisbane to Dobodura at the end of January, and then to Finschhafen, which had been captured by the Allies in early October, three weeks later. It also maintained a detachment at Port Moresby in February and March, until the whole squadron moved to Nadzab at the end of the latter month, and then to Hollandia, on New Guinea's north coast, in June 1944.

In late November 1943, 1 PRU's F-4 A55-1 was attached to the RAAF's 75 Squadron, a Kittyhawk unit based in New Guinea. Several of the 75th's fighter pilots used it to photograph Japanese installations on New Britain. After it was returned to 1 PRU, A55-1 soldiered on until September 1, 1944, when it was destroyed in a crash-landing in Australia. By that time, the RAAF had received De Havilland Mosquito PRs to replace the F-4s. (A55-3 had been lost to a similar accident in Australia on December 5, 1943, after it was returned to the Fifth AF.)

It was also in November, shortly after its Rabaul missions, that the 39th FS, still based at Port Moresby, was forced to give up its P-38s, as it had been decided that the whole 35th FG would re-equip with Republic P-47 Thunderbolts (its other two squadrons were still flying P-39s). Among the factors in this decision were that P-38s were becoming scarcer in the Fifth AF after the losses on the Rabaul missions and the dearth of replacement aircraft—and because the Eighth AF in England then had priority for the new P-38H-5s, and then the J-5s, coming off Lockheed's assembly lines. Another was the increased availability of P-47s. (A few P-38J-5s did arrive in the SWP in December.) The 39th Squadron relinquished the last of its Lightnings, with which it had scored 121 confirmed kills, on November 19. The P-47-equipped 348th FG had arrived in New Guinea from the U.S. in June, and another Thunderbolt group, the 58th, joined the Fifth AF in November. Although the P-47 would do a lot of good work in the SWP, the P-38 was, and would remain, the theater's premier fighter.

An important innovation had been conceived by some 39th FS personnel. Its P-38s' vibration-prone cameras had been moved from the nose of the aircraft to under the right inboard wing, resulting in much improved combat film. Two P-38 groups in the MTO (Mediterranean Theater of Operations) made some similar modifications, but not until the following year.

Also forced to trade in its P-38s for P-47s, effective November 12, was the 9th FS, in its case temporarily. There just were not enough P-38s available to the Fifth AF at that time to equip six squadrons, so for a few months they would serve only with the 80th FS and the 475th FG's three squadrons. The 9th's senior pilots were given the option of returning to the U.S. at this time, and one of those who exercised it was Dick Bong, who had by then scored twenty-one of the squadron's 138 P-38 kills.

The 80th FS received a bitter blow on December 26, when its popular and highly successful CO, Maj. Ed Cragg, was killed as Fifth AF P-38s and P-47s fought off swarms of JNAF aircraft from Rabaul attempting to interfere with the American landings at Cape Gloucester on New Britain's western tip. After downing a fighter identified as a JAAF "Tojo" (Nakajima Ki-44)—though it was more likely to have been a Zeke—for his fifteenth confirmed victory, Maj. Cragg was evidently shot down by another enemy fighter, as his P-38H-1, 42-66506, was seen to crash in flames. The majority of the sixty-one USAAF victories that day were scored by P-47s of the 348th FG, but Lightning pilots of the 80th and 431st FSs were credited with ten and eleven, respectively.

Yet another top Fifth AF P-38 ace and leader was killed on March 8, 1944. This time it was Lt. Col. Tommy Lynch. Both Lynch and his good friend Capt. Dick Bong had returned to New Guinea in January from their stateside leaves and were assigned to V FC Headquarters at Nadzab. Although officially operations officers, they were given free reign to fly combat missions—either tagging along with P-38 squadrons or, more often, flying freelance sorties together, searching for both air and ground targets. Lynch had scored four more confirmed victories, bringing his total to twenty, when as he and Bong were strafing ships in Aitape Harbor, between Wewak and Hollandia, both their Lightnings were hit by anti-aircraft

This is 80th FS CO Maj. Ed Cragg's *PORKY II* (P-38H-1 42-66506) shortly after he scored his eighth victory with it on August 21, 1943. Cragg was killed in *PORKY* shortly after downing his fifteenth Japanese plane on December 26. (*John Stanaway collection*)

(AA) fire, with Lynch's receiving particularly serious damage. He bailed out of his P-38J-15, 42-103987, at a very low altitude and his parachute did not have time to deploy.

Bong continued to fly combat missions with V FC, was promoted to major, and scored seven more victories to bring his total to twenty-eight. The last three were Oscars he shot down over Hollandia on April 12 while flying with the 80th FS. Shortly thereafter, he returned to the U.S. again, this time to public acclaim as America's "Ace of Aces." Eddie Rickenbacker, the country's top World War I ace, had been credited with shooting down twenty-six German aircraft, a score that was matched by Marine Grumman F4F Wildcat pilot Maj. Joe Foss while flying from Guadalcanal. Dick Bong had now surpassed them and became a huge hero on the home front.

At the beginning of 1944, the 8th FG was unusual in that each of its three squadrons was flying a different type aircraft: the 35th P-40s, the 36th P-47s, and the 80th P-38s. However, in February, fifty-eight Lightnings were allocated to it to re-equip its 35th and 36th Squadrons. Unfortunately, many of them were well-used P-38Hs rather than the much improved Js, small numbers of which had been arriving in the theater for several months. In any event, by March, V FC had two full P-38 groups—the 8th and the 475th. The following month, the 9th FS, whose pilots had scored only eight confirmed kills with their P-47s in five months, also re-equipped with P-38s, flying its first mission with them on April 17 from its new airfield, Gusap airstrip No. 10, in New Guinea's Ramu Valley.

The 35th FS scored with its P-38s right away, when two of its pilots each shot down an Oscar near Wewak on March 15. However, it would not be until June 16 that it scored its next victory and the 36th FS its first with their Lightnings. The 36th was plagued with

Above: March 1944: Capt. Dick Bong poses with the Lightning (P-38J-15 42-103993) he was assigned after joining V Fighter Command as an operations officer, which famously displayed the name and likeness of his fiancée, Marge Vattendhal. This plane was bailed out of over New Guinea by another pilot on the 24th. (*John Stanaway collection*)

Below: After Capt. Bong's previous P-38 was lost while being flown by another pilot he flew this one, J-15 42-104380, for a short time. (He is not the person posing with it.) A rectangular space has been prepared on its nose for another picture of Marge. (*John Stanaway collection*)

Two shots of 80th FS ace Capt. Cornelius M. "Corky" Smith, Jr., and his P-38J *Corky IV*. These photos were taken shortly after Smith scored his eleventh and final victory on April 12. (*John Stanaway collection*)

considerable misfortune initially, as ten of its pilots were killed in P-38s—four in accidents and six on combat missions—from February 25 through June 2, while the 35th lost just two, both of them in accidents, on March 30 and April 9.

After more devastating attacks by the Fifth AF in mid-March, the JAAF abandoned Wewak as of the 19th, moving its air units west to Hollandia, on which the first "softening up" attacks had already been made on the 4th. The Allies bypassed and isolated Wewak but landed at Hollandia on April 22, and it was soon in their hands. Its airfield was ready for occupation by USAAF units as of May 2, and the 9th FS arrived there on the 6th. The 475th FG had completed its move to Hollandia by the 15th and the rest of the 49th FG by the 17th.

Black Sunday

On Easter Sunday, April 16, 1944, the 475th FG at Nadzab (to which it had moved a couple of weeks earlier) was scheduled for another bomber escort to Hollandia—a preliminary to the upcoming American landings there. The mission was flown despite the poor weather that had been predicted.

One of the P-38 pilots on this mission was 1Lt. Calvin C. "Bud" Wire of the 433rd FS. He recalled later:

> Normal procedure was to take off on our main tanks and as soon as we gained some altitude switch to our belly tanks. I was flying a P-38J, which had, besides the main and reserve tanks, two small 45-gallon tanks in the wings out near the tips. Where possible it was best to use this gas first, so that the extra weight on the outside wings is reduced prior to entering into any violent maneuvers.[1]

Unfortunately, for some reason, Wire's engines could not access the fuel in those wing tanks when he switched to them from his jettisoned belly tanks, so he was forced to abort the mission and return to Nadzab with his wingman—or at least to attempt to.

Even more unfortunately, a huge storm front north of the Owen Stanley Mountains had formed a massive wall of clouds from, as Wire put it, "the ground to as high as we could see." It became a challenge for most of the P-38 pilots on the mission to make it back home, and many of them could not and did not. They were forced to look for any airfield on which to immediately land, or to bail out. Wire came across a small Allied airstrip on the New Guinea coast east of Hollandia, on which he attempted to land but ended up crashing into the nearby surf, which he miraculously survived. Another 475th FG pilot bailed out safely, but six others went missing and were eventually declared deceased. Three 80th FS pilots were also lost that day. Altogether, the Fifth AF lost thirty-one aircraft and thirty-two airmen on what came to be known as Black Sunday.

The last major air action over New Guinea took place on June 16, 1944 and involved the 8th and 475th FGs. It was while they were escorting B-25s to the enemy airfields on Jefman and Samate Islands, near New Guinea's western tip. Due to the distance involved, both groups staged out of the airfield on Wakde Island, west of Hollandia, which had been captured on May 18. Twenty-six e/a, mostly JAAF Oscars, were claimed destroyed in this

Capt. Jay T. Robbins and his assigned P-38J-15 42-103988, *JANDINA III*. These photos were taken after the April 12, 1944 mission on which Robbins scored his eighteenth victory. (The score displayed on the aircraft includes one that was not confirmed.) He crash-landed this plane on an auxiliary airstrip near Saidor, New Guinea, on May 7. (*John Stanaway collection*)

fight, for the loss of one 475th FG pilot. Among the victors was 431st FS CO Maj. Tom McGuire, who was credited with a single-engined Mitsubishi Ki-51 "Sonia" light attack bomber and an Oscar, and 80th FS CO Maj. Jay Robbins (two Oscars). Coincidentally, these were the nineteenth and twentieth victories for both of them.

Also in June, the Fifth AF welcomed a very distinguished visitor: the "Lone Eagle" himself, Charles Lindbergh. Although a prewar colonel in the Air Corps Reserve, Lindbergh had resigned his commission to work in the aircraft defense industry; he was then on the payroll of the United Aircraft Corporation, whose Vought-Sikorsky Division was producing the F4U Corsair. In April 1944, he began a tour of the South Pacific as a high-profile civilian technical representative. His task was to visit some of the USMC and USAAF fighter units there to discuss with their pilots and maintenance personnel any problems they were having with the F4U and the P-38—and how to get their aircraft to perform optimally. To that end, the forty-two-year-old Lindbergh ended up flying numerous, very unofficial combat missions in both aircraft. His official flight status was that of an "observer."

After first flying missions in Marine Corsairs from the Solomon Islands, Lindbergh arrived in New Guinea on June 15 and checked out in a P-38 at Nadzab the following day. He then flew an orientation flight with the 35th FS, which was then based at Nadzab, to which the 8th FG had moved in March. On the 26th, he flew a P-38 to Hollandia, then home to the 475th FG, with which he flew his first Lightning combat mission the following day. His wingman was none other than Maj. McGuire, with whom he strafed barges along the northwestern New Guinea coast.

Still headquartered at Nadzab at that time was V FC, which would move west to Owi Island the following month. Also based there was the Combat Replacement and Training Center, where newly arrived P-38 pilots, including veterans of other combat theaters, flew

The 431st FS's CO, Maj. Tom McGuire, (on the left) and Charles Lindbergh chat on Biak Island during the summer of 1944. (*John Stanaway collection*)

some "refresher" flights and received special SWP theater training and indoctrination before being assigned to combat units.

Now that New Guinea was almost completely under Allied control and most of the Fifth AF's combat units were based at the western end of the island, they could begin flying missions to Japanese-occupied islands to the north and west in the East Indies. On July 27, the 8th and 475th FGs escorted some B-24s to enemy airfields on Halmahera Island, where their pilots shot down fifteen e/a, mostly Oscars and Tonys—of which Maj. McGuire claimed a single Ki-43 for this twenty-first victory.

The 8th FG was now flying from the airfield on tiny Owi Island in the Schoutens, off New Guinea's northwest coast, which had been occupied by the Allies on June 2, and the 475th from nearby Biak Island, the largest of the Schoutens, which had been invaded on May 27 and to which the group had moved in mid-July. The 49th FG, including the 9th FS's P-38s, had moved to Biak's Mokmer Field in early June, before the island was completely secured.

Charles Lindbergh participated in what turned out to be a very eventful mission on July 28, flying with the 433rd FS from Mokmer. Two of the squadron's flights were patrolling over the island of Ceram, southwest of New Guinea, when two Mitsubishi Ki-51 Sonias were encountered by pilots of the 9th FS, which was also operating in the area. The latter shot down one of them, but pilots of both squadrons had a hard time bringing down the other Sonia, which was obviously being flown by a very skilled pilot. Lindbergh suddenly found himself facing it, on a head-on collision course. Both pilots opened fire before they rocketed past each other with less than 10 feet to spare—the Sonias with two 7.7-mm machine guns. Lindbergh later recalled:

> Lieutenant [Ed] Miller, my wingman, reported seeing the tracers of the Jap plane shooting at me. I was so concentrated on my own firing that I did not see the flashes of his guns. Miller said the plane rolled over out of control right after he passed me. Apparently my bullets had either severed the controls or killed the pilot.[2]

Four days later, on August 1, Lindbergh participated in a four-plane fighter sweep to the Palau Islands, north of New Guinea, during which his P-38 was fired on by a Zero, which (very) fortunately missed. Inevitably, word had started to get out about his unofficial combat missions, and it finally began to dawn on the senior officers who had allowed them what the consequences would be if one of America's greatest heroes—a civilian— had been killed on a combat mission, as had nearly been the case, twice. On August 13, Lindbergh was finally informed that he could no longer fly combat missions with the Fifth AF, although he did fly another one with a USMC squadron in the Central Pacific before returning to the States.

One tangible benefit of Charles Lindbergh's brief sojourn with the Fifth AF was that he taught some of its P-38 pilots how to greatly extend the Lightning's range by carefully managing their Allison engines' power and manifold pressure settings. This knowledge was soon being put to excellent use throughout the Pacific.

The New Guinea campaign was declared officially over on August 15, 1944. The Fifth AF's P-38 pilots had by then been credited with 802 confirmed kills. Its top-scoring Lightning squadron was the 80th, with 182 victories.

The Thirteenth Air Force in the Solomon Islands

On August 7, 1942, U.S. Marines went ashore on the island of Guadalcanal in the southern Solomons. It was the U.S.'s first major land offensive of World War II and initiated an extremely hard-fought, six-month battle for its control. That same day, the Marines seized their first main objective—the airstrip that was being constructed by the Japanese, which the Americans soon named Henderson Field, after a USMC pilot who had been killed in the Battle of Midway. The first aircraft, Marine F4F Wildcats and Douglas SBD Dauntless dive bombers, arrived at Henderson on the 20th and then, on the 22nd, a P-39-equipped USAAF fighter squadron, the 67th. The Airacobra, with its poor climb rate and high-altitude performance, was not a very effective interceptor, but it did do some excellent work as a fighter-bomber in support of the ground troops.

The first eight P-38s arrived at Guadalcanal on November 12. They belonged to the 339th FS, which had been activated on the island of New Caledonia, 1,000 miles southeast of Guadalcanal, on November 3, with a nucleus of personnel, including pilots, transferred from the 67th FS, who provided it with some combat experience. It operated initially as a P-39 squadron, alongside the 67th. Sixteen Lightnings had been ferried to New Caledonia from Australia in late October, and others arrived by ship, disassembled. The latter had to be reassembled and flight tested, and the 339th's pilots who had no previous P-38 experience had to be transitioned to it, at its New Caledonian airfield, Tontouta, near the island's capital and major port, Noumea. They basically read the P-38 pilot's manual, tried to memorize the instruments, and then took off for their first flight in one. (The squadron moved elsewhere on the island to Oua Tom in mid-December, where its headquarters remained throughout most of 1943.)

The 339th FS's first CO was Capt. Dale D. Brannon, who had scored two and a half aerial victories with the 67th FS. He would be replaced by Capt. John W. Mitchell on November 25, transferred to 347th FG Headquarters and promoted to major. Mitchell had scored three of the 339th's twelve P-39 kills and would soon become one of the most famous and successful USAAF fighter pilots of the Solomon Islands campaign.

The squadron's first P-38 victories were scored on November 18, when 1Lt. Deltis H. Fincher shot down two Zeros and 2Lt. James E. Obermiller one. Fincher had already been credited with a shared victory while serving with the 67th FS, and Obermiller was one of eight former 82nd FG staff sergeant pilots who had been transferred to the SWP after training on P-38s in California—six of whom ended up flying them with the 339th FS.

An official USAAF intelligence report on the November 18 mission stated: "The P-38 is not an escort fighter, as the plane is too unmaneuverable and blind. The P-38 has not yet been sent out at its proper altitude, and the B-17s are always at poor altitude for the P-38." Maj. Brannon informed his superiors that the B-17s needed to fly their missions above 20,000 feet for the Lightnings to provide them with effective cover. This would continue to be a problem for the P-38 pilots throughout most of the Solomon Islands campaign. As to the P-38 not being an escort fighter, it would in fact soon prove itself to be one of the best.

The 339th's next victories were not scored until December 10, when its pilots were credited with three Zeros and two A6M-2N floatplane Zeros destroyed and another Zero probably destroyed. Nine days later they shot down two "float biplanes" and probably destroyed three more, including a confirmed victory and a probable by Maj. Brannon, who was flying with his

September 28, 1942: Newly arrived P-38s being transported from the docks of Dumbea, New Caledonia, through the town of Noumea to nearby Magenta Field, where they will be reassembled and flown to Tontouta, the 339th FS's base. (*USAF photos*)

old squadron that day. All these initial victories had been scored during B-17 escorts to Tonolei Harbor, far to the north on Bougainville Island, the largest of the Solomons. The 339th suffered its first combat casualty on December 15, when 2Lt. Eugene D. Woods, another former 82nd FG sergeant pilot, went missing near the Russell Islands, 30 miles northwest of Guadalcanal. Around this time, the 339th's personnel adopted a moniker for the squadron: "The Sunsetters."

By the end of 1942, there were forty-one P-38s on New Caledonia and Guadalcanal. Arriving at the former from the U.S. on November 23 was another Lightning unit, the 17th Photo Reconnaissance Squadron, which was equipped with F-5A-1s. It was part of the 4th Photographic Group, whose only other squadron at that time flew B-25s. (The group would be redesignated Photographic Reconnaissance in May.) Its ground echelon shipped out to Guadalcanal on January 13, and its pilots flew eight of its F-5s there on February 2. Its new home was the Fighter Two airstrip, at Kukum, east of Henderson Field, where it joined the 339th FS. The 17th's CO, Capt. John E. Murray, flew its first photo mission, to the southern tip of New Georgia Island, on the 5th. The following day, its official designation was changed to Photographic Squadron (Light). On the 7th, 1Lt. Harold W. Ervin failed to return from a sortie—the squadron's first operational casualty.

The new Thirteenth AF, to which all USAAF units operating in the Solomon Islands would now be assigned, was activated at New Caledonia on January 13, 1943, as was its XIII FC. Their 347th FG, which had been activated there on October 3, was comprised of the 67th, 68th, 70th, and 339th FSs. When the 18th FG's H.Q. moved to Guadalcanal from the island of Espíritu Santo, north of New Caledonia, in mid-April, it was assigned the 12th and 44th FSs, and the 70th was also transferred to it.

Over the next year, throughout the Solomon Islands and Rabaul campaigns, these squadrons would operate a mixture of P-38s, P-39s, and P-40s—and sometimes two types concurrently. Only the 67th and 68th Squadrons did *not* fly P-38s during that time. To make the situation even more confusing, pilots of one squadron would often fly combat missions with another. With their P-38s, which they received in early 1943, the 12th and 70th Squadrons would score five and twelve confirmed victories, respectively, from February through June, in addition to those they racked up with P-39s.

New Caledonia was initially the rear echelon administrative area for the Thirteenth AF's fighter squadrons operating from Guadalcanal. That is where they arrived initially; then their aircraft would be reassembled and flight tested and their personnel briefed and given additional training prior to the movement of their air echelons to Guadalcanal. The same was true of replacement aircraft and personnel, including pilots.

Capt. John Mitchell, the 339th Squadron's CO, became a hero to the troops on Guadalcanal on the night of January 29. Ever since the Americans first landed on the island the JNAF had sent bombers over it nearly every night. They did do some physical damage with their bombs, but the greatest damage was to morale and efficiency, as a result of personnel spending many fearful, sleepless nights in uncomfortable foxholes. These bombers—twin-engined Bettys—received the nickname "Washing Machine Charlie" due to the racket caused by their unsynchronized engines. Mitchell was as fed up as anyone with this situation, and he finally asked for permission to try to intercept one of the bombers with a P-38 in the predawn hours, which he received. He took off, spotted a Betty right after it had dropped its bombs, opened fire, and sent it flaming into the sea for his seventh victory.

Above: F-5A-1 42-12670 being serviced by 17th Photographic Squadron ground crewmen on Guadalcanal sometime in 1943. (*USAF photo*)

Below: This colorful P-38H-1, serial number 42-66683, named *PLUTO* after the popular Disney cartoon character, served with the 12th FS on Guadalcanal in 1943. (*USAF photo*)

P-38Gs being reassembled in New Caledonia prior to their assignment to Thirteenth AF fighter squadrons. (*USAF photo*)

Judging from their pristine appearance, P-38G-13s 43-2190 (in the rear) and 43-2191 have just arrived in the South West Pacific. No. 43-2191 joined the 339th FS on Guadalcanal, was given the squadron number 115 and was assigned to Lt. Albert Farquharson. The meaning of its unusual name, *HAD V Unlimited*, is not known. (*Michael Bates collection*)

Two days earlier, Capt. Mitchell had shot down two Zeros during a JNAF attack on Guadalcanal, bringing his score to six (three with a P-38) and making him the Thirteenth AF's first ace. He scored one more, a "float Zero," on February 2, while covering B-17s bombing ships in Shortland Harbor, on Shortland Island, just below Bougainville.

The Air Forces units on Guadalcanal were initially under the operational control of its Marine air group commander. The Allies' air war in the Solomon Islands was a multi-service and an international endeavor, with USMC, USN, and USAAF units working together closely, along with several RNZAF Kittyhawk squadrons. Effective February 16, 1943, six days after Japanese resistance on Guadalcanal had ceased, all these units, including the Thirteenth AF, were consolidated under and became subordinate to Command Air Solomons (COMAIRSOLS), which was overseen by two USN admirals during its first five months, before Maj. Gen. Hubert R. Harmon, CO of the Thirteenth AF, assumed its command.

The 339th FS's mission on February 14 was a particularly tough one. Ten Lightnings and a dozen Marine Corsairs escorted some PB4Y bombers (the Navy version of the B-24) to the passage between Bougainville and the Shortland Islands, where enemy ships were once again attacked. As the PB4Ys came off their bomb runs, they were attacked by thirty Zeros and fifteen floatplane Zeros, precipitating a vicious air battle. The P-38 pilots were credited with three Zeros destroyed and three probably destroyed and the Vought F4U Corsair pilots with two Zeros and a floatplane. The Zero pilots gave as good as they got, however. One PB4Y was shot down over the target and another had to ditch in the sea on the way home, while two Corsairs and three of the P-38s also went down, although one of the latter's pilots was rescued after ditching near the Russell Islands—which would be occupied by the Allies a week later for the construction of an advanced airfield.

Late in 1942, the Allies had adopted a standard new system of code names for Japanese aircraft, under which fighters received men's names and bombers and reconnaissance aircraft women's. Thus, for example, the Zero became the Zeke and the float Zero the Rufe. The name "Zero" was ingrained in the minds of Allied servicemen, however, and would remain in popular usage, including by fighter pilots, for some time.

The 339th FS's pilots would score a total of 102 confirmed air victories in the Solomon Islands campaign, from November 1942 through November 1943. It also lost more than a few aircraft and pilots, much of which had to do with tactics. When the P-38 was utilized properly, its victory-to-loss ratio was quite positive. All Allied fighter pilots knew (or should have known) not to dogfight with the agile Zero, and specifically not to get into a turning fight with one at low speed and low altitude. This was particularly true of the big Lockheed fighter. The P-38s were normally assigned as high cover for bomber escort missions, with the Marine and Navy F4Fs, F4Us, and Grumman F6F Hellcats providing medium cover and the P-39s and P-40s lower, close cover. Of course, it did not always turn out that way. Sometimes the Lightnings would be assigned lower cover, or have to assume closer support of the bombers when other fighters failed to show up or were diverted from their assigned position in the formation for some reason. The 339th Squadron had generated thirteen Missing Aircrew Reports (MACR) by the end of April 1943, but only another eight during the following seven months.

According to Bill Harris (his full name), who became the squadron's top scoring pilot, "we learned the high price of using P-38s at too low an altitude without effective top cover. Most of our losses (64%) came on six TBF/SBD escort missions. The usual altitude on these jobs ranged from 15,000 feet down to 2,000 feet—much too low for comfort and well-being."

The 339th's main job was, and continued to be, escorting COMAIRSOLS bombers up "The Slot," the water passage running through the middle of the Solomon Islands, to their targets. Until daylight air attacks on Guadalcanal finally ceased that summer, its pilots also helped defend the island against them. They also flew some ground attack missions. For example, on March 29, a 17th Squadron PR pilot spotted more than two dozen JNAF floatplanes at their moorings in the Shortlands. The next day, 339th FS P-38s and Marine F4Us strafed them and claimed to have destroyed eight.

April was a very active month for the Thirteen AF's P-38 pilots. On the 7th, sixty-seven Val dive bombers escorted by 110 Zeros attacked Allied shipping off Guadalcanal. In the huge air battle that ensued, the Allied fighters that had been scrambled—a mixture of F4Fs, F4Us, P-38s, P-39s, and P-40s—claimed to have shot down twelve Vals and twenty-seven Zeros, of which the P-38 pilots were credited with eight Zeros destroyed plus one probably destroyed. Capt. Thomas G. Lanphier of the 70th FS shot down three of them and 1Lt. Rex T. Barber of the 339th FS two. The remaining three P-38 victories were scored by other pilots of the 12th, 70th, and 339th Squadrons. The victorious 12th FS pilot was Maj. Paul S. Bechtel, who had previously scored two kills and a probable flying P-39s and another with a P-38. As an operations officer with XIII FC, he scored his fifth and last victory in a Corsair while flying with a Marine squadron.

During the second week of April 1943, the first XIII Fighter Command awards ceremony was held on Guadalcanal. XIII FC CO Brig. Gen. Dean Strother, on the left, congratulates Maj. John Mitchell, to whom he has just awarded a DFC. The aircraft in the background, No. 110, was P-38G-13 43-2187, normally flown by Capt. Rex Barber (the score on its nose is the aircraft's, not Barbers). (*USAF photo*)

Getting Yamamoto

Eleven days later, pilots of those squadrons flew what turned out to be one of the most famous fighter missions of World War II, and certainly the most famous P-38 mission. American cryptographers had already broken the Japanese communications codes after the Allies captured some of their codebooks, as a result of which, it was learned from Japanese radio transmissions that Admiral Isuroku Yamamoto, the architect of the Pearl Harbor attack, was going to be flown from Rabaul to the small island of Ballale, just south of Bougainville, within a very precise timeline on the morning of April 18. A mission was organized to intercept it with equal precision. It consisted of eighteen P-38s (the only Allied fighter on Guadalcanal that had the range to fly there and back) led by Maj. John Mitchell.

Almost miraculously, the interception was made just as the two Betty bombers carrying Yamamoto and his staff, escorted by six Zekes, approached Ballale. Although there were only two of them, three Bettys were claimed to have been shot down, plus three Zekes (none of which were, in fact, lost). Capt. Tom Lanphier of the 70th FS (flying P-38G-13 43-2338), the 339th Squadron's 1Lt. Rex Barber (flying G-13 43-2264), and Barber's squadron mate 1Lt. Besby F. Holmes (in G-1 42-12690) were all credited with one Betty and one Zeke. These were Lanphier's sixth and final victory and Barber's fifth. First Lieutenant Raymond K. Hine, Holmes's wingman, was MIA, evidently shot down by the Zeros. Mitchell, Lanphier, Barber, and Holmes were all awarded the Navy Cross for this amazingly successful mission, as it was flown under the direction of the USN. The controversy over whether Barber or Lanphier actually shot down Yamamoto's Betty has been argued, *ad nauseam*, ever since, with no final resolution in sight—or likely—seventy-six years later.

P-38G-13 43-2264 (No. 147/*Miss Virginia*) of the 339th FS crashed on Guadalcanal in late April 1943. Earlier that month, on the 18th, Capt. Rex Barber had flown this plane on the Yamamoto intercept mission. (*USAF photo*)

John Mitchell returned to the States in May and subsequently served another combat tour as a group commander with VII FC, providing escort to the B-29s bombing Japan from the Marianas. He scored three more victories flying North American P-51 Mustangs from Iwo Jima and shot down four MiG-15s while commanding a North American F-86 wing in the Korean War, bringing his final total to fifteen.

A USAAF night-fighter unit, Detachment "B" of the 6th Night Fighter Squadron (NFS), had arrived on Guadalcanal at the end of February. However, its radar-equipped P-70s (modified Douglas A-20 bombers) turned out to be too slow to intercept the Bettys. They scored a single victory, in April, and that was it. So, it had been decided to officially utilize P-38s as night fighters, as John Mitchell had done successfully four months earlier, and some experienced Lightning pilots were selected for that special duty. It paid off on the late evening of May 13, when 1Lt. William E. Smith of the 12th FS shot down a Betty and damaged another that he had caught in Guadalcanal's searchlight beams. On the night of May 18–19, seven P-38s were sent up in relays. One of them was flown by Maj. Louis R. Kittel, the 70th FS's CO, who spotted two Bettys in the beams and by their exhaust flames and shot them both down—for which he was awarded a DFC.

The P-38 pilots also continued to help counter the large daylight air raids. One of the biggest was on June 16, when fifty Vals, escorted by sixty-eight Zeros, attacked USN transports near Guadalcanal. More than 100 Allied fighters, including a dozen P-38s of the 339th FS, were scrambled to intercept them, the Lightning pilots wading into the Zekes. Second Lieutenant Bill Harris was credited with two, the fourth of his eventual sixteen victories (he had scored his first two—both also Zekes—on June 7, during a JNAF raid on the Russell Islands.) Second Lieutenant Murray J. Shubin shot down five Zekes and probably destroyed another, bringing his score to seven of an eventual eleven confirmed victories, for which he was awarded the DSC. The 339th scored a total of eleven kills in these actions, of the ninety-seven credited to the Allied fighters.

The daytime attacks on Guadalcanal ceased in July, and the 339th, now the Thirteenth AF's only P-38 squadron, could henceforth focus on its offensive bomber escort missions and on providing cover to Allied invasion forces as they gradually moved up the Solomon Islands chain. U.S. Army soldiers and Marines landed on New Georgia's southern coast on June 21, and nine days later, they invaded nearby Rendova Island. Their main initial objective was the Munda airfield on New Georgia, which, due to extremely stiff resistance, was not captured until August 5. Munda would then soon be utilized by the Thirteenth's P-38s.

On July 3, forty Zekes flew a fighter sweep over Rendova that was intercepted by sixteen 339th Squadron pilots, who downed five of them but lost three of their own. On the 17th, seventy-eight COMAIRSOL bombers, escorted by 114 fighters, attacked enemy shipping off Buin, on Bougainville's southern coast. Numerous Zekes from the nearby Kahili airfield intervened, and a huge air battle ensued. Forty-four Zekes and Rufes were claimed destroyed, six of them by the 339th FS, which lost two of the five U.S. aircraft that failed to return from this mission.

Around this time, there was a serious shortage of P-38s; as of July 9, XIII FC had just twenty-nine, total. They were by now concentrated in the 339th FS, the 12th and 70th Squadrons having reverted back to P-39s exclusively. As the summer progressed and the situation became even more critical, some of the 339th's pilots were forced to fly Airacobras with the 68th FS.

Above: P-38 pilots on Guadalcanal pose for a photograph in the spring of 1943. The bearded pilot in the second row is the 70th FS's CO, Maj. Louis Kittel. To Kittel's left is Maj. Paul Bechtel, an ace and CO of the 12th FS. (*Author's collection*)

Below: Lt. Murray J. Shubin of the 339th FS poses with his assigned aircraft, P-38G-13 43-2242, with which he shot down five Zekes and probably destroyed another over and near Guadalcanal on June 16, 1943, for which he was awarded the DSC. Shubin had a final total of eleven confirmed kills. (*USAF photo*)

Nocturnal Lightnings

The 6th NFS detachment on Guadalcanal had received some P-38s in June to supplement its ineffective P-70s. These were regular Lightnings borrowed from the day-fighter squadrons, which its pilots used in coordination with the searchlights on Guadalcanal and the Russell Islands. Their first success was on the night of July 12, when 1Lt. Ralph F. Tuttle shot down a Betty over the Russells. First Lieutenant James A. Harrell, III, downed another on July 17, near Fighter Two, and a second on August 14, again over the Russell Islands. Second Lieutenant Henry Meigs II, who was TDY (on temporary duty) with the night-fighter detachment from the 339th FS, destroyed another Betty early the following morning, and two—one right after the other—in the predawn hours of September 21, for which he was awarded a Silver Star. They were all over Guadalcanal. (Meigs soon returned to the 339th Squadron and scored three Zekes destroyed and three more probably destroyed over Rabaul in January and February 1944.)

Detachment "B" was disbanded in November, and its pilots and aircraft were absorbed into the 419th NFS, which arrived on Guadalcanal that month from Florida and was attached to the 18th FG. The 419th sent a detachment to Bougainville in late January 1944. Its Lightning pilots did not score any air victories but were quite successful in the night intruder/ground attack role.

The next important Japanese-held island to fall to the Allies, in September, was Vella Lavella, northwest of New Georgia. Its Barakoma airfield was soon also being used by Allied aircraft.

Last on the Allies' list of major objectives in the Solomons was the capture of Bougainville. It was decided to target Cape Torokina on its south central coast. Once that area was secured an airfield would be built there to be utilized in COMAIRSOLS' upcoming campaign against Rabaul, 400 miles to the northwest.

The 339th FS's situation had greatly improved by mid-September, when it returned to Guadalcanal from New Caledonia after a brief respite. It now had thirty-eight P-38s, twenty of them new P-38Hs, and thirty-three pilots, some of them also new. It would fly this tour from Munda, escorting B-24s to their targets on the islands still being held by the Japanese in the northern Solomons, most especially Bougainville and its infamous Kahili Airdrome (A/D) preliminary to its invasion, and providing cover for the Allied invasion forces—during which time it scored forty confirmed kills.

The 339th flew two eventful missions on October 10. The first was an escort of some B-24 Liberators to Kahili that morning, which was intercepted by fifteen Zekes. The P-38s were led by 1Lt. Bill Harris, whose wingman was Maj. Robert B. Westbrook, CO of the 44th FS. The 44th was scheduled to trade in its P-40s for P-38s soon, and Westbrook wanted to gain some experience flying the Lightning in combat. In this fight, five of the Zekes were destroyed and one probably destroyed without loss. Harris shot down one for his seventh victory and 1Lt. Murray Shubin two—his eighth and ninth. Maj. Westbrook also shot one down for his eighth victory, his first seven having been with P-40s. The only American loss in this action was a single B-24.

That afternoon, the 339th was in the air again, escorting a "Dumbo" air–sea rescue plane searching for the missing Liberator crew. Near Choiseul Island, southeast of Bougainville,

This fascinating series of photographs was taken shortly after 2Lt. Donald W. Livesay, a pilot of the 339th FS (seen still wearing his Mae West life preserver), crash-landed his battle-damaged P-38, H-5 42-66893, on Vella Lavella Island's Barakoma airstrip on October 7, 1943 after a fight with some Zeros. Among the obvious damage to his Lightning the external mass balance on the horizontal stabilizer has either been shot off or was broken off in the crash. (*USAF photos*)

the P-38s were ambushed by around twenty Zekes, of which five more were shot down and four probably destroyed. Harris was credited with two of the kills and shared one of the probables with Westbrook.

On October 27, the Treasury Islands, south of Bougainville, were occupied, to provide protection for Allied convoys during the upcoming battle for the latter. The JNAF sent thirty bombers escorted by fifty Zekes to attack the Allied ships that were involved. The ships' aerial protection included sixteen P-38s of the 339th Squadron, whose pilots were credited with destroying five Vals and two of the new single-engined Yokosuka D4Y "Judy" bombers. Bill Harris, newly promoted to captain, shot down one of the latter and Lt. Shubin two Vals, giving him his final victory total of eleven (he returned to the U.S. in December).

The initial landings on Bougainville took place on November 1, and the 339th covered them, scoring seven victories that day and eight more a week later, on the 8th. The vicious fighting on the ground continued for many weeks, but by December, the Allies controlled all the important terrain and their aircraft were operating from airfields on the island. The Solomon Islands campaign was over, and the 339th FS would now enjoy a two-month respite from combat.

In early October, a detachment of the 17th PRS, as it would be redesignated effective November 13, began operating from Munda, flying regular photo missions over Rabaul. At the end of January, it moved to the Piva airstrip on Bougainville. It had by then lost six of its pilots, all of whom had basically just disappeared. Since they were flying alone, over the sea, their specific fates were unknown; in one case only was debris from the F-5 recovered, by a USN ship from the surface of the water—but not its pilot.

Rabaul Finale

Rabaul had received one more big blow on November 11 when it was attacked by USN planes from five aircraft carriers in coordination with unescorted B-24s of the Fifth and Thirteenth AFs. Considerable damage was done; however, the Japanese forces there would have six weeks to recuperate and prepare for its final aerial onslaught, from land-based bombers and fighters in the Solomon Islands.

The 339th FS was rested again effective December 1, and its personnel were given leave in Auckland, New Zealand, XIII FC's primary R&R (rest and recreation) destination. Its headquarters was also finally moved from Oua Tom on New Caledonia to Guadalcanal that month.

COMAIRSOLS was ready to begin its Rabaul campaign in mid-December, with its fighters now based on airfields in the northern Solomons from which they could escort the bombers there. Comprising just two squadrons, XIII FC P-38s made up a relatively small, but vital, part of the escort—and they would not be operational at the same time. Flying from Munda, the 44th FS, which had made its transition to the P-38 in late November, would be first up to bat, and after a month, the 339th would take over the Rabaul escort duties. Besides its new aircraft, the 44th had also acquired a new name: Vampire Squadron.

The first of the 44th Squadron's Rabaul missions, on December 19, was a disappointment as the weather intervened in favor of the Japanese; very few of the B-24s were able to

Above left: Margie B. II was P-38H-5 42-66677 of the 339th FS, whose assigned pilot—posing with her here—was Lt. John R. Mulvey, Jr., who shot down two Zekes and probably destroyed another in early October 1943, including a destroyed and a probable on the 10th. (*Michael Bates collection*)

Above right and below: P-38G-13 43-2239, the 339th FS's No. 138, on Guadalcanal—before and after acquiring the name *OLD IRONSIDES*. It was assigned to Lt. Samuel T. Howie, who was credited with four confirmed air victories, including three Vals during the 339th's big fight near the Treasury Islands on October 27, 1943. (*John Lambert collection and Michael Bates collection*)

drop their bombs there. A single Zero was shot down by a Royal New Zealand Air Force (RNZAF) Kittyhawk, but the 44th's P-38 pilots encountered no e/a.

The next one, on the 23rd, was more productive. Twenty-seven 44th FS Lightnings provided top cover for two squadrons of Liberators bombing the Lakunai and Vunakanau airfields, three Marine F4U squadrons forming the rest of the escort. Sixty Zeros attacked the formation over the target, and while the Marine pilots scored eighteen kills (for the loss of three Corsairs), of the P-38s, only Maj. Westbrook's flight actually engaged them, with he and his wingman, 2Lt. Raymond M. Fouquet, each downing one. Fouquet shot his Zeke off Westbrook's tail, as his CO was trying with considerable difficulty to evade it.

The next day, Christmas Eve, seventeen 44th Squadron P-38s once again escorted B-24s over Lakunai. After the bombing, the Lightning pilots accompanied the Liberators to a safe distance on their way home and then returned to hunt for Zeros, of which they found and engaged two dozen. They were credited with eight confirmed kills and two probables, without loss. Maj. Westbrook downed two of the Zekes by himself and shared two others with 1Lt. Byron B. Bowman and 1Lt. Howard M. Cleveland, the latter TDY from the 70th FS. Bowman and Cleveland each also scored a solo victory.

The Vampire Squadron was back over Rabaul on December 25, as usual providing top cover for the B-24s. Maj. Westbrook was credited with two of the four Zekes shot down by the 44th, but he had a very close call after his second kill, when his wingman—this time Flt. Off. Rex A. Byers—once again shot a Zeke off his tail. According to the mission report:

> At the completion of this action, Major Westbrook's left engine started burning. He saw F/O Byers turn away from him and go into a cloud over Duke of York Island, pursued by three Zekes, his right engine smoking and leaking Prestone. In striving to reach the clouds, Major Westbrook, now attacked by several Zekes, was joined by an F4U, which dispersed the enemy planes. Major Westbrook cut all switches, the fire in the right engine was somehow extinguished, and he returned to Barakoma [the Marine airfield on Vella Lavella] and landed at 1430 hours.

Byers and another 44th Squadron pilot failed to return from this mission. Bob Westbrook was awarded a Distinguished Service Cross (DSC) for his leadership of and successes on these three December missions.

Although the 44th's pilots spotted numerous Zeros over Rabaul during another B-24 escort on New Year's Day, they avoided combat and the P-38s were unable to score. The January 4 mission was aborted due to the weather having "closed in," but two days later, the squadron flew its most successful Rabaul mission.

By January 6, the 44th FS had moved north to the new airfield on Stirling, in the Treasury Islands. The day's mission was an atypical fighter sweep over Rabaul along with fifty-six F4U and F6Fs. However, only eight Corsairs and sixteen Lightnings made it there through some very bad weather. This diminished formation met three dozen Zekes near Rapopo, resulting in a huge dogfight. The P-38 pilots were credited with nine destroyed and five probables for the loss of two of their own, while the Marines downed two Zeros and lost one F4U. Maj. Westbrook was credited with one destroyed plus one probable, which brought his victory total to fifteen. Lt. Col. Leo F. Dusard, the 347th FG's new CO, also scored a Zeke and Capt. Cotesworth B. Head, Jr., two, plus a probable. Head had eight previous victories flying P-40s, but this was his first with a P-38.

This was Maj. Westbrook's last mission with the 44th FS as he had completed his combat tour. Capt. Head led it on the January 9 mission, which was a bust, as the P-38s became separated from the B-24s while penetrating a "heavy cloud formation." The next Rabaul mission two days later resulted in just one confirmed and four probable victories.

The 339th FS re-entered the fray in mid-January, moving from Guadalcanal to Munda and then, on the 15th, to Stirling, where it was to relieve the 44th. It was decided that the two squadrons would fly a joint mission on the 17th, before the 44th returned to Guadalcanal. This was an escort to Navy SBDs and Grumman TBF Avenger torpedo bombers targeting ships in Simpson Harbor, by two dozen P-38s from both squadrons— of which only nineteen made it to the target. As the bombers began their runs over the harbor, the formation was overwhelmed by a mass of Zeros. In the ensuing fight, eight of the Lightnings went down, four from each squadron. In return, they were credited with destroying just six of the Zeros (three of them by Capt. Head), probably destroying six and damaging one.

The 339th was then experiencing a technical problem with its P-38s. The intake manifolds on some of their Allison engines were separating from the scroll joints, causing a fire between the cylinder banks and the engine that resulted in some aborts and the death of one of the squadron's pilots. Typically, its maintenance personnel soon solved the problem.

The 44th Squadron flew its last Rabaul mission on January 18, with fourteen of its P-38s escorting some B-25s to Tobera. Things went awry when the F4Us and F6Fs did not show up at the rendezvous with the bombers and the escort was left to the handful of Lightnings, whose pilots were forced to assume the close cover duty that was not their forte. Zeros attacked the formation on the way home, of which the 44th's pilots claimed five destroyed—one of them by Capt. Head for his fourteenth victory. Unfortunately, Head did not return; he was last seen with the right engine of his P-38 (J-5 42-67155) smoking and he then disappeared, never to be seen again.

The main reason for these P-38 losses was spelled out in a XIII FC report, which stated:

Since the P-38 first came into the theater in the fall of 1942, it had been known that this aircraft was not a low altitude interceptor, and that only above 20,000 feet could it dogfight with the Zero on favorable terms. Nevertheless, during the month of January the Lightning was used repeatedly as a low altitude interceptor, and with resultant heavy loses in aircraft and pilots to the squadrons concerned.

The report then went on to say that one of the specific problems was the low altitude from which the SBDs and TBFs bombed, requiring the escorting fighters to also fly lower. It further stated:

Marine fighter pilots did not always discharge their escort responsibilities in accordance with the prearranged plans; for time and time again our pilots report that the F4Us were either out of position or failed to maintain their assigned position in the formation. If the Corsairs were on low or close cover and left this position, which they frequently did, P-38s

P-38J-10 42-67795, seen here being utilized as a makeshift clothesline by 339th FS personnel on Guadalcanal in late 1943, was flown by that squadron and by the 44th FS on the Rabaul missions. It met its end on February 13, 1945, when it was destroyed in a crash while assigned to the 8th Service Group at Nadzab, New Guinea. (*USAF photos*)

Second Lieutenant John F. Roehm of the 44th FS was photographed on Stirling Island shortly after downing a Zero over Rabaul on January 18, 1944. (*USAF photo*)

were obliged to drop down to cover the bombers, thereby placing themselves in a highly disadvantage position.

The Vampire Squadron's Rabaul experience thus ended on a sour note. It had done an exemplary job of protecting the bombers, in the process of which it was credited with 28-13-4 enemy fighters. But it had lost eight of its pilots, including one of the very best.

The 339th Squadron went on to fly many more Rabaul missions. From January 17 through February 18, 1944, it was credited with forty-five e/a destroyed and ten probably destroyed. It suffered just five addition losses, on January 20, 22 and 28; on the latter date, three of its pilots were MIA in exchange for five Zekes confirmed destroyed and one probable. Its best day was February 10, when it shot down ten Zekes and probably destroyed one.

Capt. Bill Harris was credited with two and a half Zekes over Rabaul on February 9 and two more on the 15th. These brought his total to fourteen and a half destroyed, making him the Thirteenth AF's top-scoring P-38 pilot. He completed his combat tour later that month.

On the February 18 mission, 339th FS pilots shot down another five Zekes over Tobera. After the next day's mission, the Japanese called it quits at Rabaul, and most of its surviving aircraft were flown to Truk Island in the Carolines on the 20th.

Allied planes continued to use Rabaul, now bypassed, isolated, and blockaded, for target practice until the end of the war. The JNAF had left a handful of aircraft behind, mainly for reconnaissance purposes, and during a dive bombing mission to Rabaul on March 16, two pilots of the 12th FS, which had recently converted to P-38s, shot down a Dinah. (The 12th had arrived at Stirling to replace the 339th on February 18.) This was XIII FC's last

P-38J-15 42-104295 is well along in its reassembly process at Guadalcanal in May 1944. This plane was lost in action over the Philippines with the 12th FS in December of that year. (*USAF photo*)

aerial victory while based in the Solomon Islands, and the last of the 211 scored by P-38 pilots there since November 1942.

The Thirteenth AF's last two operational Lightning losses while based in the Solomons both occurred on April 18. A 17th PRS pilot disappeared that day during a recon to Kavieng, on New Ireland, north of Rabaul, and a pilot of the 419th NFS, while flying a daytime fighter-bomber mission against Japanese forces still active on Bougainville, was shot down and killed by AA fire.

The 67th, 68th, and 70th FSs began converting to P-38s from their P-39s in May, and by July, all six XIII FC squadrons were flying them exclusively.

During the next four months, the Thirteenth's Lightning units had little to do other than bomb, strafe, and reconnoiter the remaining isolated Japanese forces in the area, which was now a backwater to the real Pacific war taking place much farther west. They would catch up to it, however, as they would soon be joining the Fifth AF in New Guinea.

The New FEAF

The 18th FG transferred from the Solomon Islands to the Mar airstrip at Sansapor, New Guinea, in mid-August and then, in September, to the new Klenso Field on nearby Middleburg Island. The 347th FG H.Q. and its 339th FS also moved to Mar at that time, but its 67th and 68th Squadrons went to Middleburg initially. The 17th PRS transferred to Noemfoor

Newly arrived Thirteenth AF Lightnings had to go through numerous procedures before attaining operational status. These two photos, taken at Guadalcanal in May 1944, show partly disassembled and "cocooned" P-38s being offloaded from a ship and then one of them up on blocks, with its landing gear retracted, ready to have its protective covering removed prior to reassembly. (*USAF photos*)

Island, southwest of Biak, in October and also operated briefly from Sansapor before joining its parent 4th Photo Group on Morotai Island, to which the latter moved from Guadalcanal effective December 12, and where its headquarters would remain for the rest of the war.

Middleburg, off Cape Sansapor near New Guinea's western tip, had been occupied in early August and work was immediately begun on the fighter strip, which became operational on the 17th. Morotai, just north of Halmahera and 300 miles from the Philippine Islands, was invaded on September 15 and there was soon an Allied airfield on it as well.

Since the Fifth and Thirteenth AFs were now operating in close proximity from bases in western New Guinea and being assigned many of the same targets, it was almost as if they were a single air force—which they were effective August 3, 1944, when a new FEAF was activated. This entity, commanded by the Fifth AF's former CO, Lt. Gen. George C. Kenney, was an umbrella organization with administrative control over both the Fifth and the Thirteenth.

Until the upcoming invasion of the Philippines, the fighter units of both air forces would primarily be targeting enemy airfields, ports, shipping, and oil refineries in the East Indies. They would also venture to Mindanao Island, in the Philippines, which was within range of the P-38s from Middleburg.

The first of the Mindanao missions, a bomber escort to the port of Davao, on its southern coast, was flown on September 2, by P-38s of the 35th, 36th, 9th, and 432nd FSs. Tagging along with the 9th were Lt. Col. Bob Westbrook (who had recently returned to the SWP for a second combat tour, this time as the 347th FG's Deputy CO) and his wingman, 1Lt. Glenn A. Starmer of the 339th FS. A few e/a were encountered, and a Zeke, a twin-engined Kawasaki Ki-48 "Lily" bomber, and a single-engined Aichi E13A "Jake" reconnaissance floatplane were shot down. The first two were credited to 8th FG pilots and the Jake to Lt. Starmer. They were the first American fighter victories over the Philippines since April 1942. A week later, there was a USN carrier raid on Mindanao. These were the first of the air battles over the Philippines that would continue almost nonstop for the next four months.

The 49th became a full P-38 group effective September 12, after its 7th "Screamin' Demons" and 8th "Eightball" Squadrons traded in their P-40s for Lightnings.

The 6th PRG, which had moved to Biak in mid-August, was given the assignment of photographing Leyte Island in the east central Philippines, which was scheduled for invasion in late October. This involved numerous 1,500-mile-plus unescorted round trips by its pilots, often through hazardous weather fronts, from September 18 to 25, for which it received a Distinguished Unit Citation (DUC).

The oil refineries at Balikpapan on the east coast of Borneo, the source of much of the Japanese military's fuel supplies, were targeted by the FEAF from September 30 to October 14. Two of these missions resulted in numerous air victories by its fighters. On October 10, fifty-eight B-24s were escorted there by P-47s of the 35th FG and fourteen P-38s of the 9th FS, the latter staging through Morotai from Biak. The 1,700-mile round trip was accomplished by utilizing the fuel conservation techniques taught to the 475th FG by Charles Lindbergh earlier that year.

JAAF and JNAF fighters intercepted vigorously, shooting down four of the Liberators and one Thunderbolt. Of the eighteen destroyed by the American fighters, six were credited to the 9th FS. Maj. Dick Bong, who had returned the previous month for his third combat tour and was TDY with his old squadron, shot down an Oscar and a Nakajima J1N1 "Irving" night fighter—his twenty-ninth and thirtieth victories.

October 1944: Lt. Col. Robert B. Westbrook, 347th FG Deputy Commander, chats with his ground crew on Middleburg Island. He named his P-38 the *Florida Thrush*, after singer/actress Frances Langford, with whom he was personally acquainted. (*Jack Cook collection*)

An identical mission was flown to Balikpapan four days later, by the same escort fighter units plus sixteen P-38s from the 432nd FS and others from the 68th FS on Middleburg, of which only six made it to the target. A special four-plane flight consisting of leading 8th FG pilots also joined it. This one resulted in credits totaling 38-5-1, of which the 9th FS's pilots received 3-1-0, the 68th's 2-1-1 and the 432nd's two confirmed kills. The 431st Squadron's Tom McGuire had inserted himself into the 9th's formation that day, hoping to close the scoring gap with Dick Bong, with whom he was engaged in an "ace race." He shot down a Hamp, a Tojo, and an Oscar (and probably destroyed another Oscar) to bring his confirmed total to twenty-four. The only 8th FG pilot to score was Capt. Kenneth G. Ladd, formerly of the 80th FS but now CO of the 36th FS, who downed two Oscars to give him his final total of twelve destroyed. Unfortunately, Ladd, who was last seen on the tail of a Tojo, then disappeared and was never seen again.

On October 22, the 12th FS, operating from Sansapor, flew the first napalm fire bomb mission in the SWP, its pilots dropping 75-gallon belly tanks filled with it onto oil storage tanks on Ceram.

The 347th FG received a DUC for its fighter sweeps to Japanese airfields and ports on Celebes, between New Guinea and Borneo, on November 7, 20, and 22, 1944, led by Lt. Col. Westbrook. Of the sixteen e/a its pilots shot down from September 2 to November 7, Westbrook was credited with five of them, including three Oscars over an airfield near Makassar on October 23 that brought his total to twenty. On the last of the DUC missions, he was strafing ships in Makassar Bay when his P-38 was hit by intense AA fire from a gunboat and its right engine caught fire. It then crashed into the sea, killing the Thirteenth AF's top-scoring fighter pilot. Two others were MIA as well.

Above: Maj. Tom McGuire poses with his 431st FS ground crewmen on Biak Island during the late summer of 1944. (*Michael Bates collection*)

Below left: Lt. Kenneth G. Ladd poses with his colorful 80th FS P-38J, which would soon sport the name *Windy City Ruthie*, shortly after scoring his tenth victory on April 3, 1944. Ladd was later given command of the 8th FG's 36th Squadron and scored two more victories with it before he was killed in action over Balikpapan, Borneo, on October 14, 1944. (*John Stanaway collection*)

Below right: The 347th FG's leaders on Middleburg Island. *From left to right*: Maj. Leonard Shapiro, 68th FS CO; Maj. Donald H. Lee, Jr., 67th FS CO; Lt. Col. Shelby England, Group Executive Officer; Colonel Leo F. Dusard, Jr., Group Commander; Lt. Col. Bob Westbrook, Deputy Group Commander; and Maj. John Z. Endress, 339th FS CO. (*Jack Cook collection*)

Return to the Philippines

Gen. Douglas MacArthur made good on his famous promise to return to the Philippines when, on October 20, the U.S. Sixth Army landed at Tacloban and Dulag on the east side of Leyte, covered by USN carrier planes. This elicited an immediate, strong response from the Japanese on the ground, on the sea, and in the air.

Within days, airstrips were being constructed inside both beachheads. Thirty-four P-38s of the 49th FG flew in to Tacloban from Biak on October 27, and its 9th FS intercepted some Vals escorted by Oscars later that day, claiming six destroyed, one probably destroyed, and one damaged. Among the victors was Maj. Bong, who claimed an Oscar for his thirty-first victory, and Maj. Gerald R. Johnson, the 49th FG's Operations Officer, who downed an Oscar and a Val—his fourteenth and fifteenth kills.

The 475th FG then began moving to the Dulag airstrip from Biak. The 432nd's air echelon was the first to arrive, on November 2, but Tom McGuire managed to get a head start on the movement. On the 1st, his 431st Squadron was given the task of ferrying some P-38s to the 49th FG from the Buri airstrip on Morotai. There happened to be an air raid in progress when they arrived over Leyte and he shot down a Tojo for his twenty-fifth victory. The 431st would not arrive at Dulag officially until the 9th and the 433rd on the 13th.

Also on November 1, forty-two 8th FG P-38s from Morotai (to which the unit had moved from Owi in mid-September) attacked airfields on Negros Island in support of the Leyte operation. They shot down seven e/a and claimed to have destroyed about seventy-five more on the ground, for the loss of three P-38s.

In November, 6th PRG H.Q. and its 8th and 25th Squadrons moved to Dulag. The 8th would receive a DUC for the missions it flew from there late that month and in early December.

Pilots of the 9th FS shortly after their arrival at the new Tacloban airstrip on Leyte Island on October 27, 1944. (*USAF photo*)

The first P-38L-1s had arrived in the SWP in September and, with their aileron boost and anti-compressibility flaps, would prove to be very effective in numerous air battles over the Philippines. In the 475th Group, its 432nd Squadron had totally re-equipped with them by the end of September and the 431st then had a mixture of Js and Ls, but the 433rd would not receive its first Ls until November. By December, the 8th FG had begun receiving some of the new L-5s.

While the 347th FG was occupied with its missions to Celebes from Middleburg, the 18th FG moved to the Wama airstrip on Morotai from Sansapor in early November to support the Sixth Army on Leyte, mainly by attacking Japanese shipping and airfields there and on the nearby islands of Cebu, Negros, Panay, and Luzon—often encountering e/a in the process. From November 3 through December 16, the 18th Group's pilots were credited with shooting down forty-two e/a and probably destroying and damaging many more, for the loss of five of their own.

The 18th was awarded its only DUC for its actions over Ormoc Bay, on Leyte's west coast, on November 10 and 11. On the 10th, its pilots attacked a convoy there, claiming to have sunk a transport and a destroyer, two of them being lost in the process. The following day, its 12th FS encountered a large formation of Zekes in the same area and was credited with destroying eight and probably destroying four of them for the loss of one P-38.

On November 26, 9th FS pilot Lt. Norman E. Moeller described in his journal the situation at Tacloban:

A large number of Navy fighter planes landed here last night. Two of our aircraft carriers had been damaged in battles near Luzon and they had to come here to land. Our strip is still very short and soft. About thirty of the Navy fighters crashed after landing. Our airstrip has become a traffic nightmare. On our single landing strip we have operating not only our P-38s but also squadrons of P-40s, P-47s, P-61s, Navy Hellcats, Marine Corsairs, B-25s and B-24s. This was also enhanced by a stream of C-47 and C-54 cargo planes and an occasional Catalina flying boat and observation scouts. It's been so jammed up that circling the field has run past a matter of minutes into hours. One of the Corsairs taking off clipped a taxiing plane and crashed into two parked B-24s. All three burned, including the pilot. Of the twenty-five new P-38Ls that we brought up from Biak on October 27 we have only four or five left. The rest of the squadron is made up of older models that are definitely clunks.[3]

Also transferring to Leyte in November was V FC Headquarters. It would move to Mindoro two months later, then to Clark Field on Luzon in March, and finally to Okinawa in August, just before the war's end.

V FC's biggest day of aerial combat over the Philippines was December 7, while covering the Sixth Army landings at Ormoc Bay designed to help break the stalemate caused by the stubborn Japanese resistance on the island. Of the sixty-six kills claimed by the command's pilots over and near Ormoc that day, fifty were scored by the 49th's and the 475th's—twenty-two by the former and twenty-eight by the latter.

Dick Bong had just moved over to the 475th FG from the 49th (with which he had scored six victories) and was flying with Maj. McGuire's 431st FS. McGuire scored an Oscar on

Above: This 347th FG P-38 was damaged during an air raid on Middleburg Island. (*USAF photo*)

Right: A nice shot of a P-38 pilot in his flight gear prior to a mission. He is Maj. William R. Cowper, Jr., who in late 1944 was CO of the 70th FS. (*USAF photo*)

a mission over Ormoc just before noon and then downed a Tojo on another mission late that afternoon for his thirtieth victory. However, Bong also scored two: first a twin-engined Mitsubishi Ki-21 "Sally" bomber and later a Tojo in the same fight in which McGuire claimed one, bringing his total to thirty-eight. Also scoring big on December 7 were the 49th FG's Maj. Jerry Johnson (three Oscars and a twin-engined Nakajima Ki-49 "Helen" bomber, which brought his total to twenty-one) and Col. Charles MacDonald, the 475th's CO, with three "Jacks" (Mitsubishi J2Ms) bringing his score to twenty.

Ormoc fell three days later, which meant that for all practical purposes the Allies were in control of the whole island.

Maj. Bong increased his score to forty on December 17, when he shot down an Oscar over Mindoro. He was then grounded by Gen. Kenney and was soon on his way home. Bong had been presented with the Medal of Honor—for "conspicuous gallantry and intrepidity in action" from October 10 through November 15, 1944—by Gen. MacArthur at Tacloban five days earlier.

The Philippine air war was reaching its climax as Christmas approached. On Christmas Day, the 49th and 475th Groups were assigned to escort B-24s bombing Mabalacat, one of the complex of airstrips comprising Clark Field on Luzon. It was heavily intercepted, initiating a huge air battle, the results of which were fourteen victories by the 49th and twenty-eight by the 475th (one of which was its 500th) for the loss of two of its pilots. Maj. McGuire scored three Zekes, bringing his total to thirty-four, and Col. MacDonald was credited with two Jacks and a Zeke plus another Jack probably destroyed, giving him a total of twenty-four confirmed victories.

An identical mission was flown to Clark the next day, to which there was considerably less opposition. The final score was fourteen enemy fighters, of which Tom McGuire accounted for no less than four Zekes, bringing his total to thirty-eight—only two less than Bong. This time there were no losses. McGuire would be awarded a posthumous Medal of Honor for these two missions.

Although the USAAF night-fighter squadrons in the SWP had mostly re-equipped with Northrop P-61 Black Widows by late 1944, they still retained a few P-38s. The 418th and 421st NFS, which joined the Fifth AF in New Guinea from Florida in November 1943 and January 1944, respectively, had at first operated P-70s and P-38s, mainly in the night-intruder role. The 421st, which received its first two P-38s on January 22, 1944, did not score any aerial victories with them, but the 418th did. On January 13, 1944, the latter's CO, Maj. Carroll C. Smith, shot a Val down over Alexshafen with a P-38J while flying from Dobodura—the squadron's first victory. In the early morning of November 26, while flying from its new base on Morotai, to which it had moved in early October, Smith probably destroyed an unidentified twin-engined aircraft. Two nights later, on the morning of the 28th, he destroyed one Betty and probably destroyed another. Maj. Smith shot down another five e/a with P-61s to become the USAAF's top-scoring night-fighter pilot. On the early morning of December 30, 1944, Capt. Richard O. Stewart of the 419th NFS, also flying a P-38J from Morotai, shot down a Betty near Sansapor.

Once Leyte was secured, a new front was opened in the Philippines when, on December 15, landings were made by the Sixth Army near San Jose, the capital of Mindoro, the large island southwest of Luzon. Within a week, an airstrip, named Hill Field, had been built near the city,

December 21, 1944: P-38L-5 44-24850 of the 432nd FS was badly damaged by the explosion of a 1,000-lb. bomb during an air raid on Leyte's Dulag airstrip. (*USAF photo*)

This P-38J-15, named *STRAWBERRY BLOND*, was the personal aircraft of 1Lt. Sammy A. Pierce, an 8th FS ace. Over Clark Field, Luzon, on December 26, 1944 Pierce shot down three Zekes and a Frank—his only victories with the P-38. He had scored three earlier kills with P-40s in New Guinea. (*Author's collection*)

According to this photo's official caption, these 36th FS pilots at Hill Field have "just returned from a bombing mission against the remaining Jap pockets in northern Luzon" in early 1945 and are "waiting for transportation on the flight line." (*USAF photo*)

the first of four that were to be constructed on the island. Among the invasion forces was an advance echelon of the 8th FG, which moved to Hill Field from Morotai on December 20. Six days later, its P-38s were among the American aircraft on Mindoro that repelled an IJN task force from Saigon, directly across the South China Sea, that shelled the ships and facilities at San Jose, during which it lost six of its aircraft and two pilots. The group received a DUC for this action. The 8th was now in position to support the invasion of Luzon, scheduled to begin in early January. The 25th PRS moved to San Jose from Dulag effective January 3, but kept a detachment on Leyte for the next four months.

Two new F-5 photo reconnaissance squadrons arrived in New Guinea from the U.S. in mid-December. The 36th PRS was assigned to the Fifth AF's 6th PRG on Biak and the 38th PRS to the Thirteenth AF's 4th PRG on Morotai, where it went operational on February 21, and where 4th Group H.Q. would remain until the war's end.

The last major air battle over the Philippines took place on New Year's Day 1945, when the 49th and 475th FGs escorted B-24s to Clark Field once again. They were intercepted by a mixed force of Japanese fighters that included Zekes, Oscars, Jacks, and Tojos—thirteen of which were claimed destroyed. The 475th's Col. MacDonald was credited with a Tojo and a twin-engined Dinah recon, his twenty-fifth and twenty-sixth victories. A 49th Group pilot crashed into the sea while flying over it at low level in poor visibility on the way home, but he fortunately survived and was rescued. At this time, the 49th was already in the process of moving from Tacloban to San Jose on Mindoro, which it completed a few days later.

From October 27, 1944 through January 1, 1945, the Fifth AF's P-38s had been in constant action, accounting for the destruction of 439 e/a in the air—seventy-eight by the

December 20, 1944: These 36th FS P-38s had just arrived at the new Hill Field near San Jose on Mindoro Island in the Philippines, having flown there from Leyte. (*USAF photo*)

December 20, 1944: 2Lt. Francis S. "Sam" Ford of the 36th FS has just survived the crash-landing of his P-38L-5, 44-25310, on Mindoro's Hill Field. It had been damaged in a fight with some JAAF fighters. Ford was not so fortunate a few days later, when, on the early morning of December 27, he disappeared during a night flight to Tacloban on Leyte, in P-38L-5 44-25243, and was not seen again. (*USAF photo*)

8th FG, 175 by the 49th FG, and 173 by the 475th FG. Maj. Dick Bong and Col. Robert L. Morrissey from V FC Headquarters scored eleven and two kills, respectively, while flying with the 49th and 475th Groups—both of which received a DUC for these operations. Aerial victories would be hard to come by henceforth, and by the end of the war seven and a half months later, the Fifth's Lightning pilots had accumulated a combined total of only forty-three more.

After Dick Bong's departure for the U.S. and further acclaim as America's "Ace of Aces"—and now as a Medal of Honor winner—Tom McGuire was determined to beat his score. However, e/a were becoming scarce and time was short, as his latest tour (normally 300 combat hours) was coming to an end. He had relinquished command of the 431st FS on December 28 to become group operations officer. When he took off from Dulag on the morning of January 7, 1945 with three other 475th FG pilots for a sweep to Negros Island, he was determined to score.

Over Negros, they spotted a lone Oscar below them and Maj. McGuire went after it. However, the pilot of the nimble Ki-43 initially outmaneuvered the heavy P-38s and attacked his wingman. McGuire then went into a tight, full-power turn to drive the pesky Oscar off the wingman's tail, but he had made the fatal mistake of failing to first jettison his drop tanks. As he tried to position himself for a shot, his P-38 stalled, snap-rolled to the left, and crashed into the jungle upside down.

Tom McGuire would thus not be America's next "Ace of Aces." Sadly, the pilot who held that distinction, Dick Bong, was killed in a crash seven months later, on August 6, while flight testing one of Lockheed's new P-80 jets at its Burbank plant.

The 49th FG moved to Hill Field on Mindoro during the first week of January. By the end of that month, it was totally equipped with P-38Ls.

On January 9, the U.S. Seventh Army landed at Lingayen, on Luzon's west coast, and a week later, the 18th FG was operating from an airstrip there, as was the 26th PRS, up from Biak. The 18th then began flying fighter sweeps and bomber escorts to Formosa, 400 miles due north. Pilots of its 44th FS shot down three Zekes and probably destroyed another there on January 29, and the 12th FS scored two more on the 31st. The 26th PRS would be awarded a DUC for its photo sorties to Formosa on March 22. The 49th FG moved to Lingayen at the end of February and was replaced at Elmore Field on Mindoro by the 18th FG. The 49th flew its first mission from Lingayen on the 28th and subsequently flew many to the China coast, including Formosa. On March 6, its pilots shot down seven Zekes over Hainan Island.

Puerto Princesa, the capital of Palawan, the long, thin Philippine island stretching between Mindoro and Borneo, was captured by the U.S. Eighth Army on February 28, and an airfield, named after Col. Westbrook, was quickly readied for Thirteenth AF units, from which they would support the Eighth Army in the central Philippines. The 347th FG moved to Mindoro from Middleburg on February 22 and then again, just two weeks later, to Puerto Princesa, where it would remain until the end of the war—although its 67th and 339th Squadrons did operate from Middleburg and Morotai, respectively, during February and March.

On March 10, the Eighth Army landed at Zamboanga, on the southwestern tip of Mindanao, where an airstrip, named Moret Field, was soon readied, to which the 18th FG

Ground crewmen fill the drop tanks of a 44th FS P-38 (No. 475) with napalm for another firebombing mission. Napalm was a particularly effective weapon during the fighting for Luzon in early 1945. (*USAF photo*)

would transfer in early May and remain until the war's end. (Its 12th and 44th Squadrons had been operating from Westbrook Field on Palawan starting in late April.) By the middle of April, the only remaining pockets of organized Japanese resistance in the Philippines were on parts of Mindanao and Luzon.

The 547th NFS had joined the Fifth AF in New Guinea from California in September 1944 and was based on Owi Island and then on Mindoro before moving to Lingayen in early January 1945. Although equipped mainly with P-61s, it did have two very unusual P-38s—J-20s that had been modified with Navy APS-4 AI radar pods on their starboard wings and a pilot-operated radar set in the cockpit, and which were painted gloss black. While flying one of them, 44-23544, on the night of March 9, 2Lt. Francis J. Raidt was about to bomb an enemy airstrip on Luzon when he saw a "Tess" transport (a Douglas DC-2) coming in for a landing and shot it down. The 418th NFS had a modified P-38 equipped with SCR-540 radar and space for an operator but made no aerial claims with it.

The 475th FG flew eventful missions to French Indochina on two successive days, March 28 and 29, from Clark Field, which had been captured in February and to which the group had moved at the end of that month after spending the previous month at Elmore Field on Mindoro. On the 28th, while orbiting an enemy convoy that was being attacked by the B-25s it was escorting, its pilots encountered two dozen enemy fighters—a mixture of Zekes, Tojos, and Nakajima Ki-84 "Franks"—of which nine were claimed destroyed. Two 433rd FS pilots were MIA. It flew a similar mission the next day, and this time seven Zekes were shot down without loss. These were the 475th Group's last aerial victories.

The 49th FG scored *its* last victory on April 26, when its new executive officer, Maj. George Laven, Jr., flew a freelance sweep with a wingman from Lingayen to Formosa, where he

Above: Pilots of the 44th FS at Zamboanga, on Mindanao, in late 1945. (*Author's collection*)

Below: The 49th FG's CO, Lt. Col. Gerald R. Johnson (in the center, standing) poses with his assigned P-38, *Jerry*, and other prominent 49th Group pilots shortly after scoring his twenty-second and last victory, a Tojo he shot down near Hong Kong on April 2, 1945. (His plane's scoreboard includes, tongue in cheek, an RAAF Wirraway he accidentally shot down over New Guinea, plus two Rufe floatplanes he claimed over the Aleutians early in the war that were not confirmed.) Flanking Johnson are Maj. George Laven (on the left) and Lt. Col. Clay Tice. In the front row, from the left, are Capt. Bob DeHaven, Maj. Wally Jordan, and Capt. Jim Watkins. (*John Stanaway collection*)

The 9th FS's Maj. James A. Watkins not long after scoring his twelfth and final victory, near Hong Kong on April 2, 1945. His assigned P-38, *Charlcie Jeanne*, was L-5 serial number 44-26407. (*John Stanaway collection*)

claimed to have shot down a Kawanishi H8K "Emily" flying boat. He had been credited with three kills during his first combat tour with the 54th FS in the Aleutians.

In 1945, the 18th and 347th FGs flew many very-long-range missions to the Dutch East Indies, China, Singapore, and Indochina, utilizing the fuel management techniques championed by Charles Lindbergh. For example, on May 2, the latter group's 68th FS was assigned a B-25 escort to Saigon. After shepherding the Mitchells over their targets and strafing some trains (which, as it turned out, they could not really spare the fuel to do), the P-38 pilots headed for home. It was a little over 850 miles from Palawan to Saigon, but because of the constant "S" turns the P-38 pilots had to make to cover the slower B-25s, they actually flew much farther than that. One of this mission's participants, 1Lt. Richard F. Brown, remembered later:

> The P-38 factory representatives said that Lindbergh's 1600 rpm and 32 inches of manifold pressure limit was all the 1750 hp Allison engines could take. I estimated as we left the coast of [Indochina] that we didn't have quite enough fuel to make it back to Puerto Princesa. Extra fuel had been used to keep our speed up to 425 mph while strafing the targets. Then we used more extra fuel to climb back to altitude. As soon as I was at cruising level at 1600 rpm and 32 inches, I started to figure out my fuel requirements to get home. I throttled back to 1400 rpm and leaned the fuel mixture a little bit more. This was the first time I had used less than 1600 rpm, and then retarded the fuel mixtures until the engines were just barely running. At this point we could actually see our propellers slowly turning.[4]

They made it back home after an eight-hour, twenty-minute flight, having covered an estimated 1,125 miles on their return with their constant weaving.

Left: The 49th FG Operations Officer Maj. George Laven and his assigned P-38L-5, 44-25568, named *Itsy Bitsy II*, at Lingayen, Luzon, after scoring the group's last air victory on April 26, 1945. Although there are five Japanese flags on its nose, one of them represents a kill Laven claimed over the Aleutians two years earlier that was not confirmed. (*John Stanaway collection*)

Below: Lingayen, Luzon, April 29, 1945: Ground crewmen of the 433rd FS utilize a parachute as a makeshift umbrella to protect them from the tropical sun as they work on their aircraft. This P-38L-5, serial number 44-25880 and squadron number 170, was assigned to Capt. Calvin C. Wire, the 433rd's CO and a seven-victory ace, who had named it *Little Eva*. (*USAF photo*)

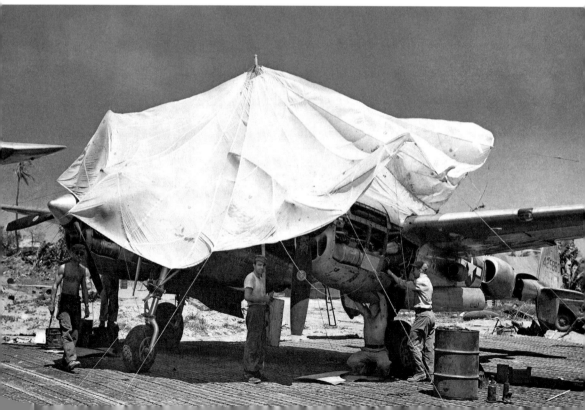

Effective May 7, the 17th PRS moved to Puerto Princesa from Morotai. It had maintained a detachment at Dulag since early February, which would remain there until the end of the war.

Once the Philippines had been secured by the Allies in early 1945 and aerial opposition had ceased, the P-38 groups based there became much more active in the fighter-bomber role, helping to destroy the few remaining pockets of enemy resistance. When Manila was liberated in March, the surviving Japanese had retreated to the hills surrounding Ipo Dam, northeast of the city, which supplied it with water. It was feared that they would blow it; therefore, Gen. Kenney ordered the FEAF's fighter groups to carry out massive napalm attacks on them, from May 3 to 26.

First Lieutenant Kenneth B. Clark of the 9th FS participated in the largest of these missions, on May 16. He recalled later that in a little over three minutes his group, the 49th, alone "dropped nearly 8,000 gallons of flaming death on a little patch about 600 yards square."

The 6th PRG and its squadrons began operating from Clark Field in mid-May. Southern Luzon was finally considered secured by June 11 and northern Luzon by July 1.

Bill Harris had returned to the SWP for his second combat tour the previous November, this time as a lieutenant colonel and deputy CO of the 18th FG, of which he would assume command on August 1. He achieved his sixteenth and final air victory by shooting down an Oscar over Celebes on June 22. Harris was flying with the 44th FS, which had moved to the small island of Sanga Sanga, off the northeast coast of Borneo, the previous week to support the Allied landings at nearby Balikpapan.

The 22nd was also the day Okinawa was declared as secured, nearly three months after its initial invasion on April 1. Some FEAF Lightning units soon began moving there, from which they would fly a few missions over the Japanese Home Islands prior to VJ Day. The four squadrons of the 6th PRG transferred to Motubo Field on Okinawa from Clark Field in July and early August, while the 8th FG moved from San Jose to Ie Shima, a small island next to Okinawa, during the first week of the latter month—as did the 475th FG, from Lingayen, to which it had moved in mid-April. The 6th Group's 25th PRS was awarded a DUC for its photo sorties to southern Japan on August 9, the day of the atomic bombing of Nagasaki.

The Thirteenth AF's last aerial victories were scored on August 4, by 67th FS pilots flying from Palawan. This was during another very-long-range fighter sweep to Singapore, which saw the seven P-38 pilots staging through the new Allied airfield at Labuan on Borneo. A Tojo was encountered near Singapore's Tengah Airfield and Capt. George T. Dubis quickly shot it down. Another one was then seen approaching the Changai Airfield with its undercarriage lowered. According to an official report, "Capt. John Holman made a frontal pass, but overshot as the Tojo turned into him. In the ensuing dogfight he registered hits on the e/a's cockpit but started no fires. A split second later Capt. Dan Shaw made a stern approach, spattering the enemy plane, which exploded and crashed into the coastal waters." Shaw received full credit for this Tojo.

The very last P-38 aerial victories—which were also the last by USAAF fighters—were scored on August 14, the day before the Japanese surrender. They were also the 8th FG's first in seven and a half months. Seven pilots of its 35th FS were assigned to provide

Luzon, May 1945: New P-38s are being brought ashore from ships in Manila Bay by barges (top) to the 5th Air Service Command Depot No. 7 at Nielson Field (bottom), where they are being reassembled and then will be flight tested. P-38L-5 44-26159, whose tail can be seen in the background, was subsequently assigned to the 475th FG's 432nd Squadron. (*USAF photos*)

Above: May 1945: This is the assigned aircraft—P-38L-5 44-25638—of the 7th FS's new CO, Maj. Clayton M. Isaacson. The four swastikas represent the victories he scored while commanding the 96th FS in Italy during a previous combat tour. He wiped out 44-25638 in a crash-landing on June 2. (*John Stanaway collection*)

Below: June 1945: The 7th FS's Capt. Robert M. DeHaven with his assigned P-38 at Lingayen near the end of his second combat tour. DeHaven had scored ten of his fourteen victories with P-40s over New Guinea. His personal insignia was, of all things, a lethal (shooting) orchid! (*John Stanaway collection*)

The Thirteenth AF's top scoring P-38 pilot, Lt. Col. Bill Harris, while serving as deputy CO of the 18th FG in 1945, during his second combat tour. (*Author's collection*)

cover for an air–sea rescue Consolidated PBY Catalina flying boat that day. Shortly after noon, near Kyushu, now reduced by aborts to five, they were attacked by eight Franks, commencing a vicious dogfight. The result was not atypical: The P-38 pilots claimed to have shot down five of the Franks, although only two were, in fact, lost, and the JAAF pilots claimed five P-38s, of which just one was lost—that piloted by 1Lt. Duane L. Keiffer. The last P-38 and USAAF fighter victory was evidently the second Frank claimed in this action by the flight leader, Capt. Raymond F. Meyer, Jr.

These brought the 8th FG's P-38 victory total to 309, of which 206 had been scored by 80th FS pilots. The 475th's total was 552, making it the top-scoring group with P-38s, the 49th's was 353 (215 by the 9th FS), the 347th's 179, and the 18th's 120. These do not include twenty-eight victories scored by V and XIII FC pilots while flying with these units.

The first American servicemen, other than POWs, to set foot on Japan proper after VJ Day were two P-38 pilots, on August 25, 1945. Two 7th FS flights had taken off from the Motuba airstrip on Okinawa—to which the 49th FG had moved from Lingayen on August 16—that morning for a sweep over southern Japan. During the mission, Flt. Off. Douglas C. Hall ran short of fuel due to his mismanagement of it, and it was doubtful that he would have enough to return to Okinawa. The flight leader, who happened to be the 49th FG's new CO, Lt. Col. Clay Tice, decided to land with Hall on the airfield at Nittagahara on Kyushu's east coast. Fortunately, they received a civil reception from the Japanese officers there, and they were soon joined, at Col. Tice's request, by an RB-17 air–sea rescue plane,

Lt. Col. Clay Tice Jr., a longtime veteran of the 49th FG, at Lingaygen shortly after assuming its command in July 1945. The skull and war hatchet on the engine cowling of his P-38L-5 *Elsie* was his personal insignia. It was this plane that he landed in Japan a month later. (*John Stanaway collection*)

This 475th FG P-38 was photographed at the Lingayen airstrip on Luzon on August 25, 1945. It is carrying both a 300-gallon and a 150-gallon auxiliary fuel tank. Note the sway bars on the larger tank. (*USAF photo*)

from which some fuel was transferred—by the Japanese—to the thirsty P-38s, after which they returned to Okinawa.

Eight days later, on September 2, the official surrender documents were signed on the USS *Missouri* in Tokyo Harbor, bringing an official end to World War II.

The Eleventh Air Force—The Aleutian Islands

When the Japanese seized the islands of Kiska and Attu, at the far end of Alaska's 1,000-mile-long Aleutian chain, on June 7, 1942, it was really a side show to the epic carrier battle near Midway Island that had taken place three days earlier, a disaster for the IJN that put the brakes on its six-month rampage across the Pacific. But still, Japanese forces had actually occupied American soil in North America.

Both the Japanese and American governments had recognized the strategic value of the Aleutian Islands and of mainland Alaska well before the attack on Pearl Harbor, by which time the U.S. was already increasing its military presence there. One result of the declaration of war was the activation of the USAAF's Eleventh AF in Alaska in January 1942.

The nearest airfield to the two captive islands—on Umnak Island—was 600 miles from Kiska and 800 miles from Attu. While Kiska was in range of USAAF and USN bombers, it was way too far for them to have any fighter escort, and that escort would be needed. Even though neither island had an airfield, Kiska's harbor was well suited as a floatplane base, and eighteen Mitsubishi A6M-Ns, the floatplane version of the famous Zero—soon to be code-named Rufe by the Allies—had been delivered there, along with a handful of Aichi E13A Jake reconnaissance seaplanes. Small batches of replacement aircraft and pilots would arrive by ship from time to time over the next nine months.

A single USAAF pursuit squadron had been based in Alaska at the time of the Pearl Harbor attack. It was then equipped with obsolete Curtiss P-36s, which were soon replaced by that company's more advanced fighter, the P-40 Warhawk. Additional fighter units would soon be on their way: two more P-40 squadrons, two Royal Canadian Air Force (RCAF) Kittyhawk (Lend-Lease P-40) squadrons, a three-squadron P-39 group, and a P-38 squadron.

The latter was the 54th FS, commanded by Maj. William M. Jackson, which was then part of the 55th FG at Paine Field in Washington State. It was reassigned to the Eleventh AF effective May 23, but there was a hitch: the squadron was equipped with P-38Es, which did not have the wing pylons and shackles that would enable them to carry jettisonable fuel tanks and bombs. These had first become available as field modifications for newly built P-38Fs and had recently been added to Lockheed's P-38F production line.

The pylons would definitely be needed in the Aleutians, as the Lightnings would have insufficient range without auxiliary fuel tanks. So it was arranged for the 54th Squadron's pilots to fly their P-38Es to the Lockheed factory in California during the last week of May to have the pylons retrofitted, after which they flew them to Elmendorf AAB near Anchorage. They arrived in Alaska on June 2, just before aircraft of the JNAF from two carriers attacked the USN base at Dutch Harbor on Unalaska Island on the 3rd and 4th, a preliminary to the landings on Kiska and Attu. They had been opposed by a single squadron of P-40s.

On June 5, 54th FS detachments were sent to Cold Bay, at the end of the Alaska Peninsula where the Aleutians begin, and to Umnak, which was 40 miles west of Dutch Harbor. In July, the rest of the squadron moved to Umnak.

The importance of having a P-38 squadron in the Aleutians was obvious. First there was the Lightning's range, which was far superior to the P-39's and the P-40's. Its twin Allison engines were also a big plus, as its pilots would mostly be flying over the icy waters of the North Pacific and the Bering Sea. If they had to crash onto or parachute into them they would most likely die of exposure within a few minutes. During the course of that long war, many Lightning pilots returned to base on one engine.

The weather in the Aleutians was among the world's worst for flying. The prevalent strong winds (called "williwas"), extreme cold and frequent thick cloud and fog caused many missions to be cancelled or aborted, and claimed many aircraft and their pilots and crews.

Four-engined USAAF B-17s and B-24s and USN Catalina flying boats commenced regular "visits" to Kiska and Attu (initially sans fighter escort, of course), and the Rufes shot down a few and damaged others. The Japanese could not reciprocate at first, but then, around August 1, six four-engined Kawanishi H6K4 "Mavis" flying boat patrol bombers were flown 800 miles east to Kiska from the JNAF base on Paramushiro, Japan's northernmost island.

On August 3, three of the Mavises, led by the unit's commander, Capt. Sukemitsu Ito, made a surprise attack on a USN seaplane tender in Nazan Bay on Atka Island, about 300 miles west of Umnak, that was servicing the Catalinas. They failed to hit it, so Ito decided to try again the following day.

The Japanese did not know that on the early morning of the 4th, three patrols, each consisting of two 54th FS P-38s and a radar-equipped B-17, had been dispatched by the USAAF commander on Umnak. The radar on board one of the B-17s, whose flight included the P-38s piloted by 2Lts. Kenneth W. Ambrose and Stanley A. Long, spotted two of the Kawanishis approaching Atka and its crew directed the Lightnings to them. When the Mavises' pilots saw the American fighters, they immediately turned tail and dove for the undercast—to no avail, as the P-38s quickly caught up to them. After several firing passes, they both went down, Long's victim plunging into the sea and Ambrose's entering the clouds engulfed in flames.

Twenty-five minutes later, a third Mavis, flown by Capt. Ito, was encountered. Both of the P-38 pilots hit it also and thought it was mortally wounded but could not claim it because it was not seen to crash or burn. In fact, Ito managed to nurse his badly damaged flying boat back to Kiska. These were the first aerial victories scored by P-38s.

A major development in the Aleutian air war was the Allies' military occupation of Adak Island, 275 miles east of Kiska, at the end of August 1942. Construction was immediately begun on an airstrip, which was ready for use by September 10. Among the first units to move there was the 54th FS. Not only would the P-38s now be able to reach Kiska—with plenty of linger time—but it was also within range of the P-39s and P-40s.

Effective September 11, the Eleventh AF activated the 343rd FG at Elmendorf Field. Assigned to it initially were the 54th FS and two P-40 squadrons, the 11th and 18th. Another Warhawk squadron, the 344th, would join it after its arrival in Alaska the

Left: Two successful 54th FS P-38 pilots on Adak. Lt. Stanley A. Long, on the left, scored one of the first two Lightning victories ever, on August 4, 1942. The second man is Capt. George Laven, the victory symbols on whose P-38 in the background represent the two Rufes he shot down over Kiska Island on February 13, 1943. (*USAF photo*)

Below: 54th FS P-38s taking off for another mission from Longview Field on Adak. P-38E 41-2232, on the left, was destroyed in a crash on March 24, 1944. (*USAF photo*)

following month. It was also in September that the 54th began receiving some replacement P-38s—much-improved "G" models plus a couple of F-5A-1 PR Lightnings.

The first mission from Adak was flown on September 13, when two P-38s escorted a B-24 on a photo reconnaissance of Kiska, during which a Lightning pilot shot down one of the Rufes that intercepted them.

The following day saw a huge—by Aleutian standards—mission to Kiska, involving fourteen P-38s, fourteen P-39s, thirteen B-24s, and a B-17. Two Rufes were shot down by the Lightnings and two more by the Airacobras, while 1Lt. George Laven, Jr., of the 54th Squadron claimed an unidentified "biplane." Tragically, Maj. Jackson and 2Lt. Dewey E. Crowe collided while pursuing one of the Rufes and were killed.

The 54th's new CO, Maj. Milton H. Ashkins, shot down a Rufe and a P-39 pilot two more over Kiska on September 28. On October 3, four P-38s and eight P-39s accompanied six B-24s to Kiska and shot down five more Rufes—two by 54th FS pilots and three by the Airacobras. Eleven days later, P-38 pilots destroyed three floatplanes on the water there by strafing, but one of them was shot down and killed.

The P-38 was also utilized successfully as a fighter-bomber in the Aleutians. The purpose of one such 54th FS mission, to Attu, on December 26, 1942, was to put at least some of the AA guns on the island out of commission just before it was bombed by B-24s. It was recalled later by one of the participants, 1Lt. Earl C. Hedlund:

I climbed into my friendly P-38E and took off with eleven other fighters for the mission. The weather was sunny but cold. We flew at low altitude to avoid wind and did not have radio

Personnel of the 54th FS pose with one of the unit's Lightnings, P-38G-10 42-13544, named *Lorna "D,"* which was destroyed in a landing accident at the squadron's new airfield on Attu Island on April 18, 1944. (*Michael Bates collection*)

Above: P-40s and P-38s of the 343rd FG undergoing maintenance at Longview Field on Adak Island in the Aleutians. P-38E 41-2239 is in the process of being brought back into service after it was damaged in a landing accident on September 23, 1942. It suffered a similar accident over two years later, on December 29, 1944, and was finally declared salvage in October 1945. (*USAF photo*)

Below: A close-up of P-38E 41-2239, taken at the same time as the previous photo. (*USAF photo*)

communication with either the other fighters or the bombers. I realized we must be near Attu when the closest aircraft dropped his belly tanks, so I followed suit and dropped my two. Both engines stopped immediately—I had not switched from belly to main tanks! But I did so quickly and both engines came back into action. I then flew my P-38 over a ridge and into the enemy naval base area ahead. The sky was full of black puffs of all sizes representing enemy fire against our approach. I selected an antiaircraft gun belching giant flames as my target and dived into the attack. I flew straight at the gun's flame, firing both the 20mm cannon and the .50-caliber machine guns. The target weapon soon ceased firing and I could see soldiers jumping to and fro.

I passed over and out into the bay, spraying fire all the way, right on the deck. I observed many smaller weapons, including riflemen firing as I sailed over them. I proceeded out over the bay, away from the fire, then I noticed smoke coming from my right engine. A quick check indicated the coolant temperature was rising, so I feathered the engine and gained a little bit of altitude.

It was all going well, although I could see where hits had been taken on aircraft surfaces. I could not locate the other P-38s and suddenly wondered about making those [250] miles back to base! I saw a B-24 that had just finished bombing and headed for it. They spotted me and allowed me to join up and fly formation back to our base. I had plenty of fuel and the Lightning flew wonderfully on one engine. I made a successful landing at Adak and felt quite relieved. The mission had been very successful and the bombers made a beautiful run, but we did lose one P-38.[5]

Back in the States after his Aleutians tour, Earl Hedlund was assigned to a new P-38 unit, the 474th FG, and went with it to Europe (the Ninth AF) as a squadron commander.

On December 30, fourteen 54th Squadron pilots escorted some twin-engined B-25s to Kiska and four Rufes rose to intercept them. Although one of them was shot down, so were two of the P-38s. Nine P-38s and six B-24s returned to Kiska the following day and this time six Rufes were encountered, one of which was shot down by two P-38 pilots, who shared the victory.

There was then a development that would mark the beginning of the end of the Japanese presence on Kiska and Attu. On January 11, 1943, the Allies occupied Amchitka Island, which was only 60 miles from Kiska, and began the construction of a new airfield, which was ready for occupancy two months later. The 54th FS moved there from Adak on March 12.

With the availability of the new airfield on Amchitka, all types of Allied aircraft could now attack Kiska practically nonstop, and it began taking a terrific beating. The Japanese floatplanes could also target Amchitka, and on February 13, while its airfield was still under construction, a P-38 from Adak shot down a Jake over it. Meanwhile, ten other Lightnings were bombing and strafing Kiska when five Rufes intervened and three of them were shot down. Two of the float Zeros were credited to now-Capt. Laven, making him, with three confirmed kills, the top-scoring Allied fighter pilot of the Aleutians campaign. (In 1945, while serving a second tour with the P-38-equipped 49th FG in the Philippines, he scored his fourth victory.)

On March 15, the 54th FS lost another pilot, 2Lt. John W. Livesay, in a particularly disturbing manner. Livesay's P-38 was hit by AA fire while strafing targets on Kiska, disabling his right engine, which he shut down. On the short trip back to Amchitka, his

In these two photos, Capt. Morgan A. Giffin is briefing the members of his 54th FS flight. Giffin, who shot down a Japanese floatplane with this P-38 near Amchitka Island on February 23, 1943, later served another P-38 combat tour with the 370th FG in Europe. (*USAF photo*)

other engine also failed and he ditched in the sea. He managed to get out of the plane before it sank, but he lost his life raft and drowned in the rough, frigid water before he could be rescued. Yet another P-38 pilot was lost to AA fire over Kiska on April 13.

U.S. forces landed on Attu on May 11 and were met with heavier than expected resistance; the island was not secured until the end of that month. On the 21st, two P-38s strafing Attu in support of the American soldiers collided, killing both their pilots.

All the floatplanes at Kiska had been eliminated by then, and no replacements were forthcoming, so they could not interfere with the Attu invasion. However, on May 23, sixteen unescorted Betty bombers were launched from Paramushiro to attack the invasion forces, evidently counting on their approach not being detected. However, a patrolling PBY did spot them and alerted the six 54th Squadron P-38s also patrolling nearby, led by Lt. Col. James R. Watt, the 343rd FG's CO.

After they spotted the bombers, the P-38 pilots dropped their belly tanks, went to war emergency power and climbed to intercept them. When the Bettys saw the Lightnings heading for them, they immediately jettisoned their bombs, tightened their formation, and dove away. Col. Watt chose the lead bomber as his target, closed on it and opened fire, whereupon it burst into flame. He then radioed his flight that he had been hit by return fire, and he was neither seen nor heard from again.

The other P-38s continued to pursue the Bettys out over the sea. Five more of them were subsequently seen to explode, catch fire, and/or crash into the sea. Seven others were heavily damaged but not seen to do so and were considered probably destroyed. In fact, just seven of the sixteen Bettys made it back to Paramushiro.

Lt. John K. Geddes hit four of the Bettys but did not receive official credit for any of them. His P-38 was hit by the return fire from two of them, the second one's blowing out the right side of his canopy. One of his engines was also put out of action, and the other then began overheating. He decided to ditch in the water near some USN ships and did so successfully. He exited the cockpit, inflated his life raft and climbed into it, shortly after which a Navy Vought OS2U Kingfisher floatplane plucked him from the frigid sea and taxied to a nearby ship, which lifted him aboard.

When American and Canadian soldiers finally went ashore on Kiska three months later, on August 15, they received quite a shock. Expecting another protracted battle with the Japanese, they instead found the island deserted. IJN ships had snuck into its harbor on the night of July 28 and taken its survivors aboard, without alerting the USN.

So, the Japanese were finally gone, and the Aleutians returned to full U.S. control. The last encounters with Japanese aircraft there were on October 23, when nine bombers made a surprise attack on Attu, and one week later when a PBY and a Betty exchanged gunfire.

Of the forty Japanese aircraft that were confirmed as shot down during the Aleutian campaign by Allied fighters, twenty were credited to P-38 pilots, who had also been very effective in the fighter-bomber role.

The other three squadrons of the 343rd FG soon began converting from their P-40s to P-38s, as they continued to guard Alaska against further Japanese attacks that never came. For the last two years of the war, their greatest enemies were the weather and boredom. The former was responsible for numerous flying accidents that destroyed and damaged many P-38s and took the lives of at least ten of their pilots.

Above left: A 54th FS armorer works on a Lightning's guns. P-38E 41-2227, in the background, was damaged in an accident on April 10, 1943 but repaired. It was damaged again in a take-off accident on April 7, 1944 and finally condemned on July 29. (*USAF photo*)

Above right: 54th FS pilot Lt. Herbert W. Hasenfus about to take off on a mission in his colorful shark-mouthed P-38. (*USAF photo*)

Below: This snow-covered 343rd FG P-38 was photographed at Ladd Field near Fairbanks, Alaska, on February 12, 1944. (*USAF photo*)

P-38 pilots of the 344th FS outside their Quonset hut Operations shack on Shemya Island in the Aleutians in 1945. (*Authors' collection*)

Interestingly, although in 1944 the 343rd FG began receiving some of the new P-38Js—and, later, some Ls—it also continued to fly the 54th FS's surviving P-38Es, now redesignated RP-38Es, until well into 1945. An 11th FS pilot bailed out of one on May 27, almost exactly three years after the first Es arrived in Alaska.

The Seventh Air Force—The Central Pacific

The Seventh was one of the USAAF's smallest overseas combat air forces as regards the number of units, aircraft, and personnel assigned to it. But its operations covered a huge area: the islands of the Central Pacific from Hawaii to, eventually, Okinawa—south of the Aleutians (the domain of the Eleventh AF) and north of the Solomons Islands, New Guinea, and the Philippines (the Fifth and Thirteenth AFs).

The Seventh AF eventually included four Lightning units. One of them was the 21st FG, which was activated in Hawaii in April 1944. It received P-39s initially but soon re-equipped with P-38s. Based first at Wheeler Field, it moved to Mokuleia Field, also on Oahu, in October.

Another Lightning unit in the Hawaiian Islands was the 28th PRS, which arrived there from Oklahoma in January 1944 and was attached to VII FC. It was based initially at Kipapa Airfield on Oahu.

The catalyst for most of the Lightning's actions in the Central Pacific was the invasion of Saipan, in the Marianas, on June 15, 1944, the main purpose of which was to provide bases for B-29s of the Twentieth AF from which to bomb Japan. On June 22, after Saipan's Aslito Airfield had been captured and readied for American aircraft, P-47s of the 318th FG (comprised of the 19th, 73rd, and 333rd FSs) were launched from two USN escort carriers and flown there. (At the end of that month, Aslito was renamed Isley Field after a USN pilot who had been killed there.) The 318th's Thunderbolts provided aerial support to the ground troops fighting for Saipan, and then nearby Tinian and Guam—and part of the islands' air defense.

By early August, the Marianas had been secured and the Seventh AF's B-24 units began arriving on Saipan from Kwajalein Island, to the east in the Marshalls. From Saipan, the Liberators continued their raids on Truk, the former IJN bastion in the Caroline Islands, south of the Marianas. Truk had been largely neutralized by USN carrier raids earlier that year, but there were still some fighters based there, and they were a major problem for the unescorted B-24s.

A new target for the Liberators was Iwo Jima, which had also been devastated by USN carrier raids (in its case the previous summer) but still maintained some aircraft—and a lot of AA guns. On October 21, 1944, the 318th FG sent some of its P-47s, operating at their extreme range utilizing large auxiliary fuel tanks, to a point 700 miles north of Saipan to cover the Liberators on their withdrawal from another attack on Iwo. But only one Japanese fighter was encountered and shot down.

Since the JNAF fighters at Truk and Iwo Jima had become a serious threat to the B-24s, and the 318th FG's P-47s did not have the range to accompany them all the way to and from those targets, an alternate plan was devised. In November, thirty-six long-range P-38s of the 21st FG were ferried by its pilots from Oahu to Saipan, where they arrived on the 11th and the 12th. Some of the 21st's pilots stayed on to fly with the 318th temporarily, and the latter's Thunderbolt pilots quickly mastered the Lightning. They were designated the Lightning Provisional Squadron within the 318th FG. After each P-47 pilot had accumulated four or five hours in a P-38, they flew their first combat mission in them on November 18, an escort to two 28th PRS F-5s photographing Iwo Jima, a seven-hour, fifty-five-minute, 1,518-mile flight.

Although the 28th PRS was still officially based in Hawaii, it had sent detachments to three islands to the west from which it could finally fly photo missions over enemy targets. The first detachment went to Kwajalein, on June 30, where it remained until September 24; the next to Saipan (July 11 to May 1945); and the last to Peleliu, north of New Guinea in the Palaus (October 5 to April 1945).

On November 22, twenty-six P-38 pilots escorted the B-24s to Truk, another seven-hour, thirty-minute mission. They encountered eight very surprised JNAF Zero pilots, four of whom were shot down by the Lightnings.

The P-38s also joined the 318th's P-47s in defending the Marianas against attacking e/a and intruding reconnaissance planes. On November 24, 73rd FS pilot 1Lt. Owen R. McCaul shot down a twin-engined Irving recon. McCaul was on a high-altitude test hop over Tinian when a strange twin-engined aircraft passed just underneath him. He quickly realized that it was Japanese, closed on it and opened fire, hitting its left wing and engine, whereupon it burst into flame and began a long descent into the ocean.

On the 27th, eleven Zekes that had staged through Iwo Jima from Japan attacked Isely Field. One of them was shot down by two P-38s that had just been scrambled from it, the credit for which they shared with a P-47—this as other P-38s were *en route* to Iwo with the Liberators.

A single-engined Nakajima C6N "Myrt" recon was shot down on December 5 by Maj. Warren K. Roeser, the 318th FG's operations officer, who happened to be on a routine

Above: In August 1944, a P-38 newly arrived on Oahu in the Hawaiian Islands is being stripped of the special coated paper that had been taped to it to protect it from the elements during its sea voyage from California. *Below:* Other P-38s in Hawaii that are well along in their reassembly process. P-38L-1 44-23993, in the foreground, later served with the 333rd FS on Saipan. (*USAF photos*)

Below: July 10, 1944: *STINKY*, F-5B-1 42-68225 of the 28th PRS, has just landed at Isley Field on Saipan in the Marianas. (*USAF photo*)

LITTLE RED HEAD II, P-38L-1 44-24008, was assigned to the 73rd FS's Lt. Owen R. McCaul, who is in the center of the bottom photo, which was taken on Saipan on November 25, 1944. The Japanese flag represents the Irving McCaul shot down over Tinian with this plane the day before. (*USAF photos*)

high-altitude calibration flight over Saipan when it was detected nearby by radar. He was vectored onto it and shot it down from 30,000 feet, later recalling that "the bullets all went home and he blew up and exploded into pieces, some of which I flew through, and which left paint marks on the P-38's nose and wings."

The B-24s had been hitting Iwo, a refueling stop for replacement aircraft being ferried to the combat zones and a staging base for others attacking the Marianas (as on November 27), since August, unescorted, and it now became their and their Lightning escorts' primary target. The 318th's P-38 pilots would fly a total of 237 sorties to the island.

Because of the air attacks on Saipan, it was decided in early December that the P-38s would commence low-level sweeps to Iwo Jima in the hope of catching and destroying some of the e/a involved in the air or on the ground by strafing. A single Zeke was claimed there on December 8 by Maj. Roeser, who was flying with the 333rd FS, and another was shot down on the 19th. Only one e/a had been destroyed on the ground by then.

The P-38 pilots swept over Iwo's two airfields once again on December 27, destroying two aircraft—and other materiel—on the ground by strafing. They also shot up a transport ship near the island, and while doing so a twin-engined Nick fighter was spotted approaching it right above the water. Maj. Roeser used his remaining ammo to set the Ki-45's right wing and engine on fire, and his wingman, the 73rd FS's 2Lt. Robert H. Reser, finished him off. (Roeser allowed Reser to receive the full official credit for it.)

Eight P-38s of the 73rd and 333rd Squadrons flew another fighter sweep to Iwo on January 5. While they were once again strafing one of its airfields, a Zeke was caught taking off and shot down. Unfortunately, as they had been flying just 25 feet over the water prior to the attack, 2Lt. Warren J. Sheneman's P-38 lost an engine, that wing dropped, and he crashed into the water and was killed.

The P-38s returned to Truk with the Liberators on January 14, the 333rd FS claiming three more Zekes but losing P-38L-1 44-24456 and its pilot, 1Lt. William R. Eustis, who was last seen chasing a Zeke down through the solid undercast. It turned out that he collided with his victim after hitting it heavily and both aircraft crashed. Eustis was able to parachute into the sea safely and made it to a nearby island, where he was captured several days later. He was liberated in Japan after VJ Day.

The landings on Iwo Jima were scheduled for February 19, and it was the 28th PRS's job to photograph its beaches and defenses—a vital part of the pre-invasion intelligence gathering. On the first such mission (February 3), twelve 318th FG P-38s escorted five F-5s, two B-24s, and two B-29s to the island. As the formation approached Iwo and the Lightnings dropped their auxiliary fuel tanks, 333rd FS pilot Lt. David G. Duket's hit the tail section of his P-38, causing him to crash into the water. Duket managed to get out of the plane before it sank and into a life raft that was dropped by a B-29 (one of the reasons they were there), but he later died. An F-5 was hit by the AA fire and then crashed into the sea, killing its pilot, 1Lt. Charles E. Decker.

The PR Lightnings eventually provided 1,170 photos of Iwo Jima, which, among other things, helped the invasion forces pinpoint and destroy many of the island's guns before they could kill more American servicemen.

The most successful mission for the 318th FG's P-38s was on February 10, when they once again escorted some F-5s and B-24s to Iwo (to take photos and drop bombs, respectively) in two waves. As the first wave approached the island e/a were seen taking off from it—some Zekes and six Betty bombers, four of which were shot down plus one of the fighters.

The second wave, two and a half hours later, found some more Zekes awaiting it, of which two were shot down. Unfortunately, one of the P-38s also went down. Capt. Cyrus M. Birney of the 73rd FS, flying P-38L-1 44-24453, disappeared after engaging a Zeke, although it was thought that he may have been the victim of the "heavy flak." It was eventually learned that he had been killed.

The 318th's last P-38 aerial claim was for a Zeke damaged on February 15, during another B-24 escort to Iwo. It flew its last Lightning mission, an uneventful trip to Truk, on the 21st.

The group's pilots were credited with a total of twenty-three kills with their P-38s. More importantly, they provided much-needed protection to the Seventh AF's B-24s and F-5s.

The 318th FG and its P-47s and borrowed P-38s returned to Hawaii at the end of February. Its pilots then converted to the new long-range P-47Ns, which they flew to Okinawa in April. At the same time, the 21st FG converted to P-51s, which it would soon be flying from Iwo Jima in support of the B-29s bombing Japan. This meant that there were now dozens of surplus P-38Js and Ls in Hawaii, most of which ended up with the Sixth AF in Panama.

The 28th PRS was still officially based in Hawaii, its H.Q. having moved to Kualoa Airfield on Oahu in October 1944. It sent a detachment to Okinawa effective April 23, 1945, and the rest of the squadron moved there on May 8. It also operated a detachment on nearby Ie Shima from May 14 to June 21. After moving to Okinawa, the 28th flew a mixture of tactical missions in direct intelligence support of the ground troops fighting a vicious battle for control of the island and long-range photo missions to the Japanese Home Islands and Korea.

As to the 28th's tactical missions, its CO, Maj. Edward H. Taylor, received an unusual request from USMC combat photographer Lt. David Duncan during the final stages of the battle. Duncan wanted to take some dramatic, close-up photos of Marine Corsair fighter-bombers attacking Japanese positions on the island. Maj. Taylor agreed to fly him on that endeavor in one of the special auxiliary fuel tanks that had been modified to enable Lightnings to transport wounded and sick personnel to rear area hospitals, including the provision of a Plexiglas window in its nose through which the patient/passenger could see and be seen. It was slung under the F-5's left wing.

Taylor flew Lt. Duncan on two such photo missions, on June 13 and 15, and they both resulted in some excellent photographs. Duncan recalled later that on one of them, "Ed nuzzled right up to each attacking Corsair as the boys blasted enemy artillery positions with broadsides of rockets and firebombs [napalm], so close I could look right over the fighter pilots' gunsights. Then Ed poured on full throttle and flew us straight through the exploding targets—at 400 mph."

One last Lightning unit joined the Seventh AF in Hawaii in April 1945; this was the 41st PRS, which transferred there from Oklahoma after completing its stateside training. It was equipped with the latest model of the F-5, the bulbous-nosed G-6, all of them in the 44-26400 serial number range. The squadron was based briefly at Kualoa until moving to Guam in June, where it remained for the rest of the war, attached first to XXI BC and then, in July, to the Twentieth AF. Unfortunately, a week after its arrival, on June 20, a typhoon

Above left: According to the camera symbols on its nose, *MISSOURI OUTLAW*, F-5B-1 42-68193 of the 28th PRS, had flown seventy-one missions when this photo was taken on Iwo Jima in March 1945. It was assigned to the squadron in Hawaii in February 1944 and flew its first operational mission from Kwajelein Island in July of that year. It was lost over Japan on July 30, 1945. (*USAF photo*)

Above right: July 10, 1945: The 28th PRS's F-5B-1 *JUNIOR* (42-68226) is about to take off for a mission over Japan from the Yontan airstrip on Okinawa. (*USAF photo*)

Below: The 28th PRS's *LUCKY LU* (F-5B-1 42-68272) was destroyed in a crash on Okinawa on June 22, 1945. The B7 on its boom meant that it was aircraft number seven of the squadron's "B" Flight. (*USAF photo*)

The Seventh AF modified 300-gallon auxiliary fuel tanks—complete with Plexiglas windows, mats, air vents, and earphones—to be utilized by P-38s for medical evacuations from front-line airfields to rear echelon hospitals. This one is being tested in Hawaii; in actual service the patient would be laying on his back, and not so far forward. (*USAF photo*)

hit the island, destroying many of the aircraft based there, including thirteen of the 41st Squadron's F-5s. It was still able to send a detachment to Iwo Jima on August 9, just six days before the Japanese surrender.

The 28th PRS was inactivated at Okinawa on May 29, 1946, and the 41st PRS at Guam on June 17.

The Sixth Air Force—The Panama Canal

Although the Sixth AF was not officially within the PTO (Pacific Theater of Operations), it did protect the western (Pacific) approaches to the Panama Canal. Like the Eleventh AF in Alaska, it was established to protect a U.S. territory in the Americas. Of course, the Eleventh saw a lot more combat. The Sixth's only contact with the enemy was when its bombers attacked German submarines operating in the Caribbean and along the northeast coast of South America. That was its secondary task, its first being the protection of the vital Panama Canal and the ships passing through it *en route* to and from the Pacific.

In early 1942, a Japanese attack on the canal seemed like a distinct possibility, but with the IJN's defeat in the Battle of Midway in June and the U.S. invasion of Guadalcanal in the Solomon Islands in August, the threat became, at best, remote. Therefore, the USAAF felt no urgency to replace the Sixth AF's increasingly obsolescent P-39s and P-40s with more modern fighters.

Finally, in late 1944, the Air Forces decided to supply the Sixth with some P-38s. The first ten (brand-new P-38L-5s) were ferried to Panama via Mexico (a U.S. war ally) from the Lockheed factory in early November. Eight of them were assigned to the 51st FS, based at Howard Field in the Canal Zone (CZ); one to H.Q., XXVI FC at Albrook Field, CZ; and another to the Panama Air Depot. There was no fighter group in the Sixth AF; its six fighter squadrons (the 24th, 28th, 30th, 32nd, 43rd, and 51st) were all under the direct command of XXVI FC.

Above F-5G-6s of the 41st PRS shortly after their arrival on Guam on June 13, 1945. No. 44-26449/21 was one of the squadron's aircraft that were destroyed on the ground by a typhoon exactly a week later. (*Jim Crow collection*)

Below: "D" Flight of the 41st PRS on Guam in September 1945. (*Author's collection*)

Howard Field, Canal Zone: P-38L-5 44-25291, named *PATSY JANE*, of the 51st FS. The tail of P-38L-5-VN 43-50266, the only Droop Snoot known to have served with the Sixth AF, can be seen on the right. (*Author's collection*)

In December, two two-seat piggy-back TP-38Ls arrived in Panama, to help the Sixth AF's single-engined fighter pilots convert to the Lightning. Another source of P-38s for the Sixth was the Seventh AF in Hawaii, when (as noted earlier in this chapter) its only P-38 unit, the 21st FG, converted to P-51s. Fifty-eight were scheduled to be transferred, the first ten P-38Js shipped from there to Panama arriving on December 31. Most of them had endured a lot of hard use, including combat with the 318th FG, and were in need of considerable repair and maintenance before they could be considered operational.

A third source of many of the Sixth AF's P-38s was the Consolidated-Vought factory in Nashville, Tennessee, which produced, under contract to Lockheed, 113 P-38L-5-VNs from January through August 1945—of which fifty-seven were ferried to Brownsville, Texas, prior to being flown to Panama.

The 51st FS was fully equipped with Lightnings by March, and the Sixth's other fighter squadrons had also begun to receive some, the plan being to assign two dozen to each. By June, a final total of 199 P-38s had arrived in Panama. Two months later, there were forty-three Js and 149 Ls in the Sixth AF's aircraft inventory. It had also received a few late-model F-5 photo reconnaissance Lightnings, six of which were assigned to its Antilles Air Command Base Flight at Borinquen Field in Puerto Rico.

In July 1945, the Sixth AF's by now well-used P-38Js were withdrawn from service, put in storage, and replaced with the newer Ls. P-38 operations ceased soon after the war ended the following month, and the remaining Ls were placed in storage as well. Most of them were eventually scrapped in Panama, although at least a dozen had been flown back to the U.S.

The 24th, 30th, 32nd, and 43rd FSs converted to P-47s in early 1946, and all the Sixth AF's fighter squadrons were inactivated in October of that year.

These P-38s at Howard Field are easily identified as 51st FS aircraft by the "S" on the tail of No. 41 (P-38L-5 44-25256) in the foreground. (*Author's collection*)

Another shot of a lineup of 51st FS P-38s at Howard Field. (*Author's collection*)

4

Lightnings in Action:
The European Theater of Operations
(Eighth and Ninth Air Forces)

Bolero

In mid-April 1942, the P-38-equipped 1st Pursuit Group, which was then training in California, was notified of its imminent overseas deployment—to England and the European Theater of Operations. It took just three days (May 17–19) for the group to vacate its bases near Los Angeles, in two echelons with two different destinations. Coincidentally, effective May 15, the USAAF had changed the official designation of its "pursuit" groups to "fighter."

The 1st Fighter Group's air echelon consisted of eighty-five P-38Fs and their pilots, sixty-five crew chiefs, an armament officer, and communications and instrument specialists. The ground echelon, which comprised the bulk of the unit's personnel, proceeded by train to Fort Dix, New Jersey, and on June 4, it departed for Scotland from New York Harbor on the British ocean liner *Queen Elizabeth*.

The air echelon would have a much more complicated and difficult journey to Britain, as the pilots were going to fly their P-38s there, with the assistance of the echelon's support personnel and utilizing two of the new 150-gallon auxiliary fuel tanks to cover the required distances. Its initial destination, after leaving California (the non-flying personnel in C-47 transports), was Dow Field, near Bangor, Maine. From there, the pilots were to commence their transatlantic hops, each individual flight consisting of four P-38s led by a B-17 for navigational assistance. Their scheduled stops were Goose Bay, Labrador; Bluie West One (BW-1) on Greenland's west coast (and/or the alternate airfield 500 miles north of BW-1, BW-8); Reykjavik, Iceland; Ayr, in Scotland; and then England. The C-47s preceded them to each of these bases, where the skeleton ground crews they transported could make minor repairs and adjustments to the Lightnings.

This was all part of Operation Bolero, the initial creation of an American strategic air force in Britain, Bolero being the code name for the U.K. It was decided that some of the USAAF units that were transferring there should fly their aircraft across the North Atlantic to England, making it faster and more efficient than the usual method of transporting them by ship. The 1st and 14th FGs' would be the only fighters to participate in this operation, which continued until January 1943.

Staggered 1st FG flights began leaving Bangor on June 27. As delays, usually weather related, accumulated at the various stops along their route, they became somewhat strung out. Other than the frequent delays, the operation proceeded rather smoothly, with one major exception.

On July 15, two 94th FS flights, Tomcat Green and Tomcat Yellow, which had left Labrador together on the 7th, were *en route* from BW-8 to Iceland when disaster struck. Their six P-38s (one pilot in each flight having had to abort) and the two B-17 escorts were forced to turn back after encountering an impenetrable storm front and then became lost. Eventually running out of fuel, they belly-landed on the Greenland icecap near the country's east coast. Although the aircraft were lost, all the men survived and were rescued eight days later.

When the first 27th FS pilots arrived in Iceland on July 6, they received some very unwelcome news: the squadron's air echelon was to remain there temporarily, based at the airfield at Keflavik, as part of the island's air defense. The Bell P-39 Airacobras and Curtiss P-40 Tomahawks and Warhawks already based in Iceland could not, of course, match the P-38's performance as an interceptor. The Luftwaffe's four-engined, ultra-long-ranged Focke-Wulf 200C Condors were operating in the area. They bombed the island and convoys passing nearby *en route* to Britain and Russia and acted as spotters for German submarines, which were taking a frightful toll of Allied ships.

By the end of July, the air echelons of the 71st and 94th Squadrons had joined their ground echelons at their new English bases. The 71st's (and 1st FG Headquarters') was Goxhill (USAAF Station 345), in Lincolnshire, on England's east central coast, and the 94th's was Kirton-in-Lindsey (Station 349), a satellite of Goxhill.

The 14th FG began *its* Bolero journey at the end of June, also from California, when its air echelon, including the pilots in their new P-38Fs, flew to Bradley Field in Connecticut, where it spent the next several weeks. A month later, the group's ground echelon traveled to Fort Dix and then to England, also on an ocean liner.

The experience of the 48th FS flight led by Capt. Andrew J. Bing was typical of the 14th Group's Bolero experience. These four P-38 pilots and their B-17 guide left Bradley Field for Presque Island, Maine, on July 25. On the 26th, they proceeded to Goose Bay, from where they took off again later that same day for BW-1. After a three-day layover in Greenland, they flew to Reykjavik on July 29. On August 3, they made it to Ayr and then to their new English base, Atcham (Station 342), near Shrewsbury in Shropshire, the following day.

By the end of August, 164 P-38s had successfully crossed the Atlantic from the U.S. to Britain.

Atcham would be the 14th FG's home for the next three months. Not the whole group's, however, as it had been decided by some higher authority that its 50th FS would replace the 27th FS in Iceland, effective August 18. The 50th was detached from the group permanently and ended up serving there until February 1944. It became part of the new 342nd Composite Group in September 1942. Its pilots would shoot down just two e/a: a twin-engined Junkers Ju 88 on April 24, 1943 and an Fw 200 on May 8. Coincidentally, the only P-38 pilot lost during the Bolero operation, 1Lt. Herbert A. Goodrich, was a member of the 50th FS. Goodrich went missing between Greenland and Iceland on August 1; he was last seen entering a huge cumulous cloud.

One of the issues that kept the P-38s from becoming operational right away in England was the need to replace the crystals in their SCR-522 VHF radios to make them compatible

Two photos of 27th FS Lightnings shortly after their arrival in Iceland on July 6, 1942. Seen in the bottom photo are P-38F-1s 41-7540, 41-7594, and 41-7598. No. 41-7540/42 was flown by Lt. Elza Shahan, who later scored the first P-38 victory in the ETO. No. 41-7598 was lost in action over Tunisia on December 3, 1942. (*USAF photos*)

These two 50th FS P-38 pilots, 2Lts. Harry R. Stengle (left) and James M. McNulty, Jr., shared in shooting down a Ju 88 over Iceland on April 24, 1943. (*USAF photo*)

with those used by the British air control system in the U.K. that was utilized by both the RAF and the USAAF. There was also found to be a problem with radio antennas and nosewheel doors breaking off at high speed and/or during violent maneuvering that likewise created some delays. The antennas were replaced with more robust Spitfire masts until suitable American made parts could be obtained. As to the nosewheel doors, it was found that the problem was faulty adjustments to their safety catches, which allowed the door to be forced open slightly during those violent maneuvers and then broken off by the air pressure.

Since the Eighth AF, to which the two P-38 groups were now assigned, had been in England only a few months, was just a shadow of the "Mighty Eighth" it would later become and had very little combat experience to date, the 1st's and the 14th's personnel received most of their briefings and intelligence from the RAF, which had been fighting the Germans for nearly three years. It had, in fact, established liaison teams at USAAF installations in the British Isles that provided information on such subjects as the locations of friendly AA gun zones and barrage balloon areas, and aircraft recognition. Also, USAAF personnel were sent to RAF schools for instruction on subjects such as the aforementioned British air traffic control system, and experienced RAF fighter pilots briefed the rookie American pilots on how to fight the Luftwaffe.

Back in Iceland, the 27th FS's only air action there took place on August 14, when an Fw 200, flying from Norway, appeared over the island. The squadron's CO, Maj. John W. Weltman, and a wingman, 2Lt. Elza E. Shahan, took off to intercept it, which they did, both pilots scoring some hits. As Weltman recalled later, during his third firing pass, his "guns jammed and one engine got a bit rough on me." He then landed and found that two bullets from the bomber had damaged his ammunition cans and another had shot 5 inches off a propeller blade.

Shahan, along with a P-39 and two P-40s, continued to pursue the Focke-Wulf. The Airacobra pilot hit it next, whereupon its left inboard engine caught fire. Shahan then scored some hits in its fuselage, and the Condor's left wing crumpled and exploded. The official credit was split between these two pilots. This (shared) victory was the first for a P-38 in the European Theater, and Shahan was awarded a Silver Star for it.

Maj. John Weltman's 27th FS Lightning, P-38F-1 41-7601, displaying the damage inflicted on it by an Fw 200 gunner over Iceland on August 14, 1942. (*USAF photo*)

The 27th Squadron's air echelon left Iceland on August 22 and arrived at its English base, High Ercall, via Scotland, four days later. High Ercall (Station 346) was a satellite airfield of Atcham. On August 24, 1st FG H.Q. and the 71st FS departed Goxhill for Ibsley (Station 347) in Hampshire, near the English Channel. The 94th moved there from Kirton-in-Lindsey three days later.

The 1st FG flew the first combat missions by P-38s from England on August 29. Two of its Lightnings were dispatched to patrol off the French coast while two others were scrambled to intercept e/a, with which there were no encounters. For the next six weeks, it would regularly fly both fighter sweeps and bomber escorts to targets in France and the Low Countries.

By early September, there were 133 Lightnings in the U.K.—eighty with the 1st FG, forty-six with the 14th FG, and the rest in reserve. Later that month, the two P-38 groups were informed that, as they had suspected, they were not going to remain in England as part of the Eighth AF but would soon be transferred to the Twelfth AF, which had recently arrived in England and with which they would move to North Africa right after the upcoming Allied invasion of Vichy French Morocco and Algeria. The 1st FG was officially transferred to the Twelfth on September 23 and the 14th FG a week later, although they would continue to operate from their English bases under the direction of the Eighth AF and the RAF.

It was in mid-September that the 27th FS moved to its new base, Colerne, an RAF Fighter Command airfield near Bath in Wiltshire. Its pilots arrived there from High Ercall on the 15th.

The mission the 1st FG flew on October 2—an escort of some B-17s to Méaulte, France—was somewhat eventful. Although it encountered no air opposition, Lt. William Young of the 71st Squadron went missing. It was later learned that he was a POW. Young was the first P-38 combat casualty in the ETO, although two 1st FG pilots and one 14th FG pilot were killed in accidents in England.

The 1st's last mission from England, on October 9, to Lille, France, was target support for Eighth AF B-17s and B-24s. Some Focke-Wulf Fw 190 fighters and plenty of flak were seen, but there were, once again, no actual aerial encounters by the P-38s.

The 14th FG did not fly its first combat mission until October 15, when it escorted RAF Bostons (Lend-Lease Douglas A-20s) to Le Havre, France. It was assigned just two more, on the 21st and the 25th. The 14th FG flew a total of seventy-four combat sorties from England and the 1st 273 sorties.

One of the many aspects of the preparations for the imminent move to North Africa was an important modification to the P-38s. In his diary entry for October 27, 1Lt. William F. Schottelkorb of the 48th FS noted:

Air filters are being installed on our planes, under the booms and in the wheel wells. When the wheel doors are closed, when the plane is flying, the normal air intake scoop on the side is in operation. When a landing is affected and the boom doors or wheel doors are open, then a separate air intake is put into operation by means of opening a butterfly valve and closing the valve to the main air inlet. This second air opening is a screen mesh affair that is about a foot high and two feet long.[1]

The purpose of these and other extra filters was to keep the North African sand out of the moving parts of the Lightnings.

Late in October, the groups' ground echelons boarded some ships, on which they would remain for over two weeks until they finally disembarked in Algeria. The 1st FG's

This damaged P-38 and the portion of an "assault barge" to which it was lashed were being transported on a ship that was sunk in late October 1942 while crossing the Atlantic to the British Isles. Found floating in the ocean, they were towed by a British corvette 300 miles to the port of Belfast, Northern Ireland, arriving there on November 25. (*USAF photo*)

Cargo carried by ship convoys traversing the Atlantic Ocean from the U.S. to Britain included Lend-Lease LCTs (Landing Craft, Tank)—also referred to as "assault barges"—that were being supplied to the Royal Navy. To facilitate shipping, the LCTs were disassembled into three sections, and in some cases, to make use of all available space, a P-38 was lashed to each section. This photo shows one carrying P-38LO 40-751. (*USAF photo*)

air echelon moved to its departure base in southern England—Chivenor, Cornwall—on November 6. The following day, the 14th FG's air echelon arrived at Portreath, Devon. They would be leaving the British Isles from those airfields in a little over a week.

The ETO's First USAAF Photo Recons

There was also a Lightning PR unit in England briefly before it moved on to North Africa. This was the 5th PRS, which had arrived from the States in mid-June. It was based first at Molesworth (Station 107), Huntingdonshire, and moved to Podington (Station 109), Bedfordshire, in September. It was while at Podington that it was attached to the 3rd Photo Group, assigned to the Twelfth AF and finally received some aircraft: 13 F-4-1s. The 3rd PG, which had arrived at Membury (Station 466), Berkshire, from the U.S. in early September, was based at Steeple Morden (Station 122), Cambridgeshire, for a few days in late October and early November before moving to Algeria.

Meanwhile, back in California, in early September, a third P-38 group, the 82nd, whose squadrons were then based at three airfields in the Los Angeles area, was notified of its upcoming deployment to England. Since the 82nd would not be participating in Operation Bolero, all its personnel traveled by train to the East Coast, with the exception of a few pilots who delivered P-38s there, also for shipment to the British Isles.

The men of the 82nd FG sailed from New York on the British liner *Queen Mary* on September 27 and arrived in Greenock, Scotland, on October 3. There they were transferred to two smaller ships, which transported them to Belfast, Northern Ireland. From Belfast, they traveled by train to their new base at Eglinton (Station 344), near Londonderry. Its 97th FS would operate from a satellite field at nearby Maydown. They were now, temporarily, part of the Eighth AF.

It would be a month before the 82nd received any P-38s in Ireland, but in the meantime, its personnel were the recipients of plenty of instruction from the RAF. It even borrowed a few of its aircraft, including some Spitfires, with which its pilots were able to sharpen the flying skills they had not been able to utilize for the past several weeks.

The group's first P-38s finally arrived on November 13. They included both the F models they had flown in the States and some of the newer Gs. They had been shipped to Liverpool, from where they were transported to a nearby air depot, reassembled, flight tested, and flown to Ireland. The 82nd received a total of ninety-eight Lightnings. Also, while it was in Ireland, some new pilots were assigned to the group, including several Yanks who had been serving with the RAF and the RCAF but chose to transfer to the USAAF now that America had entered the war. The 1st and 14th FGs had also been assigned a few of those men.

After receiving their new Lightnings, the 82nd's pilots, inevitably perhaps, challenged some RAF Spitfire pilots to mock aerial "duels." According to a 96th FS pilot, his CO, Maj. Harley C. Vaughn, a future ace, "went up in a P-38 and a Limey went up in a Spitfire and they had a dogfight over the field. Vaughn whipped him, and we really razzed the Limeys."

It was not long after its arrival in Ireland that the 82nd FG learned that it too would eventually be serving with the Twelfth AF in North Africa. By mid-December, it was deemed ready, and on the 16th, fourteen pilots of its 95th and 97th Squadrons flew their P-38s to the embarkation point, St. Eval, Cornwall, for their imminent move to North Africa. The last such flight was by four 96th Squadron pilots on the 24th—the day after the group's first formation flight to Algeria.

It was also on December 16 that the 96th FS's 2Lt. Scott K. Giles, flying P-38G-1 42-12753, decided to buzz the base air depot (BAD) operated by Lockheed at Langford Lodge, just west of Belfast, where their planes had received their modifications for service in North Africa—mainly the aforementioned filters. (BADs specialized in aircraft overhaul, modifications, repairs, and parts supply.) According to one of his fellow pilots, Giles "dove on the field doing about 500 miles an hour and pulled up into what we thought was going to be an Immelman, but when he got to the top and was supposed to roll out he sort of hesitated, as if something was wrong, and then started to pull it through into a loop. He didn't pull it through fast enough and he hit right in the middle of the runway, going straight down and doing about 400 miles an hour." This was a tragic example of the fact that, even in a combat theater, the Axis were not the only threat to a P-38 pilot's life and well being.

Langford Lodge, a former RAF landing ground, had, starting in early 1942, been transformed into the USAAF aircraft maintenance depot that became operational in September, with most of its operation subcontracted to the Lockheed Overseas Corporation. The first P-38 arrived there on November 16, and by the time the Lockheed contract was terminated in July 1944, more than 1,000 had passed through the facility.

Several weeks before the 82nd FG departed England, another P-38 group, the 78th, arrived there from California. Two trains carrying the group's men and equipment had left for the East Coast on November 10, 1942. They arrived at Camp Kilmer, New Jersey, on November

Above: These Lightnings are undergoing modifications for service in North Africa by the Lockheed Overseas Corporation at Langford Lodge. P-38F-15 43-2136 subsequently served there with the 95th FS, 82nd FG. The aircraft next to it displays RAF-style camouflage paint on its wing, indicating that it, too, is an F-15, all of which had originally been ordered by the RAF as Lightning IIs. (*Lockheed photo*)

Below: December 1942: P-38s of the 82nd FG in the process of being modified at the Langford Lodge air depot for their upcoming service in North Africa, including the addition of yellow outlines to their national insignias to make them more visible. P-38F-15 43-2102, on the right, which was assigned to the 95th FS, had an unusually long operational career; it finally met its end on May 24, 1944, when it was destroyed in a landing accident in Italy. (*USAF photo*)

Above: More P-38s at Langford Lodge. They will soon join the 82nd FG at nearby Eglinton and Maydown—including, in the foreground, P-38F-5 42-12610. While flying this Lightning from England to Algeria on December 23, 1942, 97th FS pilot 2Lt. Theo S. Miller crashed it just across the border inside Spain as he was attempting to land at Gibraltar. (*USAF photo*)

Below: USAAF personnel and Irish civilians in the process of towing a P-38 "down a narrow Irish rural road" from the docks of Belfast to Langford Lodge. Note that the propellers and outer wings have been detached for shipping—and that sealing tape and insulation still cover parts of the engine cowlings and the nose. (*USAF photo*)

15 and sailed for England on the *Queen Elizabeth* eight days later. The 78th arrived at Greenock on the 29th, and on December 1, it moved onto its new English base, Goxhill, which had previously been occupied by the 1st FG. It was made clear from the beginning that it was going to remain a part of the Eighth AF, providing escort for its bombers.

The 78th Group's first P-38Gs were delivered from an air depot on December 15, and by the end of January, there were fifty-eight on hand. Its CO, Col. Arman Peterson, announced that it would become operational in February, from its new base at Duxford, Cambridgeshire, to which it would soon be moving. Although it did not seem particularly significant at the time, the 78th, to which were then assigned most of the P-38s in England, was designated the strategic P-38 reserve for the Tunisian campaign in North Africa.

A 78th FG air echelon was sent to a B-17 base on January 13 to practice bomber escort procedures and techniques, and after a week and a half, it was ready to fly an actual combat mission with the Flying Fortresses. However, that was canceled due to a startling new development.

What had happened was that on January 14, at the Casablanca Conference of the Allied heads of state and their military leaders, Gen. Henry "Hap" Arnold, commanding general of the Army Air Forces, was disturbed to learn that, due to attrition and insufficient replacements, the three vital P-38 groups in Algeria were considerably under strength (they each then had only about thirty aircraft). He therefore ordered that the Eighth AF's P-38 "strategic reserves" (basically, the 78th FG's aircraft) be flown to North Africa by the 78th's pilots to resupply them. The decision was announced to the group's personnel on January 25.

Above left: A ground crewman steam cleans a P-38 somewhere in the British Isles. Note the yellow surround to the national insignia, indicating that it has been designated for service in North Africa. (*USAF photo*)

Above right: January 9, 1943: Partially disassembled P-38s are being towed through the foggy streets of Liverpool from its docks to its airport, Speke, where they will be reassembled and flight tested. (*USAF photo*)

This process began immediately. The first step was to have the group's P-38s modified with the special air filters at Langford Lodge. On January 26, forty-five of its pilots flew their Lightnings to Ireland for that purpose, during which flight two of them were killed in a midair collision.

An even bigger bombshell was dropped on February 7 when it was announced that all the group's junior pilots—more than sixty of them—were also being transferred to North Africa to reinforce the 1st and 82nd FGs and to rebuild the 14th, which had recently been relieved from combat for that purpose. They ferried the P-38s to Algeria on February 13, in three separate flights, after which they were reassigned to one of the above-mentioned units. The 78th FG soon received new pilots and aircraft (P-47s) and finally commenced its bomber escort duties with the Eighth AF in April.

As of mid-February 1943, there was only one Lightning unit based in England. That was the Eighth AF's first permanent photo reconnaissance squadron, the 13th, which had replaced the 5th PRS at Podington on December 1 but had yet to fly an operational mission. It had trained at Colorado Springs as part of the 3rd Photo Group but was now, temporarily, an independent squadron. It had left Colorado for New Jersey in mid-October, shipped out from New York Harbor a month later, and arrived in Scotland at the end of November.

The 13th Squadron received it first thirteen Lightnings (F-5A-3s, of which Lockheed had built just twenty) in England on January 9. They had been delivered by ship to Liverpool and from its docks were transported to that city's airport, Speke, then an RAF installation, where they were reassembled by Lockheed personnel and flight tested. They were then flown to the base air depot at Burtonwood (BAD 1) in nearby Lancashire, where their SCR-274-N HF radios were replaced with Bendix SCR-522-A VHF sets before being delivered to the squadron at Podington.

BAD 1 was one of three base air depots established by the USAAF in Britain. Their main tasks were to reassemble, modify as necessary and test fly newly arrived aircraft before releasing them to combat units in the ETO. Since the planes, including P-38s and F-5s, arrived by ship, it was important that the BADs be located close to major ports. Thus, Burtonwood and Warton (BAD 2), both in Lancashire, were near Liverpool, and Langford Lodge (BAD 3) was close to Belfast. When P-38s were eventually replaced by P-51s in the Eighth AF, the now surplus Lightnings would be sent to a BAD to be prepared for transfer to either the Ninth or the Fifteenth AF, including any needed maintenance and/or repairs.

The 13th Squadron moved from Podington to Mount Farm (Station 234) in Oxfordshire—a satellite of the RAF photo recon base at Benson—on February 16, ten days after its designation had been officially changed to 13th Photographic Squadron (Light). Prior to commencing operations from Mount Farm the squadron's pilots were briefed by experienced RAF PR pilots.

The 13th PS's CO, Maj. James G. Hall, a World War I bomber pilot, flew the unit's first operational mission on March 28, 1943 to targets along the coast of France. It suffered its first operational loss on April 4, when 1Lt. Jack R. Campbell did not return from a mission to Antwerp, Belgium; it was later confirmed that he had been killed.

On May 19, forty-seven-year-old Maj. Hall became the first USAAF photo recon pilot to photograph Paris. (He is believed to have been the oldest operational Lightning pilot.) That same day, another pilot flew the squadron's first mission to Germany.

Col. James Hall, the World War I bomber pilot who commanded the 13th Photographic Squadron when it arrived in England in February 1943 and who was given command of the 7th Photographic and Mapping Group when it arrived there in July. At the age of forty-seven, he is believed to have been the oldest operational Lightning pilot. Note the early type P-38 control wheel. (*USAF photo*)

Problems with the F-5

Some design and production flaws did not fully manifest themselves on the F-5As until they were being utilized operationally in overseas combat theaters. For example, the 13th PS soon became aware that its photos were not as sharp as those taken by RAF PR units. Therefore, its photo lab technicians began an investigation. They removed the protective glass window over each camera port and found that none of them met specifications (i.e., were 100 percent flat), which caused some distortion.

They then tested the F-5s' K-18 cameras, with the assistance of the RAF's technical branch, the Royal Aircraft Establishment, at Farnborough Airfield in Hampshire, which was the equivalent of the USAAF's Technical Data Laboratory at Wright Field, Ohio. It was discovered that although their lenses were of high quality, their filters had been poorly ground. A British optical company then reground the faulty filters (95 percent of them) while another company replaced the glass. The head of the 13th Squadron's photo lab filed reports on these deficiencies and they were eventually corrected at the sources.

Another serious problem involved both the cameras and the radios. Noise (interference) emanating from the cameras when they were being operated often made it impossible for the pilots to hear radio transmissions, and as a result they frequently turned their sets off. British radio technicians traced the problem to ignition leaks, which they fixed with bonding and filters.

The Eighth AF was assigned two more photo reconnaissance squadrons during the late spring of 1943. The first was the 14th PS (Light), which arrived at Mount Farm on May 12. The second was the 22nd PS, whose ground echelon, which had left New York on the *Queen Mary* on May 31, showed up there on June 8 and was greeted by its pilots, who had been flown to England by the USAAF's Air Transport Command. Both squadrons—like most of the PR units that moved to England and North Africa from the U.S. in 1942 and 1943—had until then been training at Colorado Springs.

The 22nd PS flew its first mission on June 24, but the 14th's operational debut was delayed, due to its pilots not arriving in England, also via air transport, until July 14. (Its ground echelon had left Colorado Springs on April 24 and New York on May 5.) In the meantime, the 14th Squadron's ground crews were assigned five well-used RAF Spitfires to repair and maintain. Perhaps not coincidentally, later that year it would be flying Reverse Lend-Lease Spitfire PRs operationally.

The 7th PRMG was transferred from Colorado Springs to Mount Farm effective July 7, and the three PR squadrons then based there were assigned to it. James Hall, now a lieutenant colonel, was appointed its CO. At that time, the 13th and 22nd Squadrons had a total of only eleven operational Lightnings, due to combat and operational losses and a lack of replacements. The whole group never had more than twenty F-5As on hand at any given time.

The USAF reference book *Air Force Combat Units of World War II* describes the 7th PRMG's primary tasks as "to obtain information about bombardment targets and damage inflicted by bombardment operations; provide mapping service for air and ground units; observe and report enemy transportation, installations, and positions; and obtain data on weather conditions." Its major job was, and would remain, obtaining damage assessment photos of VIII Bomber Command targets.

The 7th Group's F-5s experienced yet another vexing problem when flying at high altitude over northern Europe. There was a standing order that they fly no lower than 24,000 feet on their photo missions, as they were considered to be too vulnerable to AA fire below that altitude. However, when flown at the higher operational altitudes (typically at least 30,000 feet) their Allison engines often experienced premature detonation and carburetor overheating.

In the early model P-38s and F-5s, super hot compressed air from the superchargers passed through the intercooler system in the leading edges of the wings before entering

This rare F-5A-3, 42-12786, then named *Eclipse*, was assigned to the 13th Photo Squadron in July 1943, then to the 22nd Photo Squadron and finally to the Ninth AF's 34th PRS. (*Michael Bates collection*)

the engines' carburetors, and that system did not always work well. The intercoolers often failed to reduce the supercharged air's temperature to the proper level, which sometimes resulted in the fuel mixture exploding in the cylinder before the piston reached the top of its compression stroke. Those explosions typically blew out the piston head and caused the bearing to fail and/or the connecting rod through the crankcase to break, requiring an engine change—assuming the pilot had been able to bring the aircraft back on the other, hopefully unafflicted, engine. They could also backfire through the intercooler, damaging the aluminum alloy baffle plates that prevented turbulence in its ducts.

These engine explosions also usually resulted in metal particles contaminating its lubrication system, requiring the replacement of the oil coolers. Replacement coolers for the group's newer F-5A-10s were almost impossible to obtain, so those from salvaged aircraft were often utilized, or F-5A-3 cores—which, oddly enough, *were* available—were modified to fit the A-10's shells.

Yet another problem was occasional turbo-supercharger failure, a dramatic example of which happened on July 4 to Capt. Norris E. Hartwell of the 22nd PS. As he crossed the English Channel at 30,000 feet *en route* to his target the right engine's supercharger turbine wheel disintegrated. Pieces of it sheared 18 inches off a propeller blade, severed a hydraulic line, and destroyed the radio. Hartwell immediately shut down the engine and feathered the prop, and fortunately then made it back to Mount Farm.

Although some temporary solutions were devised, most of these problems were not really resolved until the introduction of the P-38J and its PR equivalents the F-5B and C, with their new cooling system and other improvements.

While the early P-38s and F-5s performed well in the warmer climes of the Pacific and Mediterranean Theaters, the higher altitudes at which they were flown in the frigid, damp northern European skies made their operation there much more problematic. Another problem was the Lightning's poor cockpit heating system, which caused their pilots extreme discomfort at altitude, no matter how many layers of clothing they wore, thereby reducing their operational efficiency. (The availability, starting in early 1944, of the General Electric F-3 electrically heated two-piece flying suits did help.) Even at its best, the system never was ideal, since the heat for the cockpit had to be ducted a considerable distance from the engines—and some of it was directed to the guns and the cameras, to keep them from freezing up. In a single-engined aircraft, the heat-generating engine was, of course, right in front of the cockpit, which made possible a much simpler and more effective system.

As a result of some of these problems, effective July 15, 1943, the 7th PG's pilots were temporarily restricted to a 300-mile operational radius until they could be solved or at least mitigated. This reduced the number of missions they could be assigned and placed an added burden on the RAF's PR units.

On July 24, the RAF and the USAAF teamed up for a comparative performance test of their three primary PR aircraft—the F-5, the de Havilland Mosquito, and the Supermarine Spitfire, in which the Spitfire proved to be faster than the twin-engined aircraft and had a better climb rate. While making a turn during the test, the F-5A-3, serial number 42-12781, piloted by the 13th PS's Capt. Thomas B. O'Bannon, suddenly disappeared into the haze below. It was soon learned that O'Bannon had crashed and was killed.

The crash site investigators found the tail assembly a considerable distance from the rest of the wreckage, and that the elevator trim tab control rod had evidently broken

First Lieutenant Thomas B. O'Bannon, Jr., of the 13th Photo Squadron checks the Bailout Breathing Oxygen equipment in the cockpit of his F-5 at Mount Farm. (Note the rearview mirrors on either side of it.) O'Bannon was killed in a flying accident in England on July 24, 1943. (*USAF photo*)

off, overstressing the tail until it too broke away. There was a similar incident on August 18, when Flt. Off. Malcolm D. Hughes of the 22nd PS had to bail out of his F-5 (A-10 42-13099) over England when his tail assembly also detached while he was flying through a storm. An examination of the wreckage showed that the problem had once again been the failure of the trim tab control rod, which had caused elevator flutter and a loss of control.

The result of this second accident was the actual grounding of all the 7th Group's F-5s, from August 23 until September 3. Lockheed technical representatives had been asked to stress test some of the rods, and they found that during extreme compression they bent and then sheared off. The Lockheed Overseas Corporation began to manufacture modified rods at Langford Lodge to replace the faulty ones, but not fast enough to suit the group. By September 7, the 14th Squadron had received just two of them. They were eventually all replaced, however, and the problem was subsequently resolved at their supply source back in the States.

The 14th PS had finally become operational on August 7, after receiving seven F-5A-10s. The squadron commander, Maj. Marshall Wayne, flew its first official mission on the 18th. Capt. James M. Campbell, the only pilot who accompanied its ground echelon to England, had by then flown five missions in 13th Squadron aircraft.

The Eighth AF greatly expanded its operations during the summer of 1943, flying more and more bombers farther and farther into Axis-controlled Europe. However, its losses were heavy. The Luftwaffe's home defense *jagdgeschwadern* (fighter wings) were equipped with large numbers of both single- and twin-engined fighters, including the latest models of the formidable Bf 109 and Fw 190, the majority of whose pilots were experienced, skillful, and aggressive.

As of August, the B-17s and B-24s were being escorted by just four P-47 groups. Although several more would soon become operational with VIII Fighter Command, there still would not be enough of them to provide sufficient protection to the bombers, and their range was limited. They could not accompany the bombers all the way to their more

Above: F-5A-10 42-13319, named *Kay*, is seen here painted in what was then the 7th Photo Group's standard aircraft color scheme of RAF PR blue. It was originally assigned to the group's 22nd Squadron, in September 1943, but was transferred to the 14th Squadron briefly two months later. In December, it was sent to Italy, where it joined the 5th Photo Squadron of the 3rd Photo Group, with which it was lost in action over that country on February 14, 1944. (*USAF photo*)

Below: Lt. Harlan J. Fricke (center), a 14th PRS pilot, describes to his crew chief (on the right) and a fellow officer his just completed mission to Germany on November 9, 1943, in this plane, F-5A-10 42-13313. On December 11, Fricke was killed when he crashed while trying to land at Mount Farm in thick fog after returning from a weather recon to France. (*USAF photo*)

distant targets, and it was after they had to turn back that the majority of the losses to enemy fighters took place.

VIII Bomber Command incurred its worst single-day's loss to date on August 17, during separate missions to Schweinfurt and Regensburg, Germany. Sixty B-17s failed to return, many of them falling to enemy fighters after the P-47 escorts reached the limit of their range and were forced to leave them.

Return of the P-38s

At that time, the only USAAF fighter with the range to accompany the Eighth's bombers all the way to most of their targets and back was the P-38. Its H model, which Lockheed was delivering to the Air Forces at that time, had, with its 300-gallon internal fuel capacity, a radius of action only about 25 miles more than the P-47, with its gas-guzzling Pratt & Whitney radial engine—200 *versus* 175 miles. However, the Lightning could carry two 150-gallon drop tanks, increasing its range to about 400 miles, whereas the early model P-47D then in use carried just one 100-gallon auxiliary tank, which gave the P-38 a 100-mile advantage. (The P-47D's range was later increased, with additional internal fuel capacity and the use of larger drop tanks, but it never matched that of the Lightning and the Mustang.) In any event, it was decided that it was time to transfer some P-38 groups training in the U.S. to England.

The first to make the move was the 20th FG, then based at March Field in southern California. Its squadrons were the 55th, 77th and 79th. It left California on August 11 and arrived in Scotland on the 25th. The following day, it began to occupy what would be its home for the duration of the war, Kings Cliffe (Station 367), Northamptonshire.

The Eighth AF's other new P-38 unit was the 55th FG, which was based at McChord Field in Washington State. It was comprised of the 38th, 338th, and 343rd FSs. The 55th left McChord on August 23, 1943, sailed to England from New York on September 5, and arrived at its new base, Nuthampstead (Station 131), Hertfordshire, nine days later. On October 5, the 55th became part of the Eighth AF's 66th Fighter Wing (FW), and the following day, the 20th FG was assigned to its 67th FW. Both groups were initially equipped with P-38H-1s and -5s, which were processed through Langford Lodge after arriving by ship. Some of the leaders of both groups were P-38 veterans of North Africa on their second combat tours. This one would be very different from their first.

The 55th FG received its first P-38s in England on September 27. Frank E. Birtciel of the 343rd FS later recalled his and most of his fellow pilots' level of preparedness: "We wondered what type of tactics we would be using at high altitude since we had no training in that area. The squadron had little aerial gunnery practice, with the exception of some ground gunnery at Muroc [California]."

Even though it had arrived in England after the 20th FG, because its pilots were more experienced the 55th was the first to become operational, flying its initial combat mission, a sweep over the Dutch Islands, on October 15. This was just a few days short of a year since the last previous P-38 mission from England, by the 14th FG. The 55th flew its first bomber escort the following day and suffered its first loss on the 18th, when 2Lt. Hugh E.

Above: August 1943: P-38s arriving in Belfast, Northern Ireland, on the deck of an oil tanker. Note the protective coverings, and that they are carrying 150-gallon drop tanks. (*USAF photo*)

Below: A P-38H of the 38th FS, 55th FG not long after the unit's arrival in England in August 1943. (*USAF photo*)

Gillette of the 38th FS, while returning from the day's mission, bailed out of his burning P-38H-1, 42-66719, into the English Channel. He was not recovered. Gillette was the first of forty-eight 55th FG pilots who would be killed while flying P-38s from England—most of them during combat missions but some as the result of non-combat-related accidents.

The 20th FG was declared operational on October 26, but it would be a while before it flew a full-group mission. In the interim, one of its squadrons at a time would fly a few missions with the 55th FG to gain experience. There would not be enough P-38s available to fully equip the 20th Group until well into December. Some 79th FS pilots arrived at Nuthampstead on November 3 and flew missions with the 55th Group on the 5th, 7th, and 11th, later on which day it was replaced by the 77th FS, which flew missions with the 55th on November 25, 26, 29, and 30 and December 1. Two 55th FS pilots joined them on the latter mission, and the rest of that squadron replaced the 77th at Nuthampstead on the 2nd. The 55th Squadron then flew just two more missions with the 55th Group, on December 8 and 11.

The first Eighth AF P-38 victories were scored by the 55th FG on November 3, during target support for a B-17 wing to Wilhemshaven, Germany, which was heavily contested by the Luftwaffe. The results were quite positive for its Lightning pilots, who were credited with four enemy fighters destroyed, one probably destroyed, and five damaged (4-1-5) for no loss to themselves. Lt. Col. Jack S. Jenkins, the deputy group commander, who was leading the 343rd Squadron that day, was credited with the Eighth's first confirmed P-38 victory, a Bf 109, and he also probably destroyed an Fw 190. The 343rd's 2Lt. Robert L. Buttke, a future ace, shot down two Fw 109s. Only seven bombers were lost, four of them to mid-air collisions. The following day, the group received a commendation from the commander of the B-17 wing, which stated:

> The heavies were escorted in such fashion as to indicate the P-38 pilots had a personal interest in the safety of each bomber crewman. When hostile fighters appeared below and to the side, the P-38 pilots immediately dove to the attack, scattering the Hun fighters to

An armorer and another ground crewman work on P-38H-5 42-67015 of the 38th FS, coded CG-D. This plane was damaged in a crash-landing on November 3, 1943, the day the 55th FG scored the Eighth AF's first P-38 victories. (*USAF photo*)

the four winds. Their mission today has well deserved the highest praise of the bomber forces.

The score on the 5th was 5-2-2 e/a, all by the 55th's 38th FS, during a B-24 escort to Münster, Germany. On the debit side, the -50-degree temperature at altitude (25,000 feet and higher) caused engine trouble that resulted in some of the P-38s aborting the mission. At that temperature, oil became thick and sluggish, and the sudden application of full power in a combat situation, especially in a climb, often caused the Allisons' piston rod bearings to break up. At high altitude, the engines also began to throw oil, increasing their consumption and thereby reducing typical engine life to a little over eighty hours—less than one half the norm. Moisture, especially from aircraft vapor trails that accumulated behind the engine exhaust stacks, created problems with the turbo-supercharger regulators by getting into the balance lines and freezing. The vapor trails were also problematic in another way, in that the Luftwaffe pilots could immediately identify those emanating from the twin engines of the P-38 and thus forewarned could initiate the most effective tactics against them.

Although there was no aerial action on November 7, the 20th FG lost two of its senior pilots. Maj. John G. Wilkins, the deputy group commander, had a delayed take-off and he was not seen again after departing late and alone. Capt. Herbert W. Cumming of the 79th FS lost an engine and had to bail out over the English Channel; he too then disappeared.

The P-38s did well enough during their first few missions, but the one on November 13, to Bremen, Germany, would be a cold splash of reality. The Luftwaffe pilots were particularly aggressive that day, shooting down seventeen B-24s and B-17s and ten of the escorting fighters—seven of them from the 55th FG, whose pilots were credited with 6-4-6 e/a in return. Once again, the bitter cold was a huge problem for both the pilots and the aircraft. Donald E. Penn, a 38th FS pilot, later described some of their challenges:

The General Motors Allison V-12 engines with the 1710 inch displacement were extremely unreliable. The supercharger was operated by gases from the engine, so when you pushed the throttle up or down the impeller speeded up and put more power or less power in the engine, although it took about 125 horsepower for the engine to drive the supercharger. The P-38s had a turbo supercharger on them which was put on as an after thought. This [was the] kind of Mickey Mouse way they had of harnessing the supercharger to the throttle linkage, and the rpm was, at best, lousy. We called them "Allison time bombs." We actually lost pilots with both engines quitting over Germany, and guys were killed on takeoff because they lost an engine when the plane was heavily loaded, and they didn't have enough experience to fly it on one engine and it got away from them.

I was on a mission pretty deep in Germany and we saw some German fighters coming from a long distance away, so we dropped our belly tanks and turned on our gun switches. Second Lieutenant Wilton Erickson touched the throttle on his P-38 at about 35,000 feet, and, before he could do anything else, one engine went up to seventy inches [of manifold pressure] and he hit 3000 rpms and full power on the engine, flipping him over on his back. There was a big flash and pieces flew off one engine. He got it righted and feathered, and decided to head home with some escorts. When the engine exploded, it blew a hole in the side with the pistons flying right out. The hole was so big two men could stick their heads through. I was really amazed that his P-38 didn't catch fire.[2]

This overall lack of confidence in their aircraft, the terrible cold inside the P-38's cockpit at high altitude, and their often being outnumbered by experienced and aggressive Luftwaffe pilots would make the winter of 1943–44 a long and very difficult one for the Eighth AF's Lightning pilots. (The cold also often caused windshield fogging, which was another problem that had to be dealt with.) But despite these difficulties, they would persevere in their task of protecting the bombers, in which success was not measured only by the number of enemy fighters they shot down, as regardless of which they were a deterrent to attacks on the bombers by enemy fighters by their mere presence.

Most discussions about the Eighth AF's problems with the P-38 that winter have seemed to focus only on the aircraft. Certainly, as has been amply noted, the Lightning did have some design deficiencies and technical problems that needed to be resolved when it first began to be utilized in combat in large numbers starting in late 1942. But, as has also been noted, they were gradually revealed, acknowledged, and solved by Lockheed engineers and test pilots in the States and maintenance personnel overseas, and by the summer of 1944, the latest P-38 models, the J-25 and the L-1, followed soon after by the L-5, would compare favorably with the front-line fighters of any air force, Allied or Axis.

Although the extremely cold temperatures at high altitude in the ETO received much of the blame, P-38 pilots in Italy were flying similar missions over other parts of Europe at the same time with fewer problems—and they were equipped with the old "F" and "G" models, plus a few of the Eighth AF's castoff Hs. In fact, at least some of the problems that resulted in the Lightning's relatively poor performance there were caused by inadequate leadership, maintenance, and pilot training.

For example, Lt. Col. Cass Hough, when he was head of VIII Fighter Command's Operational Engineering Section (OES), stated that many of the Eighth's P-38 pilots failed to follow instructions to utilize high manifold pressure and low rpm (revolutions per minute) to improve their aircraft's range and reduce stress on the engines because "it gave them a rough ride."

On the technical side, it was learned in early 1944 that more than half of the Champion spark plugs that were being delivered to overseas combat units were faulty. It was also discovered that much of the British fuel supplied to the Eighth AF was improperly blended, and that its tetraethyl lead compound separated from it in the Allison engine's manifold. In March 1944, the 55th FG would test the new 150-octane fuel that had recently become available, with some positive results. Also, it was not revealed until July of that year, as the Eighth AF was phasing out its P-38s, that there was a fuel metering problem at high altitude, which could cause incipient detonation leading to engine failure. One cause of this was vapor lock, which was then minimized by modifying the fuel lines to eliminate—or at least reduce—sharp bends. For the Eighth's P-38 pilots, it was a matter of too little too late.

As to the fairly common turbo-supercharger failure, because of the hydraulically actuated regulators, the low temperatures thickened its oil, causing the turbine to go out of control. One solution to this problem, which would be initiated in late February 1944, was to make the penetration flights into enemy territory at 22,000 feet or less. Maximum cruise speed for the F-5s and P-38s was 240 mph at 28,000 feet, utilizing 35 inches of manifold pressure and 2,600 rpm. Their pilots were instructed to increase power settings to 45 inches and 3,000 rpm for thirty seconds every twenty minutes to keep the oil sufficiently warm; blocking part of the intercooler radiator intakes to reduce the amount of cold air entering them was also tried. The 20th FG experimented with piping hot air from the engine exhaust to the supercharger regulator. They both helped but did not totally eliminate the problem.

The bottom line was that no matter the attempted solutions, earlier models of the P-38 only operated above 25,000 feet with considerable difficulty, which was obviously problematic for high-altitude bomber escort duty.

The 20th FG broke into the scoring column for the first time on November 26, when the 55th FG, including the 77th FS, was assigned to target support for bombers attacking Bremen. As the 77th rendezvoused with the bombers, five twin-engined Dornier Do 217s were spotted and the squadron commander, Maj. Herbert E. Johnson, Jr., shot one of them down. (Johnson had flown an earlier tour with the 14th FG in North Africa.) The 343rd FS scored two kills and the 38th made one damaged claim.

The 55th Group flew another really tough mission on November 29, when it was once again assigned to escort the bombers to Bremen. A combination of bad weather and an attack by a large number of Bf 109s in the target area resulted in the loss of six P-38s and their pilots, four of whom were killed and the other two captured. In return, the Lightning pilots were credited with just two of the enemy fighters destroyed, one probably destroyed, and two damaged.

The Eighth AF received its and the 7th PG's last photo reconnaissance squadron in November. This was the 27th, which arrived at Mount Farm from Colorado on the 4th of that month. The whole squadron, including its pilots, had sailed from New York on October 21. It flew its first operational mission on December 20.

The lack of F-5A replacement aircraft was one of the reasons the 7th Group began to also operate PR Spitfires on loan from the RAF later that year, the first dozen arriving at Mount Farm on November 3. The Spitfire could actually fly higher, farther, and faster than the early F-5s, although it could not carry the selection or number of cameras the Lightnings could—various combinations of the K-17, K-18, and K-22.

It was also during November 1943 that the official designations of the photo recon units were changed, again. Effective November 30, the 7th Group's squadrons became just Photographic Reconnaissance, and on the 29th, it became Photographic Group (Reconnaissance).

In December, the 7th received ten of the new F-5B-1s, the PR version of the P-38J-5. Unfortunately, despite some definite improvements, they and the F-5C-1s (actual modified J-5s), the first examples of which reached Mount Farm in January, still had some engine problems. They did have more powerful Allisons, whose increased allowable supercharger speed also increased their reliability. However, Lockheed recommended redline rpm limits to prevent engine and supercharger damage. Interestingly, the new wing leading edge fuel tanks that were to have replaced the intercoolers had not been installed in the F-5Bs at the factory, and this had to be done at Langford Lodge as the tanks became available there. This was accomplished during February and March, although two aircraft were fitted with them at Mount Farm by the group's attached 381st Service Squadron. The wing tanks did

December 12, 1943: Lightnings of the 55th FG's 338th Squadron preparing to take off for another bomber escort mission. P-38H-5 42-67042 (CL-L) was one of the few Hs to survive the war in England; it was declared salvage there shortly after VE Day.

Taken in December 1943, this photo shows 338th FS P-38s resting on their hardstands at Nuthampstead. (*USAF photo*)

Left: A Spitfire and an F-5 of the 7th Photo Group flying over the English countryside. The group received its first Spitfire PR XIs in November 1943, and by January, its 14th PRS was operating them exclusively. (*USAF photo*)

Below: Zola, F-5A-10 42-13289, joined the 22nd PRS in November 1943. The following May, it was transferred to the Twelfth AF in Italy and assigned to the 3rd PRG's 12th PRS. (*Michael Bates collection*)

increase both the F-5's and the P-38's range considerably, especially when combined with the 150-gallon drop tanks.

Effective January 7, the 14th PRS became exclusively a Spitfire squadron; it received all the rest of the 7th Group's Spits and passed its F-5s on to the other three squadrons.

It was also in December that the 20th and 55th FGs began receiving the latest (J-5) model of the P-38. It too was definitely an improvement, with its increased fuel capacity and better engine cooling, but the Lightning's high-altitude performance over northern Europe remained problematic, as did its poor cockpit heating, which continued to be a major problem until the pilots were issued the electrically heated suits in March. The last of their Hs had been replaced in both groups by the end of January. Some of them were transferred to Italy and others went to the Eighth AF's new P-38 operational training unit, the 554th Fighter Training Squadron (FTS).

The 495th and 496th Fighter Training Groups (FTG) had been established in December—the former at Atcham and the latter at Goxhill—and became operational in January. Their purpose was to provide both conversion and refresher training to replacement fighter pilots arriving in the ETO, for both the Eighth and Ninth AFs. The two 495th Group squadrons, the 551st and 552nd, trained P-47 pilots, while the 554th Squadron of the 496th Group trained P-38 pilots and its 555th Squadron P-51 pilots. These courses lasted two to four weeks, upon the completion of which the pilots would usually be assigned to operational units. In August 1944, with the increased number of P-51 units, the whole 496th FTG would switch to Mustangs and P-38 training was transferred to the 495th FTG's 555th FTS.

A green-and-gray P-38J-5 or 10 at a base depot in the U.K. in early 1944 prior to being assigned to a fighter group there. It was early in the J-10's run on the Lockheed assembly line that Lightnings ceased to be painted. (*USAF photo*)

Since late 1942, Atcham had been home to a USAAF replacement pool that trained newly arrived fighter pilots in both operational theater procedures and gunnery. It was when the 20th and 55th Groups arrived in England in August 1943 that the unit, then designated the 2906th Observation Training Group (Fighter) (Provisional), received its first P-38Hs. During that same period, Goxhill was also operating as a fighter training base, where the pilots of newly arrived fighter units were likewise given instruction on operational procedures in the ETO.

Another non-combatant unit that flew Lightnings in the ETO was the 27th Air Transport Group (ATG), which included, as of the autumn of 1943, three ferrying squadrons (FRS), the 310th, 311th, and 312th, whose pilots ferried P-38s and F-5s from air depots to the operational units' airfields. The 310th was based at Warton (Station 582), Lancashire, the home of BAD 2, and the 311th and 312th at Maghaberry (Station 239), Northern Ireland, the latter two moving to nearby Langford Lodge in May 1944. In November 1944, the 310th FRS was transferred to the 31st ATG of the Ninth AF in France. Another Ninth AF unit that ferried P-38s and F-5s was the 326th FRS, also assigned to the 31st ATG, and then, as of September 1944, to the 1st Transport Group (Provisional).

The 20th FG finally flew its first independent mission on December 28, 1943—a fighter sweep over Holland. No longer would its individual squadrons have to tag along with the 55th FG on its missions, and there would be six instead of four P-38 squadrons available to escort the bombers.

Both P-38 groups had another rough day on January 5, when seventy Lightnings escorted the B-17s and B-24s to Kiel, Germany. *En route*, the 55th's pilots spotted some twin-engined Me 210 fighters, which were evidently decoys, as they were then bounced from above by an estimated thirty Bf 109s. The P-38s immediately formed two defensive Lufbery Circles, going in opposite directions, and during the twenty-minute fight that ensued five of the Messerschmitts were claimed destroyed, but four of the Lightnings failed to return. The 20th's pilots were also bounced, by a mixed formation of Fw 190s and Bf 109s that shot down two of their P-38s. Another was lost to AA fire. The group's only claim was for a single damaged 190.

The 55th FG experienced one more eventful mission on January 31—another fighter sweep over Holland. After being bounced by some very savvy Bf 109 pilots, who used dive, fire, and zoom tactics very effectively, six of the P-38s were shot down, all from the 38th FS, but the group's pilots gave as good as they got, claiming seven of the 109s destroyed in return.

A week later, the 55th's CO, Lt. Col. Jenkins, wrote in his personal diary: "We have had seven long missions in eight days and we are tired. We've lost about thirty-five percent of our group since we arrived. Not good at all."

The 20th FG's mission on February 11 was definitely "not good at all." It provided target and withdrawal support to some B-17s attacking targets in western Germany until the P-47s took over on the way home. According to the group's Intelligence Bulletin: "From rendezvous to landfall out the group was continuously bounced by small units of single engine fighters." They took a heavy toll, as eight of the P-38 pilots were MIA, including the mission leader, Deputy Group Commander Lt. Col. Robert P. Montgomery, who was flying his assigned aircraft, P-38J-10 42-68036. They were able to claim only two e/a destroyed,

Mr. Dinc, P-38H-5 42-67026, coded CL-P, was assigned to 338th FS flight leader Capt. Chester A. Patterson. "Chet" Patterson was one of the 55th FG's most successful P-38 pilots, having scored four confirmed kills by the end of January 1944. The following month, 42-67026 was transferred to the Fifteenth AF in Italy and assigned to the 1st FG's 27th Squadron. It was destroyed in a crash-landing there on July 28, 1944. (*USAF photo*)

one probably destroyed, and two damaged in return. (Lt. Col. Montgomery went down over France and was helped by French partisans to evade capture; he returned to England in June.)

Second Lieutenant Arthur W. Heiden coincidentally joined the 79th FS that same day. He later described what it was like for the 20th FG's pilots that winter:

There were disastrous incidents of ignition breakdown because of high-tension ignition leakage. The oxygen systems were woefully inadequate. This is what they put into the airplane and the pilot was stuck with what he had. It just wouldn't do the job. No one liked 30,000 feet anyway. There had been no training for it. There had never been any need for it. It was too cold and the windows frosted up. All this piled up on the Eighth AF pilots, but there they were at 30,000 feet plus and sixty below zero. It was miserable.

Then things really started to come apart. Now, suddenly, superchargers were running away. They were blowing up engines on the basis of one engine blowup *every seven hours*. Intercoolers were separating the lead from the fuel and the result was lowered octane. Hands and feet were freezing; pilots were calling their airplanes airborne ice wagons, and they were right. Frost on the windows got thicker than ever. The most disgusting of all was the leisurely way the German fighters made their way straight down.

It was around this time that a legendary P-38 pilot arrived in England. He was not a USAAF officer, but rather Anthony "Tony" LeVier, the civilian Lockheed test pilot, who had been asked there to do some P-38 engine test work and to put on some special training and demonstration flights, the latter mainly for the benefit of the somewhat demoralized Lightning pilots in the U.K.

During his four months in England, LeVier would visit most of the operational P-38 and F-5 units in England, as well as VIII Fighter Command H.Q., the OES at Bovingdon, the

P-38 training squadron at Goxhill and Langford Lodge. The pilots really appreciated his flight demonstrations, which showed them what they could do with the P-38 once they had mastered it. They were similar to the ones he put on for P-38 operational training students back in the States.

While at Langford Lodge, LeVier was assigned a special P-38J-10, serial number 42-68008, which had the name *Snafuperman* and some colorful artwork on its nose. It had received some upgrades that would not appear on production aircraft for several months. They included the special new dive flaps that would soon make their appearance on the J-25 model, and which finally solved the P-38's compressibility problem once and for all. While LeVier was there, 200 dive flap retrofit kits were sent to England from the States on a C-54 transport to be installed on the Eighth AF's earlier model P-38Js. Tragically, the C-54 was shot down by an "overzealous" RAF Spitfire pilot, who mistook it for a German Fw 200. P-38J-25s would not reach England until July, and those flaps would have come in very handy in the interim.

As of January 1944, there were still some targets beyond the range of Allied PR aircraft in England. So, the first "shuttle" mission was planned, whereby a 7th Photo Group pilot would photograph a distant target or targets and then land at an Allied airfield in the MTO. This was flown on January 29 by Maj. Hartwell of the 22nd PRS. After photographing the Dijon area of southern France, Hartwell landed at Pomigliano, Italy, then home to the Twelfth AF's 3rd Photographic Group (Reconnaissance). On his return trip to England two days later, he photographed the ball bearing works at Annecy, France.

As of February 18, 1944, the 7th Group became part of the new 8th Reconnaissance Wing (Provisional), commanded by Col. Elliott Roosevelt, who had previously been CO of the Mediterranean Allied Photo Reconnaissance Command. This unit became the 325th Reconnaissance Wing effective August 9.

Like many of the 7th Photo Group's Lightnings, *BEV.*, F-5A-10 42-12979, served with more than one of its squadrons. Shown here in its RAF PR blue paint job while assigned to the 14th PRS, it was lost on January 15, 1944 when Lt. Thomas M. Connor of the 27th PRS bailed out of it over England. (*Michael Bates collection*)

Tactical Lightnings

In October 1943, the Ninth AF, which had been serving in North Africa, was transferred to England. It was going to be the USAAF's tactical air force supporting the upcoming Allied invasion of France. Among its many other units the new Ninth would be assigned three P-38 groups—the 367th, 370th, and 474th—and five F-5 photo reconnaissance squadrons.

The 370th FG, comprised of the 401st, 402nd and 485th FSs, was the first to arrive in England, from Connecticut, on February 12 as a P-47 group. It had just moved into its temporary new home at Aldermaston (Station 467), Berkshire, west of London, when it received the shocking news that it would not be receiving new P-47s there but would be transitioning to the P-38. William M. Davis, then operations officer of the 485th FS, still remembered it well many years later:

> We had an advanced party that met us when we got to Aldermaston, and they indicated that there had been a change in our aircraft. There were a hundred P-38s sitting on this field. We were quite surprised, of course, as almost nobody in the group had ever flown a P-38, much less the maintenance people, who had a real problem because the aircraft was so different.
>
> As far as flying was concerned this brought up a tremendous problem because flying a twin-engine, a hot airplane, versus a single engine, there was a world of difference. For example, if you lost one of those two engines close to the ground and you weren't really sharp on single-engine procedure, you could easily lose several hundred feet before you could bring your aircraft under control and stabilize it. Maybe you didn't have several hundred feet to lose, so you could be in the ground.[3]

The 370th's pilots flew their new P-38s to what would be their first of many operational bases, Andover (Station 406), Hampshire, near England's south coast, on February 29. After some much-needed additional training, it would fly its first combat mission on May 1. At the end of that month, it was assigned to IX Tactical Air Command (TAC) and its 71st FW.

The 10th Photo Group (Reconnaissance) also joined the Ninth AF in February, moving from Mississippi to Chalgrove (Station 465), Oxfordshire, accompanied by the 30th PRS. It was joined there by the 31st and 34th PRSs in March and by the 33rd PRS in April—all of them from Will Rogers Field in Oklahoma City. The 30th Squadron flew the group's first mission, to France's Cherbourg Peninsula, on February 25.

Meanwhile, another P-38 group selected for the Eighth AF—the 364th—had left California for England on January 14. The unit arrived at its new base, Honington (Station 375), Suffolk, near England's southeast coast, during the second week of February and was assigned to the 67th FW. Three long-range Rolls-Royce/Packard Merlin-engined P-51 groups had also been added to the bombers' escort force by the end of February, so the protection of the B-17s and B-24s on their longer missions would henceforth no longer be the sole responsibility of the P-38 pilots.

The 364th FG flew its first mission, withdrawal support for bombers returning from Germany, on March 2. It was led by Maj. Mark K. Shipman, an experienced 55th FG pilot. On the following day, P-38 pilots of the latter unit had the distinction of flying

April 29, 1944: An F-5 of the 34th PRS about to take off from its base at Chalgrove, England. It has not yet had its unit markings applied. (*USAF photo via Mike Tovani*)

the first Allied fighters over Berlin, even though the bombers did not make it there due to the miserable weather. On the 5th, during a mission to Bordeaux, in southern France, Capt. Paul S. Miller, its assistant group operations officer, became the 364th's first combat casualty when he crash-landed in that country after running out of fuel. Miller evaded capture and made his way to Spain and eventually back to England.

The Eighth AF was finally able to complete its first major mission to Berlin on March 6. The 364th FG encountered e/a for the first time that day, on its fifth mission, when seven Bf 109s attacked the bombers under its care near Steinhuder Lake. Future ace Capt. John H. Lowell of the 384th FS destroyed one and probably destroyed another, and a squadron mate damaged one. One of the group's pilots was MIA. The only other P-38 victory on this mission—of the total of eighty-one credited to VIII Fighter Command units—was by a 20th FG pilot.

The 474th FG, comprised of the 428th, 429th, and 430th FSs, arrived at Warmwell (Station 454)—also called Moreton, after the nearby village—from California on March 12 and was assigned to the Ninth AF. Warmwell was located just 5 miles from the English Channel in Dorset.

When the personnel of the 367th FG (made up of the 392nd, 393rd, and 394th FSs), which was also assigned to the Ninth AF, arrived at its new English base, Stoney Cross (Station 452), just south of Andover, on April 5, they were in for a shock similar to that experienced by the 370th FG two months earlier. Expecting to be flying P-51s (they had trained on P-39s in California), they found P-38s awaiting them instead. Only four of its pilots had flown one before.

The sixty or so P-38Js the 367th had been issued were all well used and most of them required considerable maintenance before they were combat (or even training) worthy,

Right: P-38J-10 42-68043 had quite a combat history. Coded N2-D, it was assigned initially to Capt. George F. Ceuleers of the 383rd FS (posing with it here along with his ground crew), who named it *Connie & Butch Inc.* When the 364th switched to P-51s in July, 1944, 42-68043 was transferred to the Ninth AF's 393rd FS, 367th FG, becoming Lt. Robert R. Greene's *Greenhornet.* When the 367th converted to P-47s in February 1945, it was transferred to the 428th FS, 474th FG, and coded F5-U. It was destroyed in a crash-landing in Germany three months later, on May 11. (*USAF photo*)

Below: Pilots of the 430th FS pose with Lt. Raynor H. Roberts' *SECOND FRONT,* P-38J-10 42-67473, coded K6-D. (*474th FG Association collection*)

but the pilots soon commenced learning to fly them. Morale took a big hit when the group suffered its first P-38 pilot loss. The officer in question was twenty-two-year-old Capt. James E. Peck of the 394th FS, one of only a handful of pilots in the 367th FG with previous combat experience. He had flown Spitfires with both the RAF and the USAAF in the MTO and had come as close as a fighter pilot could to being an ace without achieving that distinction, having been credited with a total of four and a half confirmed air victories, four probables, and no less than nine and a half e/a damaged.

Peck took off from Stoney Cross on the afternoon of April 11, and proceeded to put on an impressive air show for the benefit of the group's personnel, thoroughly wringing out his P-38, J-15 43-28337. Upon landing, he came in too high and applied full power to go around again, but then his left engine failed. He had just managed to retract his landing gear and flaps when the Lightning stalled and crashed. The aircraft's explosion on impact threw Capt. Peck clear of it, but he soon died of his injuries. Although this incident did not exactly fill most of the group's other pilots with confidence, it turned out that he was the only fatality during their transition to the Lightning.

In March, a small VIII Fighter Command detachment comprised of two P-51s and two P-38s were TDY'd to Little Snoring, in Norfolk, which was home to several RAF night-fighter squadrons. They were used to fly low-level nocturnal "intruder" missions over the Continent, as RAF fighters had been doing for several years. It was finally decided that it would not be worth the effort to expand the program, especially after one of the P-38 pilots, 1Lt. James H. Corbet of the 79th FS, was MIA on April 12. Corbet had taken off in P-38J-10 42-67862, which was painted a dull black, for Ijmuiden, in the Netherlands, and neither he nor his aircraft were seen again. It was assumed that he had crashed into the North Sea.

The 474th FG flew its first combat mission, a fighter sweep over France, on April 25. On the previous afternoon, Tony LeVier had showed up at Warmwell to give a demonstration of the P-38's new dive flaps. Robert D. Hanson, a 428th FS pilot, remembered it well many years later:

> Tony LeVier did more than demonstrate the dive flaps. He really showed us how the P-38 could perform by doing maneuvers such as completing a takeoff on single engine, slow rolls at low altitude on one engine and more amazing tricks than I can remember. The primary purpose of his demonstration was to instill confidence in the airplane. The Eighth AF units which were flying P-38s were having trouble with airplane confidence among their pilots and groundcrew members.[4]

Prior to its first combat mission, also a sweep to France, on May 9, the 367th FG received fourteen replacement pilots with an average of 100 hours each in P-38s—far more than any of the group's original pilots at that time. Later that month, both groups were assigned to IX TAC's 70th FW.

Things really began changing for the better for the fighter units of the Eighth and Ninth AFs with the arrival of spring. The weather was improving and more fighter groups were joining VIII FC, which reached its final total of fifteen in May. Also, Gen. James H. "Jimmy" Doolittle, who had assumed command of the Eighth AF in January, was determined that its fighter pilots become more aggressive, with the goal of achieving air superiority over the European Continent—which would, in fact, be accomplished well before its upcoming invasion.

As to the P-38 units, the warmer weather was certainly a relief, as were the lower-level missions to which they began to be assigned more frequently. Their surviving pilots were now more experienced, both in combat and in actually flying the Lightning, and their later model P-38Js incorporated some welcome improvements.

With more fighters available, some began to be utilized for offensive sweeps ahead of the bombers, intercepting the Luftwaffe fighters before they were able to reach them, while others provided close support to engage those that did. Also, the Eighth AF's fighter pilots were now being encouraged to attack the enemy's fighters on the ground at their airfields. As an incentive, they were even given official credits for such strafing "victories"—although these were recorded separately from their aerial credits.

A good example of these new low-level airfield strafing missions was the one flown by the 20th FG on April 8, for which it was awarded a DUC. Lt. Col. Harold J. Rau, the group CO, had been given permission to attack ground installations and airfields over a large area of central Germany. Its 79th FS's pilots destroyed thirteen e/a on the ground at the Salzwedel airfield and shot down a huge Heinkel He 177 bomber that was in its landing pattern. The squadron, which Lt. Col. Rau was leading, was then bounced by seven Bf 109s, of which five were shot down for the loss of two P-38s and their pilots.

The 77th FS strafed another airfield southeast of Salzwedel, destroying eight more e/a on the ground and two in the air, while losing one of its pilot to AA fire. All three squadrons strafed additional targets such as trains, bridges, and buildings, doing lots of damage. A 55th FS pilot was also MIA.

The 364th FG flew a very similar mission a week later, on the 15th. Its individual squadrons strafed airfields and other targets of opportunity near the Elbe River and Hamburg in northwestern Germany. Considerable damage was done, but at a huge cost: eight of the group's pilots were missing in action, victims of the vicious AA fire.

Such low-level strafing missions by VIII FC pilots—especially those targeting airfields— were to become increasingly more common as the war progressed, and the numerous and skilled German AA gunners were to exact a huge toll of USAAF fighters, including P-38s.

It was also in April 1944 that the RAF lost one of its *bona fide* heroes, oddly enough while he was flying a USAAF aircraft. Wg. Cdr. Adrian Warburton had become its premier photo recon pilot while serving in the MTO from 1940 to 1943. In early 1944, Col. Roosevelt, with whom he had become friendly in North Africa, requested Warburton for his new command in England, which was made up of both USAAF and RAF strategic PR units. On April 1, he was appointed RAF liaison officer to the 7th PG.

Eleven days later, Warburton and another pilot took off from Mount Farm for a shuttle mission to Sardinia, *en route* to which they would photograph targets in southern Germany. The wing commander was flying F-5B-1 42-67325, which was assigned to the 27th PRS. The two pilots split up to cover their individual targets and Warburton was not seen again, at least by any Allies. His precise fate was unknown until the wreckage of his Lightning and some of his remains were recovered from a crash site in Germany in 2002. The evidence suggested that he had been shot down by AA fire from a nearby airfield.

Above left: Shortly after assuming command of the Eighth AF in January 1944, Lt. Gen. "Jimmy" Doolittle (seen here in the cockpit) was assigned this P-38, H-5 42-66972, for his personal use. It was later transferred to Italy. (*USAF photo*)

Above right: Gentle Annie, P-38J-10 42-67722, coded MC-R, was assigned to the 79th FS but was flown by 20th FG CO Lt. Col. Harold J. Rau, pictured here with it, their ground crew and his dog. The "R" stood for Rau and the swastikas represented the five e/a he and *Annie* destroyed on April 8, 1944—one in the air and four on the ground. Unfortunately, she was destroyed on the 18th of that month, in a crash-landing while being flown by another pilot. (*USAF photo*)

Above left: April 20, 1944: Lt. Earl H. Miller and his 384th FS ground crew pose with their assigned aircraft, P-38J-5 42-67217, named *HETTIE*. This Lightning had served previously with the 55th FS of the 20th FG as KI-W. It was destroyed in a crash-landing on September 10, 1944 while assigned to BAD1 at Burtonwood. (*USAF photo*)

Above right: Armorers of an unidentified Eighth AF P-38 unit are readying 1,000-lb. demolition bombs for another mission for *Nuey V* by attaching a tail fin to one of them. (*USAF photo*)

F-5B-1 42-67348, the 13th PRS's *Yankee Doll*, went missing along with its pilot, 2Lt. John R. Leaser, who failed to return from a photo mission to Lyon, France, on May 8, 1944. (*USAF photo*)

Effective April 16, the 55th FG moved from Nuthampstead to Wormingford (Station 159), Essex. Later that month, there was an exchange of pilots between the 15th Combat Mapping Squadron (CMS) at Bari, Italy, and the 7th PG in England. Three of the former's pilots were TDY with the latter for three weeks, and when they returned to Italy they ferried some new F-5s there. At the same time, five 7th Group pilots were flying missions with the 15th CMS.

The Droop Snoot

It was also in April 1944 that a new type of Lightning made its combat debut in England. This was a highly modified P-38 called the "Droop Snoot." It was the brainchild of the aforementioned Lt. Col. Cass Hough and of Lt. Col. Don Ostrander, an armament and ordnance specialist. When this project commenced, Hough was CO of VIII Fighter Command's Flight Research and Engineering section at Bushey Hall, Watford, but in February 1944, he became deputy CO of the new Operational Engineering Section for the Eighth and Ninth AFs at nearby Bovingdon.

The idea behind the Droop Snoot was to use P-38s as fast high-altitude bombers. The plan was that the Droop Snoot, which carried a bombardier and a Norden bombsight inside its Plexiglas nose, would act as the lead bomber at the head of a group or squadron of Lightnings, which would all drop their bombs on the command of the Droop Snoop bombardier. Once the P-38s did so, they could defend themselves against enemy fighters. The Droop Snoots were designed to carry two 1,000-lb. bombs but could carry six 500-pounders.

Work on the Droop Snoot prototype, P-38J-10 42-68184, had begun at Bovingdon in January, but it was completed and test flown at Langford Lodge late the following month, with the help of some Lockheed engineers. The first Droop Snoots were delivered to the 20th and 55th FGs at the end of March, and they flew them on their first missions on April 10, to the airfields at Gütersloh, Germany, and Coulomiers, France, respectively. Eventually, each Eighth and Ninth AF P-38 squadron was assigned a Droop Snoot, and even the famous P-47-equipped 56th FG flew one of them on a few missions. Several dozen of them were eventually produced at Langford Lodge.

During May 1944, as the Allied invasion of northern France approached, the photo recon units of the Eighth and Ninth AFs were focused on obtaining clear low-level photos of its beaches. (Those where the landings would not take place were actually given more attention, to mislead the Germans.) The 7th PG began flying fewer of its long-range, high-altitude strategic sorties in favor of tactical missions in support of the invasion forces—until the Allied offensive on the Western Front bogged down late in September after the failure of Operation Market Garden, of *A Bridge Too Far* infamy. Special attention was also given to locating and photographing Noball targets—the launching sites in France and the Low Countries for the V-1 rocket bombs that would create havoc in England that summer.

The first low-level photos of the Normandy beaches in preparation for the invasion were taken on May 6, by 2Lt. Albert Lanker of the 31st PRS. This dangerous type of mission was called "dicing" by the RAF, from its pilots' expression "a dicey situation," which was adopted by USAAF photo recon pilots. Lanker was assigned a 20-mile strip of beach from Le Tréport to Berck-sur-Mer—his third mission. According to the 31st PRS history, he "was somewhat nervous and apprehensive as he lifted his F-5 off the runway at Chalgrove and headed toward the Channel." It then described the mission itself:

> At Dungeness he was flying at fifty feet above the trees when he circled his aircraft and shot across the Channel ten to fifteen feet above the waves. Near Berck-sur-Mer Lt Lanker turned around a sand dune to lessen his possibilities as a target (photos later revealed the sand dune to be an enemy gun emplacement), and then gaining speed in a short dive started his photo run. At this point Lt. Lanker said his nervousness left him and he began to enjoy himself immensely. During the four minutes his cameras were operating he encountered five groups of workmen building defenses on the beach and later related, "I headed straight for every group just to watch them scatter and roll. They were completely surprised—didn't see me until I was almost on top of them." Near the end of the run he scaled a cliff with the wingtip six feet from the top, and a German soldier fired a rifle at him. This was the only opposition he encountered during the entire mission.

Lanker was killed in action later that year during the Battle of the Bulge.

With the invasion quickly approaching, VIII FC was directed to concentrate on destroying rail lines on the Continent—and the locomotives and cars they carried—to prevent additional German troops, supplies, and equipment from reaching Normandy. It was called Operation Chattanooga Choo-Choo, after the popular wartime song. This was a far cry from all the high-altitude escort missions the P-38 groups had flown the past winter, and even more dangerous.

Above: The first Droop Snoot,
P-38J-10 42-68184, photographed
at Langford Lodge shortly
after its completion there in
February 1944. (*USAF photo*)

Right: May 28, 1944: F-5E-2
43-28329 of the 34th PRS, whose
crewmen are not identified.
(*Michael Bates collection*)

The 55th FG flew its first Choo-Choo mission on May 21, destroying twenty-three locomotives, plus two Bf 109s on an airfield, and shooting up buildings, rolling stock, and even river traffic. The cost was high, however, as seven P-38s and their pilots were lost to the terrible AA fire. The 364th FG also flew a strafing mission that day, its targets some airfields east of Berlin. It claimed twenty e/a destroyed on the ground for the loss of two pilots.

The 364th had a rougher mission four days later, when the targets of both the bombers and the fighters were railroads and airfields in eastern France and Belgium. While the 383rd FS was covering some B-24s on their withdrawal, it was bounced by at least ten Fw 190s. The ensuing fight was a draw, with three shot down on each side, all the missing P-38 pilots surviving to become POWs. The 385th Squadron lost three more pilots to AA fire while strafing an airfield south of Paris; one was killed and the other two taken prisoner. It destroyed some trains but no aircraft.

It was also in May that the 479th FG, comprised of the 434th, 435th, and 436th FSs, showed up in England; it was the fifteenth and last fighter group assigned to VIII Fighter Command, as well as the last to arrive in the ETO. The 479th left California on April 15 and reached its English base, Wattisham (Station 377), Suffolk, exactly one month later. It was assigned to the 65th FW.

The 479th flew its first combat mission—a fighter sweep over Holland and Belgium—on May 26. It was led on its first few by Maj. John Lowell from the 364th FG. Its first pilot loss overseas was Capt. William A. Walker, CO of the 436th FS, who crashed and was killed during a training mission on the 25th.

At 6 a.m. on D-Day, June 6, the 7th Photo Group's new CO, Lt. Col. Clarence A. Shoop, and Lt. Col. Norris Hartwell, now the deputy group commander, took off from Mount Farm to photograph the Normandy invasion beaches and the nearby city of Caen under the low overcast. Shoop later reported that, at one point, "Suddenly little red golf balls started floating by my wings—light caliber flak. I yelled at Hartwell and he turned one way and I turned the other. The air was pretty full of lead for a few seconds."

The 10th PG received a DUC for the pre-invasion photo missions it flew from May 6 to 20, 1944, and the 7th PG was also awarded one for its missions in support of the Normandy invasion from May 31 to June 30.

P-38s of both the Eighth and Ninth AFs were among the hundreds of Allied fighters covering the invasion forces, starting well before dawn. Lightnings had been chosen to fly cover for the ships because their unique profiles reduced considerably the risk of "friendly" fire emanating from the nervous gunners on board.

The 479th FG suffered its first two combat losses on June 17; ten more of its pilots would be lost during the remainder that month. Its first air victory was scored by 1Lt. Clarence O. Johnson of the 436th FS, who shot down a Fiesler Fi 156 liaison aircraft he spotted over France during a fighter-bomber mission on June 22. Johnson had been credited with four e/a destroyed during a previous combat tour with the 82nd FG in North Africa, so this victory made him an ace. He transferred to the P-51-equipped 352nd FG in August and scored two more aerial victories before he was KIA on September 23.

As the American ground forces slowly fought their way out of the Normandy beachhead area after D-Day, against the Wermacht's determined opposition, they were well supported

P-38s of the 38th FS on a mission during the spring of 1944. In the foreground is CG-H, P-38J-10 42-67713. Its regular pilot was Lt. Kenneth C. Underwood, but Lt. Bert R. Shepard was flying it on May 21 when he was shot down over Germany and taken prisoner. In the background is J-10 42-68132, coded CG-I, which was destroyed in a crash-landing on May 27, partly due to the battle damage it had sustained. (*USAF photo*)

After Lt. Byron P. Yost of the 364th FG's 384th Squadron returned from a mission on May 30, 1944 with battle damage, the nose gear of his plane, P-38J-10 42-67980/5Y-F, collapsed on landing, with this result. Yost was killed in the same aircraft on July 15 when he collided with another P-38 over France. (*USAF photo*)

Above left: June 2, 1944: Lt. Lee S. Ayoub, a P-38 pilot of the 383rd FS, points to the name of his assigned aircraft. Ayoub had shared in shooting down a Bf 109 on April 15 and destroyed an Fw 190 on May 25. (*USAF photo*)

Above right: Cpl. Joe Diaz, an armorer of the 436th FS, loads a belt of .50-cal. ammo for one of the guns of P-38J-15 43-28640/9B-O, named *Lil' Venus*. When the 479th FG switched to P-51s in September 1944, 43-28640 was transferred to the 552nd Fighter Training Squadron. It was destroyed in a crash on October 27. (*USAF photo*)

Below: This F-5A-3, 42-12786, looked very different when it was photographed earlier while serving with the 7th Photo Group. Now with the Ninth AF's 34th PRS, it has been stripped of its RAF PR blue paint and given a new name, *My Little De-Icer*. (*Michael Bates collection*)

Mary, F-5B-1 42-68229 of the 34th PRS, which was then assigned to Lt. Glen Tovani, photographed on June 10, 1944. (*USAF photo*)

by the Ninth AF's fighter-bombers, including those of its three P-38 groups. The Lightning proved itself to be very effective in this role. It could carry a heavy load of bombs, and the cone of fire from the four .50-cal. machine guns and the 20-mm cannon in its nose was devastating against enemy ground targets. Its liquid-cooled Allisons were more vulnerable to AA fire than the P-47's rugged radial engine, but it did have two of them, and there were many Ninth AF P-38 pilots who returned safely from a mission on just one.

The ubiquitous German AA batteries, consisting of multiple rapid-fire cannon and manned by experienced and skilled gunners, claimed hundreds of Allied fighter-bombers—including dozens of P-38s of the Ninth AF, and, initially, the Eighth AF—on the Western Front from D-Day to VE Day.

The mission flown by the 367th FG on June 22 illustrated just how serious this threat was. Although it was touted up front as a "milk run" against the port and fortress of Cherbourg, at the tip of the eponymous French peninsula, on which American ground troops were moving, it turned out to be anything but. The group's forty-eight P-38s were among the 557 Ninth AF fighter-bombers participating in these attacks. As its pilots approached their individual targets at very low level, they ran into a "wall" of AA fire unlike anything they had previously encountered. The mission was an "unqualified disaster" as seven of the group's pilots were killed and only eleven of its aircraft returned to Stoney Cross undamaged.

As soon as airfields became available for them in France, Ninth AF units would begin moving there from England, to be able to give better support to the American armies during their liberation of France and their subsequent move into Germany. It had been decided that, to have more balanced and efficient reconnaissance units available for the invasion, the 10th PRG and the 67th Tactical Reconnaissance Group (TRG) would be consolidated. Each sent the other two of its squadrons—the 10th's 30th and 33rd PRSs going to the 67th Group in exchange for two of its F-6 Mustang tac recon squadrons.

The first to leave England for France was the 30th PRS, which arrived at Le Molay (A-9D), near the Normandy beachhead, on July 3. (All Allied continental airfields received a similar letter/number code.) It would be typical of the Ninth AF units on the Continent after D-Day; following the front, it would move to Toussus le Noble, France (A-46), on

This P-38 of the 367th FG, J-10 42-68071, was the first Lightning to land in France after D-Day—on a temporary landing ground that had just been bulldozed out of the beachhead—on June 10. (*USAF photo*)

Chalgrove, England, July 4, 1944: 34th PRS pilot 1Lt. J. L. Sanders poses with his ground crew and their colorful Lightning, *BLOOMER CRICKET*, F-5B-1 42-68243. (*Michael Bates collection*)

Two great shots of the colorful *Sky Queen/Miss Deane*, F-5E-2 44-23240. In the first one, its pilot, Capt. Paul R. Miller, is posing with it solo and in the second he is doing so with some of his fellow 33rd PRS pilots. No. 44-23240 was assigned to the squadron in early August 1944, when it was still based at Chalgrove, England (it moved to France two weeks later). It was destroyed in a take-off accident at Eschwege, Germany, on July 19, 1945, by which time the squadron had been reassigned from the 10th PRG to the 363rd RG. (*Michael Bates collection*)

August 31; to Gosselies, Belgium, on September 22 (and operate from A-78, Florennes, Belgium, temporarily from December 8 to 18); to Vogelsang, Germany, (Y-51) on March 24, 1945; to Limburg, Germany, (Y-83) on April 2 and to its final European base, Eschwege, Germany, (R-11) on April 10.

Next to make the move, to A-6/Beuzeville, was the 367th FG, on July 22, followed two days later by the 370th FG, to A-3/Cardonville. In early August, the 474th FG transferred to A-11/Neuilly, followed, in the middle of that month, by the 34th PRS—and then the 31st PRS—to A-27/Rennes, while the 33rd PRS joined the 30th PRS at Le Molay on the 15th.

By the time summer arrived in England, the USAAF leaders there had decided that all of VIII Fighter Command's groups that were not already flying the P-51 would convert to it. There were several reasons for this. One of them was that since the Merlin-engined Mustang's combat debut in December 1943, it had gradually proved itself to be the most successful high-altitude escort fighter—at least in Europe. The P-51's range and speed equaled the P-38's, and it was more effective in a dogfight at the higher altitudes at which the Eighth AF's escort fighters normally operated. Also, the P-38, with its two engines and complicated systems, was more difficult to maintain, and the P-51 required one less ground crewman. Another important factor was that the logistics would be greatly simplified if the Eighth AF operated just one fighter type.

This transition had actually begun in late February, when the 4th FG traded in its P-47s for P-51s, quickly followed by two more Thunderbolt groups. The process was not completed

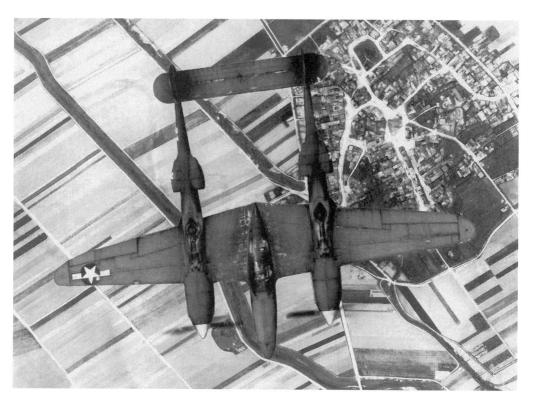

An F-5A of the 30th PRS over Germany. (*USAF photo*)

until December, when the 78th FG relinquished its P-47s and also began flying Mustangs. The famous 56th FG was an exception in that it was allowed to keep its P-47s until the end of the war in Europe, at which time VIII FC had fourteen P-51 groups plus the 56th's Thunderbolts.

Ironically, demonstrating just how much the performance of the Eighth AF's P-38 groups and their pilots and aircraft had improved over the past few months, the 20th and 55th FGs both had one of their most successful days in aerial combat thus far just before the switch to P-51s. This was July 7, when they escorted some B-24s to Bernburg, Germany, which mission was strongly opposed by enemy fighters. According to the 20th Group's Intelligence Bulletin:

> Hell broke loose in the target area when fifty Me 410s with approximately 100 Me 109s and FW 190s stacked in layers as top cover made aggressive and determined attacks on the bombers. Twenty of the fighters bounced the 55th Squadron and in the resulting battle three Me 109s were destroyed for no loss. The 77th bounced Me 410s and [single-engined] enemy fighters as they prepared to attack the bombers. Two Me 410s and two FW 190s were destroyed and two FW 190s and one Me 109 damaged.

The 20th's only loss was Capt. James M. Morris of the 77th FS, who shot down one of the twin-engined Me 410 *Zerstörer*s but was himself shot down by the Messerschmitt's rearward firing, remotely controlled machine guns mounted in "barbettes" on the sides of its fuselage, to become a POW. This was Morris's seventh confirmed kill—plus a one-third share of another—which made him the top-scoring P-38 pilot in the ETO.

The 55th FG was even more successful, its 38th and 338th Squadrons being credited with a total of 19-1-2 enemy fighters. The day's top scorer was 38th FS CO Maj. John D. Landers, with three Me 410s destroyed. Landers was on his way to becoming a legendary ace and fighter leader. During his first combat tour, flying P-40s in Australia and New Guinea with the Fifth AF's 49th FG, he scored six kills. His three on July 7, 1944 gave him a total of four with the 55th FG. Soon thereafter, he was transferred to the 357th FG briefly and then became CO of the 78th FG, scoring another four and a half air victories with the two Mustang groups.

The 20th and 55th FGs began their transitions to the P-51 shortly thereafter. The 20th flew its first Mustang mission on July 19 and its last Lightning mission two days later. The 21st was also the day the 55th flew both its first P-51 mission and its last P-38 mission. The 55th's final P-38 loss was on July 13 and the 20th's was on the 19th. Their last P-38 victories were scored on July 7 and 14, respectively. The 20th FG had been credited with destroying eighty-nine e/a in the air and had lost eighty-seven pilots to various causes. The 55th FG had scored 102 confirmed kills with its P-38s. Forty-eight of its Lightning pilots had been killed, eight of them in non-combat-related accidents. Many others had become POWs and a few were able to evade capture after going down in enemy-held territory— usually with the help of local partisans. The 20th FG generated eighty P-38 MACRs and the 55th seventy-eight.

A week later, it was the 364th FG's turn to switch to P-51s. Two missions were flown by the group on July 27. The first was comprised of a mixture of P-38s and P-51s and the second was with Mustangs only. The 364th had generated fifty-three MACRs (which did not include pilots and aircraft lost in non-combat-related accidents) while scoring just thirty-seven confirmed air victories with its Lightnings.

Above: Capt. Roy M. Scrutchfield of the 55th FS, 20th FG poses with his ground crew and their assigned P-38J-15, 43-28430/KI-N. This plane was destroyed in a crash on June 16, 1944 while being flown by another pilot. (*USAF photo*)

Below: Lt. Russell W. Bebout, a 79th FS pilot, pictured here with his ground crew, shot down an Fw 190 with this, his assigned P-38—J-15 43-28689/MC-Y—on June 28, 1944. He scored two more victories later with a P-51. When the 20th FG switched to Mustangs in July, 43-28689 was transferred to the Ninth AF. (*USAF photo*)

Above left: The 79th FS' Capt. Merle B. Nichols poses with his ground crew and their P-38J-10, *Wilda*, 42-67868. (*USAF photo*)

Above right: The 79th FS's 1Lt Arthur W. Heiden, his ground crew and their P-38, J-15 42-104086, *Lucky Lady*, coded MC-H. When the 20th FG converted to Mustangs in July 1944 this Lightning was transferred to the 402nd FS of the Ninth AF's 370th FG. It was lost in action over Belgium on December 26, 1944, during the Battle of the Bulge. (*USAF photo*)

Below: Kentucky Kernel IV, P-38J-15 43-28718/MC-A, was the fourth Lightning then-79th FS CO Maj. Delynn E. "Andy" Anderson had named after his home state. (He also flew a P-51 with that name before completing his combat tour.) When the 20th FG transitioned to Mustangs, 43-28718 moved to the Ninth AF's 474th FG and became its 429th Squadron's 7Y-F. (*USAF photo*)

Second Lieutenant Donald A. Schultz of the 13th PRS watches as S/Sgt. Charles Mader and Cpl. Morris Berkoff remove the film with which Schultz has returned from a photo mission during the summer of 1944. The official caption states: "In short time, these photographs will be developed, printed and ready for study." (*USAF photo*)

Despite the 7th Photo Group's problems with its earlier model F-5s, there were exceptions. One was F-5C-1 42-67114, named *Maxine*, which seems to have led a charmed life. Assigned to the 22nd PRS in February 1944, in July, it became the first 7th Group Lightning to complete fifty sorties, and it went on to fly fourteen more before it was "retired" from the group in November. After being reconditioned, it was transferred to the French Air Force, effective April 29, 1945.

Frantic

From early June to mid-August 1944, the Eighth and Fifteenth AFs participated in Operation Frantic, the "shuttle" missions from and to England, Italy, and Russia (Ukraine). The only Eighth AF Lightnings involved in that operation were F-5s of the 7th PG, which would, along with a few more from the 5th PRG in Italy, serve as the photo reconnaissance "eyes" for Frantic's bombers and fighters.

The first two 7th FG pilots had arrived at Poltava, Ukraine, on May 25 via Italy. Ground echelons had already established some facilities there, including a photo lab. Although the Soviets did provide bases for the USAAF units involved in Frantic, they made the process very difficult. For example, American planes entering Russian airspace had to follow very specific routes and schedules and could only land at the designated airfields.

In a nearly tragic case of what was assumed to be misidentification, the 22nd PRS's Lt. David K. Rowe, who had been TDY in Italy with the 15th CMS and was now flying from

Right: This photo of F-5C-1 42-67128, the 22nd PRS's *DOT+DASH*, was taken shortly after its arrival at Poltava, Ukraine, on May 25, 1944 to participate in Operation Frantic. Posing with it are its pilot, Lt. Everett A. Thies, and its crew chief, T/Sgt. Daniel Noble. This Lightning was lost on October 6 when it was shot down by an Me 262 jet fighter over Holland, its pilot, Lt. Claude C. Murray, Jr., managing to escape capture with the assistance of the Dutch underground. (*USAF photo*)

Below: A nice close-up of *DOT+DASH*'s colorful artwork. (*Michael Bates collection*)

Poltava, was shot down during a photo mission on June 26—ironically by a Lend-Lease Soviet P-39. His plane caught fire and Rowe was seriously burned before he was able to bail out; he fortunately survived his injuries.

By the end of August, the F-5s had flown around 100 PR sorties *en route* to and from Poltava. Sometimes the 7th Photo Group's pilots flew directly from England to Russia, or *vice versa*, and sometimes they would stop in Italy or Sardinia *en route*, depending on their targets.

Earlier in August, the 7th PG had received four specially modified P-38J Droop Snoots (one per squadron), in the noses of which the usual bombardiers and bombsights had been replaced with electronic monitoring devices and their operators. These were ELINT (Electronic Intelligence) aircraft, whose main purpose was to monitor the Germans' radar defenses by locating and recording the sources of their beams so that methods could be utilized to confound and subvert them.

It was the British who devised and oversaw this program, which was called Radio Countermeasures (RCM). Its primary operational unit was the RAF's 100 Group (similar to a USAAF wing). The 7th PG's ELINT aircraft, P-38J-15s 43-28479 and 44-23156 and J-20s 44-23501 and 23515, and their crews were TDY with 100 Group's 192 Squadron, based at Foulsham in Norfolk, on a rotational basis. The first USAAF ELINT mission was flown by a 27th PRS pilot on September 1. There was one loss during these missions, on October 26, when the 13th PRS's Capt. Fred B. Brink, Jr., and his operator, 2Lt. Francis I. Kunze, crashed into the North Sea in 44-23515 due to engine failure and were killed.

Also in the summer of 1944, the RAF obtained three Lightnings from the USAAF that were evidently the only ones flown by British pilots operationally. They were all based at Coningsby, an RAF Bomber Command base in Huntingdonshire, and assigned to 5 Group Marker Force. P-38J-20 44-23517 arrived there on July 20, from Langford Lodge. After flying a few daylight missions over occupied Europe, it was returned there the following

The 7th PRG's Lt. Ellis "Bruce" Edwards and the ELINT Lightning P-38J-15 44-23156, a modified Droop Snoot. (*Author's collection*)

month to be converted to a two-seater. It was collected on September 16 and, when back at Coningsby, was painted in standard RAF photo recon blue with RAF roundels. It then flew a few night missions and remained in the RAF's inventory until after the end of the war.

P-38J-20 44-23482, which was not modified, also arrived at Coningsby in July and was briefly tested as a target marker for the RAF's night bombers before being returned to the USAAF; in September, it was transferred to the 82nd FG in Italy. P-38L-1 44-24360, a Droop Snoot, arrived on August 6 for a one-month stint with the RAF, shortly after which Wg. Cdr. Guy Gibson, who had been awarded a VC for leading the famous "Dam Busters" mission, flew it on a daylight reconnaissance mission to Holland with a navigator on board.

As the liberation of France was proceeding to its successful conclusion, the remaining Luftwaffe airfields in that country became prime targets of the Allied air forces. One such mission took place on August 18, when the 479th FG escorted some B-24s to the Nancy-Essey airdrome (A/D) in eastern France. When the bombing was over the 479th's CO, Col. Hubert Zemke (formerly the famous commander of the P-47-equipped 56th FG), flying at the head of the 435th FS, decided to check the results and found that only two aircraft had evidently been hit by the bombs and approximately seventy remained undamaged. So while the 436th FS returned home with the B-24s, he led the 434th and the 435th on a strafe of the airfield. This attack resulted in credits for forty-three e/a destroyed plus many others damaged—and the first of the group's DUCs—for the loss of one P-38 and its pilot, who was killed.

On August 22, the 430th FS flew the 474th FG's first Droop Snoot mission. The following day, the group earned its only DUC, for its attack on retreating enemy forces in the Falaise-Argentan area of France. Its pilots spotted a huge concentration of them massed along the Seine River, and despite extremely heavy AA fire, they repeatedly bombed it, thereby disrupting the evacuation and enabling American ground troops to capture many Wermacht soldiers and a great deal of their equipment. Three P-38s were shot down in those actions, all of their pilots becoming POWs.

A historic event took place on August 25, 1944: the liberation of Paris from its four-year German occupation by American and Free French soldiers. The Wermacht and the Luftwaffe continued to withdraw eastward toward Germany and Belgium, while being harassed relentlessly by Allied forces on the ground and in the air.

All three Ninth AF P-38 groups continued the attacks on German airfields in northern France that day. The targets of the 367th FG's squadrons—which had recently moved from Beuzeville to Criqueville (A-2), also near the Normandy beachhead—were in the Laon area, northeast of Paris, which they hit shortly after noon. After completing their bomb runs, the 394th FS's three flights spotted thirty Fw 190s below them near St. Quentin. One flight then shot four of them down, but all four of *its* pilots were lost in return. Two more 394th Squadron pilots were shot down before the group's other two squadrons were able to answer their calls for help.

By the time the fight was over and the surviving Fw 190s had scurried away, another P-38, from the 392nd Squadron, had also gone down, but the 367th's pilots were subsequently credited with sixteen Fw 190s destroyed, plus many more as probably destroyed, damaged, or "unconfirmed." The 393rd Squadron's Capt. Laurence E. Blumer scored five of the confirmed kills. Of the group's seven missing pilots, it was determined later that two were killed, one became a POW (but later escaped) and four managed to evade capture with the help of the French underground.

The plane Capt. Blumer was flying was his assigned P-38J-25, serial number 44-23590, which he had named *Scrapiron IV*. The J-25s, with the new aileron boost and dive flaps, had finally arrived in England the previous month. All the ones that were sent overseas went to the Ninth AF, except for two that were initially assigned to the Eighth AF's 479th FG and later passed on to the Ninth. Certainly, they—and the "L" models that soon followed—gave their pilots an extra advantage in dogfights.

The 474th FG saw even more action that afternoon, about an hour after the 367th, which resulted in August 25, 1944 henceforth being referred to by the group's veterans as "Black Friday." Its 428th and 429th Squadrons were each assigned an airfield to attack east of the Seine River, but neither made it to their destination.

They were flying together near Beauvais, *en route* to their targets prior to splitting up, when they were alerted by their ground controller that e/a were in the area. They soon spotted fighters at nine o'clock heading in the opposite direction at the same altitude. These were thirty-plus Bf 109s of the Luftwaffe's III./JG 76 accompanied by a dozen Fw 190s of I./JG 26. The German pilots immediately dropped their external fuel tanks and the P-38 pilots their bombs, and they attacked each other head-on. Several aircraft from both sides went down in that initial pass and then the melee disintegrated into numerous individual dogfights. Soon thirty-two more Fw 190s, of II./JG 26, came along and also waded in.

The 428th FS, which was flying lower than the 429th, lost eight of its P-38s—two-thirds of the squadron—in this fight. Five of the missing pilots survived, three as POWs and two as evaders, but three of them were later determined to have been killed, as was one from the 429th Squadron. Two more of the latter's pilots were shot down but also evaded capture.

It turned out that the Lightning pilots had given a lot better than they got, which was amazing considering that they had been outnumbered three to one. It took some time to sort through all the claims by the returning pilots, as it was a while before all the evaders got back to the group, which moved to St. Marceau (A-43) on August 29. The final, official tally for the 428th FS was twelve confirmed destroyed, while the 429th was credited with nine—plus, once again, many more e/a probably destroyed, damaged, or unconfirmed.

The 367th FG flew another eventful mission that afternoon. This time, its targets were enemy airfields in southern France, which had been invaded by Allied forces ten days earlier. Its 392nd Squadron, accompanied by the 402nd Squadron of the 370th FG, found an airdrome near Dijon full of Ju 52 transports. It destroyed sixteen of them by strafing and the 402nd five. The 367th FG received its only DUC for its successes that day, including the bombing of the airfields at Clastres, Peronne, and Rosieres that morning.

The 479th FG flew two more successful strafing missions on September 5, this time to Germany—for which the group earned its second DUC. The 434th Squadron spotted twenty-plus planes on the airfield at Ettingshausen, and strafed them, nineteen being confirmed destroyed. Meanwhile, the 436th Squadron strafed the nearby Mershausen A/D, on which one its pilots destroyed two e/a, and then the Friedberg A/D, where it destroyed seventeen more.

The group returned to the same area late that afternoon, for the same purpose, this time dive bombing with 500-pounders as well as strafing. The 434th FS destroyed eight more e/a

Above: Maj. Robert C. Rogers, CO of the 392nd FS, and his assigned P-38J-25 44-23677, which he had named *Little Buckaroo* and was coded H5-A. Rogers scored no aerial victories; the five swastikas represented enemy aircraft he destroyed on the ground by strafing. When the 367th FG switched to P-47s in February 1945 this aircraft was transferred to the 370th FG. (*USAF photo*)

Below left: September 30, 1944: Capt. Laurence E. Blumer of the 393rd FS and his assigned P-38, J-25 44-23590/8L-C, *SCRAPIRON IV*, with which he had shot down five Fw 190s in a single action near St. Quentin, France, on August 25. (*USAF photo*)

Below right: Taken at A-68 on the same day as the previous photo, this one shows Capt. Linton A. Moody of the 393rd FS and his ground crew with their P-38J-25 44-23488, named *REBEL II*. A little over a month later, on November 21, another pilot was killed when he crash-landed it. (*USAF photo*)

Above: October 7, 1944: 393rd FS pilot Lt. Donald P. Buchanan and his ground crew with their P-38 *Barb IV*, at A-71, Clastres, France. (*USAF photo*)

Below: *Omar* was the P-38J-25, serial number 44-23577, that was assigned to Capt. Owen Hansen of the 392nd FS, pictured here with it and its ground crew on October 12, 1944. No. 44-23577 was lost over Germany on January 19, 1945, after Capt. Hansen had completed his combat tour. (*USAF photo*)

October 14, 1944: Capt. Robert B. Moorhead, a 392nd FS flight leader, shakes hands with a member of his ground crew in front of their P-38, J-15 42-104128, *Mattie II*, at A-68, Juvincourt, France. (*USAF photo*)

at Ettinghausen, four of them by 1Lt. James M. Hollingsworth, who had destroyed two on the morning mission. (Hollingsworth had flown a previous P-38 tour in North Africa with the 14th FG.) An additional Bf 109 was destroyed on another nearby airfield. The 435th Squadron lost Maj. Raymond S. Carter at the heavily defended Langenselbold A/D, when his P-38 (J-15 44-23177) was hit by the AA fire there and he crashed and was killed. The 435th claimed just one e/a destroyed, at Hochst Oberau, while the 436th Squadron destroyed eight on the Hanau A/D.

The time had finally come for the 479th FG to relinquish its P-38s and convert to the P-51. The first Mustangs arrived at Wattisham at the end of August and were assigned to the 435th FS, which flew the group's first mission with them on September 12. For the next three weeks, the group would fly its missions with both aircraft as its other two squadrons completed the conversion process. Ironically, two of its final P-38 missions, in late September, were the group's most successful with the Lightning in aerial combat.

On the 26th, the 479th FG was assigned a fighter sweep over the Dutch–German border to cover Operation Market Garden. After patrolling for a while, its pilots moved farther into Germany and soon spotted and bounced forty-plus Bf 109s near Münster. In the fifteen-minute dogfight that ensued, they were credited with twenty-nine destroyed for the loss of a single P-38 and its pilot. Another 479th pilot crash-landed his damaged plane in Allied territory near Brussels, Belgium. Ten e/a were claimed destroyed by the 435th Squadron's Mustang pilots, while the 434th and the 436th, flying P-38s, were credited with seventeen and two, respectively. Three 434th FS pilots each scored a triple: Lt. Col. James M. Herren, Jr., the squadron commander (three Bf 109s); future twelve-victory ace 1Lt. George W. Gleason (also three Bf 109s); and 1Lt. Quintin S. Pavlock (two Bf 109s and an Fw 190). The group was awarded its third DUC for this mission.

Two days later, the 479th FG flew what turned out to be another big one—target support for B-17s bombing Magdeburg, Germany. The 434th FS, which had received its first P-51s on September 8, was flying its first mission in them, but with just one section (two flights);

its other section was flying P-38s. Shortly after rendezvousing with the Flying Fortresses, the 434th and 436th Squadrons spotted and engaged two large formations of enemy fighters. The result of this fight was a score of 13-0-6, without loss. The 434th's P-38 section claimed only a single e/a damaged, but the 436th's Lightning pilots were credited with 9-0-4 Fw 190s, including three kills each by 1Lts. Donald A. Dunn and Victor Wolski. (The 436th FS was credited with only fifteen confirmed air victories with P-38s, total!)

The 436th Squadron received its first Mustangs on September 29 and flew the group's (and the Eighth AF's) last P-38 mission on October 3. The 479th's Lightnings were flown to the Burtonwood air depot (BAD 1), and most of them ended up with the Ninth and Fifteenth AFs. The group's P-38 pilots were credited with a total of fifty-two confirmed air victories—thirty-five of them by the 434th Squadron, including five by Capt. Robin Olds, the 479th's only Lightning ace, who had an eventual total of thirteen. Forty-one of its pilots were missing in action.

The Jet Threat

On August 2, 1944, while photographing targets near Halberstadt, Germany, 1Lt. Gerald M. Adams of the 27th PRS spotted an aircraft about 5 miles away, above him. After completing his photo run, he noticed that it had already halved the distance between them—and then it was firing at him. He managed to evade the enemy fighter, which he described as "a really weird looking airplane with little puffs of smoke coming out of its tail," by diving into some clouds, fortunately without being hit. The strange aircraft was the new, experimental, rocket fighter, the Me 163, which was used by the Luftwaffe in very small numbers with minimal success.

Four days earlier, on July 29, some P-38 pilots of the 479th FG had also had an encounter with an Me 163, during a bomber escort to Merseburg, Germany. The 434th FS flight led by Capt. Arthur F. Jeffrey, a future fourteen-victory ace, spotted a "stubby little fighter" making a pass at the crippled B-17 they were escorting home. Jeffrey and his wingman went after it while his other element provided top cover. The Me 163 was evidently flying without power after diving from a higher altitude (a common tactic), and when its pilot spotted the P-38s, he first went into a shallow dive and then started a steep climb. At this point Capt. Jeffrey opened fire and saw some strikes. It then circled to the left and he turned inside it and got in a good deflection shot. The rocket fighter then split-S'd into the clouds below at around 3,000 feet, while receiving more strikes from the P-38. In his Combat Report Jeffrey stated: "It is my opinion that no ship and no pilot could pull out of an 80- to 90-degree dive from 3,000 feet, indicating 550 miles per hour or better," and he was given credit for its destruction.

Although no German record of an Me 163 being lost that day has been located, it was evidently at least damaged. This was the first and only confirmed P-38 victory over a German jet or rocket aircraft.

The Luftwaffe's other radical new fighter, the twin-jet Me 262, was a different story. It had recently also become operational and would soon prove to be amazingly successful—its successes being limited only by its relatively small numbers and by Hitler's insistence that they be utilized as bombers.

By this time, the Reich's territory was being devoured by Allied offensives on both the Eastern and Western Fronts, and its cities, factories, airfields, and transportation systems were under constant surveillance, photographically and visually, by the Allies' many reconnaissance aircraft, which the Germans considered to be a major threat. In late 1944 and early 1945, F-5s and Mosquito and Spitfire PRs became prime targets of the Luftwaffe, and especially of its jet pilots, such was their importance to both the Allied air and ground campaigns. Although the Me 262, which was more than 100 mph faster than the Lightning, did not actually shoot down that many F-5s (nine are known to have been lost to them, plus two or three times that many Spitfire and Mosquito recons), they did intercept them on numerous occasions, at the very least interfering with their missions and sometimes causing their pilots to abort them.

The very first F-5 kill by an Me 262 was a 7th PG aircraft that went missing on October 6, 1944. Two pilots of its 22nd PRS were on a mission over Holland that day when they were attacked by the jets. One of them managed to escape, but 2Lt. Claude C. Murray, Jr., was shot down. After bailing out safely, he was rescued by members of the Dutch underground, who helped him avoid capture.

The next loss of an F-5 to an Me 262 took place on October 29, when 2Lt. Eugene S. Williams of the 22nd PRS was shot down during another photo mission to northwestern Germany and Holland. He was later reported to be a POW. Williams was the victim of *Leutnant* Alfred Schreiber of *Kommando Nowotny*, an experimental jet unit whose *Kommandeur* was its namesake, Walter Nowotny, one of the Luftwaffe's leading *experten* (aces).

In early November, the 27th PRS was detached from the 7th PG temporarily to operate alongside Ninth AF PR units on the Continent. Its new base was Denain/Prouvy (A-83), in northern France near the Belgian border, where it would remain for the next five months. On one of its first missions from A-83, to Stuttgart, Germany, on November 26, one of its Lightnings was shot down by an Me 262 of the Luftwaffe's new jet fighter *gruppe*, III./JG 7. Its pilot, 1Lt. Irvin J. Rickey, never saw the jet and thought his aircraft, F-5E-2 43-28619, had been hit by AA fire. He bailed out to also become a POW.

As encounters with the jet fighters increased, solutions were sought. The first was to send the F-5s out in pairs, their two additional eyes hopefully enabling the pilots to spot the speedy Me 262s in time to avoid or evade them. Another was to provide them with fighter escort. In January 1945, the 7th PG received some P-51s of its own to use as escorts to its Lightnings and Spitfires. Two months later, a 22nd PRS F-5E-2, 43-28577, was equipped with two experimental .50-cal. gun packs for self protection, but this was not a success, mainly because it slowed the aircraft down too much.

As of the end of October 1944, the 10th PRG's only remaining F-5 squadron was the 31st, as its 34th PRS had been transferred that month to the Ninth AF's new Provisional Reconnaissance Group, which was created to support the U.S. Seventh Army, moving up from southern France. (Effective April 20, 1945, the 34th was transferred again, to the 69th TRG, which had arrived in France from the U.S. the month before.) All three of the Ninth's P-38 groups were now part of IX TAC's 70th FW.

The 370th FG's productive fighter-bomber work was rewarded with a DUC for the mission it flew on December 2, during the Battle of the Hurtgen Forest. According to its citation, "despite bad weather and barrages of AA fire, the group dropped napalm bombs on a heavily defended position in Bergstein, setting fire to the village and inflicting heavy casualties on enemy troops defending the area."

F-5E-2 43-28974 of the 31st PRS photographed over France in October 1944. (*USAF photo*)

SanDot IV, another 485th FS P-38—J-25 44-23670, coded 7F-B—was shot down by AA fire over Germany on December 6, 1944. (*Michael Bates collection*)

Battling the Bulge

On the early morning of December 16, 1944, the Wermacht launched a huge, surprise counteroffensive against American forces along the Siegfried Line in the Ardennes Forest, a large, heavily wooded area stretching across the borders of France, Belgium, and Luxembourg. Its initial objective was the Meuse River in France, and it made quick progress against the lightly held American lines. Eighth and Ninth AF F-5s and Ninth AF P-38s would play a major role in what became the six-week Battle of the Bulge, named after the large protuberance into the American lines created by the German offensive—the recon Lightnings locating and photographing the enemy ground forces and their supply columns and the fighters doing their best to destroy them.

On December 17, the Ninth's fighter-bombers were out in force to attack the advancing German army, and equally large numbers of Luftwaffe fighter pilots did their best to stop them from doing so and to attack American ground forces. There were constant aerial clashes over and near the battle zone, in which the P-38 and P-47 pilots were credited with seventy-five confirmed kills, eighteen of them by the Lightnings.

The 370th and 474th FGs, which were then based together at Florennes, Belgium, (A-78) were particularly busy that day, bombing and strafing the enemy and their supply lines, plus battling Luftwaffe fighters on five separate occasions. Twelve of their P-38 pilots were MIA, six from each group; eight were killed in action, and four became POWs.

Another 7th PG F-5 was lost to an Me 262 of III./JG 7 on December 23, despite a P-51 escort. The formation was jumped by six of the jets after making photo runs over Magdeburg. As three of them distracted the three Mustangs, the others attacked the two Lightnings, of the 22nd PRS. One of the latter's pilots evaded their fire, but the right engine of 1Lt. Robert F. Calgren's F-5E-3, 44-23603, was hit and exploded. Calgren bailed out to become a POW.

More of the jets were encountered by 27th PRS pilots, also flying in pairs, the following day, Christmas Eve. Second Lieutenant Jeryl D. "Jerry" Crowell, flying F-5E-2 43-29026, was shot down and killed by an Me 262 over the Ardennes in Belgium. On another mission, to Nürnburg, Germany, 1Lt. Ira J. Purdy, flying in tandem with 1Lt. Robert N. Florine, was also attacked by a 262. He later described what happened:

[The F-5] had a blind spot low and behind the pilot. This is where the Me 262s hit us from, just as I started my camera run over Nürnburg. When on the mapping run it was necessary to keep the photo platform as steady as possible, so we were probably not watching as closely as normal; each pilot was supposed to cover his buddy's blind spot. But these guys came up so fast we never knew what hit us.

My aircraft was badly hit in the port wing and engine by cannon shells, and I was about to bail out when it seemed that the aircraft was still flyable. Lieutenant Florine's was not hit and he spent the next minutes keeping the two jets off my back by diving into them each time they tried to close and finish me. There is little doubt that he risked his own life to save mine.

Purdy made it back to A-83 on his remaining engine and belly-landed there. He ran, unharmed, from his Lightning as it burst into flame.

Above: Lt. John T. Curtis of the 394th FS, 367th FG poses with his assigned P-38J-25, 43-23694, coded 4N-N, at Juvincourt, France, in December 1944. (*Author's collection*)

Below: Juvincourt, France, during the winter of 1944–45. According to this photo's official caption, "Pilots of the 367th Group, cooperating with US Third Army troops, have contrived a sleigh train for transportation from briefing hut to dispersal areas. A jeep crammed with pilots and towing three sleigh loads arrives at the line ready to discharge its passengers for change to speedier and deadlier transportation." The P-38 in the background is a J-15, serial number 43-28528, the 393rd Squadron's 8L-U. (*USAF photo*)

Below: F5-W of the 428th FS receiving outdoor maintenance at Florennes, Belgium, during that cold winter of 1944–45. (*USAF photo*)

Pilots of the 370th FG's 402nd Squadron walk to their planes at their base in Belgium during the winter of 1944–45. (*USAF photo*)

Mary Rose II, P-38J-10 42-67780 of the 370th FG's 485th Squadron, is being serviced at Florennes, Belgium (A-78), in the fall of 1944. Its assigned pilot was Lt. Harold E. Erschen, but another pilot was shot down and killed in it over Belgium on December 27, during the Battle of the Bulge. (*USAF photo*)

The 485th Squadron's 7F-M, P-38J-10 42-67940, parked at A-78 in the fall of 1944. Second Lieutenant Jack M. Jarrell, Jr., went missing in this plane on December 14 when it was hit by a Bf 109 and he bailed out of it, never to be seen again. (*USAF photo*)

Some 485th FS P-38s taking off from A-78 for another mission during the Battle of the Bulge. (*USAF photo*)

By the end of January, the Bulge had been eliminated and the Wermacht was back where it had begun its offensive—minus a lot of men and materiel. The Western Allies were now free to proceed to the west bank of the Rhine, through the Ruhr River Valley, and into Germany's heartland.

Also in January, the Ninth AF received its last F-5 PR squadron, the 39th—which was also the last Lightning unit to arrive in the ETO—when it moved from Oklahoma to Valenciennes, France. At first, its individual flights were attached to the Ninth's three tactical air commands, until the whole squadron joined the 10th PRG at the end of February. A month later, it was transferred to the Provisional Reconnaissance Group. The 39th PRS followed the typical Ninth AF continental "gypsy" lifestyle, as it and its flights operated from three more airfields in France, two in Belgium, and one in Holland before moving to Wiesbaden, Germany, on April 20.

In late 1944, at least sixteen bulbous-nosed Pathfinder Lightnings, highly modified P-38Ls carrying H2X AN/APS-15 ground scanning radar sets (called "Mickeys") and their operators, arrived in England, to help develop blind bombing techniques for dark or cloudy conditions. The Eighth AF's 654th Bomb Squadron, of the 325th RW's 25th Bombardment Group (Reconnaissance), utilized one of them, 44-23880, for experimental night sorties in January and February 1945. This program was discontinued on February 13, as it was found that modified B-17s could handle the job more efficiently, as they had scanners that swept a full 360 degrees, whereas the H2X in the Pathfinder could only sweep 210 degrees.

Also in February, shortly after its move to St. Dizier (A-64) from Juvincourt (A-68), France, the 367th FG completed its conversion to the P-47 that had begun in December, when its pilots began to slowly accumulate the required minimum of five hours in the aircraft before they could fly it in combat. This process was delayed by poor flying weather, the limited number of Thunderbolts available to them, and the group's busy combat schedule during the Battle of the Bulge. (December was also the month during which the 367th had been transferred from IX TAC to XIX TAC, which was supporting Gen. Patton's Third Army.) As of February 11, its 392nd FS had finally received the last of its full complement of P-47s, and for the next two weeks, the group operated both types, until sufficient Thunderbolts had been assigned to the 393rd and 394th Squadrons. By the end of the month, its Lightnings were all gone, mostly transferred to the 370th and 474th FGs.

The 367th's pilots were initially not at all happy with the change, citing, among other things, their beloved P-38's superior acceleration compared to the P-47 and its two engines. But most of them eventually came to appreciate the good points of the Thunderbolt—especially its super rugged Pratt and Whitney R-2800 radial engine.

Yet another 7th PG F-5 was lost to a German jet on February 21. Second Lieutenant Grover P. Parker of the 13th PRS was photographing his target, Stettin, Germany, escorted by two P-51s, when he was suddenly attacked by an Me 262. The fighter leader called out to Parker to break, but it was too late—his Lightning's right engine burst into flame. The Mustang pilot then hit the jet, which also burst into flame, and exploded. The only Me 262 known to have gone missing that day belonged to II./KG(J) (*Kampfgeschwader(Jagd)*) 51, a fighter-bomber unit. The P-51 pilots last saw Lt Parker's F-5E-3, 44-23718, heading east, toward the Russian lines. He made it there, landed, and was assisted by the Soviets.

Commandant (Maj.) Rene Gaoille, CO of the French Air Force's photo reconnaissance unit GC/II 33 (center), and another officer chat with USAAF S/Sgt. John Oltmanns, its liaison line chief, sometime in the winter of 1944–45. GC/II 33 was then part of the 1st Tactical Air Force. (*USAF photo*)

Amazingly, Lt Parker had gone missing twice during the previous September, while serving with the 27th PRS, on both occasions eventually returning to England. On the 9th, he belly-landed in occupied France after running out of fuel and was rescued by members of the French underground. Ten days later, he was hit by AA during a mission in support of Market Garden and crash-landed on the coast of Belgium near the Dutch border. This time, he was actually captured by the Germans but soon escaped and was then assisted by the Dutch underground. He had somehow managed to persuade his superiors to allow him to continue flying missions.

As the Allied armies on the Western Front moved up to the Rhine to prepare for the final push into Germany they got a huge break. The U.S. Army's 9th Armored Division, after penetrating the Siegfried Line, reached the river sooner than had been expected. Arriving there on March 7, its men were astonished to see the Ludendorff Bridge across it still standing. Although it was badly damaged, the Germans had failed to destroy it as they had the forty-six other bridges spanning the Rhine. American troops immediately took possession of it and established a bridgehead on the opposite side of the river. The Germans became determined to destroy them both and the Luftwaffe immediately began its attacks. The 474th FG's P-38s were among their defenders.

Enemy planes first attacked the bridge on March 8, and the 474th commenced its patrols over it the following day, but it did not see any real action until the 13th. Just before 1 p.m., its 429th Squadron caught several bomb-carrying Fw 190s heading for the bridge and claimed one destroyed, two probably destroyed and three damaged. Unfortunately, two of the P-38s collided during this action; one of their pilots managed to return to A-78 despite considerable damage to his aircraft, but the other crashed and was killed. A third pilot, last seen chasing a 190, was also later determined to have been killed.

An hour later, the 430th FS bounced eight more Fw 190 fighter-bombers attacking the bridge and claimed 4-1-0, although one of the "destroyed" was not confirmed. Two of *its* P-38s also collided, but both of their pilots were able to bail out successfully and survived.

On March 14, 428th FS pilots claimed to have damaged three "Me 262" jets attacking the bridge. These were, in fact, twin-engined Arado Ar 234 jet bombers, two of which were, as it turned out, actually shot down by the P-38s, their crews bailing out after their aircraft had been hit by them. The 474th FG flew its last Remagen mission on March 17, and a week later, it moved from A-78 to A-59, near Strassfeld, Germany.

On the evening of February 28, Lt. Col. Morgan A. Giffin, the 370th's deputy group commander (who, two years earlier, had flown P-38s with the 54th FS in the Aleutians), announced to its pilots that they would be transitioning to the P-51, much to their surprise and displeasure. They were also puzzled, since they knew the Mustang was not nearly as effective a fighter-bomber as either the P-38 or the P-47. The answer was that it was to join the Ninth AF's only other P-51 group in escorting the Ninth's bombers and flying armed reconnaissance missions.

The 370th, which was then based at Zwartberg, Belgium, (Y-32) had been transferred from IX TAC to XXIX TAC in January. It flew its first Mustang mission on March 22 and its last in P-38s three days later. It also suffered its final P-38 loss on the 25th, when the one being flown by the 485th FS's 1Lt. Kenneth J. Busse, L-5 44-25537, was hit by AA fire while he was strafing a marshalling yard. He bailed and was captured. Busse's was the group's eighty-third P-38 MACR filed since April 23, 1944. Many of these pilots became POWs and a few managed to evade capture, but the majority were KIA. Other 370th FG Lightning pilots were killed or seriously injured and their aircraft destroyed in non-combat-related accidents. The 367th FG's MACRs had totaled seventy-four (from May 19, 1944 to February 21, 1945) and the 474th's eventual total was 107 (from April 9, 1944 to April 20, 1945). Piloting a Ninth AF P-38 was a dangerous business!

Most of the 370th Group's Lightnings were passed on to the 474th, which was now the only P-38 group in the ETO.

Around April 1, the 14th PRS returned all its Spitfires to the RAF and re-equipped with F-5s. The 7th PG was then in the process of moving from Mount Farm to nearby Chalgrove, the former home of the Ninth AF's 10th PRG. Its 22nd PRS was the first to make the move, on March 24, and it was completed by April 8. Later that month, the 27th PRS finally returned to England after flying its last missions from France on April 20.

On April 7, Luftwaffe *experten Oberleutnant* Walter Schuck of III./JG 7 shot down the F-5E-3, 44-23715, flown by Capt. William T. Heily of the 30th PRS, which was then based at Limburg, Germany, (Y-83) as he was photographing a portion of the autobahn near Seesen, Germany. Heily bailed out and was captured, but he was liberated by American soldiers eight days later. On the following day, another Ninth AF F-5, E-2 44-23229, was shot down by an Me 262 of I./JG 7 as it photographed a target at Stendal, Germany. Its pilot, Capt. John G. Austin of the 33rd PRS, then based at Venlo, Holland, (Y-55) was killed.

This F-5E-2, 43-28988, was assigned to the 14th PRS when it traded in its Spitfire PRs for F-5s in April 1945. Its pilot was Lt. Donald W. Werner, who named it *Betty Jane* after his wife. (*Author's collection*)

Ninth AF fighters were credited with shooting down nine e/a on May 8, the last day of the war in Europe—three of them by pilots of the 474th FG, which had been operating from Langensalza, Germany, (R-2) the past two weeks. The very last USAAF air victory in the European Theater was scored just after 8 p.m. when 2Lt. Kenneth L. Swift of the 429th FS claimed a transport aircraft near Rodach, Germany. According to a news release about this incident, "Lt Swift fired a short burst across the bow of the enemy plane as warning. Promptly the Heinkel [actually a Siebel Si 204] peeled off and crash-landed in a nearby field. Ten Germans scrambled out of the smashed plane waving handkerchiefs." This was the 496th confirmed kill by a P-38 in the ETO—282 by the Eighth AF's and 214 by those of the Ninth AF.

The German surrender went into effect at 12.01 a.m. on May 9.

The 474th FG and its P-38s were assigned to occupation duty in Germany until late November 1945, when it returned to the U.S., where it was soon inactivated. The 30th PRS had returned to the States in July, and the 33rd and the 39th did so the following month. All three were also inactivated there, while the 31st and 34th PRSs were inactivated in Germany in November. Most of the Lightnings still in the ETO had been scrapped by the following year, although a few late model F-5s were transferred to the French Air Force shortly after VE Day.

April 10, 1945: The 430th FS's Droop Snoot taking off from its base at Strassfeld, Germany (Y-59). (*USAF photo*)

Lt. Robert H. Deecken crashed the 429th FS's 7Y-P (P-38J-10 42-67799) while taking off from Bovingdon, England, on April 11, 1945. This Lightning had originally been assigned to the 20th FG. (*USAF photo*)

Lightnings in Action:
The Mediterranean Theater of Operations
(Twelfth and Fifteenth Air Forces)

Operation Torch

On the early morning of November 8, 1942, American and British forces, covered by Allied naval aircraft from carriers, landed on the beaches of Morocco and Algeria, near Casablanca, Oran, and Algiers; the Allied invasion of Vichy French Northwest Africa— Operation Torch—had begun. The subsequent fighting was short-lived, as the French capitulated three days later.

Captured French airfields were immediately made ready for use by Twelfth AF units waiting in England, including the 1st and 14th FGs. Their P-38s had been flown from their operational English bases to two others in the southern part of the country and were now ready to proceed to Algeria, in small formations usually comprised of two flights of Lightnings led by a single twin-engined Martin B-26 Marauder for navigation. The pilots flew at 500 feet across the Bay of Biscay to avoid German radar on the French coast, then climbed to 5,000 feet along the coast of Spain. They tried to avoid crossing that Axis-friendly country, but most of them did fly over neutral Portugal. The airfield at Gibraltar, the British colony on Spain's southern coast, was available for emergency landings and refueling. The 1,500-mile trip took about eight hours.

Pilots of the 1st FG's 27th Squadron were the first to leave England, on November 12, and the flights continued for the next six days. Some of the 1st's P-38s and pilots did not make it to North Africa from their embarkation point in Cornwall. Its largest flight was made on the 15th, and it was quite eventful. One Lightning crashed in Spain, killing its pilot. The 94th FS's 1Lt. Jack Ilfrey, a future ace, lost one of his two 150-gallon auxiliary gas tanks and was forced by the resulting shortage of fuel to land at Lisbon's airport. The Portuguese had a policy of confiscating aircraft of foreign countries that landed there, but eventually repatriating their pilots.

Ilfrey was detained by government authorities at the airport, and his plane (P-38F-1 serial number 41-7587) was refueled, with the intention of having it flown to a nearby military air base. He was asked to give a Portuguese Military Air Service (*Serviço Aeronáutico Militar*, or SAM) pilot some basic instruction on how to fly the Lightning. While Ilfrey sat in its cockpit pointing out the various controls—as the engines were turning over—another P-38 came in for a landing. This distracted the Portuguese pilot, and Ilfrey immediately "gave it full power," the prop wash knocking him off the wing where he had been squatting, and took off straight across the field. He then flew to Gibraltar.

The other P-38 pilot, Ilfrey's squadron mate 1Lt. James Harmon, was not as fortunate. His plane, P-38G-1 42-12738, was confiscated, and he was interned for several months before being allowed to rejoin his unit (he was later killed in action in North Africa). No. 42-12738 was integrated into the SAM and repainted in its colors and markings. It remained in service until 1944, when it was scrapped.

The pilots of the 14th FG's 48th Squadron left Devon for Algeria on November 14, and those of its 49th Squadron followed four days later. Their flights to North Africa were less eventful than the 1st Group's, and most of them made a stopover at Gibraltar *en route*. The 48th landed initially at Oran's La Senia A/D and then had to take off again for both groups' actual destination, Tafaroui, a few miles to the south.

At Tafaroui, the P-38 pilots were reunited with the rest of their air echelons—including their ground crews—which had flown in on C-47 transports, and the ground echelons, which had arrived by ship. The two groups were initially assigned to XII Fighter Command, which would soon be absorbed by the tactical XII Air Support Command (ASC).

A week after their arrival in Algeria, the 1st FG moved from Tafaroui to Nouvion, on the Mediterranean coast east of Oran, and 14th FG H.Q. and its 48th FS to Maison Blanche, Algiers' airport. On November 18, the 48th escorted some C-47s to Constantine, Algeria, while 1st FG pilots flew some area patrols—the P-38's first combat missions in North Africa.

On the night of November 16, 1942, Luftwaffe bombers attacked the airfield at Maison Blanche, near Algiers, and destroyed or damaged seven of the 14th FG's P-38s that had arrived there that day. (*USAF photo*)

The Germans and Italians reacted to the takeover of Algeria by moving more of their forces—including air units—from Italy and Sicily into neighboring Vichy French Tunisia, the Allies' next objective.

The 14th FG flew its first mission over Tunisia on November 19; it was a B-17 escort by the 48th FS from Maison Blanche to El Aouina. The following morning, a detachment of that squadron was dispatched to the desolate landing ground at Tebessa, in eastern Algeria near the Tunisian border. Late that afternoon, six of its pilots strafed the enemy airfield at Gabes, on Tunisia's southeast coast, destroying a Junkers Ju 52 transport on the ground—the first claim for an e/a by a P-38 in the MTO. Unfortunately, they all became lost in the encroaching darkness on the way back to Tebessa and were forced to crash-land their Lightnings in the desert (the pilots were all recovered). It was then determined that this base was inadequate to operate P-38s from.

Two days later, the P-38's first air combat in North Africa took place as the 48th FS was escorting the B-17s to Tunis, the Tunisian capital. Enemy fighters were encountered, and 2Lt. Carl T. Williams, Jr., claimed to have shot down a Bf 109. (Williams would himself be shot down and killed twelve days later.) A squadron mate's P-38 was badly shot up and he crash-landed it back at Maison Blanche. The supposed Bf 109s were actually Macchi MC.202s of the *Regia Aeronautica*'s 155° *Gruppo Caccia* (Fighter Group), none of which were, in fact, lost.

On the morning of the 22nd, two 48th FS pilots shared in shooting down a twin-engined reconnaissance Junkers Ju 88 near Maison Blanche. Both 14th FG squadrons moved to Youks les Bains, a few miles northwest of Tebessa, later that day. Shortly after their arrival, another 48th FS pilot shot down a twin-engined Italian aircraft during a reconnaissance over the front.

Although most of Algeria's desert airfields scarcely deserved that name, Youks was particularly undeserving; it was just a flat, desolate expanse in a valley surrounded by mountains, with absolutely no facilities. All supplies and materiel had to be flown in, and the group's personnel were forced to improvise and scrounge to survive. Also, Youks soon became the target of Axis bombers.

The 24th was the P-38's first big scoring day. That morning, during a strafing mission to Tunisia, some 48th FS pilots spotted a Ju 88 and one of them shot it down. That afternoon, the 49th Squadron flew a fighter sweep to the Axis airfields at Gabes and Sfax. Its pilots claimed to have destroyed twenty-six aircraft on the ground at Gabes by strafing, and then, *en route* to Sfax, just to the north, a three-plane flight spotted nine trimotor transports they identified as Ju 52s but were in fact Italian Savoia Marchetti S.82s. One of the P-38 pilots was on single engine, having lost the other to the AA fire at Gabes, but his squadron mates, 1Lts. James E. Butler and Virgil W. Lusk, waded in, Butler subsequently claiming four and Lusk five destroyed (seven were actually lost). This made Lusk not only the first P-38 ace, but an "ace-in-a-day." He had also destroyed three Ju 87s on the ground at Gabes.

On the 28th, two other 48th FS pilots each shot down a Ju 88 during a reconnaissance of the Gabes area. Later that day, while on another sweep, four P-38 pilots, from both 14th FG squadrons, encountered some actual Ju 52s over Lake Bizerta, near Tunisia's northern coast. The 48th Squadron's 1Lt. Irvin C. Ethell shot down four of the Junkers and a 49th Squadron pilot another before they were attacked by some Bf 109s. Ethell managed to escape after hitting one of them (credited to him as probably destroyed), but the 49th's Jim Butler, who had been so successful four days earlier, was shot down and killed, as was 1Lt. Carl F. Skinner of the 48th FS. They were the 14th FG's first combat casualties.

The following day, the 1st FG scored for the first time, when a mixed formation of pilots from the 48th FS and its 94th FS (which had joined the 14th FG at Youks les Bains the day before) spotted a pair of twin-engined Bf 110 fighters after once again strafing the Gabes airfield. The 48th's Capt. Ralph J. Watson shot one of them down and the other was shared by Capt. Newell O. Roberts and 1Lt. Jack Ilfrey of the 94th.

Portions of all three 1st FG squadrons were based at Maison Blanche by the middle of December.

Another Twelfth AF Lightning unit making the move to North Africa from England was the 3rd Photographic Group, commanded by the president's son, Col. Elliott Roosevelt, whose headquarters arrived at Algiers in mid-December. As with the three P-38 groups, it was assigned to XII ASC. One of its three squadrons was the 15th Photographic Reconnaissance, which was then equipped with B-17s but would convert to F-5s during the coming year. Its two Lightning squadrons at that time were the 5th and 12th PR, both of which had arrived in North Africa in November, the former at Algeria and the latter at Morocco, where it spent three weeks before joining the rest of the group at Algiers.

The 82nd FG was finally deemed ready for service in North Africa in December. Starting on the 16th, its pilots flew their planes from Ireland to Cornwall. One week later, fifty-one of its P-38s took off for Algeria, with a B-26 leading each of the four sub-flights.

As a 95th FS formation approached the middle of the Bay of Biscay at low level, it was attacked by four twin-engined Ju 88 fighters of 14 *Staffel*, *Kampfgeschwader* (Bomber Wing) 40. They immediately shot down a twin-engined Douglas A-20 that was "tagging along" with the formation and then the "tail-end Charlie" P-38. After recovering from his initial shock, the squadron commander and formation leader, Maj. Robert E. Kirtley, led

Ground crewmen and a camera technician of the 3rd Photographic Reconnaissance and Mapping Group handle their assigned duties with one of the unit's F-5s in North Africa. (*USAF photo*)

his flight after the Junkers, which were by then re-entering the cloud layer from which they had emerged before their attack. Years later, he recounted what happened:

> As I came out of the overcast I was dead astern of the Ju 88 and closing fast. At 100 yards I fired one burst—50 rounds per [.50-cal.] gun. His left engine exploded, pieces came off and he leveled out right on top of the overcast. I throttled back and flew formation with the aircraft for a minute or so, having exhausted my ammo. He re-entered the overcast, straight and level, and I followed him down. He hit the sea in a nose-down position and came apart.[1]

The element leader in Kirtley's flight, 2Lt. Arthur V. Brodhead, Jr., also downed one of the Ju 88s, after a long chase, but he then became lost and ended up belly-landing his plane, P-38F-15 43-2098, on a beach in the Irish Free State. He was later allowed to rejoin his unit in North Africa.

There were other casualties. The 96th Squadron's Capt. Buddy A. Strozier made an emergency forced landing in Portugal, damaging his plane, P-38G-5 42-12825, in the process. He was interned there but was later released, and returned to his squadron. Most of the 82nd's pilots landed at Gibraltar, unable to make it to their actual destination, Tafaroui, because of the deteriorating weather. One pilot with engine trouble crashed his P-38 in Spain, just across the border from the British colony. The aircraft was badly damaged and he was injured but later bribed his way into Gibraltar. Another pilot crashed into a mountain in Algeria and was killed.

The 82nd FG flew its first missions in North Africa (two convoy protection patrols) on Christmas Day. It then received the disconcerting news that, due to the 1st and 14th FGs' heavy loss of aircraft, it had to transfer half of its P-38s to those units, its pilots personally flying them to their airfields. On December 28, they delivered twenty-two of them—mostly the latest "G" models—to the 14th FG at Youks les Bains.

The 14th lost its top-scoring pilot two days later, when 1Lt. Virgil H. Smith was killed in a fight with some Bf 109s of III *Gruppe* of *Jagdgeschwader* (Fighter Wing) 53 (III./JG 53) near Gabes. Smith had scored his first victory on November 28, when he shot down a Ju 88. He became an ace when he destroyed an Fw 190 on December 12 for his fifth victory and had added another Bf 109 to his score on the 28th.

The 82nd FG moved up to the front on New Year's Day—specifically, to the airfield at Telergma, in northeastern Algeria. Most of the 1st FG had moved to Biskra, a popular prewar oasis resort southeast of Algiers, on December 14; the 27th and 71st Squadron detachments at Maison Blanche joined it there a week later. By January 9, 1943, the 14th FG had transferred from Youks les Bains north to Berteaux, which was a few miles east of Telergma, the 48th FS being the first to move there, on the 5th. On January 22, the 71st FS moved to Ain M'Lilla, near Constantine.

All three P-38 groups were scoring steadily, but at a considerable cost in aircraft and pilots. Their combat inexperienced pilots had been tossed into the fray against some extremely experienced Luftwaffe pilots, requiring a steep learning curve on their part if they were to survive and succeed—which some did not. The survivors gradually gained the necessary experience and learned how to utilize the Lightning's strong points (speed, maneuverability, and firepower) to their advantage and minimize its problematic aspects—most especially by avoiding steep dives, either on or away from e/a. In the early days of the Tunisian campaign, they were frequently outnumbered and complained that the Bf 109s always seemed to be attacking them from above, which put them at a distinct tactical disadvantage.

By mid-January, the 14th FG was in poor shape, partly because it had just two squadrons so could put up fewer aircraft for missions, but also because of some apparent bad luck. Although it had scored a respectable number of victories and done its job satisfactorily, the 14th's losses had been particularly heavy. By January 23, thirteen of its pilots had been killed, five were POWs, and eight had been wounded or injured badly enough to have been unable to continue operational flying. The 48th FS's mission that day broke the proverbial straw. Its pilots were ambushed—once again from above—by Bf 109s of II./JG 51 while strafing Axis road traffic near Medinine, Tunisia. Five of them were shot down and killed and another was forced to crash-land his badly damaged Lightning. Only one of the Messerschmitts was claimed in return.

The 14th now had so few experienced pilots and aircraft, and morale was so low, that it was decided at XII ASC H.Q. to relieve it temporarily so it could be reorganized. It flew the last mission of its initial combat tour on January 28, during which it scored its sixty-first confirmed air victory and suffered its final loss, a 49th FS pilot who had to bail out of his burning P-38 and became a POW. Its surviving original pilots were then sent home, and its replacement pilots and its few remaining P-38s were transferred to the 82nd FG. Its CO, Lt. Col. Troy Keith, led the group's non-flying personnel to Mediouna in Morocco to begin its rebuilding process.

In mid-February, there was a major reorganization of the Allied air forces in the MTO. The Twelfth AF became a subsidiary of the new Northwest African Air Force (NAAF), which included American, British, and Free French units, and its bomb wings became part of NAAF's Northwest African Strategic Air Force (NASAF), commanded by Maj. Gen. Doolittle, previously CO of the Twelfth AF. The Twelfth's P-38 groups were now assigned to the bomb wings whose aircraft they escorted—the 1st (and later the 14th) to the 5th BW (B-17s) and the 82nd to the 47th BW (twin-engined B-25s and B-26s). Also in the middle of that month, the 1st FG moved from Biskra northeast to Chateaudun du Rhumel, near Constantine. It was joined there by the 71st FS from nearby Ain M'Lilla.

It was also in February that the Twelfth AF's bombers began attacking strategic targets in Sardinia and Sicily, often escorted by P-38s, and the following month Axis shipping became a primary target of NAAF. All three P-38 groups soon became proficient in both dive- and skip-bombing. The 82nd FG's pilots became particularly adept at skip-bombing ships, as they not only escorted the B-25s and B-26s on their anti-shipping missions but joined in the attacks.

Due to continued attrition and insufficient replacements, by February the Twelfth's P-38 groups were once again short of aircraft and pilots. Thus, the decision was made to transfer all the junior pilots and P-38s of the 78th FG of the Eighth AF in England to the Twelfth AF at the end of the month, before the 78th had even entered combat.

In March, the 16th Reconnaissance Squadron, which had been in North Africa since November, became a training unit for replacement fighter pilots arriving in North Africa, operating in that capacity P-38s, P-39s, P-40s, and Reverse Lend-Lease Spitfires—as part of

Above left: Second Lieutenant William J. "Dixie" Sloan, one of the 82nd FG's original staff sergeant pilots, poses with P-38F-15 43-2064 shortly after scoring his third and fourth victories with it on February 2, 1943. He scored number five thirteen days later to became the group's first ace, and five months later, with twelve victories, he would be the MTO's highest-scoring P-38 pilot. (*USAF photo*)

Above right: P-38G-10 42-12942 was initially assigned to the 78th FG in England but was transferred to the 1st FG in North Africa in February 1943. Although maintained by its 27th FS—and squadron coded HV-A—it was flown by the group's executive officer, Lt. Col. John Weltman. When Weltman became the 82nd FG's new CO in May, he took 42-12942 with him. According to the official photo caption, the ground crewmen are "bouncing up and down on the tail of plane to get compass set at right angle for swinging the compass." (*USAF photo*)

Below: Six 97th FS pilots in the early days in North Africa. Fourth from the left is 2Lt. Thomas Ace (his actual middle name) White, who was, in fact, a six-victory ace. The pilot on the far right is 2Lt. Lloyd E. Atteberry, who had scored four victories by the time he was killed in action on March 22, 1943. (*Author's collection*)

the Fighter Training Center (FTC) at Berrechid, near Casablanca. Six months later, it was transformed into a radar detection and countermeasures squadron and re-equipped with B-17s. Its former function had by then been taken over by the 2nd Fighter Training Squadron.

By the end of March, the Allies' anti-shipping campaign was keeping desperately needed supplies and reinforcements from reaching the Axis forces in Tunisia. Thus, the Germans and Italians began relying on large formations of transport aircraft based in Italy and Sicily to get the job done, with disastrous results.

Effective April 5, NAAF commenced an operation, codenamed Flax, that was designed to counter that effort—including the institution of standing fighter patrols to intercept the transports. From that date through to April 18, many of them were intercepted by Allied fighters as they approached Tunis, and dozens were shot down. The 1st and 82nd FGs (the latter having moved from Telergma to Berteaux at the end of March) were involved in these actions, very successfully, on three different days.

The first of these interceptions was actually by chance. Around 8 a.m. on the 5th, pilots of both the 1st and 82nd FGs were escorting B-25s on sea sweeps north of the Cap Bon Peninsula on Tunisia's northeast coast when thirty-plus Ju 52s escorted by fighters were seen heading for Tunis. The 1st FG spotted and attacked them first and the 82nd joined in a few minutes later. When this melee was finally over, the Lightning pilots claimed twenty Ju 52s destroyed plus fourteen of the escort. Three 1st FG pilots and one from the 82nd were each credited with triple victories.

This action was by no means one-sided, as six of the P-38 pilots were also shot down, including 1Lt. Claude R. Kinsey, Jr., of the 96th FS. He had downed two of the Ju 52s—his sixth and seventh victories, which made him the top-scoring P-38 pilot in North Africa— before *he* was shot down, by a Bf 109. He bailed out, badly injured, and was taken prisoner. (Kinsey later managed to escape from a POW camp in Italy.)

There were two interceptions of Axis transports by P-38s on April 10. Early that morning, during a Flax patrol north of Cap Bon, some 1st FG pilots encountered a large group of "Ju 52s" (actually Italian S.82s) and claimed to have destroyed twenty of them, plus eight of their fighter escort, without loss. The 71st FS's 2Lt. Walter J. Rivers, Jr., was credited with two transports and two fighters destroyed, plus another transport damaged.

Shortly after noon, it was the 82nd FG's turn. While once again escorting some Mitchells on a sea sweep, about thirty actual Ju 52s, with the usual escort, were spotted. This time ten of the transports were claimed destroyed, plus three other aircraft, for the loss of one P-38 and its pilot.

The final aerial slaughters of the enemy transports by P-38s both took place the very next day, during two Flax sweeps. The first one, by the 95th FS, took place around 8 a.m., when twenty Ju 52s with heavy fighter escort were encountered. All the transports were claimed to have been shot down plus seven of the fighters (two pilots each scoring a triple), while three of the P-38 pilots were missing in action and another crash-landed his Lightning due to battle damage.

A couple of hours later the 96th FS flew a similar mission and also met some Ju 52s— twenty-five to thirty of them—and their escort. However, only one flight was able to engage them, and it destroyed five. The flight leader, 1Lt. William B. Rawson, who scored his fourth victory in this action, was killed, while another pilot crash-landed his damaged P-38 on his return to Berteaux.

Above: April 9, 1943: A wrecked P-38 in the "salvage dump" at the Mediouna Airport near Casablanca. (*USAF photo*)

Below left: These 27th FS pilots (from the left), 1Lt. George L. Ross, 1Lt. George A. Rush, and 2Lt. Samuel F. Sweet, are describing how they each shot down an Italian Macchi 200 fighter over the Strait of Sicily near Cape Bon on April 10, 1943. (*USAF photo*)

Below right: These four 71st FS pilots were all very successful in the 1st FG's action over the Mediterranean on April 10, 1943, being credited with a total of fourteen e/a. *From left to right*: 2Lt. Walter J. Rivers (two Ju 52s and two Mc 200s destroyed plus another Ju 52 damaged); 1Lt. John L. Moutier (two Ju 52s and an Mc 200 destroyed and a Ju 52 damaged); 1Lt. Meldrum L. Sears (four Ju 52s destroyed); and 2Lt. Lee V. Wiseman (two Ju 52s and an Mc 200 destroyed). (*USAF photo*)

Ground crewmen of the 82nd FG working on some of the unit's Lightnings in North Africa. The one with the missing engine is the 95th Squadron's AP, P-38G-10 42-13036. "A" was the code letter for the 95th FS, "B" for the 96th FS, and "C" for the 97th FS. (*USAF photo*)

Tunisian Climax

In late March, the British Eighth Army, having moved into southern Tunisia from Libya, broke through the Germans' Mareth Line, just south of Gabes, and began to fight its way up Tunisia's coast, as American ground units continued to move eastward from Algeria. During April, they gradually pushed the Axis forces into the country's northeast corner, capturing Tunis in early May and then pinning them onto the Cap Bon Peninsula, with their backs to the sea.

The reorganized and re-equipped 14th FG was now ready to re-enter the fray and its ground echelons began the move from Morocco to its new Algerian base, Telergma, on April 27. The air echelons arrived there on May 5. The group had a new squadron, the 37th, which had been assigned to it on March 1. It was previously part of the 55th FG in Washington State. Its CO, Maj. John G. Bright, was a very experienced fighter pilot, having served previously in China, first with the American Volunteer Group, better known as the "Flying Tigers," and then, as a newly commissioned Army Air Forces officer, with its successor, the 23rd FG. He was an ace with five confirmed kills and three probables to his credit.

Since the group's other two squadrons, the 48th and 49th, were devoid of combat experienced pilots and leaders, ten 1st FG veterans, who had either completed their combat tours or were about to do so, volunteered to transfer to the "new" 14th temporarily to provide that experience. (A combat tour for P-38 pilots in the MTO had originally been 200 operational hours but had been changed to fifty missions around February 1.) Their new pilots had come from the 78th FG and the FTC at Berrechid. The 14th FG flew the first mission of its second tour, an escort for some B-25s on a sea sweep, and made its first new claim for an e/a (a damaged Fw 190) on May 6.

April 13, 1943: A P-38 being unloaded from the deck of a freighter at Oran, Algeria. (*USAF photo*)

Armorers loading the guns of *BABE*, a 48th FS P-38, at Telergma in May 1943. (*USAF photo*)

An outdoor briefing of 49th FS pilots at Telergma, Algeria. The pilots are synchronizing their watches. (*USAF photo*)

The Tunisian campaign ended with the surrender of the remaining quarter of a million Axis troops there on May 13. Despite arriving in theater later than most of the others, the 82nd was then the top-scoring USAAF fighter group in North Africa, with 202 confirmed kills. It had flown 152 missions and lost sixty-four of its P-38s. The 1st FG had racked up 144 aerial victories, and the 14th had already added five to its previous score, for a total of sixty-six.

By this time, some P-38 pilots were providing a special service to XII BC: weather reconnaissance. One or two Lightnings would fly over the command's targets in Sardinia, Sicily, or southern Italy to check and report back on the weather prior to its missions. Later in the year, a special P-38 flight would be formed solely for that purpose.

Also, sometime in mid-1943, four F-5A-1s were transferred to the USN in North Africa, redesignated FO-1s and given the USN bureau numbers 01209, 01210, 01211, and 01212. No information has come to light regarding how these aircraft were utilized by the navy.

The 14th FG's dive bombing debut took place on May 24, when its pilots attacked targets in Sardinia. Capt. Herbert E. Ross, who later became a seven-victory ace and CO of the 48th FS, dropped his bomb on a large merchant ship in the harbor at Carloforte, scoring a direct hit and causing it to explode. Recon photos taken the following day showed it to be beached and still burning. Ross was awarded a DFC for this feat.

Above: Capt. Ernest K. "Hawk" Osher, CO of the 95th FS, and the ground crew of his assigned P-38, F-15 43-2112, named *THE SAD SACK* after the popular cartoon character. Osher had recently scored his fifth—and *THE SAD SACK*'s eleventh—victory, on May 11, 1943. This was one of the 82nd FG Lightnings flown to Algeria from England in December 1942. When this photo was taken it had flown eighty-six missions. By the time it flew its 183rd and last mission, on May 29, 1944— during which it was badly damaged by AA fire over Yugoslavia and was scrapped as a result—its pilots had scored five more kills. (*USAF photo*)

Below left: Five 49th FS pilots check out the squadron's scoreboard from its first tour. They would go on to score a total of twenty-two confirmed victories of their own. *From left to right:* Anthony Evans (four), Wayne M. Manlove (four), Lloyd K. DeMoss (four), Marlow J. Leikness (five), and Carroll S. Knott (five). The P-38G-15 in the background is DeMoss's *Bad Penny/The Gentleman*, with which he is known to have scored at least two of his kills, a pair of Bf 109s over and near the Millis A/D in Sardinia on June 28, 1943. (USAF photo)

Below right: These four 27th FS pilots shot down eight enemy fighters in a dogfight over Sicily on May 25, 1943. *From left to right:* 1Lt. John A. MacKay (two Bf 109s, his fourth and fifth victories), 2Lt. Samuel F. Sweet (two Bf 109s), 2Lt. Warren A. Holden (two Fw 190s), and 2Lt. Frank J. McIntosh (two Bf 109s). The colorful P-38 in the background is MacKay's G-15, 43-2308. MacKay flew a second P-38 tour with the 474th FG in Europe the following year, during which he was shot down and evaded capture with the help of the French underground. (*USAF photo*)

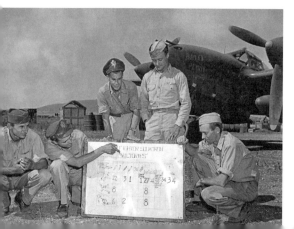

Sicily

Once all of North Africa was under the Allies' control their focus turned to Sicily, which was the gateway to their primary objective, mainland Italy, which Winston Churchill (erroneously, as it turned out) referred to as the "soft underbelly" of Axis Europe. But before they could invade Sicily, they had to deal with two much smaller Italian islands, Pantelleria and Lampedusa. The former was a particular threat, as it not only had a large airfield, with two nearly impenetrable hangars built into the side of a small mountain, but it lay directly between Tunisia and Sicily.

Pantelleria had been subjected to increased air attacks since early May, but they were greatly intensified in June. The three P-38 groups were heavily involved in this brief campaign, as both escorts to Twelfth AF bombers and in the fighter-bomber role. One highly publicized early success took place on May 8, when Lt. Col. Ernest C. Young, deputy CO of the 82nd FG, managed to skip a 1,000-lb. bomb into one of the hangars, doing considerable damage inside.

The 1st FG was involved in the P-38's most successful air combat over Pantelleria, on June 9, when a dozen pilots from its 27th and 94th Squadrons dive-bombed a gun position on the island. Some Bf 109s intervened, of which five were subsequently credited as destroyed, two as probably destroyed and two more as damaged. Three of the confirmed kills were scored by one pilot, the 27th's 1Lt. Daniel Kennedy, who later described what happened:

> I was leading the last flight of planes and we were waiting for the formation in front of us to peel off into their dives. Most of them had started down when I noticed two 109s moving in on the flight in front of mine. I succeeded in cutting in between them and forcing [one] to veer to one side and climb. I went up with him and had him in my sights all the way. Just as he burst into flames, my plane stalled and dropped away. Imagine my surprise when after I leveled off I found myself flying fifth in a formation of 109s. Before they knew what dropped in on them I had picked off the first one. I immediately went to work on the second and got him with a lucky shot that finished him before he could bring his guns around. I damaged the third and my wingman bagged the fourth.[2]

These victories brought Kennedy's total to five, making him an ace and earning him a DFC. Pantelleria surrendered on June 11 and nearby Lampedusa the following day, before any Allied troops set foot on them.

Another interesting development in June was the formation of a new P-38 squadron in North Africa, for service with the Fourteenth AF in China. It did not receive a numerical designation initially and was referred to as "Squadron X." Some of its pilots were new replacements direct from the FTC and others (also its ground crewmen) were volunteers from the Twelfth AF's three P-38 groups. Its first CO was Maj. Bob Kirtley, formerly CO of the 95th FS and then the senior P-38 instructor at the FTC. Kirtley relinquished command of Squadron X to Capt. Sam L. Palmer, previously a flight commander with the 37th FS, before it left for China in early July; he then completed his combat tour with the 1st FG.

As of April, there was another new Lightning unit in Algeria, although it was not American but rather belonged to the Free French *Armée de l'Air*. That month, its *Groupe*

Above left: Pilots of the 96th FS relaxing with coffee and donuts at their airfield, Berteaux, Algeria, after returning from a mission in late May 1943. (*USAF photo*)

Above right: May 31, 1943: A 96th FS ground crew maintaining their plane. (*USAF photo*)

In this publicity photo the 27th FS's 1Lt. Daniel Kennedy paints a swastika on his P-38 *The BEANTOWN*, named after Boston, his hometown. The last three are for the Bf 109s he shot down over Pantelleria on June 9, 1943. (*USAF photo*)

de Reconnaissance 33's II *Escadrille* (GR II/33) was provided with six F-4s for transitional training. (A French *groupe* was equivalent to a USAAF squadron and an *escadrille* to a flight.) In May, it received some F-5As, as well as a distinguished pilot, forty-three-year-old *Capitaine* Antoine de Saint-Exupéry, the famous writer, who had served with the unit during the German invasion of France in 1940 but had since been in exile in the U.S. The *escadrille* became operational with its new Lightnings in June and then moved to La Marsa, Tunisia, where it was attached to the recently redesignated 3rd Photographic Reconnaissance and Mapping Group.

The 14th FG moved to El Bathan, 20 miles west of Tunis, on June 3, the 82nd moved from Berteaux to Souk el Arba, in Tunisia just east of the Algerian border, ten days later and the 1st FG from Chateaudun du Rhumel to Mateur, also outside Tunis, effective June 29.

The Allied invasion of Sicily, codenamed Operation Husky, was scheduled for July 10. To reduce enemy aerial opposition to it, on July 2, NAAF commenced attacks on airfields in Sicily and Sardinia and on the Italian mainland. The three P-38 groups were heavily involved in this campaign, as was the 3rd PRMG, whose F-5 pilots provided vital pre-invasion photos for planning and intelligence purposes.

From July 4 to 6, while escorting the bombers to the complex of airfields at Gerbini, Sicily, P-38 pilots claimed a number of enemy fighters. The 82nd Group's 97th Squadron shot down three and damaged seven of them on the 4th. Two hours later, its 95th Squadron claimed three Macchi 202s destroyed, one probably destroyed, and one damaged. The following day pilots of the 96th and 97th Squadrons were credited with five more destroyed. The 1st FG was involved in another action over Gerbini on the 6th but was credited with only three probables and four damaged. Two 82nd FG P-38s and their pilots were lost on these missions.

F-5A-10 42-13109 of the 5th Photographic Squadron (Light) taking off from its Algerian base for another mission. It was lost in action on June 26, 1943, by which time the squadron was operating from La Marsa, Tunisia. (*USAF photo*)

Above: June 20, 1943: These 94th FS pilots have just returned from a B-26 escort to Sicily, during which they shot down seven Bf 109s. *From left to right:* 2Lt. Harold C. "Cliff" Lentz downed three; 1Lt. Leonard P. Stephan downed two; and 2Lt. Howard A. Gilliam downed two. (*USAF photo*)

Below: The 27th FS's 1Lt. Herbert W. McQuown also participated in the June 20 mission, with less positive results, as his P-38 was badly shot up by a Bf 109. Besides the damage to its tail, another shell entered the cockpit, ricocheted off the instrument panel, and wounded him in the leg. (*USAF photo*)

These 96th FS pilots were credited with a total of 16-2-6 e/a over Sardinia on June 18, 1943. The P-38 named *SPUD* in front of which they are posing was assigned to 1Lt. Joseph W. Jorda, who scored a probable on that mission to give him his final total of 4-2-1. (Unfortunately, he is not identified in the caption.) (*USAF photo*)

Pilots of the 27th FS getting ready to fly a mission from their North African base in mid-1943. Walking in front of the jeep in his flight gear is the squadron commander, Capt. James E. Pate. (*USAF photo*)

The 1st FG's experience on July 6 was not unusual. The P-38 pilots' many damaged and probably destroyed credits were symptomatic of a persistent problem: the difficulty of obtaining confirmation of their aerial victories. One factor in their dilemma was the P-38's nonexistent or inadequate gun cameras, normally an important tool in that endeavor. Harry C. Crim, Jr., a 37th FS pilot, remembered later:

> In Africa the whole 37th Squadron started with just four gun cameras. The ground temperature was so high that film melted, so from these four cameras I saw only about ten feet of developed footage. To claim a victory, you had to knock off a major piece of a plane (like a wing or the whole tail), set it on fire or see it crash. You also had to have a confirming witness. With no gun camera film, the only witness was a member of your flight.[3]

The main problem with the gun camera, even when its film did not melt, was that it was positioned in the nose, near the guns. When the four .50-cal. machine guns and the 20-mm cannon were fired, they caused the camera to vibrate severely, resulting in poor quality film that was frequently not sufficiently clear to confirm a victory. It would be another year before this problem was solved.

Operation Husky—the largest amphibious landings in history to date, supported by airborne troops—commenced on the early morning of July 10, and P-38s were covering it. That morning, after dropping 1,000-lb. bombs on rail targets, 49th FS pilots encountered some Bf 109s and shot down five of them, while losing one of their own. The 96th FS was providing cover for the landing forces late that afternoon when its pilots spotted enemy fighters taking off from the Castelvetrano and Carcittela A/Ds and immediately attacked them. They were subsequently credited with destroying ten, probably destroying two, and damaging eight during a twenty-minute air battle.

The three P-38 groups continued to support the invasion, including by giving direct support to the ground forces in their fighter-bomber role. The biggest single score in the air by Lightning pilots during the Sicilian campaign took place on July 18 and involved pilots of the 37th and 48th FSs. They were returning from an escort to an air–sea rescue aircraft that had picked up a downed B-17 crew from the sea near Naples when they spotted fifteen Ju 52s near Sicily's north coast, flying right underneath them. They were obviously delivering supplies and/or reinforcements to the island from the Italian mainland. The P-38 pilots waded into the transports and destroyed all of them, the 37th Squadron's 2Lt. Lloyd O. Hendrix claiming four.

The Twelfth AF received many replacement fighter pilots during the late spring and summer of 1943. One of them was 2Lt. Jules J. Hymel, who arrived in North Africa in July and was assigned to the FTC at Berrechid for operational training. He later recalled: "On July 25 I got some cockpit time in the P-38 airplane for the first time. On July 30 I signed up to fly the P-38. I had a choice of P-39, P-40, P-38 and the British Spitfire. On August 14 I again was asked to make a decision and I again signed up for the P-38." After the completion of his training, Hymel was assigned to the 82nd FG and its 95th Squadron.

Two other units that flew P-38s in the MTO briefly were the 81st and 350th FGs, which, in the summer of 1943, were part of the Northwest African Coastal Air Force, defending Allied ports and convoys from enemy air attack. Unfortunately, their P-39s were not quite

Above: July 10, 1943: These 96th FS pilots have just scored a total of nine kills over Sicily. *From left to right*: 1Lt. "Dixie" Sloan (an Mc 200), Flt. Off. Frank D. Hurlbut (three Fw 190s), 1Lt. Edward T. Waters (a Bf 109), 2Lt. Lawrence P. Liebers (an Fw 190), 2Lt. Lincoln D. Jones (an Fw 190), and 2Lt. Ward A. Kuentzel (a Ju 88 and an Fw 190). All but the nineteen-year-old Jones were aces. (*USAF photo*)

Right: Flt. Off. Jack Homan of the 48th FS and his P-38 *SORTA PISTOF*. The victory symbols on its nose indicate: "B." for bomber— an SM 79 he shot down on May 14, 1943; "F." for fighter—a Bf 109 he destroyed on July 23; and "T.T." for transports—the two Ju 52s he claimed in the 14th FG's aerial massacre near Sicily on July 18. (*USAF photo*)

up to that task, so in May each of their squadrons received two P-38s. Although the 81st FG did not score with them, from mid-June to early September the 350th's pilots shot down ten e/a and probably destroyed one more with their Lightnings.

By the end of July, the success of the Sicilian campaign was a foregone conclusion, and the USAAF had commenced almost daily bombings of targets on the Italian mainland, often with P-38 escort. The latter was possible because of the newly captured airfields in Sicily, where the Lightning pilots could refuel—and because they were no longer required for the tactical missions they had been flying there.

On July 25, the 14th FG moved again, this time the short distance from Bathan to Ste. Marie du Zit, southeast of Tunis.

A strange and disturbing incident took place on August 11. Some B-17s of the 301st Bomb Group were approaching the coast of Italy just south of Rome when they were attacked by a P-38 that was accompanied by an Italian Macchi MC.205 fighter. The Lightning targeted several aircraft of the group's 419th Bomb Squadron, one of which peeled off, went into a spin, and crashed into the sea. This P-38G had supposedly been captured when its pilot, who was lost and running out of fuel, landed at Capoterra Airfield on Sardinia on June 12. If so, its pilot was likely on a ferry flight. It was subsequently flown to the *Regia Aeronautica*'s Test and Research Center at Guidonia, near Rome. The pilot who used it to shoot down the B-17 was *Colonello* Angelo Tondi, the center's commander. This was the "renegade" Lightning's first and only combat mission with the *Regia Aeronautica*; the highly corrosive Italian aviation gas had reportedly ruined its fuel tanks and it never flew again.

The Axis finally conceded Sicily to the Allies on August 17, and their remaining forces there were withdrawn to the mainland across the Strait of Messina. The P-38 groups had

This 37th FS P-38 returned to its base at Ste.-Marie-du-Zit, Tunisia, in late 1943 with a bullet hole in its windshield. (*Author's collection*)

Above left: The 95th FS's 1Lt. William J. Schildt and his P-38G-15 43-2406, named *CAT SASS* and coded AX, in July 1943, shortly before he completed his combat tour. He was an ace, having been credited with six confirmed kills and two probables. (*Author's collection*)

Above right: Seven-victory 96th FS ace Lt. Ward A. Kuentzel chats with his P-38's armorer, Cpl. Howard Shaffner. Kuentzel's final score was over Italy on July 22—a Bf 109 destroyed plus another damaged. (*USAF photo*)

contributed materially to the success of that campaign. Among other things, their pilots had been credited with shooting down sixty-eight e/a from July 10 to August 17—forty-three by the 14th FG, sixteen by the 82nd, and nine by the 1st—and probably destroying or damaging dozens more. Twenty-four of them were missing in action during that period, fourteen from the 1st FG, nine from the 14th and just one from the 82nd.

The Not So Soft Under Belly

The aerial campaign against the Axis forces in Italy, a preliminary to the upcoming Allied landings there, was now greatly expanded. Three of its missions resulted in DUCs for two of the P-38 groups.

The first of those missions was on August 25, when more than 150 Lightnings from all three groups formed up over the Mediterranean Sea off the Tunisian coast, then flew at wave-top level past Sicily, across the Italian mainland and up that country's east coast to the large complex of airfields in the Foggia Plain, where they proceeded to strafe aircraft and facilities. An estimated sixty-four e/a that could have interfered with the Allied invasion of southern Italy were destroyed, and eighty-six more were damaged. Both the 1st and the 82nd (which had moved from Souk el Arba to Grombalia, near Tunis, earlier that month) were awarded a DUC. Only two dozen of the 14th FG's P-38s participated in the strafing; the rest of them escorted some B-17s on an immediate follow-up bombing of the airfields.

There was then a series of air raids on targets in the Naples area, many of them aggressively opposed by Axis fighters. On August 30, the 1st FG escorted two B-26 groups to the marshalling yards at Aversa. As they approached the target, an estimated seventy-five Bf 109s appeared above the American formation, whereupon the P-38 pilots dropped their belly tanks and broke into them. A huge dogfight ensued, during which thirteen of the Lightnings were shot down, against credits for ten of the enemy destroyed, four probably destroyed and five damaged. Amazingly, and most importantly, not a single B-26 was lost, thereby earning the 1st FG its second DUC.

Three days later, on September 2, it was the 82nd Group's turn to escort the bombers, this time seventy-five B-25s, to the Cancello marshalling yards. They were intercepted by around sixty Bf 109s from the same units (elements of the Luftwaffe's JG 3, JG 53, and JG 77) that had engaged the 1st FG on August 30. As the Mitchells made their escape to the west over the Bay of Naples after the bombing, the P-38 pilots positioned themselves between them and the enemy fighters, precipitating another massive, low-level dogfight. The result this time was ten of the Lightnings failing to return, against credits totaling 23-5-8 Bf 109s, plus one more claimed by the B-25 gunners. Once again, no bombers were lost, and the 82nd FG was awarded its second DUC.

The following day, the British Eighth Army made the first Allied landings on the Italian mainland, at Reggio di Calabria, just across the narrow Strait of Messina from Sicily. On September 8, an armistice the Italian government had signed five days earlier went into effect. However, Italian fascists in the north continued to fight alongside the Germans until the end of the war. They even established their own air force, the *Aeronautica Nazionale Repubblicana* (ANR), units of which P-38 pilots would encounter on numerous occasions.

On September 9, the U.S. Fifth Army landed at Salerno, just south of Naples—Operation Avalanche. The invasion fleet and troops were covered by the three P-38 groups, whose air echelons were operating temporarily from airfields in Sicily. (After their mission on September 6, the 1st FG's pilots landed at Dittaino, in eastern Sicily, from where they would cover the Salerno invasion for the next twelve days.) The 37th FS's Harry Crim remembered: "We did convoy and beach patrol using 1,000-lb GP bombs and belly tanks. We were under control of a Navy ship just offshore for defense, and with forward units for ground work. Flying from Sicily, we could stay in the area for two or three hours if we didn't run out of ammunition."

To help prevent attacks on the invasion forces from the air, the 14th and 82nd FGs strafed the Foggia airfields again on September 18 from their bases in Sicily, claiming to have destroyed twenty-seven e/a on the ground and one in the air and damaging many more. Two weeks later, they were captured by Eighth Army units, and on October 1, the Fifth Army took Naples.

Above left: Another 96th FS ace, Lt. Larry Liebers, interacts with his crew chief, T/Sgt. Roswell Harding, while below them the assistant crew chief, Sgt. Leroy Garman, and the armorer, Cpl. Wendell Stoltz, are hard at work. By the time he completed his tour at the end of August 1943, Liebers had been credited with seven confirmed kills plus five e/a as damaged. (*USAF photo*)

Above right: Then-Lt. James J. Hagenback of the 94th FS and the colorfully painted P-38 he flew in mid-1943. He joined the squadron in March of that year and commanded it from September until the following January. (*USAF photo*)

Below: F-5A-10 42-13071 of the 12th Photographic Squadron (Light), which was lost in action over Italy on November 11, 1943. (*USAF photo*)

Above left: La Marsa, Tunisia: Maj. Leon W. Gray, Operations Officer of the 3rd PRG, poses with his F-5, on which are displayed thirty-seven photo mission symbols. (*USAF photo*)

Above right: Maj. Gray assumed command of the 5th PRG at La Marsa, Tunisia, on October 23, 1943. The group moved to San Severo, Italy, in early December and Gray was promoted to lieutenant colonel. He is here examining the tail of F-5A-10 42-13123, which he had been flying when it was hit by a 20-mm shell. This venerable Lightning was lost on September 11, 1944 when another pilot ditched it in the Adriatic Sea off the coast of Greece. (*USAF photo*)

After having trained in Colorado for a year, the 5th PRG moved to North Africa in August and began operating from La Marsa the following month. Its only squadron at that time was the 23rd Photographic (Light), which had arrived in July and was attached temporarily to the 3rd PRMG. The 15th PS, now re-equipped with F-5s, would be transferred to the 5th from the 3rd Group in November.

The Germans' situation in Sardinia became untenable after the invasion of southern Italy and the Italian government's armistice with the Allies. On September 11, they evacuated their forces there to Corsica, which the Allies captured on October 4, and the airfields on both islands were soon being utilized by their air units. These included the 1st FG, a ground echelon of which moved to Monserrato, Sardinia, at the end of October. Its air echelon moved first to Djedeida, Tunisia, on November 6, and then to Monserrato on the 29th for a very brief stay. Also moving to Sardinia (Alghero) from San Severo, Italy, in early February 1944 was the 23rd PRS and the attached French GR II/33. A detachment of the 12th PRS from La Marsa operated from Ajaccio, Corsica, from October 18 to November 26.

In early October, the 1st and 14th FGs received a unique assignment. A Royal Navy fleet was about to conduct a special operation in the Aegean Sea near Turkey—evacuating British forces from the Dodecanese Islands after the Germans had invaded one of them. The fleet needed fighter cover to protect it from attacks by German aircraft, and the P-38 was the only Allied fighter with both the range and performance to handle that task.

On October 5, detachments of the two P-38 groups arrived at Gambut in Libya, from which they would fly their patrol missions over the British ships. One squadron would relieve another, so there would always be fighter cover present—or at least that was the plan.

They encountered e/a just once, on October 9, but it was major. Unfortunately, there was a gap in the coverage that morning between the time a 1st FG squadron departed and a 14th FG squadron (the 37th) relieved it. During this brief interval, twenty-six Junkers Ju 87 dive bombers of *Stukageschwader* 3's I *Gruppe* (I./StG 3) from the island of Rhodes attacked the British ships, sinking one and badly damaging another.

The arrival of the 37th FS a short time later coincided with another attack, by StG 3's II *Gruppe*—likewise unescorted by fighters—and an aerial massacre ensued. The P-38 pilots were credited with shooting down seventeen of the Ju 87s (plus an accompanying Ju 88), probably destroying two, and damaging three. The squadron CO, thirty-year-old Maj. William L. Leverette, was credited with seven of the confirmed victories, the biggest single-action score by any P-38 pilot. These were Leverette's first aerial claims (for which he was awarded a DSC); he later scored four more confirmed kills.

By October 15, the two groups were back at their Tunisian bases.

Strategic Lightnings

The 82nd FG was the first Lightning unit to transfer to southern Italy—San Pancrazio briefly by October 3 and then to Lecce a week later. On the 24th, it flew its first long-range, high-altitude heavy bomber escort, to Wiener Neustadt, Austria. Effective November 1, all three P-38 groups became part of the new, strategic Fifteenth AF, commanded by Gen. Doolittle—as did a P-47 group and the Twelfth AF's B-17 and B-24 groups, which, based in Italy, could now reach Axis targets throughout Southern and Eastern Europe, with fighter escort.

While at San Pancrazio, the 82nd FG flew its first three missions to Greece on October 4, 5, and 6—two B-25 escorts (on which no e/a were encountered and one of its pilots was lost) and then a strafe of the airfield at Araxos, during which it claimed to have destroyed seven e/a. The 14th FG had flown its first mission to Yugoslavia on September 27 from Ste. Marie du Zit, refueling in Sicily. All three P-38 groups would fly many more missions to the Balkans (Greece and Yugoslavia), until they were finally free of Axis control more than a year later.

At the time the Fifteenth AF was activated there was another reorganization of the Allied air forces in the MTO. The new Mediterranean Allied Air Force (MAAF) was comprised of the Mediterranean Allied Strategic Air Force (MASAF), of which the Fifteenth became a part, and the Mediterranean Allied Tactical Air Force (MASTAF), which included the Twelfth AF.

Even after transferring to the Fifteenth AF the P-38 groups escorted the Twelfth's medium bombers on occasion. For example, on November 14, the 82nd FG accompanied some B-25s to Sofia, Bulgaria—the first USAAF raid on that Axis country. They were intercepted by Royal Bulgarian Air Force (*Vazdushni Vojski*) Bf 109s, and the P-38 pilots claimed to have shot down five of them and to have probably destroyed or damaged another five, for the loss of one Lightning and its pilot.

As of the end of 1943, the 1st FG had lost 113 pilots killed, captured, or missing. Seven more had been MIA but evaded capture and returned to Allied control, six were killed in accidents and sixteen were wounded or injured so badly they could no longer fly combat missions.

On their long-range bomber escort missions with the Fifteenth AF, the P-38 pilots would be fighting Luftwaffe pilots over Germany and Austria and the occupied countries in Southern and Eastern Europe, as well as Axis Italian (ANR), Bulgarian, Croatian, Hungarian, Romanian, and Slovakian pilots.

There would be five more major Fifteenth AF raids on Sofia by the end of March 1944, all of them escorted by P-38s. On December 10, the 82nd FG was credited with nine kills there for the loss of one of its pilots. Ten days later, it claimed three victories against three losses. On January 10, the 14th FG was credited with nine victories and lost one P-38, and two weeks later, the 82nd scored two more kills (against two losses) and the 1st FG one. On March 30, all three P-38 groups claimed enemy fighters over Sofia: the 1st FG seven, the 82nd five, and the 14th one (for one loss).

After their capture, the Foggia airfields were immediately readied for occupation by units of the Fifteenth AF. The first P-38 group to move there was the 14th, which transferred to Triolo (officially, Foggia Satellite Airfield No. 7) from Tunisia during the second week of December. A month later, the 1st and 82nd FGs made the move, the 1st from Gioia del Colle, Italy, (to which it had transferred in early December, from Sardinia) to Salsola (Foggia No. 3), and the 82nd from Lecce to Vincenzo (Foggia No. 11). When the 1st FG's air echelon arrived at Salsola on January 8, it had only thirty-two operational P-38s.

The Fifteenth AF's bomb groups had begun hitting targets in Greece in the middle of November, escorted by P-38s. On five missions there from November 15 to January 11, the Lightning pilots were credited with 17-6-11 e/a. Their most successful day was December 20, on which the bombers targeted the Eleusis A/D near Athens, escorted by the 1st and 14th Groups.

As the B-17s headed for home after the bombing they were attacked by Bf 109s of III./JG 27, precipitating a nasty fight with the P-38 escort. The 14th FG's pilots were credited with 8-2-3 109s and the 1st's a lone Fw 190 destroyed. Second Lieutenant Robert K. Seidman of the 49th FS scored three confirmed and a damaged, for which he was awarded a DFC. On the debit side, three of the B-17s were lost. There were no P-38 losses over or near the target, but when they returned to Italy the weather was closing in, and four 1st FG pilots crashed into some hills and were killed.

The 82nd FG flew a particularly harrowing—and costly—mission on Christmas Day. It was a B-24 escort to the marshalling yards at Udine, Italy, near which were located several Axis fighter bases. In the target area the P-38s were attacked from above by Bf 109s belonging to II./JG 51 and II./JG 53, utilizing "hit-and-run" tactics that were extremely effective. By the time the forty-minute air battle was over, six of the Lightnings had been shot down, and two more were so badly damaged that they were scrapped after returning to Lecce—in exchange for which only a single Bf 109 was claimed destroyed. Three of the missing pilots, including the 95th FS's CO, Maj. Hugh M. Muse, were killed, and the other three became POWs.

Above: Brig. Gen. Carlyle Ridenour (center), CO of the 47th Bomb Wing, to which the 82nd FG was then assigned, visited the unit at its base at Lecce, Italy, on December 23, 1943, the anniversary of its first combat mission. (*USAF photo*)

Right: Second Lieutenant William R. Downing of the 96th FS getting ready for another mission, while wearing his coveted Ray-Ban sunglasses. Downing was shot down in P-38G-10 42-13028 by a Bf 109 during the 82nd FG's disastrous bomber escort mission to northern Italy on Christmas Day 1943, becoming a POW. (*Author's collection*)

By January 1944, the Fifteenth AF's P-38 groups had a big problem. They had not received any replacement aircraft in months, and not only were the ones they did have developing numerous mechanical problems due to their age and continued use, but there were not nearly enough of them. The 95th FS historian lamented in his war diary entry for January 9 that "Airplanes becoming very old and undependable due to lack of replacement airplanes." As early as the end of November, he had commented that "Many of our P-38s are becoming flying wrecks. Replacement pilots, having been trained in the latest types of P-38s in the States, are puzzled by the sight of our old 'F's and 'G's still being used in combat." According to a 1st FG history: "Maintaining the planes in the air became a battle of wits, scrounging and cannibalizing, particularly when we were down to such a pitiful handful."

The situation had become so serious that they had to either "pool" the aircraft of all three of their squadrons, to be able to barely put up enough for two normal-sized squadrons on a typical mission, or have each squadron operate just two instead of the usual four flights.

They did eventually receive forty-five P-38Hs from the Eighth AF, which had replaced them with the new P-38Js that were now coming off the Lockheed assembly lines—all of which were then being allocated to the ETO and the SWP. In late January and early February, pilots from all three groups were transported to England to fly these "H" models back to Italy, including eleven from the 82nd FG, who picked up theirs from the 55th FG at Nuthampstead. On February 6, they flew them to Gibraltar, guided by a B-17. After stopovers there and at Algiers, they arrived back at Foggia on the 8th. Fifteen 1st FG pilots made the same trip to Nuthampstead, as passengers in a B-17, returning to Salsola on February 12 with *their* "new" Hs.

The Fifteenth AF's Lightning pilots shared a problem with those in the Eighth: keeping sufficiently warm on their high-altitude, long-range bomber escort missions during that particularly cold winter. Their fallback solution was to wear as many layers of clothing as possible, even though it seriously restricted their movement in the cockpit. A 95th FS pilot, Barry R. Butler, later recalled the discomfort:

The P-38G's cockpit heat was almost non-existent. As I recall, the heat was diverted to the guns rather than into the cockpit. The guns would freeze due to the extreme low temperatures, and I presume that this was more important than pilot comfort.

The aircraft did have an outlet to plug in an electric flying suit, and this was supposed to solve the lack of heat in the cockpit, [but they] frequently shorted out and provided little or no comfort. The plug in the suit was located where your thigh meets your torso and caused a rather painful burn in that area when the suit shorted out.

The "well-dressed" pilot donned the following articles of clothing in an effort to keep from freezing: first, normal underwear and T-shirt. Over that a pair of long underwear, then on top of that the one-piece electric flying suit, which resembled a heavier suit of "long johns." Next came the heavy wool flying suit, topped off with a leather jacket and silk scarf. The foot protection consisted of two pairs of heavy socks, then the electrically heated "boots" (actually slippers), followed by the heavy bomber-type flying boots. On the hands, a pair of electrically heated gloves. For the head, of course, a leather flying helmet.

Thus attired, the pilot waddled out to his aircraft and prayed he didn't have a call of nature. The crew chief had to boost us up the ladder and assist us into the cockpit we were so heavily dressed.

Even with all the above clothing we were still bitterly cold at altitude. I can clearly remember stomping my feet on the floor of the cockpit and slapping my hands all over my body in an effort to keep warm.

Despite the cold, we still had to remain alert for enemy fighters, proper coverage of the bombers and, of course, navigation.[4]

Another of the Twelfth AF units transferring to the Fifteenth, in January 1944, was the 154th Tactical Reconnaissance Squadron—previously the 154th Observation Squadron and the 154th Reconnaissance Squadron (Fighter), which had been active in North Africa as a combination tactical reconnaissance/fighter-bomber unit assigned to the 68th Observation Group. It had operated a variety of aircraft that included P-39s, Allison-engined P-51As and F-6 recons, A-20s, and at least three Lightnings—a P-38 and two F-4s. Another 68th Group squadron, the 122nd Liaison, is also known to have operated several P-38s, as did its 111th Observation Squadron, which became the 111th Reconnaissance Squadron (Fighter) effective May 31.

In North Africa, an intriguing entry had been made in the 154th Squadron's history/diary regarding its engineering section's conversion of "an F-4 Lightning into an R-1 recon ship. The nacelle of the ship has been modified with an observation window and is capable of carrying an observer, who sits with a .50-cal machine gun over each shoulder. By 3 May it is completed, with several generals visiting to see it, including Twelfth AF Commanding Gen. Jimmy Doolittle."

After moving to Italy from Algeria, the 154th TRS was re-equipped with P-38s only and became a weather reconnaissance squadron (WRS) attached to Fifteenth AF Headquarters at Bari—which designation it received officially effective May 12. It flew its first weather recon mission on February 13. There had already been a Fifteenth AF Weather Reconnaissance Flight, which was absorbed into the 154th. This flight, which had been activated on November 3, 1943, was comprised of six combat-experienced pilots and twenty-two enlisted ground crewmen that had been recruited from the three P-38 groups, which continued to be a source of personnel for the 154th WRS.

The task of the weather reconnaissance pilots was simple, but challenging. Usually solo but sometimes in pairs, they would take off from Bari before dawn and fly to the vicinity of the Fifteenth AF's target or targets for the day, to check out the weather. Based on the report the weather recon pilot radioed back, the mission either proceeded as planned, was canceled, or an alternate target was chosen. Their aircraft were mostly standard P-38s, but normally with just two .50-cal. guns for self defense, which made room in their noses for an extra VHF radio and battery, a K-24 aerial camera and a radio range receiver. The 154th Squadron was also assigned a few F-5s and, later, some modified Pathfinder Lightnings.

Since the Fifteenth AF was initially assigned no essential strategic photo reconnaissance units, in January, it "borrowed" six F-5s and pilots from the Twelfth AF's 15th PRS. They too were attached to its headquarters at Bari.

Now that Corsica and Sardinia were in Allied hands, Fifteenth AF bombers were able attack targets in southern France with P-38 escort, the latter refueling on those islands. On

F-4-1 41-2148 served with the 3rd Photo Group in North Africa in 1943. These photos were taken in early 1944, by which time it had been stripped of its original green-and-gray paint job, acquired the names *Timber*!! and *Rose Marie* and was the personal aircraft of Col. Karl F. Polifka, who is seen standing on its tail. Polifka had made a name for himself as CO of the 8th PRS in New Guinea early in the war and now, as of January 1944, commanded the 90th Photographic Wing (Reconnaissance), based at San Severo, Italy. (*USAF photos*)

January 21, they targeted three A/Ds where Luftwaffe bombers were based, to keep them from interfering with the American landings at Anzio, south of Rome, the following day. Two of the targets were defended by some particularly aggressive German fighter pilots. Near one of them, Salon, the 27th and 94th Squadrons of the 1st FG claimed two Bf 109s and an Fw 190 destroyed for the loss of one P-38 and one B-17, while the 48th FS shot down three 109s defending the airfield at Montpelier for the loss of one P-38 and no bombers. Subsequent reconnaissance photos showed that a great deal of damage had been done by the bombing, and that both of the above-mentioned airfields were then unserviceable.

There was a follow-up mission to airfields in the Marseille area on the 27th that was also opposed by enemy fighters, the 1st and 14th FG pilots claiming five more destroyed for the loss of two of their own. They were also credited with two probables and twelve damaged on those two missions.

The Allied invasion of the Italian mainland had progressed well at first, but it stalled that first winter at the enemy's Gustav Line, a series of fortifications in the mountains north of Naples. It was decided to bypass those defenses with landings at Anzio, on the coast less than 40 miles south of Rome (Operation Shingle). Unfortunately, the landing forces were nearly thrown back into the sea by the Germans and the Allied offensive stalled again. Rome would not be captured until June 6.

P-38s supported the Anzio beachhead, mainly by bombing and strafing German reinforcements and supplies that were moving toward it. All three groups also participated in the huge raid by Fifteenth AF bombers and fighters against enemy airfields in the Udine area of northern Italy on January 30, to prevent their aircraft from interfering with the Shingle operation. Sixty e/a were destroyed, forty-five of them in the air, the latter mostly by P-47 pilots of the 325th FG. The 1st and 14th Groups each downed just one, but the 82nd FG claimed 6-5-2 for the loss of a single P-38.

They were also involved in Operation Argument, popularly known as "Big Week," a series of coordinated attacks by the Eighth and Fifteenth AFs on Germany's aircraft industry, from February 20 to 25. Due to poor flying weather and other commitments, the Fifteenth was only able to participate on the last four days of Big Week: the 22nd (the target Regensburg, Germany), the 23rd (Steyr, Austria), the 24th (Steyr), and the 25th (Regensburg).

There were no P-38 claims on the 22nd, and one 82nd FG aircraft was lost. On the 23rd, the 48th FS was credited with 1-2-0 e/a without loss, and on the 25th, the 14th FG claimed just 1-1-0 while the 1st and 82nd FGs each suffered two losses. Their biggest day of Argument was February 24, when the 82nd scored eight victories and the 14th two—and the 1st and 82nd each lost a single P-38. The 82nd's assignment that day was target and withdrawal support, and as its pilots moved into position over the last group of bombers, a huge swarm of 100-plus single- and twin-engined fighters were assailing them. First Lieutenant Gene H. Chatfield of the 97th FS, who shot down an Me 210 in that action, remembered this mission vividly years later:

We of the 82nd were right on schedule when we heard the bombers calling for help. We went into high-speed cruise to get there as quickly as possible. When we arrived on the scene the bombers were starting their bomb run. I could see the formations of Me 109s and Me 210/410s above and behind the B-17s. They looked like a swarm of bees. Every

Left: Lt. C. W. Herall of the 37th FS after completing his fifty-mission combat tour in early 1944. (*USAF photo*)

Below: Three 82nd FG pilots the day after they participated in the Fifteenth AF's attack on enemy airfields in the Udine, Italy, area on January 30, 1944. All three men were former bomber pilots now flying P-38s. The only one identified is Capt. Clayton M. Isaacson, in the center. The other two pilots were reportedly killed in action later. The 96th FS aircraft behind them, P-38G-15 43-2475, coded BH, was lost in action on April 25. (*Author's collection*)

few seconds eight would peel off and attack the rear bomber, sending it down in flames. We had only twenty-eight P-38s. A psychological advantage was our only hope, so rather than stay with the usual parallel flights of four planes, we strung out, wingtip to wingtip, in a broad line. This made us look like a lot more than we had. The trick worked. We plowed into the Messerschmitts, forcing them to break off their attack on the B-17s.[5]

Although the Fifteenth AF's Argument missions did do a lot of damage to the German aircraft industry, it was at the cost of seventy-seven of its B-17s and B-24s, plus the above-mentioned P-38s.

The P-38Js finally began to arrive in the Mediterranean Theater in March. The 82nd FG received its first "J" on the 20th; it had been delivered to the Foggia Main airfield, and one of the group's pilots picked it up there and flew it to Vincenzo.

There was now an air depot group in Algiers (the 36th), so the P-38Js and later model F-5s could be delivered to that city's port, offloaded from the ships that transported them across the Atlantic, moved to the nearby depot, reassembled, modified as needed, and test flown before being delivered to the MTO's Lightning units. The P-38 groups in Italy continued to operate their old Fs, Gs, and Hs in diminishing numbers for several more months until they were completely re-equipped with Js.

One of the big improvements in the P-38J was to its internal fuel capacity, which had been increased by nearly one-third, since the intercooler ducting system in the wings had been replaced with fuel tanks. The resulting increase in the aircraft's range was soon being put to excellent use on the Fifteenth AF's missions to targets throughout Southern and Eastern Europe. The major changes that set the J's appearance apart from the earlier model P-38s were its natural metal finish and the larger air intakes below the propellers for the new and more efficient core-type radiators located there.

Despite the J's obvious improvements, there were some problems with it. The 37th FS's engineering officer, Capt. James Stitt, described a couple of them, and their solutions:

We began having trouble with high-altitude engine operation due to the fact that our carburetor air intake temperature was so ungodly cold. On the new planes the intercooler doors had been moved from the wings down between the oil coolers [under the engines], and they worked very well. In fact, they worked too well. The big new radiator had so much capacity that it could drop the carburetor air intake temperature down to the point that we were not getting good fuel vaporization. We modified our planes by installing intercooler doors. They were set in front of the intercooler to close off the passing of the air to control the temperature. Control cables were run through the radiator and worked off the flap motor. They worked just fine, and eventually we educated our pilots on the operation of the doors and taught them how to maintain proper carburetor air inlet temperatures.

We also had a problem of freezing oil in the oil coolers. That was kind of a sneaky thing, because when the oil started to freeze the oil temperature gauge would go up, and the natural reaction of the pilots was to open the oil cooler door a little more. If you did that, the additional air through the coolers would freeze the oil solid, and there would be no oil, so you could lose an engine very quickly. The pilots picked up on this very quickly, and eventually we operated our P-38s at high altitude without trouble.[6]

Above left: This 1st FG P-38, F-1 41-7544, had quite a history. It joined the 27th PS in the U.S. in April 1942 and was flown across the Atlantic to England that summer, and then to North Africa in November. It was assigned to Capt. Edward S. E. Newberry, who commanded the squadron briefly in September 1943. The swastikas on *DEAR JOHN*'s nose evidently represented Newberry's four confirmed kills. It had then flown ninety-two missions, based on the symbols on its nose. No. 41-7544's end finally came on February 10, 1944, during a dive-bombing mission *to* Italy. According to the Missing Aircrew Report for its pilot, 2Lt. Thomas L. Collier, his flight leader's bomb came loose and fell into a river, and its concussion "and a large water spout caused by the explosion hit Lt Collier's plane, knocking off both tail booms and turning him over in one complete turn before the aircraft hit the bank and exploded."

Above right: Another venerable 1st FG P-38 was this colorful 94th FS F-15, whose serial number is, unfortunately, not known. When photographed in early 1944, it had, based on the P-38 symbols on its nose, flown eighty-nine sweeps and escorts, and, on the bomb symbols, forty-five bombing missions, for a total of 134. It had also evidently shot down three German planes. (*USAF photo*)

Below: March 31, 1944: These two photos show personnel of the 36th Air Depot Group at the Maison Blanche Airport, near Algiers, reassembling newly arrived P-38Js. Number 246 was J-15 42-104246, which was subsequently assigned to the 48th FS, 14th FG at Triolo, Italy—but not for long, as it went missing in action on May 12. (*USAF photo*)

The modification to P-38J intercoolers made by the 37th FS's engineering section. The new flaps are shown in both the open and closed positions. (*Authors' collection*)

Although there were numerous bomber escorts to targets in northern Italy around this time, the three P-38 groups received a very different assignment on March 18. This was a maximum-effort low-level strafing mission by about ninety Lightnings to the complex of enemy airfields in the north-eastern corner of the country. They flew over 300 miles right above the Adriatic Sea in an attempt to avoid detection; nevertheless, numerous enemy fighters attacked the 14th and 82nd Groups as they swept into the target area.

The 1st FG's P-38s were not spotted by the enemy and their pilots managed to destroy ten e/a on the ground and one Ju 52 in the air, plus other materiel, for the loss of a single P-38 that flew into a high tension wire. In a series of dogfights, the pilots of the other two groups claimed seven enemy fighters destroyed for the loss of a 97th FS pilot who had to ditch his P-38 in the sea and was taken prisoner.

During a B-24 escort to northern Italy on March 29, the first P-38J was lost in combat in the MTO when 2Lt. William B. Tucker of the 48th FS bailed out of J-10 42-68165 near Verona.

By the beginning of April, the Fifteenth AF's strategic bombing campaign was really getting into high gear, and its Lightning groups, now utilizing their new longer-ranged P-38Js, were a big part of it. On the 2nd, there was a massive raid on the ball-bearing factory, an aircraft components plant and the airfield at Steyr. The bombers were escorted by all three P-38 groups and the Fifteenth's P-47 group, the 325th, which provided staggered penetration and target support. The first enemy fighters were engaged *en route* to the target by the 82nd FG, whose pilots claimed 3-1-2. The 82nd was relieved by the P-47s, which were credited with 3-0-1 Bf 109s, and then the 1st FG took over the penetration support from them. During a thirty-minute fight, two of the 1st's squadrons were credited with ten kills.

Before the 14th FG's pilots—who were assigned to withdrawal support—even reached the target, they spotted approximately seventy enemy fighters attacking the bombers and immediately waded into them. The 49th FS skirmished with some Bf 109s, destroying two and damaging three. As the fight continued on over Steyr, the group's other two

These pilots of the 95th and 97th FSs all made claims for enemy aircraft during the 82nd FG's bomber escort to Steyr, Austria, on March 26, 1944. This was the group's first major success with its new P-38Js, one of which provides a backdrop to the photo. (*Author's collection*)

squadrons battled numerous *Zerstören* (destroyers)—twin-engined fighters—plus a few more single-engined and were credited with 18-2-2.

First Lieutenant Enoch P. Lemon of the 37th FS spotted what he estimated to be about forty enemy fighters and his section (two flights) targeted some Bf 110s, "spraying lead into the formation, trying to split them up." He then "did a wingover and came in on the tail of four 110s that split in pairs."

I got on the closest two and saw that their rear gunners were shooting at me. I said, "You son of a bitch!" and pressed the [gun] button. My tracers hit home, for there was a flash of strikes just behind the cockpit and the gunner quit firing. I closed and let him have it. Pieces peeled off its left engine and it began pouring out black smoke. Then I saw his left wing start to come apart and disintegrate from the tip inward. I switched to the other one that had turned to the left and started firing. There was a large flash under his left wing that looked like one of his rockets exploded, then his engine began to smoke and I peeled off.[7]

Lemon was credited with two of the Bf 110s destroyed and another damaged. For its valorous defense of the bombers that day, the 14th FG was awarded its only DUC. Amazingly, not a single P-38 was lost in these actions.

Salsola, Italy, March 1944: Posing with P-38H-5 42-67029 are (left to right, standing) the 1st FG's Surgeon, Maj. Emil Sposato; its CO, Col. Robert B. Richard, and 94th FS CO 1Lt. William D. Jacobsen. Kneeling are the commanders of the 27th and 71st Squadrons, Capt. Gilbert E. Butler and Capt. Lee V. Wiseman. This aircraft had served initially with the 55th FG in England. It was transferred to the MTO in February 1944, and ended up with the 154th WRS, with which it was lost in action on December 9, 1944. (*USAF photo*)

It was around this time that the Fifteenth AF began issuing two-mission credits to fighter pilots flying particularly long escort missions. Thus, sometimes their official mission totals were not precisely accurate. Also, in the spring of 1944, many of the Fifteenth's fighter pilots were completing their fifty-mission combat tours at a time when a lot of important missions were being flown, and their experience was greatly needed. Thus, some of them volunteered to fly a few more than fifty (actual) missions.

Until the Fifteenth AF entered the fight over Eastern Europe, Germany's Allies there—particularly Bulgaria, Romania, and Hungary—had been fighting alongside it against Russia, far to the east. But suddenly, their air forces found themselves having to defend their own countries from American air attacks. Bulgaria had been enduring them for nearly five months, and now it was the turn of those other two Axis countries.

The first major air raid on Hungary took place on April 3. The bombers, targeting Budapest, the country's capital, were escorted by all three P-38 groups, whose opponents included Bf 109s, twin-engined Me 210s, and a handful of Bf 110 night fighters of the Royal Hungarian Air Force (*Magyar Királyi Honvéd Légierö*, or MKHL). The Lightning pilots were credited with destroying three single-engined fighters, four twin-engined fighters, and two Heinkel He 111 bombers. No P-38s were lost, but four B-17s and a B-24 were.

It was the turn of Romania's capital, Bucharest, the following day, and its air force's fighter pilots were quite successful against what they called the "American sky terrorists," shooting down eight B-24s. The only U.S. fighter claims were by the 82nd FG, which was assigned to withdrawal support for the bombers. When its pilots reached them they were under attack by some twin-engined fighters, of which they shot down three and probably destroyed one.

Pilots of the 48th FS pose with one of their P-38s after returning from a mission in April 1944. (*Author's collection*)

Pilots of the 14th FG just returned to Triolo from a mission in the spring of 1944. (*Author's collection*)

The Fifteenth's bombers attacked five different targets in Hungary on April 13, precipitating several air battles that resulted in the P-38s of the 1st and 82nd FGs and P-47s of the 325th FG claiming to have destroyed nineteen e/a. The 1st's share was two Bf 109s and an Italian Reggiane fighter of the MKHL, and the 82nd's was five Ju 88s, three Me 210s, and two Bf 109s—plus some probably destroyed and damaged credits. Although the Hungarian pilots claimed six P-38s, none were, in fact, lost, while fifteen bombers failed to return from the mission, of which they claimed eight.

The May 10 escort mission to Wiener Neustadt was another big one, especially for the 14th FG. Its CO, Col. Oliver B. "Obie" Taylor, who was leading it at the head of the 37th FS, spotted contrails high above as they approached the target and he ordered the squadron to spiral climb up to them. Unfortunately, the P-38s also created contrails, making them highly visible. They were then bounced by two dozen Bf 109s and went into a defensive Lufbery Circle. Col. Taylor called for assistance, the 48th responded, and the two squadrons claimed a total of 4-1-8.

As the 49th FS was leaving the target area, its pilots saw some bombers under attack and immediately went to their aid, subsequently claiming 3-0-6 Bf 109s. The number of damaged credits indicates the confused nature of the fighting and, once again, the difficulty of scoring confirmed victories. Unfortunately, the Fifteenth AF lost thirty bombers that day. The only fighter loss was a 37th Squadron pilot who developed engine trouble and bailed out over Yugoslavia on the way home. As with many Allied pilots and aircrewmen lost over that country, he was rescued by its partisans, evaded capture, and eventually returned to Italy.

Effective May 12, the 122nd Liaison Squadron, still based in Algeria, was redesignated the 885th Bombardment Squadron (Heavy). Its B-17s and B-24s were used to drop leaflets behind the lines and supplies to partisans, but, as with the old 122nd Squadron, it had at least one Lightning on its roster, which it used for weather reconnaissance.

Lt. Robert K. Seidman of the 49th FS, later a five-victory ace, poses with his P-38 (whose serial number is not known), on the nose of which was the squadron's insignia. Seidman was shot down and killed by AA fire over Italy on May 14, 1944, while flying another Lightning. (*USAF photo*)

Ploesti

The 1st FG earned its third DUC on May 18, for its escort of bombers attacking some of the eleven oil refineries near Ploesti, Romania, 35 miles north of Bucharest. These provided the Luftwaffe and the Wermacht with one-third of the oil and gasoline they needed for their aircraft, trucks, and tanks, including the highest-quality 90-octane aviation fuel in Europe. Ploesti was the Fifteenth AF's highest-priority target, and the third most heavily defended in Europe, with the world's largest concentration of AA batteries and numerous German and Romanian fighters based at nearby airfields. It was nicknamed "*Festung* (Fortress) Ploesti" by Allied airmen.

The 1st was assigned to withdrawal support that day, and when its pilots picked up the B-17s as they came off their target, they were under attack by numerous enemy fighters. The P-38 pilots immediately waded into the latter, precipitating a melee lasting more than twenty minutes that resulted in credits for eleven confirmed kills, three probables, and six damaged. A single P-38 was lost when its pilot bailed out into the Adriatic on the way home. The "Fw 190s" were actually Romanian-built IAR 80s and 81s, small radial-engined fighters that were usually mistaken by American pilots and aircrewmen for the famous Focke-Wulf fighter. The IARs belonged to *Grupul 2 vânâtoare* (the 2nd FG) of the Royal Romanian Air Force (*Aeronautica Regalâ Românâ*, or ARR).

The 32nd PRS joined the 5th PRG at San Severo, Italy, from Oklahoma in May. Five months later, the group was transferred from the Twelfth to the Fifteenth AF. Its final squadron, the 37th PR, also fresh from Oklahoma, would join it in November. The group's pilots then mainly flew long-range, high-altitude photo missions to the Fifteenth's targets in southern Germany, Austria, and Czechoslovakia.

It was also in May that the 82nd FG's CO, Col. William P. Litton, instructed the group's Armament and Photographic Officer, Capt. Amos Turner, to find a solution to the P-38's continuing gun camera problem—poor quality film caused by the vibration of the guns. Assisting Turner in that endeavor was the group's civilian Lockheed technical representative ("tech rep"), Richard "Stumpy" Hollinger. Their solution was to move the camera out of the nose compartment and reinstall it in a P-38J's left wing leading edge, between the gondola and the engine. This arrangement was tested in early June and found to be satisfactory, so the modification was made to other 82nd FG Lightnings.

A 14th FG engineering officer also tackled this dilemma around the same time, and his—equally successful—solution was to move the camera to the left underwing pylon. Lockheed was notified of these field modifications and soon added the one devised by the 14th FG to its Burbank assembly lines, during their P-38J-25 run. Another modification made by that unit's personnel was the addition of sway braces to the auxiliary fuel tanks. There had been incidents in which the tanks rotated back and upward after being dropped, then struck and did damage to the flaps, and the braces solved that problem. The 1st FG's attached 94th Service Squadron also began manufacturing both the new camera mounts and the auxiliary fuel tank braces.

By mid-June, the Fifteenth AF had bombed the Ploesti oil refineries eight times, and while considerable damage had been done, the results were less than had been hoped for. In addition to their by-now legendary defenses, the refinery facilities were well dispersed

Lt. Stanley W. H. C. "Stan" Lau was a Chinese-American pilot who joined the 1st FG's 27th Squadron at the end of March 1944. He scored four confirmed kills and two damaged while flying four different P-38s. (*USAF photo*)

The P-38J *Pat III* at Triolo in early June 1944. Assigned to the 49th FS, it was flown by the 14th FG's CO, Colonel Oliver B. "Obie" Taylor, a five-victory ace. (*John Stanaway collection*)

and usually obscured by smoke produced by hundreds of generators by the time the B-24s and B-17s arrived, making accurate bombing of specific targets very difficult. The bombers were always detected, by radar and by ground observers, long before their arrival and were inevitably greeted by enemy fighters, a smoke-covered target and welcoming barrages of AA.

Given the extreme importance of this target, Fifteenth AF planners decided to try a radical tactic: attacking one of the refineries with P-38 fighter-bombers. It was hoped that they could sneak in, low and fast, before the defenses had been fully alerted. So it was that shortly after dawn on June 10, 1944, forty-six P-38s of the 82nd FG, each carrying a single 1,000-lb. bomb and a 300-gallon auxiliary fuel tank, escorted by forty-eight more from the 1st FG, sped at low level across the Adriatic Sea and then Yugoslavia and finally along the Danube River into Rumania—their target the Româno-Americană Oil Refinery, located east of Ploesti, which had emerged relatively unscathed from previous attacks.

Southeast of Bucharest, the Lightnings pivoted north toward Ploesti. By then, nine 1st FG and seven 82nd FG pilots had aborted the mission; also, one of the latter's had bailed out over Yugoslavia and another had disappeared. Shortly after the turn, numerous e/a were encountered, mostly twin-engined bombers and biplanes that were evidently fleeing from what they thought were impending attacks on their airfields. Fourteen of them were shot down by 1st FG pilots and two by bomb-carrying 82nd FG pilots, and others were probably destroyed or damaged.

The P-38s had obviously been detected, and three flights of the 71st FS, immediately after shooting down six Dornier Do 217 bombers, were bounced by IAR 80/81s of the ARR's *Grupul 6* (once again identified by the American pilots as "Fw 190s"), initiating a vicious low-level dogfight in which the P-38 pilots were at a distinct disadvantage against the nimble little Romanian fighters.

Nine of the Lightning pilots went down in this brief but deadly action. Amazingly, one of the survivors, 2Lt. Herbert B. "Stub" Hatch, Jr., was credited with five of the eight "Fw 190s" that were confirmed destroyed. He and his squadron mate 1Lt. Carl C. Hoenshell, who downed two of the Dorniers and one of the IARs, were each awarded a DSC for these actions. Although Hoenshell survived the dogfight, he was shot down and wounded by a Bf 109 over Bulgaria on his way home and died of his injuries the following day.

Meanwhile, the 82nd FG pilots continued on to Ploesti, escorted by the 27th FS and the remaining 71st FS flight. (The 94th Squadron's pilots had been delayed by their encounter with the aforementioned covey of e/a, of which they shot down seven.) They dropped their auxiliary fuel tanks, climbed to bombing altitude (6,000 feet) and dove down through the AA fire to hit their specified targets, which had not yet been totally obscured by the smoke. Among other things, their thirty-six bombs hit a cracking plant and blew up a large storage tank.

One of these pilots was thirty-two-year-old Lt. Col. Ben A. Mason, the 82nd's deputy CO, who was leading a 97th FS flight. Mason recalled later that as they climbed prior to the bombing, they "saw that the smoke screen over the target was pretty well formed."

> Their heavy antiaircraft guns, some twenty of them, formed a box barrage over the target at our diving altitude, so we had to fly into it to get into position for our dives. You try to ignore antiaircraft bursts all around you, as evasive action is ineffective; you are just as likely to turn into the next burst as away from it. You just try to find your target as soon as

possible, make your dive and get the hell out of there. For better accuracy you make your dive as steep as possible. I took some minor hits from the antiaircraft fire before making my dive—a few holes in both engine cowlings and my horizontal stabilizer shot up. After I made my dive I pulled out just above the smoke screen. After getting clear of the smoke, I got as low as possible and headed for our assembly point.[8]

Five more 82nd FG pilots were lost during or immediately after the bombing, victims of the massive AA fire. As the survivors headed southwest for Italy in small groups, they strafed targets of opportunity and encountered some more enemy planes in the air, of which they claimed 4-2-1, including a Bf 110 shot down by Lt. Col. Mason. Two more of them were MIA on the way home, and two damaged P-38s were destroyed in crash-landings back at Vincenzo.

While also strafing on the way home, the 27th FS tangled with a large formation of Bf 109s, claiming four destroyed, two probably destroyed, and four damaged but losing four of their own planes and pilots.

The 1st FG pilots were eventually credited with a total of twenty-seven confirmed kills, while the 82nd's had done considerable damage to the refinery, shot down six aircraft and destroyed three more (and much other enemy materiel) on the ground. The cost was high, however: fourteen 1st FG and eight 82nd FG pilots failed to return from this mission, for which the 82nd was awarded its third DUC.

Four days later, the 49th FS experienced one of its most grueling missions of the whole war. The 14th Group's assignment that day was to escort B-24s of the 55th BW to the Pétfürdö Oil Refinery in Hungary. Donald A. Luttrell, then a second lieutenant on his fifth combat mission, remembered later: "Standard procedure was to escort the bombers to the initial point and as they turned on the bomb run to the target we would swing wide and go around to meet them on the other side, the thinking being that the enemy fighters didn't follow the bombers through the flak so there was no reason for us to do so."

The bombers the 14th was escorting were the last in the stream, and there was already a huge smoke column emanating from the refinery when they arrived. For some reason, the 49th went around it to the west and the other two squadrons to the east, creating a wide separation between them. The 49th was soon bounced by numerous Bf 109s. Luttrell remembered that when they were called out:

All heads snapped to the left and there they were. Later estimates fell between 50 and 75, but they looked like a thousand. Talk about activity in the cockpit: drop tanks, switch gas selectors, mixtures to rich, rpm's high, throttles forward—all in a hard left turn. This was a text-book example of hours of boredom interspersed with moments of sheer panic. In seconds the situation had turned into a John Wayne movie, with airplanes twisting and turning, shooting and being shot at, and voices crackling over the radio. Someone called for the other two squadrons to come help us, but they might as well have been in the Pacific, so we had these guys all to ourselves.[9]

The 49th Squadron's two sections went into Lufbery Circles, in opposite directions. By the time the P-38 pilots were able to disengage and head for home, five of them had gone down,

P-38J-15 43-28778, coded HB—the "H" standing for H.Q.—was maintained by the 82nd FG's 97th Squadron but was flown by the group's deputy CO, Lt. Col. Ben A. Mason, Jr., who named it *Billy Boy* after his infant son. He is here posing with it and its ground crew. The two swastikas represent the Bf 109 he shot down on May 10, 1944 and the Bf 110 he destroyed during the June 10 Ploesti mission. No. 43-28778 was shot down by AA fire over Italy on April 22, 1945. (*Author's collection*)

Two 71st FS P-38 pilots relax in front of their shack at Salsola, Italy. Its wooden walls are made from belly tank crates. (*Author's collection*)

all of whom survived to become POWs. They were credited with a total of fifteen confirmed kills (one of them by Lt. Luttrell), two probables, and two damaged. The top scorer was 2Lt. Jack Lenox, Jr., with three victories, which gave him a total of five, making him an ace.

The Bf 109s were flown by both Luftwaffe pilots and MKHL pilots of the 101 "Puma" Wing, the former claiming two P-38s and the latter eight. One of the Hungarian pilots was killed.

By the summer of 1944, the Fifteenth AF had four P-51 groups and three P-38 groups to escort its bombers. Typically, the Lightnings would be used for close support, since their unique profile identified them as friendly to all but the most trigger-happy bomber gunners. Unfortunately, the P-51 looked a lot like a Bf 109 from a distance, and there had been numerous incidents in which they had been fired upon by the gunners. Thus, the Mustang pilots were usually the ones allowed to roam ahead of the bombers to intercept enemy fighters before they could reach the B-17s and B-24s—sometimes when they were forming up near their airfields—while the P-38 pilots normally had to wait until the bombers were actually attacked until they could engage them.

On July 8, however, the 82nd FG was assigned one of the fighter sweeps normally flown by the P-51s, arriving over the target, Vienna, well ahead of the bombers. Its pilots caught some Me 410 *Zerstören* climbing for altitude and forming up for an attack on the bombers approaching in the distance. One of the 82nd's squadrons attacked them from the left and another from the right, in a "pincer" movement, while the third squadron provided top cover. The result was an aerial slaughter in which sixteen of the Me 410s—plus three single-engined fighters and a stray trainer—were shot down. Two P-38 pilots were each credited with three kills.

First Lieutenant Gerald C. Osgood of the 1st FG's 71st Squadron and his assigned P-38, J-15 42-104267, which he had named *CO-PILOT*. Osgood shot down an Fw 190 on April 29, 1944 and a Bf 109 on June 16. (*USAF photo*)

Lt. Charles E. Adams, Jr., of the 95th FS scored his six air victories in four different P-38s. This one, J-15 43-28796, coded AI, which he named *Judy Ann* after his infant daughter, was assigned to him in mid-June 1944. He scored just one victory with it, his third, on the 26th of that month. (*Author's collection*)

Shuttling

From June to August 1944, the USAAF implemented Operation Frantic, a series of "shuttle" missions flown by the Eighth AF in England and the Fifteenth AF in Italy to Russia and back. After a bombing or strafing mission was completed—often to a target that was normally out of their range—the American planes would proceed to land at airfields in Ukraine, northeast of Romania, that were provided by the Soviets. From there, they would fly at least one mission to an important Axis target in Eastern Europe that they and the Soviet Air Force, due to its lack of long-range aircraft, would, again, not normally have been able to hit. After a few days, the American units would return to their bases in England or Italy, attacking other distant targets *en route*. Part of this operation was political, providing some direct U.S. support to the Russians' eastern offensive, and hopefully thereby build their trust, given the underlying level of *distrust* between the two "allies."

The first Fifteenth AF unit to participate in Frantic was the 5th PRG, which sent some of its F-5s to Poltava, the main USAAF base in Ukraine, in June. They joined others from the Eighth AF's 7th PG to provide photo reconnaissance services to the Frantic bombers and fighters

Two Fifteenth AF P-38 groups participated in Frantic 3, which commenced on July 22. It was comprised of fighters only: twenty-four P-38s from the 14th FG (the rest of which flew another mission that day), forty-eight P-51s of the 31st FG, and fifty-three P-38s of the 82nd FG. That morning this huge formation was *en route* to Romania, its targets the airfields at Buzău and Zilistea and several nearby landing grounds, where the 82nd was to strafe while the other two groups covered it.

The strafing was very successful, the 82nd Group pilots claiming to have destroyed forty-one aircraft. They also caught a few in the air, shooting down three Ju 52s, an He 111,

T/Sgt. Jack Sattler, a 97th FS crew chief, works on his assigned aircraft, P-38L-1 44-24612, at Vicenzo/Foggia No. 11. *Paddy's* pilot was Capt. George C. Marvin. (*Author's collection*)

and an Fw 190. Meanwhile, the other two groups kept a swarm of enemy fighters away from the 82nd's pilots as they strafed the airfields. The 14th FG's pilots were subsequently credited with 11-8-5, mostly Fw 190s, and one squadron of the 31st with four fighters destroyed. Some of the 190s were from II *Gruppe* of *Schlachtgeschwader* 2 (II./SG 2), a Luftwaffe fighter-bomber unit that lost five pilots in these actions, but others were actually Romanian IARs.

These successes also involved some losses—two in the 14th FG and three for the 82nd. Bf 109 pilots of the Romanian *Grupul 9 vânătoare* and the Luftwaffe's III./JG 77 claimed to have shot down six and two P-38s, respectively, and an IAR 81 pilot of *Grupul* 1 one.

The remaining American pilots then flew on to their Ukrainian bases: Poltava (the 82nd FG), Mirgorod (the 14th FG), and Piryatin (the 31st FG). On the 25th, they flew another strafing mission, to the Mielec A/D in western Poland, where both P-38 groups were to strafe while the Mustangs covered them. The 82nd's pilots were out of position as they approached the airfield and claimed no e/a on the ground but did shoot down a Ju 52, a Ju 87, and an He 111. The 14th's pilots claimed twelve e/a destroyed by strafing. In a separate action, on their way back to Piryatin, the 31st FG's pilots ran into a large formation of e/a—mostly Ju 87s—and shot down twenty-seven of them.

During their return to Italy on the 26th, the Lightning and Mustang pilots made independent sweeps of the Ploesti–Bucharest area. Near Galatz, on the Danube River, the 82nd FG ran into a swarm of e/a of various types—but mostly fighters, precipitating a huge, low-level, twenty-minute air battle. When it was over, its pilots claimed twelve destroyed, for the loss of two of their own. In another action, 14th FG pilots downed two Ju 52s.

On July 31, 1944, during a photo reconnaissance sortie from Corsica to France's Rhône Valley, which was part of the Allies' preparation for the imminent invasion of that country's southern coast, *Commandant* (Major) Antoine Saint-Exupéry went missing. No sign of him

Above left: Ground crewmen of the 37th FS pose with their P-38 No. 66, named *Sour Balls*. Note the extended access ladder. (*Author's collection*)

Above right: A temporarily unarmed 48th FS P-38 whose nose wheel is undergoing maintenance or repair at Triolo sometime in 1944. (*Author's collection*)

was found until 1998, when his ID bracelet and parts of his aircraft, F-5B-1 43-68223, were discovered in the coastal waters near Marseille. His exact fate has still not been determined.

Saint-Exupéry's unit, GR II/33, had by then been attached to the 23rd PRS for some time and had moved with it from Alghero, Sardinia, to Borgo, Corsica, on July 14. The 23rd Squadron had moved from Tunisia to Italy in November 1943, first to Foggia and then, the following month, to San Severo, before transferring to Alghero in February 1944. It (and GR II/33) moved to southern France on August 20, shortly after its invasion, and then back to Italy in October. At that point, GR II/33 remained in France, supporting the First French Army as it moved north, and soon became part of the 1st Tactical Air Force in the ETO.

The last Russian shuttle mission, Frantic 4, flown by 82nd FG P-38s and P-51s of the 52nd FG, took place from August 4 to 6. The Mustang pilots were supposed to cover the 82nd as it strafed the airfield at Focsani, Romania, northeast of Ploesti, *en route* to

Vicenzo, Italy, early August 1944: The 82nd FG's squadron commanders look on as the group scoreboard is updated. *From left to right*: Maj. Herbert L. Phillips (95th FS), Maj. Warner F. Gardner (who was about to replace Phillips), Maj. Claud E. Ford (97th FS), and Maj. Clayton Isaacson (96th FS). At 6 feet 6 inches, Isaacson was most likely the tallest P-38 pilot, and Ford was only a couple of inches shorter. (*Author's collection*)

Poltava; however, they disappeared early on and were not seen by the P-38 pilots during the remainder of the mission.

After strafing some trains and trucks on their approach to Focsani, the P-38 pilots hit the airfield in line abreast and were greeted by some extremely heavy AA fire. They were able to destroy only four aircraft, and lost their CO, Col. Litton, whose P-38 (J-15 42-104145) was hit hard by the AA fire. According to his wingman, "With both engines flaming furiously he bellied his plane in on the airfield going about 200 mph. He slid along the length of the field, finally hitting what appeared to be some buildings and blew up." It was assumed that Litton had been killed, and his men were amazed when he was repatriated from Romania at the end of the month, while recovering from serious burns.

Two other 82nd pilots were likewise shot down and taken prisoner. First Lieutenant Richard E. "Dick" Willsie's P-38 had already lost an engine to the AA on the approach to Focsani, but he nevertheless strafed the airfield, where his other engine was also hit. He knew he would have to force land and reported his plight over the radio. Willsie's squadron mate Flt. Off. Richard T. Andrews replied: "Pick a good field and I will come in after you." Willsie then did land his plane in a field and Andrews put down nearby. Willsie ran to Andrews' P-38, leapt into its cockpit and onto Andrews' lap, took off, and flew it to Poltava—a very uncomfortable two-and-a-half-hour flight for both of them. For his heroic action, Andrews was promoted to second lieutenant and awarded a Silver Star.

The final USAAF bombings of Ploesti took place on August 17, 18, and 19, as the Soviets approached it from the east. The 154th WRS was awarded a DUC for assisting them. After providing their usual pre-mission weather reports, its P-38 pilots lingered over the bombers' five distinct targets, calling out to them the positions of those not obscured by the smoke screens and photographing the results of the attacks.

From August 10 to 21, flight echelons of the 1st and 14th FGs were based in Corsica to support the Allied landings in southern France, between Nice and Toulon (Operation Anvil), which commenced on the 15th. Their task was very similar to that during the Anzio operation: mostly flying patrols over the invasion coast under the direction of controllers. The P-38s destroyed a lot of enemy materiel and killed many personnel, but at a cost of twenty-three aircraft and fifteen pilots missing in action.

By the end of August, aerial opposition to the Fifteenth AF's missions had become almost nonexistent. There were several reasons for this. For one thing, attrition from continuous combat had depleted the Axis air forces, particularly of experienced pilots. Also, they were by then concentrating their limited resources on opposing the Allied air and ground offensives on both the Western and Eastern Fronts, the former commencing with the D-Day landings in Normandy on June 6. By September, France had been liberated and the Western Allies were moving on the Low Countries and western Germany. In the east, Germany's occupied territories and its allies were being overrun by massive Russian offensives. Also by September, Romania, Bulgaria, and Slovakia had all capitulated to the Soviets—and then joined them in the fight against their former ally.

When the Eighth AF re-equipped its P-38 groups with P-51s in the summer of 1944, most of their Lightnings were passed on to the Ninth and Fifteenth AFs. This included some Droop Snoots. In mid-August, one pilot each from the 1st, 14th and 82nd FGs was sent to England to pick up the Fifteenth's first Droop Snoots and fly them across France to Italy. The 1st and 14th Group pilots turned back when they encountered a massive weather front *en route*, but the 82nd pilot, the aforementioned 1Lt. Dick Willsie, persevered and made it to Vincenzo. His aircraft flew the Fifteenth AF's first Droop Snoot mission on August 29, a successful attack on a railroad bridge in northern Italy—the rest of the 82nd FG P-38s dropping their bombs on the Droop Snoot bombardier's order. The other two P-38 groups soon received their first Droop Snoots, and bombardiers from the Fifteenth's bombardment groups were recruited to serve in that capacity on them.

After its heavy losses during Operation Anvil, the 1st FG once again found itself short of aircraft. Therefore, in September, it arranged to have some of its pilots flown to England— specifically BAD 1 at Burtonwood—as passengers in B-17s to pick up some new P-38s and fly them back to Foggia. These were in fact a mixture of brand-new aircraft and others that had already seen service with the Eighth AF.

Both of the F-5 PR groups in the MTO received a DUC for missions flown during the late summer of 1944. The 3rd Photographic Group (Reconnaissance), as it was now called, earned its on August 28, when it "provided photographic intelligence that assisted the rapid advance of Allied ground forces." On September 6, the 5th Photo Reconnaissance Group's pilots "secured photographic intelligence of German Air Force installations in the Balkans and thus enabled fighter organizations to destroy large numbers of enemy transport and fighter planes," thereby earning its DUC.

Also in September, there was a reorganization of the Fifteenth AF's fighter units, with the establishment of the new XV Fighter Command and its subordinate 305th Fighter Wing, both based at Bari. They had all been assigned to the then-new 306th FW back in March,

This brand-new P-38L-1 named *Maloney's Pony*, pictured here with its crew chief in early September 1944, was painted in the markings of eight-victory 27th FS ace Capt. Thomas E. Maloney even though Maloney would never fly it. He had been grievously wounded a couple of weeks earlier, on August 19, when he had to ditch his damaged Lightning, P-38J-15 43-28537, on the coast of southern France. (*John Stanaway collection*)

A 27th FS ground crewman gives a colleague the "OK" sign as he runs up his P-38's engines. (*USAF photo*)

Left: A 94th FS crew chief helps his pilot out of his cockpit after a long mission. (*USAF photo*)

Below: Pilots of the 94th FS load their equipment onto a jeep at Salsola (Foggia No. 3), after returning from a mission. (*USAF photo*)

but now the 306th, based at Lesina, would be comprised of the four P-51 groups and the 305th the three P-38 groups.

The first P-38Ls had arrived in Italy in August, and by the following month, many of them were flying missions with the 1st, 14th, and 82nd FGs.

While the P-38 pilots in the MTO were seeing very few e/a in the air, they did manage to claim quite a few on the ground by strafing during the late summer and fall of 1944, as indicated by the 5th PRG's DUC citation. For example, on September 3, the 14th FG's spotted several dozen, mostly Ju 87s, on the Kovin A/D in Serbia and claimed to have destroyed twenty-nine of them. They destroyed ten more, mostly Ju 52s, at the nearby Bavanište A/D. On October 6, they strafed the Salonika/Sedes A/D in Greece, destroying eighteen e/a. A week later, while returning home from a bomber escort to Blechhammer, Germany, they hit the Szombathely and Vát A/Ds in Hungary, claiming thirteen destroyed, including a Bf 109, an He 111, and a Ju 52 by the 48th FS's 1Lt. Michael Brezas, who, with twelve confirmed aerial victories, was the Fifteenth AF's top-scoring P-38 pilot.

On the following day, October 14, and for the next two, 82nd FG P-38s escorted USAAF C-47s towing gliders to and dropping British paratroopers and supplies over the Megara A/D in Greece, west of Athens. Called Operation Manna, this was part of the reoccupation of that country.

American and Russian pilots encountered each other in the air for the first time during the shuttle missions to Ukraine in the summer of 1944. Given the underlying political tensions between their governments, it was inevitable that, despite having been forced to become allies in the fight against Nazi Germany, "incidents"—some of them violent—would inevitably occur

A flight of 27th FS Lightnings. P-38L-1 44-24217 (No. 12) was assigned to the 1st FG in September 1944 and 44-24379 (No. 13) in October. The latter was lost in action over northern Italy on April 23, 1945. (*USAF photo*)

when their air forces began to meet ever more frequently as they tightened the ring around the European Axis. The worst of such unfortunate encounters took place in November.

The British had invaded Greece at the end of September, the Soviets penetrated eastern Yugoslavia the following month, and the Germans were now retreating north and west through the latter country. The 82nd FG's assignment on November 7 was to "strafe M/T [motor transport]" in central Yugoslavia.

At what the P-38 pilots thought was just north of Raška, but, due to a navigational error, was actually farther east near Niš, the group commander, Col. Clarence T. "Curly" Edwinson, who was leading the mission at the head of the 95th FS, destroyed a locomotive by strafing. As the 97th FS and the 95th's other section provided top cover, Col. Edwinson's section then shot up a nearby road convoy, the trucks in which some of the P-38 pilots soon realized were of U.S. manufacture—and that it was a Russian, not a German column. By that time, considerable damage had been done, including the death of a Russian general. (The official report on this mission noted: "There is a startling similarity between the map appearance of the briefed target and the actual target strafed.")

When attacked the Russian convoy immediately radioed the airfield at nearby Niš, where Yak fighters of the Soviet 659 IAP (fighter group) were based. The Yak pilots immediately took off and engaged the P-38s, resulting in a brief but deadly dogfight in which two of the Lightning pilots were shot down and killed, as were two of the Yak pilots (another was able to bail out successfully). The Russian flight leader, *Kapitan* Aleksandr I. Koldunov, a top Soviet ace, who reportedly claimed to have shot down three of the P-38s, then also reportedly began waggling his wings to help establish mutual identification and some P-38 pilots did the same, thus ending the confrontation.

Not surprisingly, the incident created an international political crisis. The American government apologized to the Soviets and, as a symbolic gesture, relieved Col. Edwinson of his command.

Armorers load a 500-lb. bomb on P-38L-1 44-24408 (which was delivered to the 82nd FG in November 1944) as its unidentified pilot chats with his crew chief. (*Author's collection*)

The Jet Threat

The Luftwaffe's Me 262 jet fighter had become operational that summer. Fortunately for the Allies, there would not be enough of them to make much of an impact on their bombing campaign until well into 1945. Early on, they particularly targeted the RAF's and the USAAF's fast, high-flying reconnaissance aircraft—Mosquitoes, Spitfires, and Lightnings—which had until then usually been able to avoid interception due to the Luftwaffe's piston-engined fighters having an extremely difficult time matching their speed and high-altitude performance. That was not a problem for the Me 262, however, as it was more than 100 mph faster than the P-38/F-5—and jet engines thrive at higher altitudes.

The Fifteenth AF's F-5 pilots began to encounter Me 262s that fall, mainly in the Munich area of southern Germany where many of them were based, as a result of which they were henceforth normally provided with an escort of P-38s or P-51s. No P-38 ever actually shot down an Me 262, but 82nd FG pilots did damage four of them, on November 12, December 15 (two), and February 8. They were usually able to at least distract the jets and cause them to abort or shorten their passes at the F-5s, and the Me 262 pilots were respectful of the P-38's firepower.

Two 82nd FG flights were escorting a "Photo Freddie" (F-5) near Augsburg, Germany, during the November 12 mission when an Me 262 burst out of a cloud in front of them and targeted it. They turned into the jet and 2Lt. Robert E. Berry of the 96th FS opened fire at around 500 yards, scoring hits on the 262's rear fuselage, whereupon it split-S'd away.

The 1st FG had its first encounter with an Me 262 on November 26. A 94th FS flight was returning from another F-5 escort to Munich when, near Innsbruck, Austria, one of them attacked the P-38L-1 (44-24200) flown by 1Lt. Guy J. Thomas, who was lagging slightly behind the rest of the flight. Thomas was quickly shot down, and wounded. Taken prisoner, he succumbed to his injuries eight days later. He was the victim of a pilot of III *Gruppe* of JG 7, then the only jet fighter *geschwader* (wing).

On the afternoon of December 2, 1Lt. Keith W. Sheetz of the 32nd PRS was flying an atypical solo sortie to the Munich area from San Severo when he radioed one of his squadron mates on a similar mission to say that his Lightning had been hit by a jet. He contacted a flight of P-51s ten minutes later with the same message, stating that he was headed for Italy. That was the last contact with Sheetz, who was flying F-5E-3 44-23752; it was later determined that he, too, had been killed by an Me 262 of III./JG 7.

In late 1944 and early 1945, the Fifteenth AF received fifteen modified Pathfinder P-38s, using H2X "Mickey" ground-scanning radar. They were assigned to the 15th PRS and the 154th WRS, the former receiving its first four in October and the latter flying its first Pathfinder mission on December 25. One of the 15th PRS pilots who flew them, John T. Deden, later described the aircraft and its utilization:

These Mickey planes had the elongated, bulbous nose of opaque fiberglass. Inside the nose, seated in cramped quarters entered by a small hatch on the pod's bottom, was the Mickey operator, a trained officer navigator/bombardier from a bomber group. The navigator would determine the courses and targets, with the "pilot-in-command" flying the Mickey P-38. Usually these missions were flown in instrument weather, to hopefully avoid any chance of interception. In front of the navigator were the controls for the

The 96th FS's Lt. Kenneth R. Frost in the cockpit of *BATLIN BET*, P-38J-15 42-104044, coded BB, which he named after his girlfriend back in California. Another pilot wiped it out in a landing accident on November 21, 1944. (*Author's collection*)

P-38J-15 43-28676 of the 94th FS, which was assigned to the 1st FG in November 1944. The face and feather headdress of a Native American are painted on its nose, along with the name *Lincoln Mohawks*, an evident reference to the semi-pro baseball team that was part of the Boston Suburban League. There is also a single victory marking. (*Michael Bates collection*)

medium-range ground-scanning radar. The transmitter/receiver "dish" was located in the fiberglass dome. It scanned the ground for navigation purposes and to establish bombing target information.

The mission profile was that the pilot would fly the plane to the IP (initial point) of a normal bomb run. From there the navigator would guide the pilot to the correct heading and altitude for a "bomb run" while he took pictures of his radar scope showing the ground track to the target and the target itself. After the mission the pictures would be delivered to Fifteenth Air Force Headquarters for reproduction and disbursement to various bomb groups, where navigators and bombardiers would use them to lead bomber squadrons to the targets in cases where they would be obscured by clouds—for, as it was known then, "bombing-through-overcast."[10]

Due to persistent flooding at Salsola, in mid-December, the 1st FG was forced to temporarily move its operations to nearby Lucera, home of the 301st Bomb Group. Its air echelon was "bumped" from there the following month, and on January 8, it joined the 82nd FG at Vincenzo. It returned to Salsola on February 21, and then, in mid-March, the whole group moved on to its new, semi-permanent base at Lesina, just north of Salsola.

The winter of 1944–45 was another particularly cold one, and the P-38 pilots had to wear a considerable amount of clothing on their high-altitude bomber escort missions to keep reasonably warm. This on occasion presented them with a dilemma: "answering nature's call." A 94th FS pilot, John D. Mullins, described the process:

When the need to urinate could not be put off, the P-38 was equipped to handle the situation, or at least the cockpit design people thought it was. A hard rubber funnel was fitted under the seat with a hose leading down and out the bottom of the cockpit. One simply voided into the funnel and that took care of the problem. There were a number of things wrong with that scenario.

If one really, really had to go, the parachute straps had to be unfastened, various layers of clothing had to be unzipped and/or unbuttoned and, in accordance with the laws of nature, substances contract and shrink at low temperatures. The next maneuver is best described as akin to a worm being stretched out on a lawn following a rain. One is now, in theory, ready to use the relief tube. Since this operation was rarely carried out, there is a very good chance that (a.) the tube will be kinked to stop flow, (b.) the tube will be cracked, with obvious results, or (c.) the outlet will be askew, leading to a back air pressure which will indeed blow urine all over the cockpit, where it will immediately freeze, leading to instant near-instrument conditions.

The best solution: never drink much coffee before a mission.

An Me 262 claimed another P-38 on February 5, during the escort of an F-5 to Munich by two 95th FS pilots. This time, the victim was 2Lt. Arthur B. Lewis, who was flying P-38L-1 44-24063. According to his element leader, 1Lt. Harley E. Barnhart, in his official report, the 262 attacked shortly after the Lightnings turned for home following the final photo run. Barnhart "called a break and started a turn left. Lt Lewis continued straight ahead and the jet fired a short burst from very close range. I observed Lt Lewis' left outer tank afire. He

An unidentified pilot and a "Mickey" radar operator, the crew of a bulbous-nosed Pathfinder Lightning of either the 15th Photo Reconnaissance Squadron or the 154th Weather Reconnaissance Squadron of the Fifteenth AF in Italy. These photos show very clearly how the operator accessed his obviously claustrophobic compartment. (*USAF photos*)

Two interesting shots of P-38J-15 43-28650, which was delivered to the 1st FG in May 1944. It was assigned initially to Capt. (later Maj.) Thomas F. "Rafe" Raphael, CO of the 27th FS, who named it *Sweet Sue*. It was later assigned to Capt. Chester E. Trout's—at least until another pilot crashed and was killed in it on January 20, 1945. (*USAF photos*)

turned left after the jet had passed." Barnhart last saw Lewis's plane "still bearing left from the scene, still aflame on the left wing but flying nearly straight and level." It had been hit by a pilot of III *Gruppe* of *Ergänzungsgeschwader* 2 (III./EJG 2), an Me 262 operational training unit, and he was later reported to be a POW.

Due to the almost complete lack of aerial opposition after the summer of 1944, the P-38 pilots' bomber escort missions became exercises in tedium. The antidote to their boredom was a lot more ground attack sorties. Once they were relieved of their escort duties, they often headed for the deck on the way home to attack targets of opportunity, mainly in Hungary, Austria, and southern Germany. There were also more dedicated fighter sweeps.

They especially enjoyed targeting trains—specifically their locomotives, which, when hit by machine gun and cannon fire, usually exploded spectacularly in a mass of flame and steam. "Loco busting" became a particularly popular "sport" for pilots of the 14th FG. Half of the 200 locomotives claimed destroyed by XV FC pilots in February 1945 were credited to them. They included the command's two top loco busters, Lt. Col. Hugh A. Griffith, CO of the 48th FS, with thirty-six to his credit, and Lt. Col. Charles D. Chitty, Jr., the group's deputy CO, with thirty-three.

These missions were costly, however, as the Luftwaffe's flak units were plentiful, very experienced, and deadly accurate. Many P-38 pilots were lost to them during the final Allied push against the Germans and Italian fascists in northern Italy in early 1945, as they flew numerous low-level fighter-bomber sorties in direct support of the ground forces.

Aerial opposition did increase slightly in March. The Russians and the Western Allies had Germany and its one remaining European ally, Hungary, in a vice, and their territory was quickly shrinking. Their air forces then made a final, futile, effort to at least slow down the Allied advances.

On March 21, a 96th FS pilot shot down one of the six Fw 190s seen taking off from the airfield at Pápa, Hungary, during a low-level sweep. The following day the 97th FS racked up two more kills during another sweep of the same area, likewise after a bomber escort to Vienna. The first victim was a Bf 109 that was preparing to land at Pápa, and the second was an Fw 190 encountered nearby. Both 1Lt. William H. Lancaster and his wingman, 2Lt. George L. Rivest, hit the 109, which was seen to crash, but since the 82nd FG did not award shared victories, Lancaster received full credit for it. Rivest did receive credit for the 190, however. He remembered later what happened right after they downed the Bf 109:

As I was clearing the area above me I spotted an Fw 190 heading toward the fiery crash site. I was in a good position to make a 45-degree stern deflection shot, and when I got into range I opened fire and kept firing until I saw the canopy of the Fw 190 come off. I was very close and broke off. Lt Lancaster said he saw the pilot bail out.[11]

This was the 82nd FG's 548th and last aerial victory. (The 97th FS pilots also destroyed ten e/a on the ground by strafing at another nearby airfield.) Nine days later, on March 31, the 31st FG took the lead as the top-scoring USAAF fighter group in the MTO, which record the 82nd FG had held since February 1943.

Pilots of the 49th FS also encountered e/a on the 22nd, while returning from a grueling seven-hour bomber escort to the Ruhland Oil Refinery, just 60 miles south of Berlin—the

Above: February 1945: F-5s of the 3rd Photographic Group (Reconnaissance) at Florence, Italy's Peretola Airport. (*USAF photo*)

Below: Maj. Kenneth A. Gaskin, CO of the 37th FS in the latter half of 1944, shows off his P-38's rearview mirror. (*Author's collection*)

14th FG's longest mission of the war. They were credited with destroying a "twin-engined transport aircraft" and an Fw 190, and probably destroying another 190.

The next P-38 victory, on March 30, was also by a 14th FG pilot, who shot down a "biplane trainer" during a fighter sweep to Zagreb, Yugoslavia. The following day, the 1st FG scored its first aerial victory in nearly four months, pilots of its 27th FS downing an Fw 190 and an He 111 during a fighter sweep to Vienna. On April 2, two other pilots of the same squadron shot down a Bf 109 and damaged another near Eggenburg, Austria.

An Me 262 downed one more Fifteenth AF Lightning on April 4, during yet another F-5 escort, this time by a 49th FS flight. Over Hohenlinden, just east of Munich, the jet pilot made a pass at the flight leader's wingman, 2Lt. Bill Randle, who was flying P-38L-5 44-25761. One of the other P-38 pilots saw the complete tail assembly of Randle's plane being shot off. He did not see him bail out but several minutes later spotted his chute floating down and his P-38 hit the ground. Randle was soon captured.

The 14th FG scored its 426th and last air victory on April 11. As a 37th FS flight was reforming after making a strafing attack on a railroad between Munich and Salzburg, it was attacked by some Fw 190s, one of which shot down the flight leader, 1Lt. Robert W. Whitehead, killing him. This 190 was then also shot down, by Whitehead's wingman, 1Lt. Harris R. Morris, Jr., its pilot bailing out and utilizing his parachute.

The final P-38 air victory in the MTO was scored on April 15, when 1Lt. Warren E. Danielson of the 27th FS shot down an Fw 190 he encountered while strafing a rail line near Passau, Germany. This brought the 1st FG's total to 440. The theater total for P-38s was 1,425, including ten by the 350th FG and one by the 154th WRS.

The Axis forces in Italy surrendered on April 29, and as of May 9, the war in Europe was over. The Lockheed Lightning had made a valuable contribution to the Allies' victory in the Mediterranean Theater of Operations, as an interceptor, an escort fighter, a fighter-bomber, and in the photo reconnaissance role.

The five Lightning groups in Italy continued to serve there for a few months after VE Day but were inactivated and their personnel returned to the U.S. shortly after the Japanese also surrendered, on August 15—the 14th and 82nd FGs effective September 9, 1945, the 3rd RG on September 12, the 1st FG on October 16, and the 5th PRG on October 28. The 154th WRS also returned to the States, in July, but it was not inactivated. They all left their aircraft behind in Italy, and, as detailed in Chapter 7, some of them would later see further service with the new Italian Air Force.

Above: Armorers of the 1st FG hard at work in the predawn, loading bombs for the next day's mission. (*USAF photo*)

Below left: A 1st FG ground crewman shows off the "self-styled auto" he has constructed from a 150-gallon auxiliary gas tank, complete with wheels and a Plexiglas windshield. The P-38 in the background, L-5 44-25734, No. 40, was assigned to Lt. Joseph R. Elliott of the 71st FS, who was killed in it over Italy on April 15, 1945. (*USAF photo*)

Below right: Lt. Ralph M. "Monty" Powers, Jr., of the 95th FS poses with a colorfully painted P-38L-5, 44-25713, which was assigned to the 82nd FG on March 14, 1945. (*Author's collection*)

6

Lightnings in Action:
The CBI
(Tenth and Fourteenth Air Forces)

The first Lightning unit to be assigned to the China-Burma-India (CBI) Theater—specifically to the Tenth AF—was the 9th PRS. The Tenth AF was activated at Patterson Field, Ohio, in February 1942 to serve in India and China. Its headquarters left the U.S. by ship in March and arrived at New Delhi in mid-May.

The 9th Squadron's ground echelon reached Karachi, India (now part of Pakistan), also by ship from the U.S. (Washington State), at the end of July, while its pilots were flown there from Newark, New Jersey, where they had delivered its thirteen F-4s for shipment by sea. The aircraft arrived at Karachi on September 10, were offloaded at the city's port, and then towed, *sans* their outer wing sections and propellers, through its streets and then along the road to the Karachi Air Base, where they were reassembled and flight tested. They were then flown to an air depot at nearby Agra to have their fuel tanks—which had all incurred damage—repaired. The squadron's services were badly needed to help keep track of the Japanese forces in Burma, which were a serious threat to the Allies in India.

The squadron's resources would be stretched thin for a while, as the only Lightning recon unit in the CBI. It initially served both the Tenth and Fourteenth AFs. The latter was activated in China in March 1943 under the command of Maj. Gen. Claire L. Chennault, formerly CO of the Chinese Air Force's American Volunteer Group (AVG)—better known as "The Flying Tigers." Prior to the activation of the Fourteenth AF Chennault had commanded the China Air Task Force, which was established as a subsidiary of the Tenth AF in July 1942.

The 9th PRS moved from Karachi to Chakulia, just west of Calcutta, at the end of November 1942 and flew its first mission from there on December 1. In early January, it transferred to Pandaveswar, northwest of Calcutta, where it worked closely with the B-24-equipped 7th BG, which had begun flying missions to Rangoon, Burma. Two of the squadron's F-4s flew the first photo reconnaissance mission to Rangoon on February 16, 1943. It had a detachment operating from Dinjan, far to the east in Assam State, just below the Himalayas, starting in March, and it had also established a flight at Kunming, China, on the other side of the mountains, in November 1942, from where a detachment was sent, in February, to Kweilin, 500 miles to the east in central China. Shortly thereafter, the squadron began to receive some of the newer F-5As, which could utilize two 300-gallon auxiliary fuel

The 9th PRS's F-4-1s arriving at Karachi in September 1942 on board a freighter and then on the dock after being unloaded. Note the coverings (tape and waterproof tarps and paper) that were utilized to protect them from the elements during their trans-Pacific journey, and the fact that both their propellers and outer wings had been removed. (*9th PRS Association collection*)

Above left: The 9th PRS F-4s begin their road trip from Karachi's docks. (*9th PRS Association collection*)

Above right: F-4-1 41-2160 of the 9th PRS being towed from Karachi's port to its air base. (*9th PRS Association collection*)

Below: March 4, 1943: An F-4 of the 9th PRS lands at Dum Dum, near Calcutta. (*USAF photo*)

Ground crewmen of the 9th PRS working on an F-4 somewhere in India. (*9th PRS Association collection*)

tanks that increased its range considerably. Previously, its F-4s, flying from Pandaveswar (which was 400 miles from the India-Burma border) with the old 150-gallon tanks, would have to refuel at a forward base on the way home.

Along with most of the USAAF's other photo recon units, its official designation was changed to 9th Photographic Squadron (Light) effective February 6, 1943—and then back to Photo Reconnaissance Squadron on November 13 of that year.

One of the AVG's top pilots, Frank Schiel, Jr., shot down four Japanese aircraft and destroyed three more on the ground as a Flying Tiger. After transferring to the USAAF in China, he was given the rank of major and appointed CO of the 23rd FG's 74th FS. While with the AVG Schiel had flown reconnaissance missions in a stripped-down P-40 that had been fitted with a camera. After taking command of the 74th FS, he flew a similarly converted Republic P-43 Lancer borrowed from the Chinese Air Force.

It was on November 26, 1942 that three 9th PRS F-4s, each fitted with four K-17 aerial cameras and an autopilot, arrived at Kunming, where the 74th FS was also based. Maj. Schiel was fascinated by them and immediately checked himself out in one. He flew his first photo mission in a Lightning on December 1, to Thailand. Four days later, he flew his fourth, a very long one to the island of Formosa (now Taiwan), with the F-4 flight commander, Maj. Dale Swartz. They stopped at another Chinese airfield to refuel on the way back to Kunming, and after taking off again, they became separated in some bad weather. Schiel never showed up at Kunming, and thirteen days later, his and his Lightning's remains were discovered nearby, where he had crashed into a mountain.

Above: A 9th PRS pilot prepares to fly *Stinky 2*, F-5A-10 42-13301, on a mission over Burma from Pandaveswar, India, sometime in 1943. (*USAF photo*)

Below left: Capt. William H. Weaver in the cockpit of one of the 9th Photo Squadron's F-5s. (*9th PRS Association collection*)

Below right: The official caption for this photo is "Crew chief hands a parachute up to the pilot of a Lockheed F-5A of the 21st Photographic Reconnaissance Squadron, based in China, prior to a seven-hour milk-run mission to Hainan Island." (*USAF photo*)

In July 1943, the Fourteenth AF acquired its own PR unit, the 21st Photographic Squadron (Light), which had arrived in India fresh from the U.S. in June and soon replaced the 9th PS in China. The 9th moved to Barrackpore, north of Calcutta, at the end of October. Both squadrons had a lot of territory to cover and operated numerous detachments at many different airfields in India and China throughout the remainder of the war.

The 21st Squadron's "A" (Headquarters) Flight took the 9th PS flight's place at Kunming in July, its aircraft then covering Indochina and parts of Burma, while "B" Flight was established at Kweilin to provide photo coverage of the area from Hong Kong to Shanghai to the major Japanese base at Hankow, near the confluence of the Hsiang and Han Rivers. The rest of the squadron arrived at Kunming in August and its "C" Flight was sent to Suichwan, northeast of Kweilin, in October to cover Formosa. These flights were all self sufficient and operated as small squadrons.

The First P-38s

On July 6, 1943, the pilots of "Squadron X," the new P-38 unit that had been organized in North Africa the previous month for service in China (see Chapter 5), took off from Telergma, Algeria, for their long flight to Kunming. The orders had come through on the 1st, for twenty-eight officers, fifty-eight enlisted men, and twenty-five P-38Gs, the ground crews and other non-flying personnel preceding the pilots in transport aircraft.

The trip would take several weeks and cover nearly 6,000 miles. There were twelve stops along the way: Benghazi, Libya; Cairo, Egypt; Tel Aviv, Palestine; Habbaniya, Iraq; Abadan, Iran; Bahrain Island in the Persian Gulf; Sharja, Arabia; and, in India, Jiwani, Karachi, Agra, Gaya, and Chabua, from where they would fly over the Himalayas to China. At Cairo, they joined up with a Curtiss C-46 transport that would lead most of them to Karachi.

Twenty-two of the P-38s and twenty-four of their pilots would make it to Kunming. There were the inevitable mechanical, equipment, and weather problems *en route* that delayed some of them, and three Lightnings were lost in accidents. The pilots reunited with their ground crews at Agra, and their aircraft were then serviced properly prior to their climactic and potentially dangerous flight over the Himalayas.

X Squadron's first five P-38s arrived at Kunming on July 23. The last flight from Chabua was led there over the mountains by Col. Bruce K. Holloway, CO of the 23rd FG, on August 5. It was on this flight that the squadron suffered its only pilot casualty of the trip, ironically on its very last segment. Second Lieutenant Robert J. Barrett, an 82nd FG veteran with two confirmed aerial victories to his credit, became disoriented in some clouds and crashed P-38G-10 42-13363 into the side of a mountain.

It was at Kunming, on August 2, that the unit finally received its official designation, the 449th FS, and Capt. Sam L. Palmer, who had led it to China, was appointed its CO. Effective August 26, it was attached to the 23rd FG and then moved to Lingling, nearly 600 miles east of Kunming.

Gen. Chennault had wanted some single-engined North American P-51s to replace his obsolescent P-40s and was not pleased to receive instead a squadron of P-38s. His main concern was the amount of his precious gasoline they would require, compared to the P-40 or the P-51

Chinese Army aircraft spotters examine a 449th FS P-38 carefully to memorize its distinctive lines. (*USAF photo*)

(some of which would arrive in China before the end of the year). As with most of his meager supplies, it had to be flown over the Himalayas ("The Hump") by transport planes from India. Chennault would, in fact, soon come to appreciate the P-38's contribution to the air war in China, particularly because of its range, and he highly valued his F-5 photo reconnaissance units.

The day after the arrival of the first P-38s at Kunming, on July 24, three of them were sent to Kweilin to help intercept JAAF raids on its airfield, which two of them did that morning right after their arrival, along with some P-40s. First Lieutenant Lewden M. Enslen, a 14th FG veteran, was credited with one of the six "Zeros" (actually Nakajima Ki-43 Oscars and Nakajima Ki-44 Tojos) claimed shot down along with three bombers. The second P-38, flown by a 23rd FG P-40 pilot with experience in the Lightning, was also shot down and the pilot wounded.

On the 26th, Enslen went on to down another Oscar and probably destroy one over Hengyang, a couple of hundred miles northwest of Kweilin, and scored another probable there the following day—before any of his squadron mates had been able to score at all. Although the 449th would officially be based at Lingling for the next six months, it would continue to operate detachments at Kweilin and Hengyang.

From those bases, P-38s could easily reach the Japanese occupied port of Canton, about 250 miles to the south. The 449th's missions there resulted in several air victories for its pilots, by far the most important of which turned out to be the twin-engined transport shot down by 2Lt. Billie M. Beardsley on September 9 during a dive bombing mission to Canton's docks. The converted Mitsubishi Ki-21 Sally bomber turned out to have been carrying Lt. Gen. Moritaka Nakazono, commander of the JAAF's 3rd Air Division, and members of his staff, all of whom were killed. It was Nakazono who had initiated the attacks on Fourteenth

Two very different photographs of the 449th FS's P-38G-10 42-13437, *Golden Eagle*/No. 310, which was one of the Lightnings its pilots flew to China from North Africa in July 1943. In the first one, taken at Lingling, its assigned pilot, 1Lt. Robert B. Schultz, poses with it after scoring his third and fourth victories on November 25, 1943 (he scored his fifth and last on March 4, 1944). The second photo, in which its colorful artwork has faded badly, was taken after Schultz had completed his combat tour. In it, Capt. Billie M. Beardsley (on the right) helps a ground crewman paint another bomb symbol on its nose. Shortly thereafter, 42-13437 became Lt. James Heitkotter's *Black Lace*. (*USAF photos*)

AF airfields that had commenced, coincidentally, on July 23, the day the first P-38s arrived in China, and in the defense of which they had been participating.

As of October 2, 1943, the 449th FS was reassigned, administratively, to the P-40-equipped 51st FG, which had just moved to China and the Fourteenth AF from the Tenth AF in India.

On October 30, eight 449th FS P-38s—four carrying bombs and the other four providing cover for them—flew what turned out to be a really rough mission, from Lingling. After topping off their fuel tanks at Hengyang, they proceeded northeast to dive-bomb shipping on the Yangtze River. While attacking a steamer near Kiukiang, they were bounced by Oscars of the JAAF's 25th *Sentai* (Group).

Now-Capt. Enslen, who had assumed command of the squadron on September 17, was pulling up from his dive-bombing run when he was attacked by two of the Oscars. His right engine was hit and exploded, and his P-38, G-10 42-13253, was last seen by his squadron mates with that engine "enveloped in flames." It and three other Lightnings were lost in this action, one of whose pilots, 1Lt. Tommy J. Taylor, was killed outright. Second Lieutenants Thomas D. Harmon (the former All-American college football player) and Jordan E. Robins, Jr., were also shot down but evaded capture with the help of the Chinese. Capt. Enslen's P-38 crashed 20 miles north of Kiukiang, and he was pulled from its cockpit, unconscious and severely injured, by some other Chinese. He died of his injuries on November 11. The P-38 pilots were credited with destroying six of the Oscars in this fight, which they had identified as "Zeros" and "Tojos."

Replacing Lewden Enslen as 449th FS CO, on November 9, was Lt. Col. George B. McMillan, a very experienced and charismatic fighter pilot. A prewar USAAC officer, McMillan had resigned his commission in 1941 to join the AVG, with which he had been credited with the destruction of four and a half JAAF bombers over Burma. When the AVG was disbanded in the summer of 1942, he had rejoined the USAAF.

The Formosa Raid

Due to the distances involved, until November 1943, the Fourteenth AF had been unable to attack Formosa, which the Japanese were using as a major supply and training base. However, with its new airfield at Suichwan, 125 miles east of Hengyang, and long-range fighters (the 449th Squadron's P-38s and P-51A Mustangs of the 23rd FG's 76th Squadron) now available, a strike became feasible. Photo flights over the island by 21st PRS pilots had revealed 150 aircraft at the Shinchiku A/D on Formosa's northwest coast, and a mission to it was planned.

On the late afternoon of November 24, eight 449th FS pilots flew to Suichwan, joining there eight P-51s and fourteen B-25s. Although Lt. Col. McMillan was going to participate in this important mission, he had decided to ask the squadron's original CO, Capt. Palmer, now an administrative officer, to lead it, given McMillan's lack of recent experience in China.

The thirty-plane formation took off from Suichwan on the morning of the 25th (Thanksgiving Day) and approached the island just above the surface of the Formosa Strait. The 449th's P-38s reached it first, their job being to clear away the enemy fighters ahead of the B-25s. No fighters were seen in the air over Shinchiku initially, but some bombers, identified as Sallys, were in the process of landing there and the Lightning pilots waded into them, shooting down five. (Shinchiku was a naval air base, and the bombers were actually JNAF Mitsubishi G3M "Nells.")

A variety of other enemy aircraft was encountered in the air, but very few of the base's fighters were able to take off during the attack. Capt. Palmer shot down one Zeke and the 76th FS, bringing up the rear of the formation, two. The B-25s dropped their fragmentation bombs on the airfield and then the P-38s and the P-51s strafed it. Forty-six Japanese planes were subsequently confirmed destroyed there, fifteen of them in the air, of which the 449th's pilots were credited with twelve, the 76th FS two and B-25 gunners one. The top scorer was Sam Palmer, who downed two unidentified aircraft in addition to the Zeke. The P-38 pilots were also credited with ten e/a destroyed on the ground by their strafing and the P-51s four; the rest were destroyed by the B-25's bombs.

An F-5 pilot, Lt. Edward M. Penick of the 21st Photo Squadron's "C" Flight, who had taken some of the preliminary target photos, photographed the results of the raid fifteen minutes after the bombers and fighters had departed—and after he had dropped a 500-lb. bomb on a fuel dump at Shinchiku. His photos were a major factor in the estimate of the damage that had been done there.

On December 10, Lt. Col. McMillan scored his first air victory with the 449th FS when he scrambled to intercept two fast, high-flying Dinahs reconnoitering Lingling—which had previously been pretty much immune to interception by the Fourteenth AF's P-40s. He shot down one of them and damaged the other before his guns jammed. This made McMillan an ace.

Two days later, eight of the 449th's pilots intercepted a JAAF raid on Hengyang. Concentrating on the escorting fighters, Lt. Col. McMillan shot down a Tojo and damaged an Oscar, while 1Lt. Lee O. Gregg, a future ace, destroyed one Tojo and probably destroyed another. A third P-38 pilot was credited with a probable Oscar.

On February 10, four 449th Squadron P-38s and some P-51s strafed Kiukiang, and on the way home, they encountered three twin-engined Kawasaki Ki-45 "Nick" fighters, one of which was shot down by Lt. Col. McMillan and the other by 2Lt. Keith Mahon, another future ace. The third was damaged by Capt. Rex T. Barber, who was already an ace. Barber, who had joined the squadron a few days earlier, scored five victories during his first combat tour with the 70th FS on Guadalcanal and had famously shot down a Betty bomber (believed by many to be the one carrying Admiral Yamamoto) on April 18, 1943 (see Chapter 3).

Two days later, fourteen 449th FS P-38s clashed near Suichuan with eleven Ki-44s of the 85th *Sentai* and fourteen Ki-43s of the 11th *Sentai*, of which two Oscars and four Tojos were claimed destroyed and six more probably destroyed, for the loss of one P-38 whose pilot bailed out safely. Gregg was credited with a Tojo and a probable Oscar and Capt. Barber with two Oscars probably destroyed.

The Twin Dragon Squadron

With more of the latest model P-38Hs becoming available in theater, a new fighter squadron, the 459th, was activated with them at Karachi on September 1, 1943 for service with the Tenth AF. It received a nucleus of experienced personnel, including pilots, from the Tenth's P-40-equipped 80th FG (to which the 459th FS was attached, for administrative purposes) and the 311th Fighter-Bomber Group, which flew North American P-51As and A-36A dive bombers. The 459th's first CO was Capt. John E. Fouts, Jr., a veteran P-40 pilot who had seen a lot of action with the 51st FG before transferring to the 80th. Its personnel adopted a colorful insignia for the unit—a two-headed dragon—and it soon became known as the Twin Dragon Squadron. In early 1944, its P-38s were painted with elaborate green dragons on both outer engine cowlings and booms, all the way back to their tails.

The squadron moved up to the front at Kurmitola, northeast of Calcutta, in early November. It flew its first combat mission on November 20, when four P-38s escorted some B-25s to Kalewa, Burma, and it suffered its first pilot casualty the following day when Flt. Off. Edmund J. Bovitt, flying P-38H-1 42-66714, disappeared during air-to-ground gunnery practice. No sign of him or his aircraft was subsequently seen, and it was eventually determined that he had crashed into the nearby ocean.

From November 25 to December 1, 1943, the 459th FS and the 311th Group's 530th Fighter-Bomber Squadron flew a series of bomber escort missions to Rangoon, 1,200 miles southeast of Kurmitola. Of the four P-38s that accompanied Tenth and Fourteenth AF B-24s there on November 27, only two returned. Capt. Armin J. Ortmeyer, Jr., and 2Lt. Jay R. Harlan were both MIA, victims of Oscar pilots of the JAAF's elite 64th *Sentai*. (Harlan was killed outright and Ortmeyer died later while a prisoner of the Japanese.) During another Rangoon escort mission on December 1 by fifteen P-38s, the 459th's pilots scored their first air victories when 1Lt. Hampton E. Boggs shot down an Oscar and 2Lt. Walter E. Thompson a Nick. Another Nick was probably destroyed.

On December 26, the 459th flew a notable mission that was a preview of some even more successful missions to come. It was a strafe of the enemy airfield at Anisakan, in central Burma. Three Oscars were destroyed, one probably destroyed and three damaged on the ground.

Headquarters of the 8th PRG arrived at Bally, also near Calcutta, from the U.S. at the end of March 1944, *sans* squadrons. Assigned to it there were three Tenth AF recon

Kurmitola, India, February 1944: 459th FS pilot Lt. Amel Boldman, Jr., in the cockpit of his assigned P-38, H-5 42-67002, named *Katy-Did II*. This aircraft was lost in action over Burma on March 25 while being flown by another pilot. Lt. Boldman was shot down (in P-38H-5 42-66986), wounded and taken prisoner on April 5, subsequently dying in captivity. (*Michael Bates collection*)

squadrons, only one of which, the 9th PRS, was an F-5 unit. However, another one, the 40th PRS, would join the 8th Group in July, soon after its arrival from the States. It became operational on September 6.

Back in China, on February 18, the 449th FS moved from Lingling to Suichwan, beginning a very busy period of operations during which its pilots flew a variety of missions that included strafing, dive bombing, and bomber escorts—many of them on Yangtze River sweeps.

Lt. Col. McMillan was sent to India on detached service in late March, leaving his operations officer, Capt. Barber, in temporary command of the squadron. On April 18, the Japanese launched their huge *Ichi-go* ground offensive south from the Yellow River into south-central China, which would have huge consequences for the 449th FS. Rex Barber's tour with the squadron came to a premature end eleven days later, during another river sweep near Kiuikiang while escorting two B-25s. The formation was jumped by 25th *Sentai* Oscars, and although three of them were claimed destroyed, two of the P-38s were also shot down and another, badly damaged, crash-landed back at Suichwan.

Capt. Barber was one of the downed P-38 pilots. He bailed out successfully and then barely escaped capture by the Japanese thanks to the help of Chinese civilians. However, he was severely injured, and shortly after returning to Suichwan in early June, he was sent back to the U.S.

Meanwhile, in India, in late February, the 459th Squadron's pilots underwent gunnery training at a school run by the RAF, and on March 1, the unit moved to Chittagong, southeast of Kurmitola on the Bay of Bengal near the Burmese border. There it came under the temporary operational control of the RAF's 224 Group, and during the next three months, it flew an extraordinarily successful series of long-range fighter sweeps to JAAF airfields in Burma, its objective to destroy as many e/a as possible, in the air and on the ground. On twenty-three missions from March 10 to June 6, 1944, its pilots would be credited with destroying sixty-five e/a in the air and sixty-two on the ground, plus many more probably destroyed or damaged, for the loss of eleven P-38s and their pilots. These exploits would earn the squadron a well-deserved DUC.

The 459th's most successful mission was on March 11, when twelve of its pilots caught some Oscars taking off from Aungban and picked them off one by one. They then proceeded to nearby Heho, with the same result. They also shot up some aircraft on the ground. The final tally was thirteen Ki-43s shot down and five more probably destroyed, plus five e/a destroyed and two damaged on the ground. Flt. Off. Carl M. Beardslee, flying P-38H-5 42-66997, was last seen being attacked by several of the Oscars; it was learned later that he was a POW.

On March 20, Maj. Fouts completed his combat tour and Capt. (soon to be Maj.) Verl D. Luehring, previously an 80th FG squadron commander, assumed command of the 459th FS, which position he would hold for the next year. On April 3, the squadron received its first P-38J and a dozen had arrived by the 18th. Their improved range, due to the intercoolers in the wings on the P-38Hs having been replaced with gas tanks, would prove to be very beneficial.

One of the many accounts of P-38 pilots returning from a combat mission on single engine was recorded by William Aycock, the technical representative of the Allison Division of General Motors assigned to the 459th FS. The pilot in question was 2Lt. Burdette C. Goodrich, the date was April 25, 1944 and the aircraft was P-38H-5 42-67009. The

The 459th FS's Capt. William G. Broadfoot, Jr., in the cockpit of his assigned P-38J-5, 42-67288, *HELLS BELLES II*. The five Japanese flags evidently represent the one and a half enemy aircraft he destroyed in the air and the three and a half he destroyed on the ground. (*Michael Bates collection*)

mission was a fighter sweep to Heho, during which six Oscars were destroyed in the air (one of them by Goodrich) and two on the ground. This is Aycock's rather cryptic report to the company regarding Goodrich's subsequent experiences that day:

Center intake manifold dropped on right engine during strafing pass on an airfield. Fuel intake mixture caught fire and burned between banks. Heard sound as though one machine gun was running away. First noticed loss of manifold pressure on right engine and revolutions per minute (RPM) surging, 350 to 400 MPH at time of failure. Then noticed bulge in top engine cowls. Two minutes after failure engine mixture control was cut off. A Zero then started a rear pass on Lt. Goodrich so he pushed everything full forward on the left engine and made successful evasive action. After losing the Zero, he feathered the prop on his right engine.

During the next five minutes, Lt. Goodrich climbed to 5,000 feet. He first called Capt. [Walter F.] Duke, his flight leader, and reported that he had lost an engine. Capt. Duke told him to turn right and then when he saw Lt. Goodrich was on course for home base, he told him to straighten out, and Capt. Duke dropped down to escort him. Capt. Duke then called Lt. Goodrich and told him to hit the deck and maintain as high an airspeed as possible. When Lt. Goodrich reached 0 altitude from 5,000, he was indicating 420 MPH pulling sixty inches of manifold pressure and 3,000 RPMs. Passed over an enemy airfield where small arms fire was encountered. Thirty minutes after the initial encounter at Heho, Lt. Goodrich and Capt. Duke reached the Irrawaddy River and Goodrich reduced the manifold pressure on his left engine to forty inches and 2,600 RPMs and climbed from 0 altitude to 9,000 feet to clear the Chin Hills. After crossing the hills, he throttled back to thirty-five inches of manifold pressure and 2,300 RPMs and arrived home base in another thirty minutes.

During the thirty minutes that he pulled sixty inches of manifold pressure, his oil and coolant temperatures were against the peg. When he throttled back to forty inches of manifold pressure, the temperatures returned to normal range. The cowling over the exhaust manifold just ahead of the turbo on the left engine was discolored to a bright orange.[1]

A ground crewman directs the pilot of the 9th PRS's *Miss Virginia E*, Lt. Gerald E. Chelius, out of its revetment. This aircraft, F-5B-1 42-67375, was destroyed in a landing accident in India on May 11, 1944. (*USAF photo*)

The 459th flew the last in its series of fighter sweeps to enemy airfields on June 6, just before the monsoon rains began. Twenty P-38s took off early that morning for a "beat up" of the Heho and Meiktila A/Ds. Oscars were once again encountered, and in the fight that ensued three were shot down—one each by Maj. Maxwell H. Glenn, Capt. Boggs, and 1Lt. Goodrich, the latter with his assigned aircraft, P-38H-5 42-67001, giving him a total of five and a half confirmed in the air. Unfortunately, Goodrich was also shot down and Capt. Duke was missing in action. Goodrich was captured and died in a Japanese prison camp seven months later.

Walter Duke, who was flying *his* assigned aircraft, P-38J-10 42-67626, was, with ten confirmed kills, both the 459th Squadron's and the Tenth AF's top-scoring fighter pilot. He had also destroyed eight and a half e/a on the ground. Duke's exact fate remained unknown until well after the end of the war, when some research into JAAF records indicated that after he had become separated from his squadron mates he was attacked from above by a flight of Oscars and shot down and killed. Reportedly, he downed three of the Oscars before his demise, but that could never be officially confirmed.

The Fourteenth AF was assigned another Lightning photo reconnaissance squadron, the 35th, in the summer of 1944. It left Will Rogers Field in Oklahoma in April and arrived at Guskhara, India, north of Calcutta, two months later. Its "A" Flight was immediately sent to Kunming to gain some operational experience with the 21st PRS. The rest of the squadron had joined it there by September 1, and the whole unit moved a few miles northeast to Chanyi two weeks later. It established flights at Yunnanyi, to the west near the Burmese border; at Nanning, to the southeast near the Gulf of Tonkin; then, in October, at Chihkiang, far to the northeast in Hunan Province; and, in November, at Suichwan. Many of the Fourteenth AF's units were constantly on the move by then, barely keeping ahead of the huge Japanese ground offensives in central and south China that temporarily captured many of its airfields—including Hengyang, Lingling, and Nanning.

The 21st PRS, still headquartered at Kunming, had, in April 1944, established its new "D" Flight at Liangshan, northeast of Chungking, near the Yangtze River, to cover

Above left: May 1944: 459th FS ground crewmen work on P-38J-10 42-67626, ten-victory ace Capt. Walter Duke's *Miss-V*, in which he was killed in action over Burma on June 6. (*USAF photo*)

Above right: A 21st PRS camera technician unloads film from an F-5 named *FRANTIC* at Lingling, China. It has just returned from a 1,600-mile sortie to Yawata, Japan. (*USAF photo*)

Below: An F-5 of the 35th PRS in China. (*Author's collection*)

northeast China and parts of Manchuria. It then had additional flights or detachments at Kanchow, south of Suichwan; Liuchow, southwest of Kweilin; Hanchung, far to the north near Ankang; and Luliang, a few miles southeast of Kunming. Generally speaking, the 21st's area of responsibility became north China and the 35th Squadron's south China.

During the spring of 1944, the 21st's "C" Flight at Suichwan flew some long-range, high-altitude photo missions to the Japanese Home Islands and to the Philippines. For example, Lt. John M. McNicholas completed a recon of Luzon, including Clark Field and Manila, at 30,000 feet on May 12—unopposed.

On May 6, the Fourteenth AF launched a huge (by CBI standards) raid on the Japanese supply base at Hankou, north of Suichwan. The fifty-four participating aircraft included B-25s, P-40s, P-51s, and eight 449th FS Lightnings, several of which were new P-38Js. They and the Mustangs, flying from Suichwan, comprised the formation's top cover.

It was bounced by two dozen Ki-43s of the 25th *Sentai* 120 miles south of Hankou, precipitating a huge dogfight as the American fighter pilots strived to protect the bombers. They were successful in that endeavor and the B-25s did bomb the target effectively, but the cost was high. First Lieutenant Gregg led his four-plane P-38 flight into the Oscars but it was quickly overwhelmed by their superior numbers. He and two others were shot down, while the fourth pilot managed to escape after losing an engine. Two of them were killed and Lee Gregg returned later after being rescued by some Chinese. He was credited with two Oscars confirmed destroyed, but the other 449th FS credits were for four probables and a damaged. One P-51 was also lost, and the only other confirmed victory was by a Mustang pilot.

Six days later, the JAAF sent more than 100 aircraft, in three waves, to "annihilate" Suichwan. They were not successful, however, and the P-40, P-51, and P-38 pilots claimed

These two photographs show 21st PRS Lightnings being refueled somewhere in China. The one on the left is F-5B-1 42-67388. (*USAF photos*)

seven of them shot down and many more probably destroyed and damaged, including one Oscar destroyed and another damaged by the 449th FS. Although claiming to have "wiped out" Suichwan, the Japanese in fact destroyed just one P-40 in the air and one B-25 on the ground, but their attacks did create a serious fuel shortage there.

The 449th Squadron continued its fight against the Japanese forces approaching Suichwan for the next month, climaxed by two huge blows to its morale. On June 24, Lt. Col. McMillan was attacking enemy ground troops when the right engine of his P-38, J-10 42-67673, was hit by small arms fire. While trying to put some distance between himself and the Japanese, his left engine froze as he was about to attempt a water landing on a river. The aircraft then caught fire and he crashed in flames before he could reach it.

As if the loss of their beloved CO was not enough, the squadron's personnel had to evacuate Suichwan two days later as the Japanese closed in. It moved first to Er Tong, near Kweilin, temporarily and then, in early July, to Chengkung.

It was from Chengkung, on July 29, that the 449th FS flew one of its most successful missions. This was a bomber escort to the docks and the airfield at Sanya, on the south coast of Hainan Island, where were based the Zekes of the JNAF's 254th *Kokutai* (Air Group), which had been attacking unescorted American bombers on sea sweeps along the China coast.

Seventeen 449th Squadron P-38s flew to Nanning, the closest Allied airfield to Hainan, early that morning to join up with the bombers. One aborted on the way to Nanning, another was unable to take off from there and three more had to abort *en route* to the target. The remaining twelve P-38s accompanied twenty-five B-24s to Sanya Bay, where they were intercepted by eighteen Zekes. In the ensuing fight, seven enemy fighters were confirmed destroyed, five probably destroyed, and four damaged. The Zekes were misidentified as Oscars, as they looked a lot like them and the Fourteenth AF's fighter pilots seldom encountered JNAF aircraft, which were based only at airfields along the coast of China.

Lt. Donald R. Forsythe, a 449th FS pilot, and his assigned P-38 *Sonnova Beast*, J-10 42-67846. (*Daniel Jackson collection*)

It was also in July that the 449th was ordered to send a detachment from Chengkung east to Yunnanyi, where for the next eight months it would support the Chinese Army in its Salween Campaign along the China–Burma border. Eight P-38s arrived there on the 25th.

After turning back two separate Japanese invasions of India in early 1944, the Allies began advancing from there against the enemy forces in Burma, which the 459th FS supported so effectively with its attacks on the JAAF's airfields. By the time the monsoon rains began in June, the Allied air forces had pretty much neutralized the JAAF there. The 459th had been credited with seventy-one aerial kills by then but would add just eleven more by the end of the war. Although it would continue to fly some bomber escorts, mainly to Rangoon, it would now be primarily a fighter-bomber unit. During the Allied offensive in Burma, enemy-controlled bridges became prime targets, and the 459th FS excelled at "bridge busting." During one nine-day period in February 1945, its dive-bombing P-38s put eleven of them out of commission, and a week later, it destroyed three in one day.

The 459th's pilots encountered enemy fighters on two bomber escorts to Rangoon in November 1944, claiming two Oscars and a Tojo destroyed on November 4 and another Tojo on the 13th. The squadron received its first P-38Ls, with the new dive flaps and aileron boost, later that month.

Encounters with e/a were also becoming rare in China, as the JAAF had shot its wad in the *Ichi-go* campaign, and reinforcements that would normally have gone to the CBI were being sent instead to the Philippines to counter the recent American invasion of Leyte Island. By the end of 1944, the 449th FS's main assignments were fighter sweeps and bomber escorts to Indochina, Thailand (a Japanese ally), and Burma. A unique exception to the usual lack of aerial opposition took place on November 11.

On that date, nine P-51s and eight 449th FS P-38s took off from Yunnanyi to attack the airfields at Chiang Mai and Lampang in Thailand. One P-38 pilot aborted *en route*, and as the P-51s strafed the airfields, the top cover Lightnings encountered five obsolete, fixed-undercarriage Nakajima Ki-27 "Nates" of the Royal Thai Air Force. All five of the Nates were shot down; two were claimed by P-51 pilots and two by P-38 pilots, while the fifth was shared by four pilots from both squadrons. It was not, however, totally one-sided, as the nimble little Nates managed to shoot down one of the Mustangs and damage two of the Lightnings.

The 449th's last major air action took place on January 5, 1945, when eight of its P-38s from Chengkung and a dozen P-51s from Kunming flew another sweep to Sanya on Hainan Island—one of the Lightnings and four Mustangs aborting *en route*. This mission was led by the squadron's new CO, Capt. Ralph L. Wire.

As the American fighters strafed the Sanya airfield, some Zekes began to take off from it, and in the low-level dogfights that ensued, the P-51 pilots were credited with shooting down five (claimed as Tojos) and the 449th's pilots six (claimed as Oscars)—three of the latter to 1Lt. Keith Mahon, which gave him a total of five victories and made him an ace. Capt. Wire was credited with two, which also made *him* an ace, as he had scored three victories on a previous P-38 tour with the 9th FS in New Guinea. Five e/a were destroyed on the ground by the Mustangs and one by the P-38s. One P-51 pilot was MIA and three P-38 pilots had to bail out on their return to Chengkung due to combinations of battle damage, fuel starvation, and encroaching darkness, but they all survived.

Above: Chittagong, India: 459th FS armorers load some of the then-new 4.5-inch M8 rockets into the AC-MIC launchers on Maj. Willard J. Webb's aircraft, P-38J-10 42-67842. Webb scored two of his three aerial victories in this aircraft. (*USAF photo*)

Below: Armorers of the 459th FS load a 500-lb. bomb on No. 42-67842, now *Irish Lassie*, Lt. William G. Baumeister's assigned aircraft. Baumeister was shot down and killed in it during a bomber escort to Rangoon on November 19, 1944. (*USAF photo*)

Geronimo II, P-38L-1 44-23792 of the 459th FS, was assigned to Lt. Oscar L. Garland. (*Michael Bates collection*)

Ralph Wire and Keith Mahon (who had received his promotion to captain the day before) were practicing their dogfighting skills together on February 2 when Wire's P-38 suddenly spiraled out of control. He was able to bail out but struck its tail and was badly injured. He went to hospital (where he first learned of his promotion to major) and was soon evacuated back to the States.

By early 1945, lots of the new P-38Ls were arriving in theater, and the 449th began replacing its well-used older aircraft with them. The squadron's pilots would fly the latter over The Hump to an air depot in India, pick up the brand-new ones, and fly them back to China.

The 35th PRS, whose H.Q. were still based at Chanyi, established additional flights in 1945: at Chengkung (in February); Laohwangping, between Kunming and Hengyang (also in February); once again at Kunming (in May); and at Nanning (in July), after its recapture. Following the Japanese surrender in August, the whole squadron reunited at Luliang in September to prepare for its move later that month to the U.S., where it would be inactivated in November.

The 21st PRS, still based at Kunming, moved its "C" Flight to Hsian, far to the north on the Wei River, in February 1945 and its "B" Flight to Lafieng, just west of China's capital, Chonquin, in early May. A week later, H.Q. and "A" Flight transferred to Shwangliu, in northwest China near Chengtu in Szechwan Province. "D" Flight had been based at Hanchung, just west of Ankang and south of Hsian in Shensi Province, since the previous October. The squadron had also established a flight at Ankang and one at Chihkiang, in Hunan Province northwest of Hengyang, before the whole unit moved to Hangchow, on the coast south of Shanghai, in October 1945, from where it returned to the U.S. in December. It was inactivated in January 1946.

Asian Droop Snoots

England was not the only place where Droop Snoot P-38 conversions were made (see Chapter 4). Wayne Sneddon, a Lockheed technical representative attached to the 459th FS, later recalled:

In January [1945], a Capt. Hill and I were sent to take over the Hindustani Aircraft Company to modify ten P-38s to "Droop Snoot" configuration. Capt. Hill, a stress engineer from Douglas [Aircraft Company] knew nothing of manufacturing, so he took care of the paperwork and I took care of the manufacturing. Ten Droop Snoots were made in 51 days—53 days after being told to take this operation. Several 459th personnel were enrolled in this project.

By this time India's Hindustani Aircraft facility at Bangalore was being operated by the USAAF as its 84th Air Depot, which handled the major repair and overhaul of the Tenth Air Forces's aircraft, including P-38s. The Droop Snoots created there were intended for the 459th Fighter Squadron. According to the squadron history, dated 8 April 1945, "Lieutenants [Vern] Flanders and [William] Fetner left for Bangalore today to check out the new 'Droop Snoot' airplanes the squadron will be getting. These planes are P-38s redesigned to carry a bombardier in the nose. Fetner says they are fine-looking planes."

One of these Droop Snoots, P-38L-5 serial number 44-25605, was further modified as a personal transport for Lt. Gen. George E. Stratemeyer, commander of all U.S. Air Forces in the CBI Theater.

The Tenth AF's two F-5 photo reconnaissance squadrons were both very active in support of the Allied offensive in Burma. In the late summer and fall of 1944, the 9th PRS at Barrackpore had detachments at Tingkawk Sakan and Myitkyina in Burma, and at Chittagong, where two F-5s and their pilots operated with the RAF's 224 Group. Its headquarters moved to Myitkyina in early December and then to Piardoba, near Calcutta, in early May 1945. The whole squadron transferred to Malir, India, near Karachi, in October, from which it returned to the U.S. in November. It was inactivated there in December.

The 40th PRS moved from Guskhara to Alipore, which was another in the large complex of airfields in and around Calcutta, in August 1944. It established a detachment at Cox's Bazaar, India, in December, to which the rest of the squadron moved in January. It transferred to Akyab, Burma, in February 1945, then back to Alipore in May. Its final overseas base was Kanchrapara, also just outside Calcutta, to which it moved in September and from which it returned the following month to the U.S., where it was inactivated in November.

The P-40-equipped 33rd FG had seen a lot of action in the Mediterranean Theater, from the first days of the invasion of French Northwest Africa until after the Allied invasion of Italy. It was then transferred to the CBI, arriving in India in February 1944 *en route* to China, where it became operational with the Fourteenth AF in April, now flying P-47s. The 33rd returned to India in September to become part of the Tenth AF and was based at Nagaghuli Airfield near Chabua. At the end of the year, it began converting to P-38s—its 58th FS in November and then the 59th and 60th Squadrons in January and February 1945, respectively. It moved to Sahman, in central Burma, at the end of December and to Piardoba in early May 1945.

Although the 33rd FG was primarily a fighter-bomber unit, the 58th FS did shoot down three enemy aircraft with its new P-38s on January 15, when its pilots encountered some Oscars near the Meiktila A/D in Burma.

The 459th FS utilized improvised napalm bombs in combat for the first time on January 24, and it moved from Chittagong to Rumkha, India, on February 1. During yet another B-24 escort to Rangoon ten days later, Capt. Boggs, on his second tour with the squadron, spotted a lone Tony below him and led his flight down on it. The Tony pilot evidently never

F-5E-2 43-28965 of the 9th PRS was destroyed in a crash-landing in Burma on September 28, 1944. Fortunately, its pilot, Lt. Robert H. Anderson, survived it. (*9th PRS Association collection*)

This colorful 9th PRS F-5E-2, 43-28600, was assigned to Lt. John E. Whitley, most likely one of the two pilots posing with it here. (*USAF photo*)

Above: Lt. William L. Grommett of the 9th PRS chats with his crew chief before a mission. In the background is F-5E-4 44-24902. (*USAF photo*)

Below: An F-5 over China sometime in 1944. (*Daniel Jackson collection*)

Above: This 33rd FG P-38L-5, serial number unknown, was photographed in India on July 8, 1945. Its name is *HAMMER'S DESTRUCTION* and it displays five Japanese flags. Its pilot was Lt. Samuel E. Hammer, who had scored five kills flying P-40s and P-47s with the 80th FG. (*USAF photo*)

Right: Chittagong, India, January 1945: A 459th FS armorer cleans one of the .50-cal. machine guns of P-38J-10 42-67627, named *Daddy Bear*, which was assigned to the squadron commander, Maj. Verl Luehring. (*USAF photo*)

saw them, and when Boggs, who was flying P-38L-1 44-24240, opened fire it exploded and disintegrated. Hampton Boggs had scored the 459th's very first air victory (on December 1, 1943) and now its eighty-second and last (and his ninth) a little over a year later. The squadron's last aerial claim came on February 17, when a Tojo was damaged while its pilots were dive bombing a railroad bridge in Burma.

Effective May 12, 1945, the 459th FS was reassigned from the 80th FG to the 33rd FG and moved to Dudhkundi, near Calcutta, where, on June 18, some bombardiers for the aforementioned Droop Snoots arrived. One of them, 2Lt Eli. Solop, later recalled:

> We were a group of ten bombardiers assigned to the 459th to develop techniques for dropping 1000-lb. Azon bombs from the P-38. We had ten 38's assigned to us—each bombardier was assigned to his own P-38 and pilot. My pilot was Larry Kepke. The planes were combat aircraft that had been modified to carry in addition to the pilot a bombardier and two 1000-lb. bombs. The planes had been modified by the Air Corps in [Bangalore]. When the 459th received orders to return to the States, we had not progressed to the point of dropping bombs on combat missions. We were dropping bombs on practice targets in the Bay of Bengal only, until the war wound down.[2]

The 459th returned to the U.S. in October and was inactivated there the following month. The cost of its combat successes had been high: thirty of its pilots had gone missing in action, of whom twenty-two were killed and eight captured (three of whom died in a prison camp).

The rest of the 33rd FG left for the U.S. on November 15, its 58th and 59th Squadrons from Dudhkundi, and the 60th Squadron and Group H.Q. from Piardoba, to which they had moved in May. The group was inactivated on December 8.

Back in China, the 449th FS established a detachment at Mengtze, south of Kunming, in March 1945—which its detachment at Yunnanyi soon joined—and another the following month to the east of Chengkung at Posek in April. The whole squadron was based at Mengtze by early July. It was from there that its last aerial victory was scored when a Nate was shot down over the Gia Lam A/D near Hanoi by 1Lt. William E. Dougherty on July 6. Its last aerial encounter took place four days later, when two P-38s on another sweep over Indochina were bounced by four Oscars. One of them shot out the right engine of Lt. William Jones's P-38, and then 1Lt. Joseph N. Fodor damaged the lead Oscar. The Ki-43 pilots then called it quits and Jones made it back to Mengtze, where he belly-landed his P-38.

Dougherty's victory was the 449th Squadron's seventy-fourth and last confirmed kill—plus over sixty probably destroyed and damaged credits. Its last combat-related pilot loss was on July 15, when 1Lt. William E. Shomaker bailed out over Indochina, was taken prisoner and subsequently died as such. (Shomaker had scored two air victories during his first P-38 combat tour, with the 82nd FG in North Africa.) Three more of its pilots were killed in flying accidents later in July, making a total of nineteen that were lost, in combat or in accidents. The 449th moved to India in September, and two months later, it returned to the U.S., where it was inactivated at the end of December.

7

Post-World War II Lightnings

Postwar Military Lightnings: Europe

By the end of 1945, the USAAF's Lightning units in the ETO and MTO had either been inactivated there or returned to the U.S. Most of the P-38s and F-5s that had survived the European air war had since been salvaged and destroyed, but more than a hundred of them would have postwar operational lives. As to those that did not, 1st FG pilot Harvey McDaniel later remembered: "In August [1945] we flew all remaining P-38s to Bari [Italy] for salvage. This was heartbreaking to leave almost new P-38Ls where instruments, radios, etc. were crushed and sold."

The *Armée de l'Air*'s premier photo reconnaissance squadron, II/GR 33, which later in the war was redesignated I/GR 33, had utilized F-4s and F-5s provided by the USAAF in both the MTO and ETO during its last two years. Shortly after VE Day, from May 10 to 21, 1945, it received an additional infusion of at least twenty-six late model F-5s—eight F-3s and eighteen G-6s. Postwar, I/GR 33's Lightnings were used in French West Africa, mainly for aerial mapping surveys, and in France as part of the country's NATO commitment, until replaced with RF-84 Thunderjets in the early 1950s.

In Italy after the war's end 100 Fifteenth AF P-38s and F-5s had been stored at Capodichino Airfield near Naples, reserved for the new postwar Italian Air Force, the *Aeronautica Militaire Italiana*, or AMI. They were all officially transferred to the AMI in April 1946. By the end of that year, most of them had been assigned to the 4th *Stormo Caccia* (Fighter Group) and to the AMI's training center—both at Lecce.

After the 4th *Stormo* converted to F-51s in the spring of 1948, its Lightnings were transferred to the new 3rd *Stormo* at Bari. Several of the latter's F-5s were attached to NATO's 56th Tactical Air Force at Vicenza in the early 1950s. As its inventory inevitably dwindled due to accidents and wear and tear, it too began converting to Mustangs. The last twenty Lightnings were consolidated into the 3rd *Stormo*'s 28th *Gruppo* (Squadron) in late 1951. Three years later, the remaining fourteen were transferred to the AMI training center at Bari, and in July 1956, they were scrapped.

As indicated above, these units utilized both P-38 fighters and F-5 photo recons. Six of them were modified as two-seat dual-control trainers, and the 4th *Stormo* had at least one

Droop Snoot. The Lightnings flew numerous photo reconnaissance sorties over Communist Yugoslavia starting in September 1948, and on October 27, 1948, an F-5E crashed there.

As to Yugoslavia, on April 2, 1945, Capt. Michael Brezas of the 14th FG (with twelve victories the Fifteenth AF's top P-38 ace) force-landed his battle-damaged P-38L-5, 44-25786, on the airfield at Sombor, then home to units of the new Communist Yugoslav Air Force, which confiscated it. It was repaired and then test flown by a pilot of its 111th Fighter Wing on May 19, 1945, but infrequently thereafter. The following year, it was grounded due to a lack of spare parts and dismantled. It was then moved to the country's Technical University in Belgrade and since the 1970s has been in the Yugoslav Air and Space Museum, also in Belgrade.

Postwar Military Lightnings: China

Since the early 1930s, the U.S. had supplied the Nationalist Chinese Air Force (NCAF) with military aircraft, including, during World War II, a total of over 1,200 via the Lend-Lease program. The NCAF received numerous P-40s and P-51s, with which its fighter groups fought alongside the Fourteenth AF, but very few P-38s (reportedly about fifteen), which were more difficult for its pilots to fly and for its ground crewmen to maintain. However, as the USAAF was preparing to pull out of China in late 1945, it turned at least fifty F-5s over to the NCAF, among the 1,000 aircraft that were available to it. Most of them were E-4s, and at least a few had served with the Fourteenth's 21st PRS.

In 1946, the F-5s—initially eighteen Es and Gs—equipped the NCAF's 12th Reconnaissance Squadron (RS), which began operating against the Communist Chinese from bases that included Nanking, Peiping, and Shanghai. Most of the squadron's pilots had undergone both flight training and operational photographic reconnaissance training in the U.S. late in World War II and soon afterward. By early 1950, the Nationalist government had been forced to withdraw from mainland China to the large island of Taiwan, also known as Formosa, from which the 12th Squadron's F-5s flew many sorties over the communist controlled mainland. One of its F-5Es was the first victim of the soon-to-be-famous MiG-15 jet fighter, when, on April 28, 1950, a pilot of a Russian Air Force unit based in China shot it down near Shanghai.

One of the squadron's pilots was Jude Pao, who was a member of the last small group of Chinese pilots to be trained in the U.S. during the war. After graduating with Class 45-F at Douglas, Arizona, in August 1945, he was selected for operational PR training at Will Rogers Field in Oklahoma with the 348th Combat Crew Training Station (CCTS). When that base closed down later that year, he and his three Chinese classmates transferred to the 225th CCTS at Rapid City Army Air Base in South Dakota to continue their training. After completing the PR course there, Pao returned to China in June 1946 and was assigned to the 12th RS.

Pao subsequently flew many photo reconnaissance missions from various mainland Chinese bases and then from Taiwan. He also piloted one of the first three 12th Squadron F-5s flown to Taiwan, in May 1949. In the late 1950s, its Lightnings were finally replaced with RF-86 and RF-84 jets.

Postwar Military Lightnings: The Pacific

The 343rd FG continued to operate P-38s until it was inactivated in Alaska effective August 15, 1946, although it had begun to receive some P-51s. It was replaced on Shemya Island by the 57th FG, which flew the Lightnings it had inherited from the 343rd well into the following year, as it completed the conversion to Mustangs. The 19th Air Depot Squadron at Elmendorf Field near Anchorage still had some P-38s in its inventory as of the summer of 1947.

The FEAF's Lightning units (five fighter and two photo reconnaissance groups totaling twenty-one squadrons) were based either in the Philippines or on Okinawa at the time of the Japanese surrender on August 15, 1945. Of them, the 347th FG and its three squadrons and the 6th Reconnaissance Group's 36th PRS were the only ones to return to the States right away, in December. The Thirteenth AF's other fighter group, the 18th, remained at Clark Field on Luzon, flying F-51s, F-47s, and F-80s (redesignated from "P" to "F" after the establishment of the new U.S. Air Force in September 1947), until moving to Korea in 1950 to participate in the Korean War.

As to the FEAF's other PR units, the 4th RG was inactivated, along with its 38th PRS, in January 1945, at Leyte and Clark Field, respectively. The 17th PRS was also at Clark, where it remained until returning to the U.S. in May 1946. It was then in the process of converting to F-6s, the tactical reconnaissance version of the P-51, but still had some F-5s. The 6th RG moved to Japan in September 1945 and was inactivated there the following April. Its 25th PRS also converted to F-6s during 1946 and remained in Japan until 1949. Its 26th PRS moved to Korea in September 1945 and was inactivated there the following February, while still operating F-5s. The 8th PRS, however, continued to serve in the Far East and participated in the Korean War.

The 475th FG remained in the Far East until 1949 and the 8th and 49th Groups were still there the following year at the outbreak of the Korean War, in which they both also

These P-38s of the 343rd FG were salvaged and scrapped on Shemya Island in the Aleutians about a year after the war's end. This was a common sight—particularly in the Pacific—in 1946 and 1947. (*USAF photo*)

Above: F-5 pilots of the 8th PRS at Irumagawa, Japan, in early 1946. (*John Stanaway collection*)

Below: Lt. Robert B. Maxwell, a pilot of the 475th FG's 433rd Squadron, poses with the colorful P-38 of his squadron mate Lt. Roger Palmer at Kimpo, Korea, in February 1946. (*Author's collection*)

served. The 8th and 49th spent all that time in Japan, from November and September 1945, respectively, while the 475th was at Kimpo, Korea, from September 1945 until 1948, when it too moved to Japan. The 8th FG made the switch from P-38s to P-51s rather abruptly in March 1946 while the 475th did so more gradually, from June to December 1946. The 49th FG also converted to Mustangs in 1946.

An interesting footnote to the story of Lightnings in the SWP concerns the arrival, in October 1945, of four P-38M night fighters in the Philippines. They were assigned first to the 418th NFS at Atsugi, Japan, in late January 1946. One was ditched in the ocean on the 31st and shortly thereafter the remaining three were transferred to the 421st NFS at Fukuoka, Japan. On March 8, they were flown to the 45th Service Group at Clark Field and eventually scrapped.

As to the disposal of the Lightnings based at Clark, Richard Legee, who flew P-51s and P-80s with the 18th FG in the Philippines in late 1946 and early 1947, recalled: "I could observe P-38s being cut up and burned at Clark Field. The debris pile was quite large and was south-west of the Clark Field buildings. Having RTU'd [Replacement Training Unit] in P-38s at Santa Rosa, California, it hurt to see those nearly new birds destroyed!"

Postwar Military Lightnings: Latin America

When surplus U.S. military aircraft became available after World War II, a number of Latin American and Caribbean nations scrambled to obtain some for their small air forces. These acquisitions were sometimes on the up-and-up, with the approval of the U.S. government, but in other cases, they were clandestine and illegal, involving aircraft purchased as surplus by civilians, after which they passed through numerous owners, including foreign governments. Six different countries were involved in these transactions.

The *Fuerza Aérea Hondurena* (Honduran Air Force), or FAH, was one of three of those air forces that did have the support of the U.S. government, having obtained seven Lightnings in 1947 and 1948 under the Mutual Defense Aid Program. In 1953, the USAF assigned one of its officers, Capt. Michael Alba, to the FAH as a "combat operations adviser." (Alba had flown P-38s in World War II with the 55th FG in England.)

Six of the FAH's Lightnings can be identified by their USAAF serial numbers: F-5G-6 44-26961, FAH number 504; P-38M-6 44-53056 (501); P-38M-6 44-53095 (506); P-38M-6 44-50397 (503); P-38L-5 44-53155 (502); and F-5G-6 44-53232 (505). No. 44-53155 had served previously with the Cuban Air Force, and 26961, 53095, 53097, and 53232 had all been sold as surplus at the Kingman, Arizona, air depot.

In 1957, Honduras had a territorial dispute with its neighbor, Nicaragua, which led to a brief conflict. On May 1, the Honduran Army launched an attack to recapture a village held by the Nicaraguans, supported by FAH P-38s and P-63s, which bombed and strafed Nicaraguan troops. This mini war, which ceased four days later in Honduras's favor, marked the last use of P-38s in combat. By 1960, the FAH's aging Lightnings, for which spare parts had become almost impossible to obtain, had been replaced by F4U Corsairs.

Coincidentally, Nicaragua's air national guard, the *Fuerza Aérea de la Guardia Nacional*, had, in 1949, obtained two P-38s of its own, illegally; one of them is known to have been

P-38M-6 44-27257, which had been sold at Kingman in 1946. The other was a P-38L-5, but it is not known if either of them participated in the 1957 incident.

The acquisition of five P-38s by the tiny Costa Rican Air Force (*Fuerza Aérea Costarricense*) was authorized by the U.S. State Department, but only two were subsequently sent to it. One was F-5G-6 44-26961, which arrived in November 1948 and was given the serial number GCR-01. GCR-02, a P-38L, USAAF serial number unknown, was destroyed in a crash in Texas *en route* to Costa Rica the following month. When the country's air force was temporarily disbanded shortly thereafter, 44-26961 was sold to Honduras.

Bolivia obtained at least one Lightning, F-5G-6 44-26927, which was originally sold at the Walnut Ridge, Arkansas, air depot. Another, P-38L-5 43-50281, had been earmarked for the Bolivian Air Force (*Fuerza Aérea Boliviana*) but was not in fact delivered to it.

The Dominican Republic's *Campania de Aviacion* (Aviation Company)—which became the *Cuerpo de Aviacion Militar Dominica* or CAMD in February 1948—obtained a dozen P-38s and F-5s in 1947 and 1948, most if not all of them clandestinely, without export licenses. As civilian aircraft, they were not armed, and the CAMD had to scrounge some 0.30-cal. machine guns to install in them in place of their usual .50s. (None of the Latin American Lightnings ever carried 20-mm cannon.) Attrition and a lack of spare parts soon took their toll, however, especially given the inexperience of the Dominican pilots. (The government ended up hiring nine American pilots to fly them.) P-38L-5 44-53167, which carried the CAMD serial number 501, was written off in a crash on July 28, 1947, as was another Lightning on July 21, 1948. Yet another force-landed in neighboring Haiti on August 2, and a fourth was sold to Nicaragua. There were just eight Lightnings in the CAMD's inventory as of January 1949, of which only three were described as airworthy, the other five being beyond repair. The last of them were cut up and disposed of in October 1950.

Perhaps the most interesting and unusual of the Latin American Lightnings were those utilized by the Cuban Air Force (*Cuerpo de Aviación del Ejército de Cuba*, or CAEC). These were actually confiscated by the Cuban government in August 1947 from a clandestine military group called the *Legión de Caribe* (Caribbean Legion), which was based on the island of Cayo Coco off Cuba's northern coast and whose purpose was to overthrow the government of Dominican dictator Rafael Trujillo. Before this operation was shut down, they had assembled sixteen aircraft, including a half-dozen illegal Lightnings, which were numbered 121 to 126 in CAEC service. They were P-38L-5 44-27145 (which was originally sold at the Altus, Oklahoma, air depot), P-38M-6 44-27258, P-38L-5 44-53010 (#126), F-5G-6 44-53012 (#122), P-38M-6 44-53082 (which was purchased at Kingman), and P-38M-6 44-53100.

Postwar Civilian Lightnings

P-38s continued to be built at the Lockheed and Consolidated-Vultee plants right up to VJ Day—and ceased immediately thereafter. The USAAF had already decided that the Lightning was not going to fit into its postwar plans, which were obviously going to be centered on jet-propelled aircraft. It would take more than a decade for the new USAF to achieve an all-jet fighter force, however, and in the interim, P-47s and P-51s, not P-38s, would fill in—especially Mustangs, which would see a lot of action in the Korean War.

So, what was to be done with all the hundreds of P-38s and F-5s in the USAAF's current inventory? Those still serving overseas would not be coming home, as their likely fate—salvage and destruction—would be the same no matter where they were based. There were Lightnings all over the U.S. during the latter part of 1945—at the factories, the Dallas Modification Center, Ferry Command bases and air depots, and in training units. Many, particularly older models, were salvaged where they were at the time. William Nickloff, a crew chief with the 535th Twin Engine Flying Training Squadron at Williams Field in Arizona, remembered when they destroyed that unit's well-used Lightnings: "They would hoist them up, retract the gears, lower the plane to the ground, roll over them with large tractors, then cut them up with torches."

Valuable parts that could be reused—guns, engines, radios, instruments, tires, etc.—would typically be removed and the remaining, mostly aluminum, parts were melted down into ingots of reusable metal. At overseas bases, where there were few if any salvage facilities, they were typically crushed, burned, buried, and/or dumped into the ocean.

Many of the stateside P-38s were brand new, or nearly so, often with only the flight time required for them to be flown from a factory or the modification center to an air base/depot, where they would sit and wait for disposition. It was decided that the government would make them available for sale to civilian buyers (most of them salvagers) to get at least a small portion of its investment back. It would ask just $1,250 for a P-38 that cost it nearly $100,000.

It was the Reconstruction Finance Corporation (RFC), a subsidiary of the War Asset Administration (WAA), which facilitated this sales program. Five USAAF bases around the country, often then referred to as "aircraft boneyards," were chosen by the RFC, to which the planes would be ferried for temporary storage and then sale or scrapping. The ones that handled most of the P-38s and F-5s were Kingman AAF in Arizona, Altus AAF in Oklahoma, and Walnut Ridge AAF in Arkansas. At one time during the summer of 1946, there were 478 Lightnings in storage at Kingman.

A good example of the movement of military aircraft around the U.S. in late 1945 and early 1946 was the deactivation, effective November 30, 1945, of Santa Rosa Army Airfield in California, where the 434th Base Unit had been providing operational P-38 training for the past eighteen months. From October 29 through December 31, eighty of the unit's Lightnings were transferred elsewhere, including forty to the Kingman RFC depot and thirty-three to Altus.

At least seventy-four Lightnings are known to have been sold at the RFC depots and continued to be flown rather than scrapped. Most of them had very interesting subsequent "lives," with multiple owners and uses. The majority have by now been destroyed in various mishaps and/or scrapped. Some, as noted earlier in this chapter, ended up in small air forces south of the U.S. border, and the utilization of most of the rest initially fit into two categories: entertainment (air racing and airshows) and the aerial mapping business.

The USAAF also donated a few surplus P-38s to aeronautical schools around the country and to certain communities as outdoor monuments, the latter including P-38L-5 44-53236, which has been part of the Richard I. Bong Memorial in his hometown of Poplar, Wisconsin, since 1949. By 1947, most of its Lightnings had been disposed of, and of the 10,038 that had been built only a few hundred still existed—in some foreign air forces and in civilian hands. Two former WASP pilots who had ferried P-38s during the war had each purchased one: Nadine Ramsey F-5G-6 USAAF serial number 44-53193 and civil registration number

Above: These war surplus P-38s were photographed at one of the government's many postwar aircraft "bone yards," in this case Augusta, Georgia, in October 1945. *Jolie* (P-38LO 40-744), in the foreground, was a very rare and unique Lightning; looking closely, a second cockpit can be seen on its left boom. This experimental modification was utilized during the war to study the effects of aerial maneuvering on a human subject sitting away from the aircraft's center of gravity. (*Michael Bates collection*)

Below: When photographed here, F-5G-6 44-27002 had the civil registration number N53753, but it was later sold to Mark Hurd Aerial Surveys, becoming its N503MH. (*Michael Bates collection*)

N34993 and Nancy Harkness-Love, former leader of Air Transport Command's Women's Auxiliary Ferrying Squadron, F-5G-6 44-53247/N90813.

Another, very unusual, owner of a surplus Lightning, in his case F-5G-6 44-53026, was William P. Lear, Jr., son of the founder of Learjet. Bill, Jr., paid for it at Kingman on May 20, 1946, at a bit more than the $1,250 asking price by including two 165-gallon drop tanks in the sale. Also included were full internal gas tanks containing over 400 gallons of fuel. Lear, whose eighteenth birthday was forty-five days away, had never flown a P-38; his first flight in one was his trip back to his home airport in southern California. He flew his Lightning in the 1946 Bendix Trophy Race, finishing fourteenth, and in various air shows around the country until crashing it during a show in Idaho on September 16 of that year. Bill Lear, Jr., is believed to be the youngest Lightning pilot ever.

The popular prewar National Air Races in Cleveland, Ohio, comprised of both pylon and cross-country events, made a comeback in the four years after the end of World War

Teenage pilot Bill Lear, Jr., flies the second Lightning he owned, F-5G-6 44-53183/civil registration number NX56687, over San Francisco Bay during the 1947 Oakland Air Show. (*Author's collection*)

Another shot of Bill Lear Jr.'s No. 74, on the ground. (*Michael Bates collection*)

II, mostly featuring modified war surplus aircraft, including P-38s and F-5s. Twenty-six Lightnings are known to have competed in these races, with varying degrees of success.

The most successful Lightning air race pilot was none other than famed Lockheed P-38 test pilot Tony LeVier, flying his bright red modified F-5G-6, 44-27002/N21764. LeVier had purchased this plane, the first Lightning sold at Kingman, on January 23, 1946. He finished second in the 1946 Thompson Trophy Race (closed circuit pylon), first in the 1947 Sohio Trophy Race (a special P-38 pylon event sponsored by Standard Oil of Ohio) and fifth in the 1947 Thompson. N21764 subsequently served as an aerial mapping aircraft with Mark Hurd Aerial Surveys from 1953 to 1965.

The most unusual of the P-38 air racers was a rare "F" model, 43-2181/N5010N. While departing the Van Nuys, California, Airport on the 1947 cross-country Bendix Trophy Race—flown by James Rubel, a USAAF veteran—it lost the special P-80-type auxiliary fuel tank that was attached to its right wing tip, and then a turbo supercharger fire resulted in Rubel baling out of it over the Arizona desert. Amazingly, 43-2181 had served with the 82nd FG in North Africa, its various pilots scoring five confirmed aerial victories with it.

Undoubtedly the most unique P-38 to survive past 1946, RP-38E 41-2048 had been heavily modified by Lockheed during the war to assist in the investigation of the Lightning's compressibility problem. It was popularly known as "Swordfish" due to its strange needle-nosed appearance. It continued to be used by the company after the war, until it was sold to Hycon Aerial Surveys, which modified it again for aerial mapping, which task it performed until 1960.

Several civilian Lightnings were used for some special weather-related tasks. In 1957, Jim Cook, of Dallas, Texas, a former airline pilot, purchased F-5G-6 44-27087, previously a photo mapping aircraft, which he radically modified for his research on the use of airborne radar to detect weather phenomena, which work he carried out over the Midwest from Love Field in Dallas until 1983.

F-5G-6 44-53242/N57496 also had a very unusual postwar occupation: cloud seeding. It was utilized by the California Electric Power Company to generate rainwater over the Sierra Nevada Mountains along the California–Nevada border for the rivers feeding its hydroelectric power plants. It was flown by a pilot named Robert F. Symons, starting in 1948. In 1955, N57496 was sold to Weather Modifications, Inc., which used it for the same purpose until it crashed near the Bishop, California, Airport in 1958, killing its pilot.

There was a post-World War II boom in aerial surveying and mapping, for which the F-5 was obviously particularly well suited. A number of highly modified war surplus Lightnings were used by various aerial survey companies such as Mark Hurd and Hycon, mostly in the U.S. and Canada, and they mapped a lot of the little known parts of the world at that time, particularly Alaska and parts of Africa and South America, until more modern jet aircraft became available.

In the 1960s, quite a few surviving P-38s and F-5s became available for the burgeoning warbird movement, which involved recovering and restoring vintage military aircraft, especially World War II types. The Latin American air forces that had been utilizing them were replacing them with more modern fighters and the aerial survey companies were replacing their faithful old F-5s with jets. As there were fewer and fewer Lightnings available and their and the warbird movement's popularity continued to increase, the relatively few survivors have become valuable commodities.

The official caption for this photo states: "Tony LeVier—Examiner Air Show—Mines Field 6/3/46." Mines Field, a WWII P-38 training base, later became LAX. Tony must have performed some very strenuous maneuvers during this show to have required a "G-suit"! This Lightning was the one (P-38L-5 44-53078) LeVier purchased at the Kingman, Arizona, RFC depot several months earlier, which, painted a brilliant red, he flew later that summer in the 1946 Thompson Trophy Race at the Cleveland National Air Races, finishing second. (*Michael Bates collection*)

Above: F-5G-6 44-26961 served with the Honduran Air Force in the 1950s and was then briefly part of Ed Maloney's Air Museum. In the late '60s, with the civil registration number N74883 and refitted with a "fighter" nose, it was purchased by WWII P-38 pilot Larry Blumer, who had it painted to look like the P-38J-25 with which he shot down five Fw 190s in a single action over France. It was destroyed in a take-off crash on April 9, 1981, killing its then-current owner. (*American Aviation Historical Society collection*)

Below: This colorful war surplus Lightning, P-38L-5 44-27147/NX4530N—which had been purchased from the Walnut Ridge RFC depot—placed third in the 1947 Sohio Trophy Race (for P-38s) at the Cleveland National Air Forces. It was destroyed in a crash-landing on September 23, 1952 while being ferried to its new owner in Mississippi. (*Michael Bates collection*)

Above: This F-5G-6 with the colorful shark mouths on its engine cowlings was 44-53038/N62828, which was flown to a third place finish in the 1946 Sohio Trophy Race. It was destroyed in a crash in Ohio in the early 1950s—which was the fate of so many surplus Lightnings. (*Michael Bates collection*)

Below: Built as a P-38L-5 (serial number 44-53170) and converted to an F-5G-6, this Lightning (civil registration number NX61121) received some radical modifications to prepare it for the 1947 Cleveland Air Races, in which it placed fourth in the Sohio Trophy event. Among other things, its wings had been clipped and its "photo" nose replaced by one fabricated from a 300-gallon auxiliary fuel tank. After the postwar air races came to an end it was donated to the Teterboro, New Jersey, School of Aeronautics. (*Michael Bates Collection*)

Below: F-5G-6 44-27026 was purchased from the Kingman, Arizona, depot in April 1946 and subsequently received the civil registration number N70005. It became an air racer, finishing ninth in the 1946 Bendix Trophy Race, but it crashed and was destroyed during the time trials for the 1949 Cleveland Air Races. (*John Stanaway collection*)

The *PAUL BUNYAN* was F-5G-6 44-53173, which received the civil registration number N70087, and a painting of the famous fictional lumberjack and his blue ox "Babe" on its nose. It finished eighth in the 1946 Bendix Trophy Race and was subsequently sold for scrap. (*Michael Bates collection*)

PUNKIN, P-38L-5 44-26545/N66692, was ill-fated as an air racer. It was entered in the 1946 Bendix Race but failed to complete it and was scrapped for spare parts sometime in the early 1950s. (*Michael Bates collection*)

As a P-38J-10 converted to an F-5C-1, 42-67574 (civil registration number N49721) was a rare postwar bird. During the war, it had served in the training role with the 2nd PRG at Will Rogers Field near Oklahoma City. It was purchased at the RFC depot at Bush Field, Georgia, in March 1945 and became an air racer. It placed sixth in the 1946 Sohio Trophy Race, was forced to abort the 1947 Sohio due to mechanical problems, and ostensibly won that event in 1948 but was disqualified for low flying. It was scrapped not long after. (*Michael Bates collection*)

This is the venerable, highly modified "Swordfish" Lightning, P-38E 41-2048, that Lockheed purchased back from the USAAF in 1946. The company continued to utilize it for flight testing with the civil registration number N91300 until it was sold in 1954 to Hycon Aerial Surveys, Inc., which used it for aerial mapping until 1960, as pictured here. (*Author's collection*)

This F-5G-6, serial number 44-26612 and civil registration number N5056N, was purchased from the Altus, Oklahoma, RFC depot in October 1946 by Kargl Aerial Surveys of Midland, Texas, and was also subsequently utilized by Aero Exploration of Tulsa, Oklahoma. In 1952, it was bought by the Minneapolis-Honeywell Regulator Company to test advanced auto-pilot systems. It was destroyed in a crash at San Antonio, Texas, shortly after being acquired by Jack Ammann Photogrammetric Engineers, Inc. (*John Stanaway collection*)

Two of Mark Hurd Aerial Surveys' F-5s. (*Michael Bates collection*)

Above left: Mark Hurd pilot Raymond Miller in the cockpit of one of the company's F-5s. The cameraman is not identified, but this photo clearly shows his access hatch. (*Author's collection*)

Above right: Former USN pilot Paul Stiles flew for Fairchild Aerial Surveys after the war. He is seen here posing with one of the company's surplus F-5s, with which he helped map the whole country of Panama and parts of Alaska in the 1950s. Fairchild purchased five Lightnings, two of which were utilized for spare parts while two others (including this one) were modified with extended noses that had room for three cameras and a cameraman, to be used for high-altitude mapping. They were painted a bright orange. (*P-38 National Association collection*)

Below: Another Fairchild Aerial Surveys F-5, photographed at Billings, Montana, in August 1946. Neither the pilot nor the cameraman are identified. (*Michael Bates collection*)

Lightnings: The Good and the Bad/ Problems and Solutions/Comparisons

What were the best and the worst aspects of the Lockheed Lightning at different periods in its development, particularly according to the pilots who flew it? Here are arguably the top three in each category.

The Good

1. Most former P-38 and F-5 pilots have mentioned the benefit of having two engines, mainly because so many of them had returned to their airfield on single engine, due to battle damage or to a mechanical problem, on at least one occasion. Especially appreciative of those twin Allisons were the pilots who flew them long distances over water—everywhere in the Pacific, over the Mediterranean in 1943 and over the North Sea from England to the European Continent and back.
2. Its battery of nose-mounted guns, which made for much easier aiming and shooting, and produced a deadly cone of fire.
3. Its counter-rotating propellers, which, along with its tricycle landing gear, made it much easier to taxi and take off than single-engined fighters, more stable and maneuverable in the air and easier to land.

There were obviously many other good points about the P-38—for example, its mild stall characteristics. William C. Phelps, who flew Lightnings with the Sixth AF in Panama, remembered: "Actually, it never stalled out. You could put the yoke clear back in your gut and hold it there. The P-38 simply slowed down, nosed over, picked up speed, [then] started flying all over again—and would repeat this maneuver over and over."

How about visibility? According to P-38 ace Bill Harris:

Cockpit visibility was good except for ten o'clock and two o'clock down at a twenty-degree angle. The only other blind spot was directly to the rear because of the armor plate, which could easily be looked around if you moved your head a little to the side. I preferred this inconvenience to removing the armor plate! Ground visibility on takeoff and landing was excellent, as there was no engine in front and the tricycle landing gear lowered the nose.[1]

Harris also liked the P-38's control wheel, because "they were less tiring to use over long flights than some other fighters with between-the-legs sticks."

Richard F. Brown, who flew Lightnings in the Pacific with the 68th FS, liked the fact that "the P-38 was a very quiet plane, because its exhaust exited through the turbo-superchargers on top of the plane in the tail booms to the rear of the cockpit." On ground attack missions, "many times nobody heard us or knew we were there until it was too late for them."

The Bad

1. Restricted dives due to the threat of compressibility and the possibility of becoming unable to recover from one because of it, which problem was often more psychological than technical but could definitely be a restraint in combat.
2. Poor cockpit heating. This was a particular, huge problem at high altitudes over Europe in the winter of 1943–44, but it could create some discomfort even at slightly lower altitudes and/or in the warmer climates of the Mediterranean and the South Pacific. According to Bill Harris: "Early cockpit heating was poor. Even in the tropics, at altitudes over 25,000 feet the cockpit windows would frost over. Throughout my entire time in the various P-38 models I was never warm enough."
3. Poor gun camera film, caused mainly by the vibration of the guns, which were located too close to the camera.

George B. Seeberg, who was a P-38 pilot with the 18th FG in the Pacific, later shared some of his negative impressions of the Lightning, based on his experiences:

> Remember skinned knuckles or torn flight gloves on your right hand as you tried to adjust the slide coolant temp controls of the F and early G models? The cockpit heater that did a great job except for your feet that just about froze at altitude? [Losing an] engine on takeoff with a full load of fuel, ammo and belly tanks? Turbos that almost never cut in at the same time and made close formation flying a thrill? The miserable retractable ladder, especially when wearing a survival pack and chute? The cockpit fluorescent lights that were impossible to adjust? The fun of hand pumping our gear down when the hydraulic system wouldn't? What about that compressibility thing before the dive flaps on the J and L models? There never has been a perfect aircraft and, in all likelihood, never will be. [Still,] to me the P-38, even with its variety of faults, was one exceptionally fine aircraft. That second engine kept me from having to make a couple of very long swims back to base, and even back then I was not a very good swimmer.[2]

As to that retractable ladder about which Seeberg complained, it was stored in the bottom rear of the gondola and extended by pulling a recessed lever on top. The pilot then climbed up the ladder utilizing its stirrups and hand holds. When finally standing on the wing to the rear of the gondola, he pushed the lever down to retract the ladder back into its compartment. It was, indeed, somewhat awkward, and the pilot often required the assistance of a ground crewman.

Above left: A Thirteenth AF ground crewman inserts a film cartridge into a P-38's gun camera on Stirling Island in the Solomons in late 1943 or early 1944. Two things are evident from this photo: the deadly—and easily aimed—concentration of fire that would emanate from its four .50-cal. machine guns and 20-mm cannon, and how close the camera was to the guns. (*USAF photo*)

Above right: An F-5 pilot of the 3rd Photo Group in North Africa mounting his Lightning's retractable ladder—about which George Seeberg complained—prior to entering the cockpit. It is obvious how difficult this process could have been for a pilot in Europe during the wintertime while wearing all the heavy clothing and equipment that would have been required. (*USAF photo*)

Problems and Solutions

When Lightnings (P-38Fs and early P-38Gs and F-4s and early F-5s) began to see a lot of action for the first time in late 1942 and early 1943, various problems, large and small, began to manifest themselves. Among the smaller ones were poorly ground camera filters and elevator trim tab rod failure on the F-5As, while the larger, more serious ones included those mentioned above. In New Guinea (the Fifth AF), there were initially problems with guns jamming, carburetor temperatures running too high, intercoolers breaking too easily, inspection panels being difficult to remove, and oil and coolant lines vibrating free and leaking. Nevertheless, the P-38 was then indisputably the USAAF's premier fighter, as evidenced by its growing score of enemy aircraft.

These and other technical problems that are discussed in detail in this book were gradually solved on succeeding models of the P-38, the solutions often including improved maintenance procedures. From the time the last of the P-38F-5s were delivered to the Air

This is a nice shot of Maj. Tom McGuire, CO of the 431st FS, in the cockpit of his last assigned P-38, L-1 44-24155 *Pudgy (V)/#131*, taken on Leyte Island in the Philippines in November 1944. Note the small aperture of the gun camera installation inside the shackle beneath the wing, which was pioneered by the 14th FG in Italy and first appeared on the Lockheed assembly line with the P-38J-25. (*John Stanaway collection*)

Forces in March 1943 until the first P-38L-5s rolled off the Lockheed assembly line in October 1944, virtually all the Lightning's deficiencies, large and small, had been resolved. It is true that its cockpit heating system never became totally satisfactory, but at least it was improved somewhat starting with the "J" models.

Diagnosing and solving these problems was very much a collaborative process, involving Lockheed engineers and test pilots in California and P-38 mechanics, engineering officers and civilian Lockheed and Allison technical representatives in the field. In England, the Eighth and Ninth AFs also received considerable assistance from both RAF personnel and civilian technicians.

A good example of such problem solving involved the above-mentioned gun camera film, which issue is discussed in more detail elsewhere in this book. The personnel of least three overseas P-38 groups tackled this dilemma and they all came up with the same basic solution: moving the camera from the nose to a wing. All three were slightly different, but they all worked. The one devised by the 14th FG in Italy in the spring of 1944 was placing the camera inside the left wing pylon, which modification Lockheed soon added to its P-38 assembly lines starting with the J-25, the first of which was built in June of that year.

Compressibility

Then there was compressibility, to which the P-38 has been closely linked for eighty years. Based on his analysis of the P-38's projected speed and airflow, and mathematical equations involving a new concept called "Mach number," after the Austrian ballistics expert who discovered it, Lockheed design engineer Kelly Johnson came across what was to become a serious problem for the new generation of fast, heavy fighters—and most especially the P-38—when they entered steep, sustained dives from very high altitude.

Johnson warned about this phenomenon in a report to the USAAC in 1937: "As airplane speeds and operating altitudes increase to the values to be encountered with the Model 22, consideration must be given to the effect of compressibility."

So, what is compressibility? Air passing over an airplane's surface, especially at very high altitudes where the air is thin, has to speed up to get around its bumps or curves. To get around the larger "bumps" on the P-38, Johnson determined that the airflow's velocity could increase by as much as 40 percent and reach the speed of sound (Mach 1), at which point strange things start to happen, including the forming of a shock wave that in its wake creates a "compressibility burble" that adversely effects the airflow over the aircraft's control surfaces.

One of the USAAC test pilots checking out the YP-38s at Selfridge Field in 1940 was Maj. Signa A. Gilkey. One day he took one up, rolled it over on its back, and entered a steep dive at 35,000 feet. It soon began to vibrate violently and reached the vertical as its speed increased to 500 mph, with severe buffeting setting in at 400 mph. Gilkey suddenly found that he could not pull the control wheel back no matter how hard he tried. He then had a timely inspiration: as he hurtled earthward, he started cranking "nose-up" trim on the elevator trim tab, a small flap utilized to position the elevator for either climb, dive, or level flight so the pilot did not have to exert continuous heavy pressure on the yoke. Nothing changed, however, until he reached the heavier air at 12,000 feet, when the plane suddenly pulled out of its dive, so violently that the top of the canopy and one of its side panels blew out and Maj. Gilkey lost consciousness briefly.

This and other, similar, incidents definitely caught the attention of both Lockheed and the Air Corps. In England in 1942, two P-38 pilots also went into compressibility during high-altitude dives, one of whom failed to recover from it and was killed, while the other was actually torn out of his cockpit by the slipstream, breaking both his legs. He reported that, as had been the case with Maj. Gilkey, once the speed had built up, the aircraft would not respond to the controls.

Maj. Cass Hough, the head of VIII Fighter Command's Office of Flight Research, was informed of these incidents and decided to investigate. Over England on September 17, 1942, he dove a P-38F from 43,000 feet, reaching 525 mph at 35,000 feet. He later determined that a vacuum had built up aft of the plane's center section, depriving the elevators of airflow and thereby adversely affecting their function. He was able to recover by utilizing a degree and a half of tail-heavy trim.

Lockheed's chief test pilot, Milo Burcham, commenced dive tests in a P-38 and also confirmed what Maj. Gilkey had found: that the Lightning pilot who found himself in compressibility needed to wait until he entered the thicker air at lower altitudes and then carefully apply the elevator trim tab. He and fellow Lockheed test pilot Tony LeVier then began to spread the word about how to recover from compressibility, especially among novice USAAF pilots. Of course, knowing what to do was one thing; actually remembering to do it, as a pilot was, say, in a screaming dive from high altitude with a Bf 109 on his tail and an unmovable control wheel, was something else again.

The real solution to the compressibility problem was the new electrically operated dive brakes that Lockheed had developed by early 1944, which modification first appeared on its assembly lines with the P-38J-25. With these flaps, the Lightning pilot could dive from any altitude and pull out with no difficulty.

It was Burcham and LeVier who did most of the test flying, in 1943, of the P-38G-10, serial number 42-12947, that was fitted with the experimental dive flaps, which were the brainchild of Lockheed design engineer Ward Beman. They worked off 1⊠-hp electrical motors that activated a screw mechanism that extended the flaps full down (35 degrees) in a second and a half. The control switch was located on the left side of the yoke.

So, why did these flaps work? Basically, it was because at very high speeds and altitude the suction on the lower surface of the wing was so great that it overwhelmed the normal lift force on the top of the wing, and the flaps restored that balance.

Comparing the Lightning to Other World War II Aircraft

In late July 1942, Col. John N. Stone, CO of the 1st FG, flew one of his unit's P-38Fs to the Royal Aircraft Establishment at Farnborough, England, to compare its performance with that of a captured German Fw 190A fighter. In that test, the Lightning did well in turns and low-altitude maneuvering but could not match the Focke-Wulf's rate of climb or acceleration. The following month the RAF's Air Fighting Development Unit examined the performance of another P-38F flown by the aforementioned Maj. Hough. The results were mostly positive, as the P-38 was found to be as fast as the Spitfire Mk IX at all but the very highest altitudes and to have at least as good a rate of climb.

On July 24, 1943, the RAF and the USAAF teamed up for a comparative performance test of their three primary photo reconnaissance aircraft—the Lockheed F-5, the de Havilland Mosquito, and the Supermarine Spitfire PR. In this case, the Spitfire was found to be faster and have a better rate of climb than either twin-engined aircraft.

When the Eighth AF's P-38 groups switched to P-51s in the summer of 1944, there was a lot of discussion about and controversy over which was the better fighter. An interesting anecdote in this regard comes from former 479th FG pilot Albert S. J. "Al" Tucker, who was a proponent of the P-38. During that brief period when the 479th had examples of both aircraft on hand, he, in a Lightning, "jousted" with Lt. Richard D. Creighton—newly assigned to the group and a P-51 proponent—in a Mustang. According to Tucker: "In the P-38 I was able to demonstrate that in his Mustang Dick Creighton couldn't keep up with me, couldn't climb with me, couldn't turn with me and couldn't get me off his tail. He had to admit after a few failures to out-joust me with his P-51 that the P-38 was 'better than I thought,' but he wouldn't concede that it was truly the better of the two airplanes until he had a chance to switch and see for himself."

They did switch, and Creighton was reportedly impressed with "how good and fast the big P-38 was and how easy it was to out-turn the Mustang without any fear of snap rolling. Nevertheless, stubborn to the end, he said that the Mustang still had one important advantage over the heavier P-38: acceleration." So, they decided to test that theory in an aerial drag race, flying side by side and then applying full power simultaneously. Tucker admitted that he "didn't truly know which airplane would pull away quicker, but to my surprise the P-38 shot ahead immediately and didn't stop pulling away." This contest was between a P-38J and a P-51D.[3]

Another former 479th FG pilot, Herman C. Hoversten, flew both types on long-range bomber escort missions. As to their respective ranges, he stated that he "would gladly wager a large amount that given the two airplanes with full drop tanks, the P-38 would be airborne for at least an extra hour longer than the P-51."

A comparison of the official flight specifications for the P-51D and the P-38L is revealing, although not definitive. They credit the Mustang with a maximum speed of 437 mph and the Lightning with 414 mph, both at 25,000 feet. Their service ceilings were close, but the P-38 came out slightly ahead this time, 44,000 feet to 41,900 feet. Its climb rate was also slightly better, the P-38's time to 20,000 feet being exactly seven minutes, while the P-51's was an additional eighteen seconds. The Lightning could carry 410 gallons of fuel internally and the Mustang just 269, although the latter's range on internal fuel only was 950 miles while the Lightning's was just 850. Of course, such factors as weather (especially wind) and the pilots' fuel management procedures would effect the actual range on any given mission.

The Republic P-47D-30 was a contemporary of both those other USAAF fighters in the fall of 1944. Its top speed was rated at 433 mph and its service ceiling at 43,000 feet. By that time, the Thunderbolt's internal fuel capacity had been increased to 370 gallons and its range, officially, without drop tanks, was 800 miles. Its official climb rate was 3,180 feet per minute, or less than seven seconds to 20,000 feet—this due to the Thunderbolt's powerful 2,500-hp Pratt and Whitney R-2800 Double Wasp engine and its large paddle-blade propellers that could really take hold of the air.

Now for evaluations of the P-38 by two of its opponents—first, Luftwaffe *experten* Franz Stiegler, who often encountered Lightnings while flying Bf 109s with JG 27 in the MTO in 1943:

[They] could turn inside us with ease and they could go from level flight to climb almost instantaneously. We lost quite a few pilots who tried to make an attack and then pull up. The P-38s were on them at once. They closed so quickly that there was little one could do except roll quickly and dive down, for while the P-38 could turn inside us, it rolled very slowly through the first five or ten degrees of bank, and by then we would already be gone. One cardinal rule we never forgot was: Avoid fighting a P-38 head on. That was suicide. Their armament was so heavy and their firepower so murderous that no one ever tried that type of attack more than once.

Johannes Steinhoff, a 176-victory *experten* who commanded JG 77 in the MTO, remembered about the Lightning: "It was fast, low profiled and a fantastic fighter, and a real danger when it was above you. It was only vulnerable if you were behind it, a little below and closing fast, or turning into it, but on the attack it was a tremendous aircraft. One shot me down from long range in 1944."

One of their opponents, Pincus P. "Phil" Taback, a former 82nd FG pilot, made his case for the P-38:

[Its] tricycle gear was much faster for scrambling takeoffs, also less prone to accidents. The P-38 had counter-rotating props, which in turn gave you no torque. I can't begin to tell you the value of that—no snap rolls and no spins, especially on the deck in tight turns. Talk about gun patterns: four .50-caliber machine guns and a 20mm cannon all in the nose in a seven-foot pattern. In the single-engine fighters the guns were in the wings so they had to cross at a point at 600 feet (approximately). Do I have to explain the difficulty compared to the straight pattern of the P-38? I never heard of a P-38 losing both engines at the same time. I can't begin to tell you how many pilots came home on one engine, whether it was engine failure or shot out.[4]

The P-38 and the Lufwaffe's two main fighters, the Bf 109 and the Fw 190, were overall fairly well matched. By mid-1944, the 190 was being utilized primarily as a bomber destroyer and as a fighter-bomber. In the former role, its most numerous model was the A-8, which had increased armament to help it shoot down the bombers and added armor to protect its pilot from return fire. This added weight made it a less effective dogfighter, but it could still be a tough opponent in the hands of an experienced pilot, especially at very high altitudes, where it was more agile than the P-38. The Fw 190A-8 had a reported top speed of 408 mph, a service ceiling of 37,400 feet, and a climb rate of just 2,362 feet per minute. Usually providing cover for the Focke-Wulfs attacking the bombers were the Bf 109s, whose main task was to distract the American fighters. By the fall of 1944, its latest model was the G-14, whose A/S (high-altitude) version had a maximum speed of 422 mph at 25,000 feet, a service ceiling of 41,000 feet, and a climb rate of 3,030 feet per minute. As to the P-38Js fighting these e/a, most often it came down to numbers, tactics, and, most especially, the skill and experience of their pilots. According to British aviation historian Roger Freeman:

> In actual combat [in late 1943 and early 1944], what had proved to be the case in Africa was found to apply [in Europe]—below 18,000 feet the P-38 was a better machine in most respects than the Me 109G and stood up well against the Fw 190A. Above that its performance fell off and it could neither pursue an enemy with much chance of success above 28,000 feet, nor out-dive the Messerschmitts and Focke Wulfs at such heights. Once the fight was brought down to 18,000 feet then the tables were turned in these respects.[5]

When it came to battling the JNAF's famed A6M Zero (Zeke) and the JAAF's even more nimble Ki-43 Oscar, the tactics were pretty much set in stone. Since the P-38 was much faster than either of these opponents and they were much more maneuverable—and given the Lightning's superior firepower and much sturdier construction—its pilots always strived to maintain their altitude and speed by utilizing dive and zoom tactics whenever possible. The A6M3's top speed was 332 mph and the P-38J's 415 mph, while their service ceilings were 36,250 feet and 44,000 feet, respectively. As to range, with drop tanks the Zeke's was 2,030 miles and the Lightning's 2,600.

Both Japanese fighters were notoriously deficient in fuel tank protection, and when hit by the heavy firepower of a P-38, they usually burst into flame, especially when incendiary bullets were used. The Lightning pilots did their best to avoid individual low-speed, low-level turning dogfights, since a competent and alert Zeke or Oscar pilot could easily avoid them in that situation—and quite possibly end up on their tails. With the introduction by 1943 of heavier, faster, and more sturdy Japanese fighters, such as the Ki-61 Tony and the Ki-44 Tojo, the P-38 pilots' tactics were modified accordingly. Of course, when the new aileron boost was introduced on the P-38 in the summer of 1944, their pilots could confidently dogfight (turn) with any enemy fighter.

9

The Survivors

Of the 10,038 Lightnings that had been built by August 1945, two years later, only several hundred still existed, most of those that had survived the war having been scrapped. A few that had been purchased as surplus by civilians continued to be flown, but most of the survivors were serving with the air forces of France, Italy, and China. At the time of this writing, seventy-two years later, they have dwindled down to several dozen, residing in various air museums and aircraft collections. Of them, the following nine are currently flying.

1

P-38F-1 serial number 41-7630 (civil registration number N17630) is undoubtedly the most famous, and certainly the most rare, surviving P-38. On July 15, 1942, its pilot was forced to crash-land it, along with five other P-38s of the 94th FS, plus two accompanying B-17s, on Greenland's icecap, while *en route* to Iceland as part of Operation Bolero, the transfer of USAAF aircraft from the U.S. over the North Atlantic to England. Although the aircrews were rescued, their damaged planes had to be abandoned, and there 41-7630 resided, underneath an ever-growing layer of ice (eventually 260 feet of it) until it was recovered in 1992 by the Greenland Expedition, during the seventh such expedition since 1981. Its disassembled parts were lifted by helicopter to a nearby port and then shipped to Savannah, Georgia, from where they were trucked to the Middleboro, Kentucky, Airport for restoration at what became, in 1996, The Lost Squadron Museum, owned by Roy Schoffner, who financed it. It flew again for the first time on October 26, 2002. *Glacier Girl*, as it was named during its restoration, has subsequently been a staple at air shows throughout the country. Since 2007, it has been owned by Rod Lewis's Lewis Air Legends in San Antonio, Texas.

2

P-38F-5 serial number 42-12652 is another amazing P-38 restoration, in that, like *Glacier Girl*, it was not one of those that survived World War II intact. In September 1942, it was delivered to the 39th FS in Australia, with which it became White 33. It saw a lot of action in the New Guinea campaign until early 1944, when, now serving with the 475th FG, it was badly damaged when its nose gear collapsed on Dreger Field, near Finschafen,

Famed warbird pilot Steve Hinton enters the cockpit of *Glacier Girl* at the Chino, California, Airport. (*P-38 National Association photo*)

White 33 during a Chino air show. (*Hayman Tam photo*)

and it was abandoned there. In 1999, its remains were recovered by an Australian aircraft recovery group and removed to Melbourne. In 2003, they were moved again, to WestPac Restorations at the Rialto, California, Airport, where its long rebuild (which required many spare and newly manufactured parts) began. In 2009, WestPac moved to Colorado Springs, Colorado, as did 42-12652/White 33. This historic P-38 flew again there on October 29, 2016 with famed warbird pilot Steve Hinton at its controls. Originally intended for Paul Allen's Flying Heritage Collection at Paine Field in Seattle, it is now on display at and flying from the National Museum of WWII Aviation in Colorado Springs.

3

In 1945, P-38J-20 44-23314, which currently carries civil registration number N138AM, was donated by the USAAF to the Hancock Field School of Aeronautics in Santa Monica, California, which sold it to a private collector nine years later. In 1959, it was donated to Ed Maloney's The Air Museum in Claremont, California, which by the time it moved to the Chino, California, Airport in 1973 was called Planes of Fame. It was on static display from 1962 to 1987, when it began to be restored to airworthy status by Steve Hinton's Fighter Rebuilders, flying again for the first time on July 22, 1988. As *Joltin' Josie*, it was a fixture at the Palm Springs Air Museum from 1989 to 1998, when it rejoined Planes of Fame. In 2003, it was repainted as *Porky II*, the Lightning flown by 80th FS ace Edward Cragg in New Guinea, and then again, in 2006, as *23 SKIDOO*, 475th FG ace Perry Dahl's P-38.

4

P-38L-5 44-26981/N7723C, which was converted to an F-5G-6 photo reconnaissance Lightning at Lockheed's Modification Center at Love Field near Dallas, has had a long and complicated history since being sold at the Kingman, Arizona, War Assets Administration air depot in 1946. It was utilized by several companies for aerial surveying until 1962, after which it went through numerous other owners prior to being seriously damaged in a landing accident in 1971. After it was purchased by Jay Silberman in 1979, a restoration was begun, and it finally flew again in September 1985. It went on display at the Museum of Flying in Santa Monica, California, in 1989 and was fitted with a new fighter nose the following year, shortly after which it was sold for $1.5 million to William Lyons' Martin Aviation at the John Wayne Airport in Santa Ana, California (formerly the Orange County Airport). In 1995, it returned to the Museum of Flying and then, in 2002, became part of the Commemorative Air Force at Midland, Texas. It was purchased by Vintage Fighters in 2005 and is currently part of Jack Croul's Allied Fighters, based at the Chino Airport. It carried the name *Honey Bunny* for several years.

5

No. 44-27083, another P-38L-5/F-5G-6 conversion—now registered as N2114L—was operated by Mark Hurd Aerial Surveys from 1948 to 1968, when it was retired. After being in storage for twenty-six years, it was acquired by Jack Erickson, who restored it, as *TANGERINE*, for his Tillamook Air Museum in Oregon. It flew again for the first time in September 1996. It is currently on display as part of the Erickson Aircraft Collection in Madras, Oregon.

The 23 SKIDOO. (*Hayman Tam photo*)

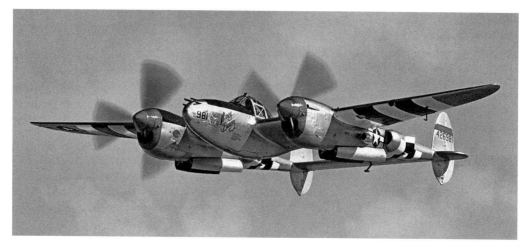

Above: The Allied Fighters' P-38, formerly named *Honey Bunny*. (*P-38 National Association photo*)

Below: TANGERINE. (*Hayman Tam photo*)

6

No. 44-27231/N79123, also a P-38L-5/F-5G-6 modification, participated in the 1946 Cleveland Air Races shortly after it was purchased from the War Assets Administration depot at Altus, Oklahoma. It then passed through many more hands before it was acquired, in 1976, by warbird collector and restorer Dave Tallichet, who kept it at the Chino Airport for four years before beginning its restoration, in Tulsa, Oklahoma, and then back at Chino, during which it was refitted with a fighter nose. It flew again in November 1995. It was then painted in the markings of one of Dick Bong's P-38s, *Marge*, and was based at the P-38 National Association's hangar at March Field, California, from 1998 to 2001. It was then sold to Paul Allen's Flying Heritage Collection briefly and again in 2003 to The Fighter Collection at Duxford, England. In 2004, it was purchased by Ron Fagen for his Fagen Fighters WWII Museum in Granite Falls, Minnesota. Originally appearing as *Ruff Stuff*, an 80th FS Lightning in New Guinea, it was repainted in 2015 as *SCAT III*, which was a P-38 flown by ace Robin Olds with the 479th FG in England.

7

No. 44-53095/N9005R, a P-38L-5 that was converted to a P-38M-6 night fighter at Lockheed's Modification Center, was acquired by the Honduran Air Force in 1948. In 1960, it was sold to an American collector, who stored it at the Blythe, California, Airport for nine years before selling it to William Ross of Illinois, who flew it as *Der Gabelschwanz Teuful* (Fork Tailed Devil). In 1988, it was purchased by the Lone Star Flight Museum in Houston. It was damaged in an accident in 1997 and by 2006 was being restored by Comanche Fighters, also in Texas. It is currently owned by the Friedkin family of Houston, and after appearing as *Putt-Putt Maru*, the P-38 flown by 475th FG ace Charles MacDonald, for a while has, since 2009, been displayed in the markings of *Thoughts of Midnite*, another 475th FG Lightning.

SCAT III in flight. (*Fagen Fighters WWII Museum photo via the P-38 National Association*)

Thoughts of Midnite. (*Hayman Tam photo*)

The Evergreen Aviation Museum's P-38 before it was purchased by the Collings Foundation. (*Hayman Tam photo*)

8

No. 44-53186/N505MH, another P-38L-5/F-5G-6 modification sold at the Kingman air depot in 1946, did aerial survey work until it was retired by Mark Hurd in 1967. It was part of Harrah's Automobile Collection in Reno, Nevada, from then until 1982. Dave Tallichet acquired it for his restoration company in 1985, rebuilt it and sold it, in 1987, to Doug Arnold's Warbirds of Great Britain collection. It was delivered to England in 1989 and flew there with the name *Miss Behavin'* until the following year, when it was purchased by the Evergreen Aviation Museum and flown back across the Atlantic. It was on display at Evergreen's facilities in Marana, Arizona, and McMinnville, Oregon, until it was purchased, in 2015, by the Collings Foundation, which is currently (2019) restoring it for its flying collection of World War II aircraft.

9

Yet another P-38L-5/F-5G-6 conversion, 44-53254 was flown, after being heavily modified, in the postwar Cleveland Air Races with the name *Sky Ranger*. It was acquired by the Confederate Air Force (which in 2002 changed its name to the Commemorative Air Force) in Texas in 1964. For many years, it was flown extensively by CAF co-owner Melvin "Lefty" Gardner in air races and at air shows as *White Lightnin'* with the civil registration number N25Y. It was distinctive for the early model P-38 air intakes under its engines. After a serious crash in 2001, it was sold to the Red Bull company for its aircraft collection, the Flying Bulls, in Salzburg, Austria, and was restored by Ezell Aviation in Breckinridge, Texas—becoming airworthy again in 2008. Now known as the Red Bull P-38, it appeared after its restoration in a striking polished aluminum finish. It is a favorite at air shows throughout Europe.

There are also currently a dozen Lightnings, either restored or at least complete, on static display in air museums and other venues. They comprise the following aircraft.

P-38G-10 42-13400, which served with the 54th FS in Alaska. In 1999, it was recovered from where it had crash-landed on Attu Island in the Aleutians in 1945. Beautifully restored for static display the following year, it can be viewed at Joint Base Elmendorf-Richardson (formerly Elmendorf AFB) in Anchorage, Alaska.

The remains of P-38H-5 42-66841, named *Scarlet Scourge*, which served with the 475th FG in New Guinea, were recovered from there in 1992. It was part of the Papua New Guinea National Museum until 1997, when it was acquired by the Classic Jets Fighter Museum in Adelaide, South Australia. After many years of painstaking work, it is now beautifully restored to non-flying, static-display status.

P-38J-10 42-67638, another 54th FS aircraft, crash-landed in Alaska in 1944 and was subsequently utilized as an air-to-ground target. It was recovered by the Air Force Heritage Foundation in 1994 and after its restoration was delivered to Hill Air Force Base in Utah in 1996. It is currently on static display there at the Hill Aerospace Museum.

P-38J-10 42-67762 is displayed at the National Air & Space Museum's Steven F. Udvar-Hazy Center in Chantilly, Virginia, near Washington, D.C. It is unrestored but complete. This Lightning spent most of the war serving as a test aircraft at the USAAF's research and development center at Wright Field, Ohio. Postwar it was selected to be an exhibit at a proposed USAAF museum and was in storage from 1946 until 1960, when it was acquired by NASM.

The two manifestations of F-5G-6 44-53254 as a highly modified postwar air racer with the civil registration number N25Y—as *Sky Ranger* in 1947 and in a colorful Inca Bronze paint scheme for the 1948 races. It finished second in the 1947 Miami Air Races and in that year's Sohio Trophy Race at Cleveland, but mechanical problems kept it from placing in the 1947 and 1948 Thompson Trophy Races. The following year, in the final Cleveland National Air Races, it placed fifth in the Tinnerman Trophy Race. (*Michael Bates collection*)

Above left: White Lightnin' in 1990, displaying its beautiful paint job. Inside the red lightning bolt is its name—in white, of course. (*Author's collection*)

Above right: P-38J-10 42-67762, currently on display at the National Air & Space Museum. (*Hayman Tam photo*)

Below: The same plane much more recently as the immaculate Red Bull P-38. (*P-38 National Association collection*)

P-38L-5/F-5G-6 44-27053 is currently on display at the War Eagles Air Museum in Santa Teresa, New Mexico. Although potentially airworthy, it is on static display only, with the name *Relampago*. This was another postwar aerial survey aircraft, and it was also utilized by Jim Cook for weather research in the Midwest during the 1950s and '60s. In 1969, it was purchased by Gary Levitz and the Confederate Air Force and was their air racer *Double Trouble Too* until it was damaged in a landing accident in 1983. It was repaired and then went through two more owners before being acquired by War Eagles in 1994.

P-38L-5/F-5G-6 44-27183, which is part of the Yanks Air Museum in Chino, California, is the only currently restored photo reconnaissance Lightning. Although airworthy, it is on static display only. This aircraft was used extensively for aerial survey work from 1946 to 1969. After passing through several other owners, it was acquired by Charles Nichols for his Yankee Air Corps (which was later renamed the Yanks Museum) in 1990 and was then restored to its original F-5 configuration.

P-38L-5/F-5G-6 44-53015 is currently on outside static display at the front gate of Joint Base McGuire-Dix, in Lakehurst, New Jersey, as a memorial to P-38 ace Thomas McGuire, after whom the base is named. It is painted in the markings of his 475th FG Lightning named *Pudgy V*. This aircraft participated in the Cleveland Air Races after the war and did aerial survey work from 1955 to 1962, when it was acquired by the Tallmantz Movieland of the Air Museum at the Orange County, California, Airport. Dave Tallichet obtained it for his Yesterday's Air Force at Chino in 1970 and fitted it with a fighter nose. It was acquired by the USAF Museum in 1981 and flown to what was then McGuire Air Force Base for display.

P-38L-5/P-38M-6 44-53087 is featured at the Experimental Aircraft Association's AirVenture Museum in Oshkosh, Wisconsin, painted as Dick Bong's *Marge*. This Lightning passed through many owners after the war and was mostly utilized as a modified aerial survey aircraft. The EAA Aviation Foundation acquired it in 1981. It is reportedly airworthy but is not flown.

P-38L-5/P-38M-6 44-53097 is on display at the Museum of Flight at the King County International Airport near Seattle, Washington, with the name *Lizzie V*, the Lightning flown by 475th FG ace John Purdy. This aircraft served with the Honduran Air Force in the 1950s and '60s and then passed through the hands of numerous American collectors until acquired by the Champlin Fighter Museum in Mesa, Arizona, in 1983. It was purchased by the Museum of Flight in 2000.

P-38L-5/F-5G-6 44-53232, another ex-Honduran Air Force Lightning, is on static display at the National Museum of the USAF at Wright-Patterson Air Force Base in Ohio. It was an air racer after the war and following its sojourn in Honduras was acquired by what was then the USAF Museum in 1961. It is displayed in the colors of a 20th FG P-38 in England.

P-38L-5 44-53236 is the centerpiece of the Richard I. Bong Veterans' Historical Center in Superior, Wisconsin. It appears in the markings of one of Bong's P-38s that was named after his then-fiancée, *Marge*. It is beautifully restored but not airworthy. It was donated by the USAF to the Richard I. Bong Memorial in the American Ace-of-Ace's hometown of Poplar, Wisconsin, in 1949 and was displayed there and at another air museum in Minnesota until the Historical Center opened in 2002.

When it comes to surviving Lightnings, P-38J-15 43-28570, which served with the 44th FS on Guadalcanal, is a most unusual case. On June 5, 1944, while attempting to land

The Yanks Air Museum's 44-27183, the only currently restored F-5. (*Author's photo*)

F-5G-6 44-53015 was purchased from the Kingman, Arizona, RFC depot in 1946 by the famous race car driver Rex Mays and acquired the civil registration number N9957F. With the name *MACMILLAN METEOR*, it was entered in the 1946 Bendix Trophy Race, in which Mays placed thirteenth. After going through numerous other civilian owners, including Hycon Aerial Surveys, it was donated to the Air Force Museum in 1981 and became a gate guard display at McGuire AFB, New Jersey, where it remains as of this writing, in the colors of Tom McGuire's P-38 *Pudgy*. (*Michael Bates collection*)

Above: In the late 1960s former P-38M 44-53087 (civil registration number N1107V) was owned by the Wilson Flight Training Center at the Fairfax Airport in Kansas City. It had previously spent many years doing aerial survey work for Spartan Air Services and Hycon Aerial Surveys, for which it had received its huge modified photo nose. (*American Aviation Historical Society collection*)

Below: No. 44-53087 looking very different, indeed, as the AirVenture Museum's *Marge*. (*EAA photo*)

P-38L-5 44-53236, which is now the centerpiece of the Richard I. Bong Veterans' Historical Center in Superior, Wisconsin, while part of the Polar Aviation Museum in Anoka County, Minnesota. (*Author's collection*)

on single engine at the squadron's airfield at Kukum, its CO, Maj. Peyton S. Mathis, Jr., disappeared and was subsequently listed as MIA—and, eventually, as KIA. No. 43-28570, it turned out, had crashed into a swamp, on its back, in 7 feet of water, from which it was found impossible to recover Maj. Mathis's body. As the war moved on, it was abandoned and forgotten. Flash forward to 2012, when a local resident, with a large crew, finally recovered the P-38 and the remains of its pilot after four months of intensive labor. The aircraft, which was found to be remarkably well preserved, was disassembled, cleaned up, and then reassembled. It is now stored in a warehouse on Guadalcanal, awaiting restoration.

There are portions of other P-38s recovered from New Guinea in storage at several facilities in Australia, plus, in the U.S., parts from crashed Lightnings, which may be used for future restorations. One example of the former is P-38G-13 43-2195, which has already been partially reassembled by Hopper Warbirds in Townsville, Queensland, Australia.

A similar example is that of P-38L-5 44-25786, which 14th FG ace Michael Brezas force-landed in Yugoslavia on April 2, 1945. It was confiscated by that country's new communist government, flown briefly by its air force and ended up, disassembled, in the Yugoslav Air and Space Museum in Belgrade, where it reportedly is awaiting restoration.

Also reportedly in storage and awaiting restoration is P-38L-5/F-5G-6 44-26761, which is owned by Kermit Weeks' Fantasy of Flight in Polk City, Florida. This P-38 had a long history of aerial survey work before Weeks obtained it for his Weeks Air Museum in Tamiami, Florida, in 1981. Unfortunately, it was badly damaged by Hurricane Andrew in 1992.

P-38J-15 42-103988 and P-38H-1 42-66534 (the latter located in Wilmington, Delaware) are also reportedly awaiting restoration. No. 42-103988 is a particularly interesting case, as

F-5G-6 44-26761 passed through many hands after it was purchased at the Altus, Oklahoma, RFC depot in October 1947, mostly doing aerial survey work. It received the civil registration number N6190C when it joined Hycon Aerial Surveys in 1956. In 1981, it was purchased by Kermit Weeks for his air museum near Miami. Damaged by Hurricane Andrew in 1992, it is reportedly still awaiting restoration. (*Michael Bates collection*)

it was 80th FS ace Jay T. Robbins's assigned aircraft, *Jandina III*. Robbins crash-landed it near Saidor, New Guinea, on May 7, 1944, and it was abandoned there. It was recovered in 1999 and transported to Australia and then, in 2002, to WestPac Restorations in California. Unfortunately, the government of Papua New Guinea declared it an illegal recovery, for which reason its whereabouts and status have been kept secret. It is reportedly part of the Flying Heritage Collection, but the museum will not confirm it.

Then there is the Flying Heritage Collection's P-38J-15 42-104088, which is definitely in storage and awaiting restoration. Sold as surplus after the war, it passed through several owners until Gary Levitz acquired it as a "hulk" in 1969 and restored it to airworthy condition. It was badly damaged in a crash-landing in 1974, acquired by the Confederate Air Force the following year and then rebuilt, flying again on February 28, 1992 as *Scatterbrain Kid II*—still fitted with its aerial survey nose. It crashed again in 1994 and has supposedly been in the process of a rebuild ever since.

P-38 Production Models, Modifications, Conversions, and Experiments

XP-38

LAC Model 022-64-01, construction number (C/N) 2201 and USAAC serial number 37-457. The X, of course, stood for experimental. It was powered by an Allison V-1710C-9 (-11) engine rated at 1,150 hp on the left side, turning in that direction, and an opposite-turning -15 on the right. Only one was built; its construction began in July 1937 and was completed in December 1938. It flew for the first time on January 27, 1939 and was destroyed in a crash-landing on February 11.

YP-38

LAC Model 122-62-02, C/Ns 2202 to 2214/USAAC Nos. 39-689 to 39-701. Y was the USAAC's designation for a prototype. Thirteen were built and delivered from September 1940 to May 1941.

The Air Corps was so impressed with the XP-38 that it ordered these YP-38s, some of which were service tested by the 1st Pursuit Group at Selfridge Field, Michigan. They were powered by the new F series V-1710s, specifically the F-2 -27 and -29 engines, with General Electric B2 turbo-superchargers, also rated at 1,150 hp. This was quite different from the C-9 engine utilized by the XP-38 in that the F-2's crankshaft was moved up several inches from the centerline of the engine block, resulting in the propellers being mounted higher and the top of the engine cowling being flatter and less streamlined than before.

The proposed armament for the YP-38 was two .50-cal. and two .30-cal. machine guns and a 37-mm cannon, but in fact none were fitted and the gun ports were faired over. The larger radiator scoops on its booms and the new oil cooler air intakes below the engines created some increased drag, resulting in a slight reduction in its official top speed from that of the XP-38—405 *v.* 413 mph.

Lockheed test pilot Milo Burcham in the cockpit of the first YP-38, serial number 39-689, over Pasadena, California, in late 1940. (*Lockheed photo*)

P-38-LO (no model designation)

LAC Model 222-62-08, C/Ns 2215 to 2232/USAAF Nos. 40-744 to 40-761 and 2234 to 2244/40-763 to 40-773. Twenty-nine were built, and they were delivered from June to August 1941.

The -LO (Lockheed) designation is often used with this P-38 variant since it had no model letter and might be confused with another model, although it was not utilized uniformly until the P-38F-1. Its armament was to have been four .50-cal. machine guns and a 37-mm cannon, but they were seldom installed, and sometimes dummy barrels were fitted instead. From a visual standpoint, its spinners were not as pointed as those used on the XP-38 and the YP-38, and it was the first to be painted in the USAAF's new Olive Drab and Neutral Gray scheme.

Many P-38-LOs were supplied to the 1st, 14th, and 82nd Pursuit Groups, which were training in southern California in late 1941 and early 1942. The survivors later received the RP (Restricted Pursuit) designation, indicating that they were "restricted" from combat service, and to training and other duties only.

XP-38A

LAC Model 622-62-10, C/N 2233/USAAF No. 40-762. Modified from a P-38 (no model designation) to test a pressurized cabin; it was delivered in December 1942.

A P-38-LO, of which only twenty-nine were built. They had no model letter and most of them, including the one in this photo, had no guns. (*Michael Bates collection*)

P-38D

LAC Model 222-62-08D, C/Ns 2245-2280/USAAF #s 40-774 to 40-809. Thirty-six built were built, and they were delivered from June to September 1941.

The P-38Ds had armor plating to protect the pilot, bulletproof glass, self-sealing fuel tanks, a new low-pressure oxygen system and flow regulator, and some minor airframe modifications. Not all of them were armed and those that were had just the four .50-cal. machine guns; no cannon had yet been installed on a P-38. The Ds are easily recognized by their unique gun enclosure tubes that protruded from their noses. Used initially by the 1st, 14th, 78th, and 82nd FGs while they were training in southern California before moving to England in mid- and late 1942. Some of them were later reassigned to the 329th and 360th FGs—P-38 OTUs also based in southern California—and the survivors received the RP designation.

P-38E

LAC Model 222-62-09, C/Ns 5201 to 5315/USAAF Nos. 41-1983 to 41-2097, 5318 to 5338/42-2100 to 41-2120, 5390/41-2172/, 5437/41-2219 and 5439 to 5510/41-2221 to 41-2292. A total of 210 were built, and they were delivered from November 1941 to April 1942.

Other than the lack of wing pylons and shackles for bombs and/or auxiliary gas tanks, the P-38E was combat ready, and that deficiency was solved by retrofitting many of them. This model was the result of literally hundreds of improvements and upgrades, both large and small, that had been implemented by Lockheed over the past year, including improved electrical and

This is a great shot of a 1st PG P-38D, taken in late 1941 or early 1942. (*Michael Bates collection*)

This photo of P-38E 41-2081 was taken in the U.S. sometime in early 1942. Its unit is not known, but it is known that it showed up with the Eighth AF at the Langford Lodge air depot in Northern Ireland later that year. (*National Archives photo*)

hydraulic systems and better radios and flight instruments. The large scoop on the top of each boom was now a thing of the past, replaced by two smaller ones. A retractable landing light was also now in place under the left wing. Toward the end of the E's production run, its hollow steel Hamilton Standard propellers were replaced with Curtiss Electric duralumin props, which reportedly contributed to a noticeable improvement in performance. It also, finally, had the P-38's full intended armament: four .50-cal. machine guns and a 20-mm cannon. It was powered by the new V-1710-F4 (-27/-29) engines, as were the F-4-1s, the F-4A-1s and the single F-4A-2. (No. 41-2014 was, atypically, actually converted to an F-4-1.)

At least twenty-seven P-38Es are known to have served with the 54th FS in the Aleutians and later with other squadrons of the 343rd FG there. They had been upgraded to P-38F configuration with the addition of the under-wing pylons at the Lockheed factory. Es served with many P-38 combat units training on the West Coast. The RP designation was given to most of the survivors in October 1942.

P-38F (no numerical designation)

LAC Model 222-60-09, C/Ns 5511 to 5539/USAAF Nos. 41-2293 to 41-2321, 5541 to 5576/41-2323 to 41-2358, 5601 to 5604/41-2383 to 41-2386/, 5606 to 5610/41-2388 to 41-2392, 5613 to 5623/41-7486 to 41-7496, 5625 to 5640/41-7498 to 41-7513, 5643 to 5651/41-7516 to 41-7524, 5653 to 5657/41-7526 to 41-7530, 5659 to 5661/41-7532 to 7534, 5663 to 5665/41-7536 to 41-7538, 5669/41-7542, 5670/41-7543, 5672/41-7545, 5674/41-7547, and 5678/41-7551. A total of 126 were built; they were delivered in March and April 1942.

All P-38F models were powered by V-1710-F-5 (-49/-53) Allisons. The "F" was the first really combat ready Lightning, as it was the first model to be equipped with the 2,000-lb. pylon and shackle under each wing for the carrying of bombs and/or fuel tanks of either 75- or 150-gallon capacity. After this upgrade was introduced on the assembly line, kits were made available to retrofit them to P-38Fs that had already been built, and to some P-38Es. The new 150-gallon tanks, which could, in fact, hold as many as 165 gallons, were an aerodynamic laminar flow design by Kelly Johnson. They made the P-38 the USAAF's only operational long-range fighter for well over a year. There were, however, some problems associated with the tanks initially. One was that there was no gauge to let the pilot know how much fuel was left in them, so he had to make an educated guess as to when they might run dry and then switch over to the main tanks before they did—or he could just wait until they did actually run dry and then make the switch, and restart the now-dead engines. Also, the empty tanks could at that time only be safely jettisoned at 160 mph or less, lest they do some damage to the aircraft after their release, requiring the pilot to first slow down considerably.

One visual difference on the P-38F was the installation of the antenna for its SCR-552-A radio under the nose in place of the pitot tube, the latter having been moved to under the left wing—except for the F-4A-1, and future Lightning photo recons, on which the antenna was remounted on top of the fuselage so as not to interfere with the coverage of the vertical cameras in their noses. It was also on the "F" model that the canopy was redesigned to open up and back, rather than to the right. The canopy itself was reinforced at this time, after some of them, or at least parts of them, had come off during steep dives. These modifications were covered by Lockheed Service Bulletins (tech orders)—one of them, dated April 14, 1942, adding steel side window cross bracing and another, dated May 5, adding a steel reinforcing strap to the top.

Most of these early P-38Fs were used for stateside training, by both combat units preparing for overseas duty and by OTUs, but a few served with the 1st FG in Iceland, England, and North Africa.

P-38F-1-LO

LAC Model 222-60-15, C/N 5540/USAAF No. 41-2322, 5577 to 5579/42-2359 to 42-2361, 5600/41-2382, 5605/41-2387, 5611/41-7484, 5612/41-7485, 5624/41-7497, 5641/41-7514, 5642/41-7515, 5652/41-7525, 5658/41-7531, 5662/41-7535, 5666 to 5668/41-7539 to 41-7541, 5671/41-7544, 5673/41-7546, 5675 to 5677/41-7548 to 41-7550, and 5679 to 5807/41-7552 to 41-7680. (Nos. 41-2382, 41-2387 and 41-7484 were actually Model 222-60-12s.) A total of 151 were built; they were delivered from May to July 1942.

Most P-38F-1s were assigned to the 1st, 14th, 78th, and 82nd FGs in California in 1942 prior to their transfer to England. The 1st's and the 14th's pilots flew theirs across the North Atlantic that summer and the others were shipped to air depots in England and Northern Ireland. Most of them subsequently served with the Twelfth AF in North Africa.

P-38F-5-LO

LAC Model 222-60-12, C/Ns 7001-7100/USAAF Nos. 42-12567 to 41-12666. A total of 100 were built; they were delivered from June 1942 to March 1943.

Most P-38F-5s through serial number 42-12620 were assigned to the 1st, 14th, and 82nd FGs in the U.K. and then served with them in North Africa. At least twenty-eight, with serial numbers in the 42-12572 to 42-12613 range, served with the 50th FS, first as part of the 14th FG and then with the 342nd CG, in Iceland. Most of the rest of the F-5s went to the Fifth AF in the SWP and were assigned to the 39th and 80th FGs in late 1942 and early 1943.

P-38F-13-LO

LAC Model 322-60-19, C/Ns 3144 to 3172/USAAF Nos. 43-2035 to 43-2063. Twenty-nine were built; they were delivered from August to October 1942.

These were initially ordered by the RAF as Lightning IIs, but reverted to the USAAF when the order was canceled. They were used almost exclusively for training in the U.S., by fighter groups preparing for overseas combat duty plus the two P-38 OTUs, the 329th and 360th FGs. No. 43-2035, which was originally Lightning II AF221, was utilized by Lockheed as a test aircraft investigating the possibility of P-38s launching torpedoes.

P-38F-1 41-7586 was serving with the 1st FG in California when this photo was taken in 1942. It was assigned to the 445th FS of the 50th FG at Orlando AAB, Florida, when it was destroyed by a fire on June 29, 1943. (*Lockheed photo*)

P-38F center sections fill one of Lockheed's assembly hangars sometime in mid-1942. (*Lockheed photo*)

P-38F-15-LO

LAC Model 322-60-19, C/Ns 3173 to 3293/USAAF Nos. 43-2064 to 43-2184. A total of 121 were built; they were delivered in September and October 1942.

The P-38F-15s were also originally ordered by the RAF as Lightning IIs. This model introduced a major improvement in the utilization of Lockheed's Fowler flaps involving an actuator modification that allowed them to operate at up to eight degrees of deflection at speeds up to 250 mph, which increased the aircraft's ability to turn tightly without stalling and also acted as brakes to help make slower, safer landings. These "combat" flaps formed part of the trailing edge of the wing and when needed they could be moved backward and rotated downward to improve lift through increased camber and wing area. Also, a retractable landing light was installed under both wings of the F-15, not just under the left one as before, and three identification lights—colored red, blue-green, and amber, from front to rear—were added to the back of the gondola, replacing the flares that had been used on the earlier models.

Almost all the F-15s ended up in North Africa with the 1st, 14th, and 82nd FGs. Many served first with the 78th FG in England until it converted to P-47s in early 1943 and all its P-38s were transferred to the Twelfth AF.

P-38G-1-LO

LAC Model 222-60-12, C/Ns 7121 to 7200/USAAF Nos. 42-12687 to 42-12766. Eighty were built; they were delivered from August to October 1942.

All P-38Gs were powered by the V-1710F-10 (-51 and -55) engines, as were the F-5As. Although generating the same horsepower as the earlier -49s and -53s, they featured improved controls and were better suited to fast, long-range cruise. The Gs were also equipped with an improved low-pressure oxygen system with greater capacity for longer-range flights at higher altitudes.

Around two dozen G-1s were sent to the SWP and assigned to P-38 squadrons of the Fifth and Thirteenth AFs, but the majority were shipped to the British Isles and subsequently served with the Twelfth AF in North Africa.

P-38G-3-LO

LAC Model 222-68-12, C/Ns 7221 to 7232/USAAF Nos. 42-12787 to 42-12798. Twelve were built; they were delivered in September and October 1942.

Several G-3s served in North Africa with the 1st, 14th, and 82nd FGs, but the majority were utilized in the U.S. for training purposes.

P-38G-5-LO

LAC Model 222-68-12, C/Ns 7233 to 7300/USAAF Nos. 42-12799 to 42-12866. Sixty-seven were built; they were delivered from August to October 1942.

Most of the G-5s in the 42-12799 to 42-12834 serial number range served with the three P-38 groups in North Africa, some of them via the 78th FG in England. A few were assigned to training duties in the U.S., while most of the remainder equipped the 9th and 39th FSs in New Guinea.

P-38G-10-LO

LAC Model 222-68-12, C/Ns 7304 to 7400/USAAF Nos. 42-12870 to 42-12966, 7421 to 7500/42-12987 to 42-13066, 7561 to 7700/42-13127 to 42-13266 and 7761 to 7991/42-13327 to 42-13557. A total of 548 were built; they were delivered from October 1942 to May 1943.

Commencing with the G-10s, the center wing sections and their pylons were strengthened to carry the new 300-gallon auxiliary fuel tanks (which initially were used mainly for ferrying purposes) or a 2,000-lb. bomb load. The majority of this model ended up in North Africa with the 1st, 14th, and 82nd FGs, many of them via the 78th FG in England. At least twenty-one were assigned to Squadron X in North Africa, which flew its P-38s to China for service with the Fourteenth AF, where it became the 449th FS. Many G-10s were utilized for training in the U.S., and a few were assigned to the Thirteenth AF in the SWP and to the 54th FS in the Aleutians, replacing some of its P-38Es.

This P-38G-10, 42-12926, photographed in England in January 1943, was assigned to 82nd FS CO Maj. Harry J. Dayhuff, who named it *Mackie*, after his wife. It was subsequently sent to North Africa and later assigned to the 2nd Fighter Training Squadron at Berrechid, near Casablanca. It was destroyed in a crash in Tunisia on December 8, 1943. (*Author's collection*)

P-38G-13-LO

LAC Model 322-68-19, C/Ns 3294 to 3467/USAAF Nos. 43-2185 to 43-2358. A total of 174 were built; they were delivered from November 1942 to January 1943.

Both the G-13s and the G-15s were originally ordered by the British as Lightning IIs. The early G-13s were mostly sent to the Pacific Theater, including at least seven that were assigned to the 54th FS in the Aleutians. Most of the later G-13s were sent to North Africa, via England.

P-38G-15-LO

LAC Model 322-68-19, C/Ns 3468 to 3500/USAAF Nos. 43-2359 to 43-2391 and 3502 to 3668/43-2392 to 43-2558. A total of 200 were built; they were delivered from January to March 1943.

Most of the G-15s went to North Africa, although a small number were assigned to training duties in the U.S. and about a dozen to the 9th and 80th FSs in New Guinea.

P-38H-1-LO

The H-1 prototype was LAC Model 422-81-20, C/N 1105 and USAAF No. 42-13550, which was delivered in March 1943. The production models, also 422-81-20s, C/Ns 1013 to 1237/USAAF Nos. 42-66502 to 42-66726—of which 225 were built—were delivered from May to August 1943. They and the H-5 were powered by V-1710F-17 (-89 and -91) engines, which featured a small increase in horsepower, from 1,150 to 1,240, mainly due to improved turbo-supercharging. Also, automatic radiator cooling flaps had replaced the old manual ones, to eliminate pilot error.

P-38H-5-LO

LAC Model 422-81-20, C/Ns 1238 to 1612/USAAF Nos. 42-66727 to 42-67101. A total of 375 were built; they were delivered from June to December 1943.

Most of the H-5s in the serial number block 42-66754 through 42-66816 were assigned to training units in the U.S. Twenty of them, from 42-66734 to 42-66753, were assigned to the new 475th FG in Australia, and other H-5s also went to the Fifth AF—and to the Thirteenth AF—in the SWP. Nos. 42-66914 through 42-66976 were utilized mostly for training in the U.S. Nos. 42-66978 through 42-67014 went to the 449th FS in China and the 459th FS in India, while most of the remaining H-5s were assigned to the 20th and 55th FGs of the Eighth AF in England.

F-4-1-LO

LAC Model 222-62-13, C/Ns 5316 and 5317/USAAF Nos. 41-2098 and 41-2099, 5339 to 5389/41-2121 to 41-2171, 5391 to 5436/41-2173 to 41-2218 and 5438/41-2220. Ninety-nine were built, and they were delivered from March to August 1942.

P-38H-5 42-67079, flown by Lockheed test pilot Jimmie Mattern, was photographed over southern California by Lockheed photographer Eric Miller. Note the feathered prop. (*Lockheed photo*)

The F-4-1 PR model was based on the P-38E but not converted from it, with the exception of 41-2014, which was actually converted to an F-4-1. Three or four K-17 cameras replaced the armament in their noses. A few of them arrived in Australia with the 8th PRS in April 1942, and they flew the Lightning's first combat missions anywhere over New Guinea early the following month. It received a total of seventeen F-4-1s, of which two (41-2158 and 41-2159) were loaned to the RAAF for its 1 Photo Reconnaissance Unit, which later received 41-2122 as well. Fourteen were assigned to the 9th PRS in India (the Tenth AF) in the summer of 1942. Most of the rest were used for PR training in the U.S., although at least two are known to have served with the 3rd PG in England and North Africa.

F-4A-1-LO

LAC Model 222-60-13, C/Ns 5580 to 5599/USAAF Nos. 41-2362 to 41-2381. Twenty were built; they were delivered in August 1942. The majority of the F-4A-1s were used for PR training in the U.S., but, as with the F-4-1, at least two served with the 3rd PG in England and North Africa.

F-5A-1-LO

LAC Model 222-68-16, C/Ns 7101 to 7120/USAAF Nos. 42-12667 to 42-12686. Twenty were built; they were delivered from August to December 1942.

At least seven F-5A-1s (42-12670, 42-12675, 42-12676 and 42-12678 to 42-12681) served with the 17th PRS on Guadalcanal in early 1943, and at least two (42-12685 and 42-12686) with the 54th FS in the Aleutians. Approximately half of them served in the training role in the U.S.

F-5A-2-LO

LAC Model 222-62-16, C/N 5375 and USAAF No. 41-2157. Only one was built (converted from an F-4-1), and it was delivered to the USAAF in July 1942.

F-5A-3-LO

LAC Model 222-68-16, C/Ns 4201-4220/USAAF Nos. 42-12767 to 42-12786. Twenty were built; they were delivered in October 1942. At least thirteen F-5A-3s served with the 7th PG in England, and at least one is known to have been assigned to the 17th PRS on Guadalcanal.

F-5A-10-LO

LAC Model 222-68-16 and C/Ns 7401 to 7420/USAAF Nos. 42-12967 to 42-12986, 7501 to 7560/42-13067 to 42-13126, and 7701 to 7760/42-13267 to 42-13326. A total of 144 were built; they were delivered from November 1942 to March 1943.

Aside from those retained in the U.S. for training duties, F-5A-10s served in every overseas combat theater.

F-5B-1-LO

LAC Model 422-81-21, C/Ns 1823 to 1912/USAAF Nos. 42-67312 to 42-67401 and 2703 to 2812/42-68192 to 42-68301. A total of 200 were built; they were delivered in December 1943 and January 1944.

F-5B-1 42-67332 and P-38J-5 42-67183 on a publicity photo flight over southern California. The F-5B-1 was in fact derived from the J-5. This PR Lightning joined the 7th Photo Group's 27th PRS in England in January 1944 and then in June was transferred to its 13th PRS. It was destroyed in a forced landing in France on February 9, 1945 while being flown by a pilot of the 326th Ferry Squadron. (*Lockheed photo*)

These were the last of the F-4 and F-5 photo recons to be built at the Burbank plant, for a total of 500. Henceforth P-38Js and Ls would be ferried to the Dallas Modification Center to be converted to later model F-5s. The majority of the early F-5B-1s were assigned to the 7th PG in England, but they also served in every other combat theater.

P-38J-1-LO

LAC Model 422-81-14, C/Ns 1001 to 1003/USAAF Nos. 42-12867 to 42-12869 and 1006 to 1012/42-13560 to 42-13566. Experimental prototypes for the new P-38J-5s. Ten were built; they were delivered from March to October 1943. All the P-38Js (and the F-5Bs and Cs) used the same engine as the Hs, but they had been re-engineered to produce 1,425 hp—1,600 at War Emergency Power (WEP).

No. 42-13562 later served with the 329th FG, the California OTU; 42-13564 was converted to an F-5C-1 photo recon and served with the 3rd PRMG in the MTO; and 42-13565 was assigned to the Cold Weather Test Detachment in Alaska, where, among other things, it was equipped with skis in place of wheels in one experiment.

P-38J-5-LO

LAC Model 422-81-14, C/Ns 1613 to 1822/USAAF Nos. 42-67102 to 42-67311. A total of 210 were built; they were delivered from August 1943 to April 1944.

The "J" models were quite different from the previous Hs in many ways. For example, the carburetor intercoolers were moved from the leading edges of the wings to between the oil radiators in the lower front of the engine nacelles, which now featured much larger chin scoops to accommodate more coolant air. They were replaced by 55-gallon fuel tanks, thereby increasing the aircraft's range considerably. The old three-quarter circle control wheel was redesigned with a pistol grip on either side, giving the pilot more control. There was also a new, flatter, windscreen that reduced distortion, plus improved defrosting and cockpit heating. The biggest change visually, starting with the P-38J-10, was the lack of paint—all Lightnings would henceforth be delivered in their natural aluminum finish.

Most of the J-5s were delivered to the MTO and to the ETO, although a handful went to the CBI and about four dozen to the SWP. Forty-six of them became the first P-38s to be converted to photo reconnaissance aircraft (F-5C-1s) at Lockheed's Modification Center at Love Field, near Dallas. The F-5C-1 conversions were 42-67105 to 67134, 42-67236 to 42-67239, 42-67241 to 42-67248, 42-67249, 42-67250, 42-67253, and 42-67254.

P-38J-10-LO

LAC Model 422-81-14, C/Ns 1913 to 2702/USAAF Nos. 42-67402 to 42-68191. A total of 790 were built; they were delivered from October to December 1943.

P-38J-10 42-68008 was photographed for publicity purposes over southern California. This was the Lightning that was later assigned to Lockheed test pilot Tony LeVier in England, which he named *Snafuperman* and with which he put on many flight demonstrations there. When LeVier returned to the U.S., 42-68008 was assigned to the Eighth AF's 479th FG, and specifically to the CO of its 434th FS, Lt. Col. James M. Herren, Jr., who named it *Touché*. Its squadron code was L2-A. When the 479th FG switched to P-51s in September 1944, it was transferred to BAD 3 at Langford Lodge, Northern Ireland, which declared it salvage shortly after VE Day. (*Lockheed photo*)

Aside from several small batches of J-10s that were shipped to the Pacific and the CBI, and a few that found their way to the Fifteenth AF in Italy, the vast majority were assigned to the Eighth and Ninth AFs in England. Forty-eight are known to have been modified as F-5C-1s, about half of which remained in the U.S. to be utilized for PR training. They were 42-67426, 42-67529 to 42-67569, and 42-67572 to 42-67577.

P-38J-15-LO

LAC Model 422-81-22, C/Ns 2813 to 3262/USAAF Nos. 42-10379 to 42-104428, 3263 to 4062/43-28248 to 43-29047, and 4063 to 4212/44-23059 to 44-23208. A total of 1,400 were built; they were delivered from December 1943 to May 1944.

The P-38J-15 was the first model that was completely equipped with the new leading edge wing tanks at the factory; this installation had been hit and miss with the J-5s and -10s, and they often had to be retrofitted by means of kits in the field. The J-15s were produced in three very different serial number blocks. As to the first one, most of its early aircraft, through 42-104040, went to the Fifth AF's 475th FG and 9th and 80th FSs, and then, through 42-104334, primarily to the ETO and MTO, with the rest also being shipped to the PTO and the CBI.

P-38J-15 44-23109 was destroyed in a landing accident in Hawaii on September 13, 1944 while assigned to the 21st FG. (*Michael Bates collection*)

P-38J-15 44-23139 at the Lockheed factory after being modified to Pathfinder configuration. (*Lockheed photo*)

Most of the second block of J-15s went to the ETO and MTO, with several smaller blocks being delivered to the PTO and CBI, while most of the last aircraft in this block, starting with 43-28888, were retained in the U.S. for training purposes. At least 168 were converted to F-5E-2s: 42-104081, 43-28285 to 43-28334, 43-28577 to 43-28625, 43-28872, 43-28909, 43-28933, 43-28938, 43-28963 to 43-28965, 43-28968, 43-28970, 43-28972 to 43-28974, 43-28977 to 43-28980, 43-28990, 43-28992, 43-28993, 43-289995 to 43-29002, 43-29004 to 43-29009, 43-29015, 43-29016, 43-29018 to 43-29037, and 43-29044.

As to the last block of J-15s, the first of them, through 44-23145, went mainly to the Pacific and the CBI and the rest mostly to the ETO and MTO.

P-38J-20-LO

LAC Model 422-81-22, C/Ns 4213 to 4562/USAAF Nos. 44-23209 to 44-23558. A total of 350 were built; they were delivered in May and June 1944.

Seventy-seven J-20s were converted to F-5E-2 photo recons: 44-23211 to 44-23216, 44-23218 to 44-23247, 44-23249 to 44-23281, and 44-23283 to 44-23290. Most of those in the 44-23402 to 44-23471 serial number range were assigned to base unit OTUs in the U.S., and those from 44-23479 to 44-234525 ended up in the ETO and the MTO.

P-38J-25-LO

LAC Model 422-81-22, C/Ns 4563 to 4772/USAAF Nos. 44-23559 to 44-23768. A total of 210 were built; they were delivered from June to November 1944.

P-38J-20 44-23425 was assigned to the 434th Base Unit, an operational training unit at Santa Rosa AAB in northern California. (*Author's collection*)

The J-25 was the first production P-38 to be fitted with Lockheed's new electrically operated dive flaps and hydraulic aileron boost. The pilot's control input was now much lighter and the Lightning's roll rate and maneuverability noticeably improved. The aileron boost utilized the aircraft's hydraulic system pressure, which kicked in when the pilot applied only about a tenth of the actual force required to the control yoke.

Nearly all the J-25 fighters were assigned to the three P-38 groups of the Ninth AF in Europe during the summer of 1944, although two of them went briefly to the Eighth AF's 479th FG before it had completely re-equipped with P-51s. One of them, 44-23559, the first built, was converted to a Pathfinder Lightning, with the ground-scanning H2X radar and its operator. Eighty-nine J-25s were converted at the Dallas Modification Center to F-5E-3 photo recons: 44-23602 to 44-23611 and 44-23687 to 44-23768. Most of them were shipped to the ETO and MTO; only a handful ended up in the PTO and the CBI. Since they had to be modified, they arrived in the combat theaters much later than the J-25s did.

P-38K-1-LO

LAC Model 422-87-23, C/N 1004 and USAAF No. 42-13558. An experimental high-altitude P-38 with broad-bladed Hamilton Standard propellers and special V-1710-F-15 (-75/-77) high-output engines, it was delivered in September 1943. Although the "K" did not demonstrate an appreciable increase in performance over the P-38J, some of its improvements were incorporated into the P-38L.

P-38L-1-LO

LAC Model 422-87-23, C/Ns 4773-6062/USAAF Nos. 44-23769 to 44-25058. A total of 1,290 were built; they were delivered from June to November 1944.

The Ls featured an increased fuel capacity and the new V-1710-F-30 (-111/-113) engines that were still rated at 1,425 hp but had more efficient turbo-superchargers, which boosted their performance. An innovation that appeared on some of them was AN/APS-13 tail warning radar, which covered a cone of 30–60 degrees to the rear and would signal the pilot by means of a bell and a light should another aircraft approach his from that direction. Its antenna was positioned on the bottom of the right vertical tail. The P-38L-1s and 5s and their modified F-5 versions served in every USAAF combat theater.

At least fourteen P-38L-1s were converted to Pathfinders, which saw service in the ETO and MTO. They were 44-23875 to 44-23880, 44-23883, 44-24634, 44-24637, 44-25011, 44-25018, 44-25033, 44-25040, and 44-25054.

There were also large numbers of F-5s modified from P-38Ls, first a few more F-5E-3s, then F-5E-4s (the first of which was former P-38L-1 44-24082); F-5F-3s (the first former P-38L-1 44-24732); and, finally, F-5G-6s (the first former P-38L-5 44-25173). The E-3s and 4s were very similar to the E-2s, while the F-3s featured a distinctive raised chin camera portal and the G-6 a redesigned, bulbous, nose section. They are extremely hard to track, but this writer/researcher has determined that there were at least 705 F-5E-3s, 371 F-5E-4s,

P-38L-1 44-24524, while serving with the 434th BU at Santa Rosa. On October 29, 1945, this Lightning was transferred to the Kingman, Arizona, RFC depot, where it was evidently scrapped. (*Author's collection*)

F-5G-6s of the 41st PRS on Guam in 1945, displaying their large and unique noses, including that of *LUSCIOUS! LUCILLE*, 44-26421. Unfortunately, *LUCILLE* was destroyed by the typhoon that hit the island on June 20. (*Author's collection*)

Lockheed employees pose proudly under their plant's famous net camouflage with one of its "products," P-38L-1 44-23855, during the summer of 1944. After leaving the factory, this Lightning was assigned to the 433rd Base Unit, an operational P-38 training squadron based at Chico AAF in northern California. It was destroyed in a landing accident there a few months later, on December 8. (*Michael Bates collection*)

111 F-5F-3s and 357 F-5G-6s, in addition to the earlier 123 F-5C-1 and 166 F-5E-2 modifications. When you add in the 500 F-4s and F-5s that were built at the Lockheed plant, the total of PR Lightnings comes to at least 2,133, or 21 percent of all the Lightnings that were built, although that number is almost certainly incomplete and understated due to a lack of sufficient data.

It was hard to tell a P-38J from a P-38L, they were so similar in appearance. The most visible difference concerned the landing/taxiing light on each. The J's was a retractable unit under the left wing, while that on the "L" was fixed in the leading edge of that wing.

P-38L-5-LO

LAC Model 422-87-23, C/Ns 6063 to 8262/USAAF Nos. 44-25059 to 44-27258 and 8263 to 8582/44-53008 to 44-53327. A total of 2,520 were built; they were delivered from October 1944 to August 1945.

Booster pumps were added to the fuel tanks of the P-38L-5s; they were housed in small fairings beneath the wings. Also, after considerable experimentation with various rocket launching installations, the one that came to be called the "Christmas tree" launcher was used fairly extensively late in the war on the "L" models. These consisted of vertical racks each carrying five rockets that did look a bit like the eponymous tree; they utilized two mounting points under each wing and had their own firing circuitry.

Seventy-five L-5s were converted to P-38M-6 night fighters, which had a separate cockpit for the radar operator, behind the pilot's, and carried an AN/APS-6 radar unit in a pod under its nose. Their serial numbers were 44-26831, 44-26863, 44-26865, 44-26892, 44-26951, 44-26997, 44-26999, 44-27000, 44-27108, 44-27233, 44-27234, 44-27236 to 44-27238, 44-27245, 44-27249 to 44-27252, 44-27254, 44-27256 to 44-27258, 44-53011, 44-53017,

P-38M-6 night fighter serial number 44-27234 being test flown over southern California. (*Lockheed photo*)

44-53019, 44-53020, 44-53022, 44-53023, 44-53025, 44-53029 to 44-53032, 44-53034, 44-53035, 44-53042, 44-53050, 44-53052, 44-53056, 44-53062, 44-53063, 44-53066 to 44-53069, 44-53073, 44-53074, 44-53076, 44-53077, 44-53079, 44-53080, 44-53082 to 44-53090, 44-53092 to 44-53098, 44-53100, 44-53101, 44-53106, 44-53107, 44-53109, 44-53110, and 44-53112. Four P-38Ms arrived in the Philippines in October 1945, but the rest remained in the U.S., of which a number were sold as surplus after the war and flown again. When P-38L-5s were sent to the Dallas Modification Center, they were converted to either F-5G-6s or P-38Ms, usually in a rather random fashion—evidently pretty much the same way they were sent there.

P-38L-5-VN

Assigned USAAF serial numbers 43-50226 to 43-50338, 113 P-38L-5-VNs were produced at the Consolidated Vultee plant in Nashville, Tennessee, from January to August 1945 and were delivered to the USAAF from May to August. Fifty-seven of them were ferried to the Sixth AF in Panama, via Brownsville, Texas, and Mexico. Consolidated Vultee had been a Lockheed subcontractor for some time prior to 1945, constructing P-38 subassemblies.

XP-49

The XP-49 was a very unique Lightning that was powered by two Continental XIV-1430 liquid-cooled twelve-cylinder engines. Issued the USAAF serial number 40-3055, it was delivered to the USAAF in November 1943, to be used as a test bed for a proposed pressurized cockpit for the P-38, which, in fact, no production model ever received.

The XP-49, which had flown for the first time on November 11, 1942, was photographed at Wright Field, Ohio, on October 13, 1945. Its flying career long over by then, it was being utilized, ignominiously, for drop tests. *(Michael Bates collection)*

XP-58

The XP-58, known as the "Chain Lightning," was initially proposed as a two-seat, long-range bomber escort version of the P-38, but the end result did not look much like one. The original USAAC specifications, dated April 12, 1940, called for an aircraft only slightly larger than the P-38 (of which only one had then been built), and Lockheed was asked to produce an experimental prototype. Initially it was to be armed with two 20-mm cannon and four .50-cal. machine guns, and the second crewman would operate an additional power gun turret for rear defense, but the proposed armament changed numerous times during its development, as did the USAAF's specs in general.

There was a plethora of problems with the design and construction of the XP-58, and after the prototype was finally tested in June 1944, the project was abandoned. Its performance was found to include a top speed of 436 mph, a (slow) rate of climb of twelve minutes to 25,000 feet, a ceiling of 38,400 feet and a maximum range of 2,650 miles. One of the design's problems had been the lack of a suitable engine; no less than six were considered before the Allison V-3420 -11/-13 was chosen, in February 1943. It finally became obvious that the aircraft was too large and heavy (34,000 lb.) to be a conventional air superiority fighter, so it was thought that it might be utilized instead as a bomber destroyer—and then as a low-altitude anti-tank aircraft. P-38 technical historian Bert Kinzey later described the XP-58 project as "one of the most problem plagued and incompetently run aircraft development programs in U.S. military history."

There were other strange, experimental models of the P-38. They included F-5A 42-123975, which was converted to the XF-5D, which carried a single vertical camera inside a Plexiglas nose that also accommodated a second crewman. It was armed with two

.50-cal. machine guns. P-38-LO 40-744 underwent a weird modification that consisted of a second cockpit being added onto its left boom, next to the original one, in order to study the effects of aerial maneuvers on a subject sitting away from the aircraft's center of gravity. P-38E 41-1986 received an upswept tail as part of its unrealised conversion to a floatplane, while 41-2048, which was nicknamed "Swordfish" or "Nosey" because of its elongated nose, became a highly modified two-seater used for high-speed dive tests.

The Castrated Lightnings

Then there were the aborted British Lightnings. Ironically, it was the Brits who gave the P-38 its famous name, even though, as it turned out, it was one the few World War II U.S. military aircraft it did not actually purchase, even through the very favorable Lend-Lease program. While shopping for American aircraft prior to the U.S.'s entry into the war, the British took over a French order for 667 Lockheed Model 322-Fs in June of 1940. (The "F" stood for France.) Unfortunately, they were ordered without turbo-superchargers or counter-rotating propellers, which negated much of the P-38's impressive performance. Called Lightning Is, they were LAC Model 322-61-03. The order was subsequently reduced to 143, and the remaining 524 (Lightning IIs) were to be regular USAAF type P-38s. However, all the orders were eventually cancelled unilaterally by the British government, and what were to have been Lightning IIs became USAAF P-38Fs and Gs instead.

Three Lightning IIs were actually delivered to the RAF in March 1942 for evaluation and were, understandably, found wanting. It was both their poor performance and their cost that caused the British to cancel the contract. Unfortunately, Lockheed had already begun producing their Lightnings on its assembly line, in RAF markings and camouflage colors. To avoid financial and legal difficulties with Lockheed and its new war ally, the USAAF took over the contract for what Lockheed employees had started referring to as "castrated" Lightnings because of their subpar performance. Since they were worthless as combat aircraft, the Air Forces decided to utilize them primarily as operational trainers, the majority ending up at Williams Field in Arizona, transitioning its advanced aviation cadets to the P-38. Now the recipient of the RP (restricted) designation, they were reportedly easier for the cadets to fly than standard P-38s.

These castrated Lightning Is, which retained their RAF serial numbers but in most cases were repainted in the USAAF's olive drab and gray, were built as three different customer models, the first two powered by the Allison V-1710C-15 (-33) engine that was used in the Curtiss P-40. They were delivered to the USAAF from December 1941 to July 1942. The first was the 322-B, LAC Model 322-61-04, of which only three were built, with the LAC C/Ns 3001-3003 and the RAF serials AE978 to AE980. The second model was the P-322-I, also 322-61-04s, with LAC C/Ns 3004 to 3022 and RAF serials AE981 to AE999—of which nineteen were built. Their armament was to have been two .50-cal. and two .30-cal. machine guns. Most of those used as trainers by the USAAF did not carry guns, however, unless they were specifically assigned to gunnery training. The P-322 Is were the first P-38s to come off the production line with the new fillets installed where the wing roots joined the gondola that were designed to smooth the airflow over the tail and prevent the buffeting, or flutter, that had been a problem in the earlier P-38s.

Lightning Mk I AE979 in flight over southern California in full RAF colors. It later served with the 535th TEAFTS at Williams Field, until it was scrapped in January 1945. (*Lockheed photo*)

P-322 II AF171 (Lockheed construction number 3092) on the compass rose at the Lockheed factory. This aircraft later served with the 535th Twin Engine Advanced Flying Training Squadron at Williams Field, Arizona—until a student pilot bailed out of it on December 15, 1943. (*Lockheed photo*)

P-322 II AF105 was one of the three sent to England in March 1942 for evaluation by the RAF. It was returned to the USAAF there in July 1943 and declared salvage by BAD 1 at Burtonwood in October 1944. (*Lockheed photo*)

The P-322-II—LAC Model 322-62-18, LAC C/Ns 3023 to 3143 and RAF codes AF100 to AF220—was by far the most numerous of the British Lightnings that were actually built, with 121 examples. These included the three that were sent to England for evaluation, AF105, AF106, and AF108, which were returned to the USAAF in England. Most of them were later retrofitted with V-1710F-2 -27/-29 engines, which meant the nacelles had to be modified slightly to accommodate them, and in those cases they were also retrofitted with counter-rotating props. None of them ever received turbo-superchargers, however. Also, the nose landing gear of the P-322-II—and all future P-38s—was redesigned by moving the drag strut from in front of the main strut to behind it, thus creating room for more ammunition in the nose compartment.

The Total

Warren Bodie, author of an excellent, technically oriented, book on the P-38 (see this book's Further Reading list), after researching actual Lockheed records found that the company had delivered 9,925 Lightnings. Adding to that the 113 delivered by Consolidated Vultee, the total was 10,038. The delivery figures for the USAAF's other primary World War II fighters were: the P-51 15,686; the P-47 15,683; the P-40 13,733; and the P-39 9,558.

P-38 Conversions

Conversions were usually made after the aircraft had been delivered to the Air Forces, sometimes officially and sometimes not, and, with a few exceptions, were not made at the Lockheed factory or at its Modification Center.

By early 1942, USAAF P-38 units training in the U.S. were unofficially converting a few of their aircraft into two-seat "piggy-backs," which practice was continued for some time, both in the States and overseas once those units began moving to combat theaters. The process was that the radio would be removed or relocated and a crude bench installed in the rear cockpit where the radio had been, right behind the pilot. Looking over his shoulder, this allowed the future Lightning pilot to observe his instructor pilot operating the aircraft, with pertinent commentary, and to get a "feel" for it.

The piggy-backs were also used to give ground crewmen and other "ground pounders" a ride in a P-38—including VIPs such as well-known USO entertainers. (Bob Hope received one in North Africa in 1943 while performing for 14th FG personnel and another two years later while visiting the 474th FG in Germany.) Lockheed actually had its own piggy-back, P-38F-1 41-7485, that one of its test pilots, James J. "Jimmy" Matern, utilized for public relations flights, which included giving reporters rides in it.

In this case what began as unofficial conversions later became official modifications. By late 1944, some USAAF fighters being used for training purposes in the U.S. were being modified into two-seaters and given the new "T" (for trainer) designation. The earliest model of such a modified Lightning to which this writer has found a reference was in an accident report for TP-38G-10 42-13534, which experienced a fire on February 7, 1945 while assigned to the 5th Ferrying Squadron at Love Field near Dallas, Texas, the home of Lockheed's Modification Center. (This was also the only TP-38 the author found that was not a converted "J" or "L.") OTUs known to have utilized TP-38s included the 434th BU at Santa Rosa, California; the 379th CCTS at Coffeyville, Kansas; and the 3028th BU at Luke Field, Arizona. When the 434th BU was inactivated at the end of November 1945 it had five TP-38Ls in its inventory. No doubt other training units were also assigned a few of them.

The most famous P-38 conversion was the Droop Snoot, which carried in its modified Plexiglas nose a Norden bombsight and a bombardier, for level bombing. It also included two hatches for the bombardier, one above and one (ventral) below him, for entry and for escape if needed. They were produced at the Langford Lodge air depot in Northern Ireland in 1944, and this writer has identified thirty-five of them by their serial numbers: P-38H-5 42-67086, P-38J-10s 42-67409, 42-67450, 42-67704, 42-67716 and 42-68184; P-38J-15s 42-104075, 42-104118, 43-28352, 43-28417, 43-28479, 43-28483, 43-28490, 43-28793, 44-23151, 44-23156, 44-23162, 44-26163, 44-23166, 44-23167, 44-23170, 44-23176 and 44-23179; P-38J-20s 44-23461, 44-23489, 44-23501, 44-23505, 44-23507, 44-23508, 44-23513, 44-23514, 44-23515 and 44-23517, P-38J-25 44-23618, and P-38L-1 44-24360.

By the end of the war in Europe, every P-38 squadron of the Eighth, Ninth, and Fifteenth AFs had operated at least one Droop Snoot. In India, ten P-38s were modified into slightly different Droop Snoots, which were delivered to the Tenth AF's 459th FS. At least one, P-38L-5-VN 43-50266, which was evidently modified in the U.S., served with the Sixth AF in Panama. There was even a conversion from the basic Eighth AF Droop Snoot that resulted in the four ELINT Lightnings, which carried radar monitoring devices and their operators in place of the bombsight and bombardier.

One P-38 conversion that never happened, but almost did, and about which many Lightning fans have speculated over the years, was the replacement of the problematic (at least at high altitude in Europe's winter skies) Allison engine with the Rolls-Royce/Packard

Above left: Lockheed test pilot Jimmie Mattern is about to give a ride in the company's "piggy-back," P-38F-1 41-7485, to Maj. Clarence A. Shoop, who was then assigned to the Lockheed plant to test fly and accept Lightnings for the USAAF as they came off the assembly lines. Shortly thereafter, in early 1944, Shoop was transferred to England, where he was given command of the 7th PRG. (*Michael Bates collection*)

Above right: The Droop Snoot *Lady Lou,* P-38J-15 43-28352, served initially with the 7th PRG in England but was transferred to Italy and the Fifteenth AF in December 1944. It subsequently served with the 82nd FG. (*USAF photo*)

Merlin that served the P-51 so well on its high-altitude, long-range escort missions. In fact, there were discussions on this subject between VIII FC and Operational Engineering officers and Rolls-Royce. As a result, P-38J-10 42-67488 was delivered to an RAF airdrome in May 1944 to test a pair of Merlins on its airframe, it having been estimated that they would increase its top speed by 38 mph and its climb rate by 1,300 feet per minute. However, this never took place and the P-38 was returned to the Eighth AF in July, the reasons seeming to have been both political and business-related.

APPENDIX II

Lightning Combat Squadrons

Listed below are all the USAAF squadrons that flew Lightnings in action against the enemy in World War II.

5th Photographic Reconnaissance Squadron, 3rd PRG, Twelfth AF. Based in England briefly and then moved to North Africa in November 1942. One of its flights was attached to the 5th PRG from March to May 1944. Operated from numerous airfields in Algeria, Tunisia, Italy, and Corsica.

6th Night Fighter Squadron, Fifth and Thirteenth AFs. During 1943, its Detachments "A" and "B" flew P-70s and P-38s from New Guinea and Guadalcanal, respectively, until the squadron was disbanded that November.

7th Fighter Squadron, 49th FG, Fifth AF. Converted from P-40s to P-38s at Biak Island, New Guinea, in September 1944. Starting in October, it operated from the Philippines Islands: Tacloban on Leyte, San Jose on Mindoro, and Lingayen on Luzon.

8th Fighter Squadron. See 7th Fighter Squadron.

8th Photographic Reconnaissance Squadron, 6th PRG, Fifth AF. Operated from Australia starting in April 1942 and moved to Port Moresby, New Guinea, in September. Assigned to the 6th PRG there in November; moved to Nadzab in March 1944 and to Biak Island in August. Transferred to Dulag on Leyte in the Philippines in November 1944, then to Clark Field on Luzon in May 1945 and to Okinawa in July 1945.

9th Fighter Squadron, 49th FG, Fifth AF. Converted from P-40s to P-38s at Dobodura, New Guinea, in January 1943. Converted to P-47s there in November 1943, then re-equipped with P-38s in April 1944, flying them from Gusap, Hollandia and Biak Island in New Guinea and from Leyte, Mindoro and Luzon in the Philippines Islands.

9th Photographic Reconnaissance Squadron, 8th PRG, Tenth AF. Arrived in India in July 1942. Subsequently operated from numerous bases there and in China and Burma. Assigned to the 8th PRG in April 1944.

12th Fighter Squadron, 18th FG, Thirteenth AF. Flew a few P-38s in addition to P-39s from Guadalcanal in early and mid-1943, then flew P-39s exclusively. Re-equipped with P-38s in February 1944 and operated from Treasury Island in the Solomons until August, when it moved to Sansapor, New Guinea. Based on Morotai Island in the Dutch East Indies from November 1944 to January 1945 and then at various airfields on Luzon, Mindoro, Palawan, Leyte, and Mindanao in the Philippine Islands.

12th Photographic Reconnaissance Squadron, 3rd PRG, Twelfth AF. Arrived at Casablanca, French Morocco, in November 1942, and it and its detachments subsequently flew from numerous airfields in Algeria, Tunisia, Malta, Sicily, Corsica, and Italy.

13th Photographic Reconnaissance Squadron, 7th PRG, Eighth AF. Based at Mount Farm, England, from February 1943 to April 1945, when it moved to nearby Chalgrove.

14th Photographic Reconnaissance Squadron, 7th PRG, Eighth AF. Arrived at Mount Farm, England, in May 1943, from which it operated until transferring to nearby Chalgrove in April 1945. As with the other 7th PRG squadrons, it flew a mixture of F-5s and Spitfire PRs from November 1943 to January 1944, when it began flying Spitfires exclusively. It returned its Spitfires to the RAF in April 1945 and re-equipped with Lightnings.

15th Photographic Reconnaissance Squadron, 3rd and 5th PRGs, Twelfth and Fifteenth AFs. Its "A" Flight served in North Africa with B-17s until November 1943, at which time its "B" and "C" Flights joined it in Italy and the whole squadron then flew F-5s. Based at Bari, Italy, from December 1943 and transferred from the 3rd to the 5th PRG in January 1944. The 5th PRG and its squadrons transferred to the Fifteenth AF in October 1944.

17th Photographic Reconnaissance Squadron, 4th PRG, Thirteenth AF. Arrived at New Caledonia in December 1942 and commenced operations from Guadalcanal in February 1943. Established a detachment at Munda, on New Georgia Island, in October and one on Bougainville Island in December. Moved to Noemfoor Island, New Guinea, in October 1944 and subsequently flew from Sansapor, New Guinea; Morotai Island in the Dutch East Indies; Dulag on Leyte Island; Puerto Princesa, Palawan; and Clark Field, Luzon.

19th Fighter Squadron, 318th FG, Seventh AF. Although a P-47 unit, it flew P-38s from Saipan from November 1944 to February 1945.

21st Photographic Reconnaissance Squadron, Fourteenth AF. Arrived in India in June 1943 and its flights and detachments subsequently operated from numerous airfields in China.

22nd Photographic Reconnaissance Squadron, 7th PRG, Eighth AF. Arrived at Mount Farm, England, in June 1943. A detachment operated from Attlebridge, England, in February and March 1944. Moved to Chalgrove, England, in March 1945.

23rd Photographic Reconnaissance Squadron, 5th and 3rd PRGs, Twelfth AF. Arrived at La Marsa, Tunisia, in September 1943 and assigned to the 5th PRG. Served alternately with the 5th and 3rd Groups until November 1944, when it was permanently assigned to the latter. It and its detachments operated from numerous bases in Tunisia, Sardinia, Corsica, France and Italy. The Free French PR unit II/GR 33 was attached to it during much of 1943 and 1944.

25th Photographic Reconnaissance Squadron, 6th PRG, Fifth AF. Arrived in Australia in November 1943 and subsequently operated from numerous airfields in New Guinea and the Philippine Islands and on Okinawa.

26th Photographic Reconnaissance Squadron. See 25th Photographic Reconnaissance Squadron.

27th Fighter Squadron, 1st FG, Twelfth and Fifteenth AFs. Based in Iceland in July and August 1942, then at Atcham, High Ercall and Colerne, England. Moved to Algeria in November 1942 and operated from numerous bases there and in Tunisia, Sicily, Libya, and Sardinia. Assigned to the new Fifteenth AF in November 1943, then moved to Italy

(Gioia del Colle in December and Salsola in January). Also operated from Corsica and from Vincenzo, Italy, until moving to Lesina, Italy, in March 1945.

27th Photographic Reconnaissance Squadron, 7th PRG, Eighth AF. Based at Mount Farm, England, as of November 1943. Moved to Denain, France, in November 1944 and then to Chalgrove, England, in April 1945.

28th Photographic Reconnaissance Squadron, Seventh AF. Based in Hawaii from January 1944 but detachments operated from the islands of Kwajalein, Saipan, Peleliu and Okinawa until May 1945, when the rest of the squadron moved to Okinawa.

30th Photographic Reconnaissance Squadron, 10th PRG and 67th TRG, Ninth AF. Arrived at Chalgrove, England, in February 1944; joined the 10th PRG and moved to Middle Wallop in May. Transferred to the 67th TRG in June and moved to France in July. It subsequently operated from two airfields in France, two in Belgium and three in Germany.

31st Photographic Reconnaissance Squadron, 10th PRG, Ninth AF. Joined the 10th PRG at Chalgrove, England, in March 1944. Moved to Rennes, France, in August and subsequently operated from three more airfields in that country and three in Germany.

32nd Photographic Reconnaissance Squadron, 5th PRG, Twelfth and Fifteenth AFs. Based at San Severo, Italy, from April 1944 and moved to Bari in August. It and the 5th PRG were transferred from the Twelfth to the Fifteenth AF in October 1944.

33rd Photographic Reconnaissance Squadron, 10th PRG, 67th TRG and 363rd TRG, Ninth AF. Joined the 10th PRG at Chalgrove, England, in April 1944. Transferred to the 67th TRG in June and went with it to France in August. Reassigned to the 363rd TRG in November. Operated from two airfields in France, two in Belgium, one in Holland and two in Germany.

34th Photographic Reconnaissance Squadron, 10th PRG, Provisional Reconnaissance Group and 69th TRG, Ninth AF. Joined the 10th PRG at Chalgrove, England, in March 1944. Moved to France in August, first to Rennes and then to Chateaudun later that month, to St. Dizier in September, to Dijon in October (when it also transferred to the Provisional Reconnaissance Group), to Azelot in November and to Hagenau in April 1945, where and when it transferred to the 69th TRG.

35th Fighter Squadron, 8th FG, Fifth AF. Converted to P-38s from P-40s in New Guinea in February 1944. Subsequently operated from numerous airfields in New Guinea, the Dutch East Indies, the Philippines Islands and Okinawa.

35th Photographic Reconnaissance Squadron, Fourteenth AF. Based at numerous airfields in China from June 1944.

36th Fighter Squadron, 8th FG, Fifth AF. Converted to P-38s from P-47s in New Guinea in February 1944. Subsequently operated from numerous airfields in New Guinea, the Dutch East Indies, the Philippine Islands and Okinawa.

36th Photographic Reconnaissance Squadron, 6th PRG, Fifth AF. Arrived at Hollandia, New Guinea, in December 1944 and subsequently based on Biak Island, Clark Field on Luzon in the Philippines and, as of early August 1945, Okinawa.

37th Fighter Squadron, 14th FG, Twelfth and Fifteenth AFs. Joined the 14th FG in French Morocco in February 1943 and subsequently operated from Telergma, Algeria, and Bathan and Ste. Marie-du-Zit, Tunisia. Transferred to the new Fifteenth AF in November 1943 and moved to Triolo, Italy, in December. Operated from Corsica briefly in August 1944.

37th Photographic Reconnaissance Squadron, 5th PRG, Fifteenth AF. Arrived at Naples, Italy, in November, 1944, and operated from San Severo from December.

38th Fighter Squadron, 55th FG, Eighth AF. Arrived at Nuthampstead, England, in September 1943; moved to Wormingford, England, in April 1944. Converted to P-51s in July 1944.

38th Photographic Reconnaissance Squadron, 4th PRG, Thirteenth AF. Arrived at Hollandia, New Guinea, in December 1944 and then moved to its operational base for the rest of the war, Morotai Island in the Dutch East Indies.

39th Fighter Squadron, 35th FG, Fifth AF. Converted from P-39s to P-38s in Australia in August 1942. Served in New Guinea from October 1942 until November 1943, when it converted to P-47s.

39th Photographic Reconnaissance Squadron, 10th PRG and the Provisional Reconnaissance Group, Ninth AF. Arrived at Valenciennes, France, in January 1945. Assigned first to the 10th PRG and then, at the end of March, attached to the 9th Tactical Reconnaissance Group (Provisional). Operated from two more airfields in France, two in Belgium, one in Holland, and one in Germany.

40th Photographic Reconnaissance Squadron, 8th PRG, Tenth AF. Arrived at Guskhara, India, in July 1944 and subsequently operated from five other airfields in India and Burma.

44th Fighter Squadron, 18th FG, Thirteenth AF. Converted from P-40s to P-38s at Guadalcanal in November 1943 and then operated from Munda, on New Georgia Island, and from Stirling Island. Moved to Sansapor, New Guinea, in August 1944 and operated from Morotai Island in the Dutch East Indies from November 1944 to January 1945. It then moved to the Philippine Islands and subsequently flew from Lingayen on Luzon, San Jose on Mindoro, Westbrook Field on Palawan, and Zamboanga on Mindanao.

48th Fighter Squadron, 14th FG, Twelfth and Fifteenth AFs. Based at Atcham, England, from August 1942. Moved to North Africa in November and based at Tafaroui, Maison Blanche, Youks-les-Bains and Berteaux, Algeria, before being withdrawn from combat to reorganize at the end of January 1943. Resumed combat at Telergma, Algeria, in May 1943 and was subsequently based at El Bathan and Ste.-Marie-du-Zit, Tunisia. Operated from Sicily in September 1943. Assigned to the new Fifteenth AF in November 1943 and moved to Triolo, Italy, in December.

49th Fighter Squadron, 14th FG, Twelfth and Fifteenth AFs. Based at Atcham, England, from August 1942. Moved to North Africa in November and based at Tafaroui, Maison Blanche, Youks-les-Bains and Berteaux, Algeria, before being withdrawn from combat to reorganize at the end of January 1943. Resumed combat at Telergma, Algeria, in May 1943 and was subsequently based at El Bathan and Ste.-Marie-du Zit, Tunisia. Assigned to the new Fifteenth AF in November 1943 and moved to Triolo, Italy, in December. Operated from Corsica briefly in August 1944.

50th Fighter Squadron, 14th FG and 342nd CG. Separated from the 14th FG in Iceland in August 1942 and reassigned to the 342nd CG in November. Moved to England in 1944 after relinquishing its P-38s.

54th Fighter Squadron, 343rd FG, Eleventh AF. Served in Alaska (the Aleutian Islands) from June 1942. Assigned to the new 343rd FG in September 1942.

55th Fighter Squadron, 20th FG, Eighth AF. Based at King's Cliffe, England, from August 1943. Converted to P-51s in July 1944.

58th Fighter Squadron, 33rd FG, Tenth AF. Converted from P-47s to P-38s at Dudhkundi, India, in November 1944.

59th Fighter Squadron, 33rd FG, Tenth AF. Converted from P-47s to P-38s at Dudhkundi, India, in January 1945.

60th Fighter Squadron, 33rd FG, Tenth AF. Converted from P-47s to P-38s at Dudhkundi, India, in February 1945.

67th Fighter Squadron, 347th FG, Thirteenth AF. Converted from P-39s to P-38s in the Solomon Islands in May 1944. Moved to Middleburg Island, New Guinea, in August 1944 and subsequently operated from San Jose on Mindoro Island in the Philippines, Morotai Island in the Dutch East Indies and Puerto Princesa on Palawan Island in the Philippines.

68th Fighter Squadron, 347th FG, Thirteenth AF. Converted from P-39s to P-38s in the Solomon Islands in May 1944. Moved to Middleburg Island, New Guinea, in August 1944, operating from there and subsequently from San Jose on Mindoro Island and Puerto Princesa on Palawan.

70th Fighter Squadron, 347th FG and 18th FG, Thirteenth AF. Assigned to the 347th FG in October 1942 and then the 18th FG in March 1943. Operated from Guadalcanal from December 1942 to October 1943, when it moved to New Georgia Island. Flew both P-38s and P-39s in early and mid-1943, then reverted to P-39s only. Switched to P-38s on New Georgia in May 1944. Transferred to Sansapor, New Guinea, in August 1944 and subsequently also operated from Morotai Island in the Dutch East Indies. Moved to the Philippines in January 1945, where it was based on the islands of Luzon, Mindoro and Mindanao.

71st Fighter Squadron, 1st FG, Twelfth and Fifteenth AFs. Based at Goxhill and Ibsley, England, from June to November 1942, then transferred to Algeria. Operated from numerous airfields there and in Tunisia, Libya, Sardinia and Sicily. Transferred to the new Fifteenth AF in November 1943, then moved to Italy (Gioia del Colle in December and Salsola in January 1944). Also operated temporarily from Corsica and from Vincenzo, Italy, until moving to Lesina, Italy, in March 1945.

73rd Fighter Squadron. See 19th Fighter Squadron.

77th Fighter Squadron. See 55th Fighter Squadron.

79th Fighter Squadron. See 55th Fighter Squadron.

80th Fighter Squadron, 8th FG, Fifth AF. Converted to P-38s from P-39s in Australia in January 1943. From March 1943 flew them from various bases in New Guinea, the Dutch East Indies, the Philippine Islands, and on Okinawa.

91st Fighter Squadron, 81st FG, Twelfth AF. Although then a P-39 unit, it operated two P-38s in the spring and summer of 1943 while part of the Northwest African Coastal Air Force, protecting Allied ships and ports in the MTO.

92nd Fighter Squadron. See 91st Fighter Squadron.

93rd Fighter Squadron. See 91st Fighter Squadron.

94th Fighter Squadron, 1st FG, Twelfth and Fifteenth AFs. Based at Kirton in Lindsey and Ibsley, England, from June to October 1942. Moved to Algeria in November and operated from numerous airfields there and in Tunisia, Libya and Sardinia. Transferred to the new Fifteenth AF in November 1943 and then moved to Italy (Gioia del Colle in December and Salsola in January). Also operated from Corsica and from Vincenzo, Italy, until moving to Lesina, Italy, in March 1945.

95th Fighter Squadron, 82nd FG, Twelfth and Fifteenth AFs. Based in Northern Ireland from October to December 1942, when it moved to Algeria, subsequently operating from five airfields there and in Tunisia. Moved briefly to San Pancrazio, Italy, in October 1943 and then to Lecce, Italy, and assigned to the new Fifteenth AF in November. Moved to Vincenzo, Italy, in January 1944.

96th Fighter Squadron. See 95th Fighter Squadron.

97th Fighter Squadron. See 95th Fighter Squadron.

111th Reconnaissance Squadron, 68th Observation/Reconnaissance Group, Twelfth AF. Operated a variety of aircraft in North Africa in 1943, including a handful of P-38s and F-4s.

122nd Observation/Liaison Squadron, 68th Observation/Reconnaissance Group, Twelfth AF. Known to have operated several P-38s, along with other aircraft types, in North Africa in 1943.

154th Reconnaissance Squadron, 68th Observation/Reconnaissance Group, Twelfth and Fifteenth AFs. Flew P-38s among other aircraft types in North Africa in 1943 with the 68th Group. Became a weather reconnaissance squadron attached to Fifteenth AF Headquarters at Bari, Italy, in February 1944 and was officially redesignated as such in May.

333rd Fighter Squadron. See 19th Fighter Squadron.

338th Fighter Squadron. See 38th Fighter Squadron.

339th Fighter Squadron, 347th FG, Thirteenth AF. Served on Guadalcanal from October 1942, first with P-39s and then, starting in November, with P-38s. Based there and on Stirling Island (from January 1944) in the Solomons until moving to Sansapor, New Guinea, in August 1944, and then to nearby Middleburg Island in September. From February 1945 it was based on Morotai in the Dutch East Indies and on Mindoro and Palawan in the Philippine Islands.

343rd Fighter Squadron. See 38th Fighter Squadron.

345th Fighter Squadron. See 91st Fighter Squadron.

346th Fighter Squadron. See 91st Fighter Squadron.

347th Fighter Squadron. See 91st Fighter Squadron.

383rd Fighter Squadron, 364th FG, Eighth AF. Based at Honington, England, from February 1944. Converted to P-51s in July 1944.

384th Fighter Squadron. See 383rd Fighter Squadron.

385th Fighter Squadron. See 383rd Fighter Squadron.

392nd Fighter Squadron, 367th FG, Ninth AF. Received P-38s at Stoney Cross, England, in April 1944. Based at six airfields in France from July 1944 and converted to P-47s at St. Dizier in February 1945.

393rd Fighter Squadron. See 392nd Fighter Squadron.

394th Fighter Squadron. See 392nd Fighter Squadron.

401st Fighter Squadron, 370th FG, Ninth AF. Received P-38s at Andover, England, in February 1944. Based at four airfields in France and two in Belgium before converting to P-51s in March 1945.

402nd Fighter Squadron. See 401st Fighter Squadron.

418th Night Fighter Squadron, Fifth AF. From November 1943 flew P-38s, P-70s and P-61s from various airfields in New Guinea, the Dutch East Indies, the Philippines, and on Okinawa.

419th Night Fighter Squadron, Thirteenth AF. Flew P-38s and P-70s from Guadalcanal and Bougainville Island in the Solomons from November 1943 to mid-1944.

428th Fighter Squadron, 474th FG, Ninth AF. Based at Warmwell, England, from March 1944. Moved to Neuilly, France, in August and then based at two other airfields in that country, one in Belgium and two in Germany.

429th Fighter Squadron. See 428th Fighter Squadron.

430th Fighter Squadron. See 428th Fighter Squadron.

431st Fighter Squadron, 475th FG, Fifth AF. Activated in Australia in May 1943 and moved to New Guinea in August, where it was based at Port Moresby, Dobodura, Nadzab, Hollandia, and Biak Island. It transferred to Dulag on Leyte Island in the Philippines in early November 1944 and was subsequently also based at San Jose on Mindoro and Clark Field and Lingayen on Luzon until moving to Ie Shima near Okinawa on August 8, 1945.

432nd Fighter Squadron. See 431st Fighter Squadron.

433rd Fighter Squadron. See 431st Fighter Squadron.

434th Fighter Squadron, 479th FG, Eighth AF. Based at Wattisham, England, from May 1944 and converted to P-51s in September.

435th Fighter Squadron. See 434th Fighter Squadron.

436th Fighter Squadron. See 434th Fighter Squadron.

449th Fighter Squadron, 23rd and 51st FGs, Fourteenth AF. Although organized in North Africa, it was activated with the Fourteenth AF in China in August of 1943. It was attached initially to the 23rd FG but was assigned to the 51st FG two months later. Flew from numerous bases in China.

459th Fighter Squadron, 80th and 33rd FGs, Tenth AF. Activated in India in September 1943 and attached to the 80th FG. From March to June 1944 TDY with the RAF's 224 Group. Reassigned to the 33rd FG in May 1945.

485th Fighter Squadron. See 401st Fighter Squadron.

547th Night Fighter Squadron, Fifth AF. Flew P-38s and P-61s from Oro Bay and Owi Island in New Guinea from September 1944 and on the islands of Mindoro and Luzon in the Philippines from January 1945.

654th Bombardment Squadron, 25th Bombardment Group (Reconnaissance), Eighth AF. Flew experimental night sorties over Europe with Pathfinder Lightnings in January and February 1945.

885th Bombardment Squadron, Fifteenth AF. Formerly the 122nd Observation Squadron; renumbered and redesignated in May 1944. It operated a few P-38s while part of the 2641st Special Group of USAAF Service Command in the MTO. Based at five different airfields in Algeria and Italy.

Note: The designations of the USAAF's photo reconnaissance units were changed numerous times during the course of World War II. To avoid confusion the author has utilized on this list only the photo reconnaissance designation, which all of them carried at one time or another.

Endnotes

Chapter 2

1 Blake and Stanaway, *Adorimini: A History of the 82nd Fighter Group in World War II* (1992), p. 1.
2 *Ibid.*, p. 4.
3 Fry, *Eagles of Duxford* (1991), p. 7.
4 Fairfield, *The 479th Fighter Group in World War II* (2004), p. 23.

Chapter 3

1 *Lightning Strikes* (P-38 National Association), dated March 2003.
2 *Ibid.*, dated May 2001.
3 *Ibid.*, dated November 2003.
4 *Ibid.*, dated November 2004.
5 *Ibid.*, dated August 2001.

Chapter 4

1 Schottelkorb, *From Model T to P-38 Lightning* (2003), p. 135.
2 Gray, *The 55th Fighter Group vs. The Luftwaffe* (1998), p. 12.
3 Jones, *The 370th Fighter Group in World War II* (2003), p. 25.
4 Steinko, *The "Geyser" Gang: The 428th Fighter Squadron in World War II* (1986), p. 63.

Chapter 5

1 Blake and Stanaway, *Adorimini: A History of the 82nd Fighter Group in World War II* (1992), p. 20.
2 *Lightning Strikes* (P-38 National Association), dated December 2000.
3 Lambert, *The 14th Fighter Group in World War II* (2008), p. 46.
4 Blake and Stanaway, *Adorimini: A History of the 82nd Fighter Group in World War II* (1992), p.139.
5 *Ibid.*, p. 149.
6 Lambert, *The 14th Fighter Group in World War II* (2008), p. 75.

7   *Ibid.*, p. 80.
8   Blake and Stanaway, *Adorimini: A History of the 82nd Fighter Group in World War II* (1992), p. 171.
9   *Lightning Strikes* (P-38 National Association), dated March 2002.
10 *Ibid.*, dated July 2011.
11 *Ibid.*, dated August 2001.

Chapter 6

1   Fiedler, *459th Fighter Squadron: The Twin Dragons CBI 1943-1945* (1993), p. 139.
2   *Ibid.*, p. 81.

Chapter 8

1   Wolf, *13th Fighter Command in World War II* (2004), p. 271.
2   *Lightning Strikes* (P-38 National Association), dated October 1997.
3   *Ibid.*, dated November 2015.
4   *Ibid.*, dated November 2001.
5   Freeman, *The Mighty Eighth* (1970), p. 94.

Further Reading

Blake, S., and DeBry, D., *P-38 Lightning: Unforgettable Missions of Skill and Luck* (P-38 National Association, 2011)

Bodie, W. M., *The Lockheed P-38 Lightning* (Widewing Publications, 1991)

Christy, J., and Ethell, J., *P-38 Lightning at War* (Charles Scribner's Sons)

Freeman, R. A., *The Mighty Eighth* (Doubleday and Company, 1970); *Mighty Eighth War Manual* (Motorbooks International, 1991)

Grantham, E. K., *P-Screamers: The History of the Surviving Lockheed P-38 Lightnings* (Pictorial Histories Publishing Co., 1994)

Johnsen, F. A., *Lockheed P-38 Lightning: Warbird Tech Series Volume 2* (Specialty Press, 1996)

Kinzey, B., *P-38 Lightning in detail & scale—Part 1 XP-38 Through P-38H* (Detail & Scale, Inc., 1998); *P-38 Lightning in detail and scale—Part 2 P-38J Through P-38M* (Detail & Scale, Inc., 1998)

Maurer, M., (ed.), *Air Force Combat Units of World War II* (Zenger Publishing Company, 1980); *Combat Squadrons of the Air Force in World War II* (Zenger Publishing Company, 1981)

O'Leary, M., *Lockheed P-38 Lightning—Production Line to Frontline* (Osprey Publishing, 1999)

Pace, S., *Warbird History—Lockheed P-38 Lightning* (Motorbooks International, 1996)

Pęczkowski, R., *Lockheed P-38 Lightning Early Versions* (MMPBooks, 2017)

Rust, K. C., *The 9th Air Force in World War II* (Aero Publishers, 1970)

Scutts, J., *Lockheed P-38 Lightning* (The Crowood Press, 2006)

Stanaway, J., *P-38 Lightning Aces of the Pacific and CBI* (Osprey Publishing, 1997); *P-38 Lightning Aces of the ETO/MTO* (Osprey Publishing, 1998)